D1209018

FORWARD FROM EXILE

Forward From Exile

THE AUTOBIOGRAPHY OF

Shmarya Levin

TRANSLATED AND EDITED

BY

Maurice Samuel

THE JEWISH PUBLICATION SOCIETY OF AMERICA

PHILADELPHIA 5728 • 1967

First Edition

Library of Congress Card Catalog Number: 67-16188

Manufactured in the United States of America

Designed by Sidney Feinberg

TO ENYA AND SAMUEL BARUCH

A Personal Note

I see him now as I saw him for the first time on the threshold of my Zionist career fifty-three years ago—a blazing figure in whose presence ordinary human beings became pallid and insipid by contrast. Tall, lean, restless, commanding, with Mephistophelian face and burning eyes—one of them with an outward cast—he held the attention of his listeners with the compelling power of the Ancient Mariner; and whether in private or on the lecture platform, he poured out his ideas, parables, illustrations, epigrams, quotations from the inexhaustible stores of a memory which he had begun to cultivate as a child. He was, many hold—I among them—the greatest Yiddish orator of his day, and he was in addition what most orators are not: a man of philosophic mind, intent on teaching rather than on sweeping an audience off its feet.

It was during his second visit to America that I came to know him. At the time of his first, in 1906, I was a schoolboy selling matches on the streets of Chicago. At the time of the second I was, as I used to put it, "on the staff of *The Maccabaean*," the official organ of the Zionist Federation of

America. As a "member of the staff" my functions were chiefly running off the mailing lists, taking copy to the printer and bringing coffee to the editor; as a special treat I would occasionally be allowed to read proofs. My entrance upon what I fondly hoped would be a dazzling journalistic career was made in an interview with Shmarya Levin. The assignment was given me not on the grounds of my journalistic competence, but because at the moment I was the only one around the office who was equally at home in English and Yiddish. The results of the interview are mercifully buried in unobtainable files of *The Maccabaean.*

Shmarya Levin's second visit to America, originally planned for a few months, was prolonged by the outbreak of the First World War for several years. It was a turning point in his Zionist life, for it shifted the center of gravity of his work and influence from the Old World to the New. In his inimitable style—a mixture of the classic maggid and the modern artist—he describes in one of his early books the dramatic moment of that transfer. He was seated at dinner one night on the German ship *Die Kronprinzessin Cecilia,* and at one point in the conversation noted idly that the moon was shining in through the portholes on his right. A few minutes later, looking up, he saw to his bafflement that the moon was shining in through the portholes on his *left.* But the moon, he argued with himself (his companions had not yet observed the strange shift) *could not* be on the left, it could not have swung round in the heavens to be shining in the north instead of in the south. He felt his right hand, then his left—and suddenly it dawned on him that the ship had quietly made a half-circle and was heading back for America. Then he understood that his life, too, had made a half-circle. He was to be in America much longer than he planned.

In those days a very large segment of American Jewry was Yiddish-speaking and Yiddish-reading. The *Forward* had a daily circulation of over 200,000; the *Morning Journal* and the *Day* (the latter recently founded) were not far behind. There was a flourishing Yiddish theater, a vigorous Yiddish intellectual life, and countless Yiddish-speaking organizations and *Landsmannschaften.* The Zionist movement was still weak in America, and Shmarya Levin's sojourn in the country was an incomparable boon to it. He was soon in demand in every Jewish community, and he threw himself into his mission with demonic energy. It may be said that he educated an older generation in Zionism, and from that older generation much of the Zionist sentiment in its English-speaking children and grandchildren derives.

The late Chaim Weizmann, first President of the State of Israel, pays glowing tribute to him in his own autobiography, *Trial and Error.* "The first place among the propagandists and leaders was occupied—practically without a rival—by Shmarya Levin. . . . He was an extraordinarily gifted orator, of the intellectual rather than the emotional type. His speeches coruscated with brilliant phrases, biblical and talmudic quotations, and penetrating analyses. Primarily a teacher rather than a politician, he was a man of the lobbies and of coteries, and took small part in the proceedings of the Congresses. Usually he would be seen in the midst of a group of cronies, whom he was entertaining with his biting characterizations of his opponents. . . . he was, despite his savage wit, utterly innocent in worldly matters, and this was his charm. Outspoken, spontaneous, he made friends and enemies as he went along, without an eye either to personal consequences or the practical results for the movement. . . . He was both teacher and artist, with the skill of the first and the temperamental quirks of the second. I could always provoke him into a rage by asking, innocently: 'Shmarya, are you making a speech tonight?' He would answer hotly: 'I don't make speeches, I give lectures.' "

It is always exasperating to be told of a certain man that he was an incomparable wit, and to be left without examples of it. Fortunately Shmarya Levin's autobiography, in Maurice Samuel's sparkling translation, abounds in examples, which the reader will find scattered like gems in the pages that follow. But it cannot be denied that some of the examples were not quotable, sometimes because they were unjust, and sometimes for other reasons. Nor can it be denied that though his autobiography brings to life a remarkable personality, the full flavor of it will never be known except to those who have tasted it as his friends.

That I could number myself among these is one of my happiest and proudest memories, the more so as it placed me in a rare company. Chaim Weizmann, Chaim Nachman Bialik, and Harry and Miriam Sacher were perhaps closest to him, and of these only the last two are still among the living. It is to Miriam Sacher, a lifelong admirer of Shmarya Levin that we owe the appearance of this volume on the hundredth anniversary of his birth. What to her is an act of piety and private friendship is also a high public service. The perpetuation of the personality and achievements of Shmarya Levin is an important addition to the annals of modern Jewry.

—MEYER W. WEISGAL.

Contents

BOOK II: YOUTH IN REVOLT

BOOK III: THE ARENA

Introduction

The name Shmarya (more properly Shmaryahu) Levin is today familiar to few outside a dwindling minority of older people who have followed or been part of the movement to create the Jewish state. In this he shares a common fate with the large majority of those devoted and gifted personalities who may be called the founding fathers of modern Zionism. The exceptions who have thus far fended off general oblivion are Theodore Herzl, Chaim Weizmann and Ahad Ha-am, and even the last has become a shadow to all but the well-informed. The names that are now to the fore, like David ben Gurion, Zalman Shazar, Golda Meir, Levi Eshkol, are of our contemporaries who have played and play a notable role, but they do not belong to the *kadmonim* or primitives. They came on the scene from a decade to a quarter of a century too late.

The complaint of the survivors of an epoch, that the exciting world they knew and wrought in is being unjustly forgotten, is as futile as it is pathetic. There is too much for the generations to remember. But here and there a particular circumstance may overcome the handicap of the historic load.

It is for instance more than likely that the writings of Ahad Ha-am and Chaim Greenberg will—to change the metaphor—emerge from temporary eclipse to become fixed lights in the constellations of Jewish thinkers; their written messages transcend the occasions which elicited them, and are relevant to enduring or recurring Jewish and all-human perplexities; their insights transformed the particular into the universal. I believe that on related grounds Shmarya Levin's autobiography will lift him permanently out of the shadows gathered about him and most of his contemporaries.

He began to write it toward the end of his life, and he did not live to complete it. When he died in 1935, he had carried the record only as far as his fortieth year. It was his and our ill-luck that the three volumes were issued separately, at intervals of one and two years, so that the force of the whole was diffused, and its impact correspondingly weakened. But there is a compensating factor in the incompleteness of the autobiography. It is truncated at a point which gives it a remarkable and impressive unity, for it closes with the ending of a separate and distinct epoch in his life, that is, when he departed from Russia in 1906, never to return.

The great work he did thereafter as a teacher and tribune certainly merits its own record, but it would add nothing to the perfect, crowded canvas of the first half of his life. It was as though he had caught himself barely in time to give us what was particular and irreplaceable in his memories. But the powerful unity of the autobiography, originally obscured by the separate publication of the three volumes now collected in one, albeit in somewhat abridged form, stands out clearly as the interlocked triple portrayal of a fascinating individual, a no less fascinating background, and a seminal historical period.

That unity, related to a specific time, place and theme—Russian Jewry and Russia from 1870 to 1906—is further tightened by its organic progression. He begins with the semi-medieval corner of the Pale of Settlement in which he spent his childhood and part of his youth, moves into the provincial areas of his later youth and early manhood, and emerges at last in the vast and tumultuous arena of Jewish and Russian general life, a leader in the Zionist movement and, briefly, a member of Russia's first Duma (parliament). And through it all he is the mirror of his surroundings, reproducing their turmoil and their tidal forces in his own emotions and in his personal problems, spiritual and practical. But this must not be taken to mean that his individuality is submerged in his surroundings; on the contrary, it asserts itself vehemently against them. He refracts, as well as reflects; he echoes, but with his own tonality. The surroundings and the man are vividly brought out by each other.

The Lithuanian village of Svislovitz into which Shmarya Levin was born a hundred years ago, is a prototype of the *shtetl*, that peculiar form of Jewish life which has become familiar—and very properly under its original Yiddish name—to thousands of Jews who have some, and to non-Jews who have no ancestral connection with it. Many descriptions have been made of it, from within and externally. It is the milieu and the material of much of the writing of Sholom Aleichem, Mendelle Mocher S'forim, Isaac Leib Peretz, Sholom Asch and other purely literary figures. It is treated more or less briefly in the memoirs of men of action like Chaim Weizmann and Zalman Shazar, the first and third presidents of Israel. It has become the subject of sociological studies in an intellectual mode which would have sorely puzzled its inhabitants. But in all these we have either fictionalized presentations—perhaps not the less instructive for that—or fragmentary reference, or a somewhat mechanical, scientific "behavioral" account. Shmarya Levin's scrupulously faithful record of his own life in the *shtetl*—the stamp of authenticity is on every page—has a unique value which cannot be derived from any other source.

He is actor and observer. As the first he is passionate and single-minded; as the second he is by turns tender, critical, objective, generous, malicious. Alternately he focuses intently on individuals and steps back to a large, illuminating view of types, groups, movements, historical perspectives. His mind is restless, his eye penetrating; and always his emotions are involved.

The picture he draws of little Svislovitz between its two rivers, of its immemorial Jewish community, of its Russian peasants, of its joys, sorrows, gaieties, worries, meannesses, nobilities and absurdities, flashes onto the screen of our minds with the brightness of an experienced reality. Nothing is "thought up." A sharp honesty of portrayal is manifest even in his most intimate relations. If he writes with reverence and love of his grave, severe, scrupulously ethical father, the intellectual Litvak, of his utterly Yiddish mother, extravagantly pious, tearfully sentimental, filled with love as a pomegranate is with seeds, he also manages to intimate their faults, their limitations and their narrownesses, and their adverse effect on his mental development.

The complete and unquestioning Jewishness of the Jews of Svislovitz is deeply moving; its manifestations are sometimes comical, sometimes harmlessly and enjoyably so, at other times disturbingly. Making the rounds of the festivals, from the most solemn to the most playful, from the High Holy Days to Purim, he introduces us to a gallery of Svislovitzers who step out of the framework of the narrative and make immediate contact with us. Some of them are old familiars—they are the stock figures that frequently occur in life—some are quite extraordinary. The *Rav* of the village we know; he conforms: learned, wise, retiring. Shmarya Levin's parents we know. But the vast and stormy widow Cherneh, baker of pancakes and guardian of the community's conscience, is unique; so in his way is her son, the thespian *manqué*, Bencheh. The variety and colorfulness of characters produces the effect of a complete world in miniature, which, indeed, Svislovitz was. The struggles which the little boy Shmarya had to survive in order to become himself were a replica both of the struggles he encountered later in the larger world, and those which faced his people as a whole in its contacts with surrounding peoples. The fate he escaped, that of becoming mentally frustrated, perhaps crippled, for the rest of his life, with his first *rebbi*, the odious little Mottye the bean, threatened him again when the vicious system of the Russian government closed the doors of higher education to him. His life was, in fact, a succession of escapes, and in that respect symbolically Jewish in the highest degree.

And yet it was in Svislovitz that his qualities of tenacity, alertness and intellectual avidity were planted in him. It was in Svislovitz that he found an excellent teacher, a *rebbi* of the modern school, who filled him with love of knowledge and an indestructible attachment to the Jewish people, its brilliant past, its complicated present and its hopes for the future. By the time he left Svislovitz at the age of fourteen, equipped with a formidable education in Bible and Talmud, but utterly innocent of modern and mundane qualifications, he was ready for the second struggle—the forcing from a hostile world, as it were at sword's point, the training which would fit him for leadership in the liberation movement of his people.

The overwhelming vitality of Jewish Svislovitz typifies the vitality of the entire Jewish people in exile, and particularly of that Russian Jewry which, potentially at least, was the greatest of all exilic Jewries. But when Shmarya Levin writes of his *shtetl*, the picture he draws has no connection with the uninformed sentimentalization of east European Jewry which has of late become a fashion among gentiles as well as Jews. "Nothing," writes Herbert Miller, "is more undignified than a past become quaint"; and nothing could be more quaint than the image of the Russian Jewish world now crystallizing in a large part of the public mind. The actuality of that world was anything but quaint. It was far more realistic, far more actual and down to earth, than one would guess from the current vaudeville and musical presentations of it.

This current distortion of the character of Russian Jewry extends beyond the *shtetl* to that enormous community—nearly seven millions—as a whole. What Shmarya Levin unfolds for us, after he leaves Svislovitz, is the panorama of an immense field of action, in which centrifugal and centripetal forces are exerted on a community just emerging into modern self-consciousness and the will to self-rule. But the historic struggle is conveyed in terms of clearly delineated individuals and groups, through arresting vignettes of localities and protagonists.

In the provincial cities where Levin, after leaving his native village, sought an education and his life's mission, he grappled with two adversaries, the Jewish exile in the Russian world and the inner exile of the Jewish people. The first denied him access to the development of his abilities in modern form, the second denied him entry into the capacities of the Jewish people, which he was determined to develop to their highest.

When we glance back at the past we foreshorten and homogenize it. Because Russian Jewry has been the channel through which American Jewry received its *Yiddishkeit*, we think of it as having been exclusively affirmative toward the Jewish heritage. Nothing could be more inaccurate. If there was a powerful focus of Jewishness in Russian Jewry, there was an almost equally powerful divergence from Jewishness. A tremendous assimilationist movement had set in, with two predominant types, the bourgeois and the revolutionary. But what matters to Jewry today is the affirmative concentration, for from it derives the personality of American Jewry. The other is naturally forgotten.

Within the affirmative concentration there was immense

variety, all of it portrayed in Shmarya Levin's record. At the center was a mass, mostly religious, which had just begun to react to modern changes. Its public relations with the outside world were in the hands of the *shtadlanim*, of whom Levin has much to say. The notion of national self-help, of democratic action by and for the Jewish people, repudiating the unasked-for intervention of wealthy or influential negotiators, was still strange to it. Such action, whether outspokenly Zionist, or simply nationalist, or even religious, was regarded as revolutionary—which it was. For within the Jewish community itself the claims of wealth and prominence to leadership were a deep-rooted tradition. The snobbery of the "big" families, their domination of internal communal affairs, was the counterpart of the *shtadlanim's* domination of "foreign policy." Shmarya Levin had to apply not less energy to breaking this internal tyranny than to the establishment of a democratic channel of communication between the Jewish and the non-Jewish worlds. And, indeed, the two processes were closely interlocked.

A fever of participation in Russian life seized Russian Jewry in the middle of the nineteenth century, when the first opportunity to modernize—soon to be withdrawn—was offered to it. On the one hand large numbers of Jews, now equipped with a modern education, entered the liberation movements of various shades, from the centrist to the extreme left. A smaller number entered into the industrialization of the country, and miniscule though that number was in relation to the Russian population, its contribution was extremely large. The successful merchants and contractors are brilliantly described by Levin, together with their relationship to the Jewish community. The majority of them were opposed to the democratization of the Jewish community, and *a fortiore* to the embryonic Zionist movement. And yet even the minority within a minority was a startling phenomenon.

After the first Zionist Congress (1897), Theodore Herzl,

whose conception of Russian Jewry, like that of most Western Jews, was one of uniform backwardness and helplessness, had to write: "There rose before our eyes a Russian Jewry the strength of which we had not even suspected. . . . What a humiliation for us, who had taken our superiority for granted! All these professors, doctors, lawyers, industrialists, engineers and merchants stood on an educational level which is certainly not lower than ours. Nearly all of them are masters of two or three languages, and that they are men of ability in their particular lines is proved by the simple fact that they have succeeded in a land where success is particularly difficult for Jews."

The men with whom Herzl came in contact were of course the delegates to the Congress, Zionists. They were the cream of Russian Jewry in respect of nationalistic consciousness, whatever its religious component. Herzl wrote of them, further: "If I wanted to summarize the impression—and it was a very strong one—I would say: they possess the inner wholesomeness which the majority of European Jews have lost. . . . When meeting them, we realized what had given our forefathers the strength to endure the heaviest ordeals. In their image our history appeared before us in its distinctiveness and vitality."

He did not meet the defecting Jews—but he would have learned nothing from them; he already knew the type as it had emerged in western Europe. Shmarya Levin also knew the type from his student days in Berlin; but meeting it on his home ground, in Russia, he was moved to special fury and contempt. For there was a difference. In western Europe there was, at least to all appearances, an atmosphere of freedom. Certainly England was comparatively free from anti-Semitism; even France, despite the passions roused by the Dreyfus trial, was essentially a liberal country. Anti-Semitism was, as Levin understood, deep-rooted in Germany, but it was not as yet an official government policy. In Russia, however, where the masses were, as a matter of fact, far less anti-Semitic than the government, persecution and oppression were written into the law, and horrible pogroms were instigated by the highest officials using for that purpose the machinery of state. When Jewish defections reached the point of baptism—and there were thousands of baptized Jews in Russia—it meant more than defection; it meant going over into the ranks of the persecutors. Revolutionaries who disassociated themselves from Judaism could plead that they were fighting the cause of all oppressed peoples, including the Jews; and Levin speaks of the revolutionaries, anti-Zionist as they were, with respect. The *meshumodim,* however, betrayed not only the Jews, but every oppressed nationality in the Russian empire.

There was a queer relationship between the apostates and the Jews of the upper economic level. Despite their repudiation, in its final and most offensive form, of Judaism, the apostates mingled almost exclusively with Jewish society. Technically Christians, with the universities open to them, entitled by law to all opportunities that were enjoyed by non-Jews, they were not welcomed by their new co-religionists. Levin describes how Menachem Mendel Ussishkin refused to have anything to do with the apostates, who were trying to make the best of both worlds; and while the majority of Jews despised and execrated them, the assimilating upper classes accepted them. Their conversion was regarded as a clever trick! Such, indeed, it was, and while the non-Jews had to yield to the letter of the law, they understood the maneuver not less than the Jews.

The reader must constantly bear in mind that this autobiography was written nearly forty years ago, and that it refers to an even earlier period, namely from the beginning of the eighteen-seventies to the opening of the twentieth century. Looking back at the beginnings of the movement for a Jewish state, one is struck by the apparent hopelessness of the outlook in those days, not simply because of external political circumstances, but because of the initial unresponsiveness of the Jewish masses and the fierce hostility of certain powerful Jewish groups. How ludicrously petty and hole-in-the-wall were the first Zionist organizational attempts, how bitterly they were fought by certain vested interests, the extreme orthodox, the collectors of funds for the *Chalukah* in Palestine, the upper classes, the *shtadlanim*. Supporters had to be won man by man, little group by little group. It needed a profound insight into the great potential of the Jewish masses, an unshakable faith in the meaning of Jewish persistence, to join the small band of initiators. It must be remembered, too, that Levin, Ussishkin, Ahad Ha-am, and the other pioneers of whom Levin provides lively vignettes, preceded the appearance of Herzl by several years. Weizmann was seven years younger than Levin. The group of students who, as members of the *Jüdisch-Russisch Wissenschaftliches Verein*, were later to make Zionist history —Weizmann, Nachman Syrkin and Leo Motzkin were among them—arrived in Berlin after Levin had left. Herzl did not begin his meteoric career until that group was already graduated and scattered.

And in the midst of their insights, the naïveté of those beginners! Their conviction that the Arabs would see the advantages of the modernization of their country by the Jews (but, for that matter, the Emir Feisal himself proclaimed that belief as late as 1918); their plans (they hadn't a penny to bless themselves with) for buying their way into the goodwill of the Turkish masters of Palestine (but Herzl, too, had illusions on that score); and, above all, their tragic belief that nothing worse than the Russian pogroms could ever happen to us in modern times. One is tempted to say that had they had a glimpse of the horrors to come they would have redoubled their efforts, but as it was they gave all they had, and many of them sacrificed brilliant prospects in the general world in order that, living precariously, often from hand to mouth, they might dedicate their total energies to the ideal. They were a remarkable group.

* * *

In some ways the preparation of this edition has been a painful task. I would much have preferred to see the three volumes of the autobiography reissued as they are. It is true that some of the passages—explanatory and propagandistic—are now rather meaningless; the arguments against Baron de Hirsch's schemes for South American colonization are now irrelevant; the proofs of the feasibility of a Jewish state no longer need to be furnished. But I have also been compelled to leave out much that reads as freshly today as it did nearly forty years ago. I have done my best to resolder the text after excisions in a way that inflicts the minimum of damage; above all, I have been guided by my loving recollection of the man who was my first teacher in Zionism, and I have tried to word the brief connecting passages in his spirit.

BOOK I

CHILDHOOD IN EXILE

CHAPTER ONE

The Place of My Birth

THE TOWNLET OF SVISLOVITZ, in the Russian province of Minsk, stood on a "mountain." We called it a mountain though it was less than a hundred feet above the surrounding country; but I will be faithful to the spirit of my childhood, and so a mountain it shall remain. On one side ran the Beresina, and along the other, parallel with it, the Svislo, which first finds historic mention in the famous chronicles of the monk Nestor, who speaks of "Minsk, on the river Svislotz." For the Svislo also ran through Minsk, but much nearer its source, so that it had a premature look about it, and suggested an irrigation canal dug by human hands. There were in fact quite a number of Minskers who did not know that their town possessed a river called the Svislo. It was best known among the poor, for it passed through their quarter; and often enough, in the early spring or late autumn, the quiet, unassuming rivulet suddenly took on character, lifted itself above its banks, and poured into the huts and hovels on either side in revenge for the contempt it suffered in normal times.

In our town, however, the Svislo was as good a river as any. There it did not have to wait for floods in order to make known its presence. Its waters were full, steady and tumultuous the year round. After running parallel with the Beresina for a certain distance it made a graceful half-turn and poured into the mother stream, proudly, as if to say: "True, I am younger and smaller, but I bring you plenty of sustenance." The Beresina, broad and majestic, swallowed her up, and flowed on unheeding to join the Dnieper.

Each of the rivers had a virtue and a defect. The Beresina was broad and splendid in some places, imposing enough to rank with the mighty Dnieper; in other places it was miserably shallow; in fact you could wade across, and I was ashamed and mortified to see peasants drive their cattle through without any precautions. The Svislo, though narrower, was deeper and swifter; and so, since the Jews of Svislovitz were passionately fond of river bathing, we made the best of the situation by allocating each river to the appropriate sex: on summer Friday afternoons the women would be lying in the shallow Beresina, cooling off, and the men would be swimming about in the deep Svislo. Between the two naked crowds the town lay deserted, waiting for its inhabitants to put on their holiday attire and flock to the synagogue for the prayers which usher in the Sabbath.

To the farther side of both rivers lay meadows. The land was unfit for cultivation, because twice a year, almost without fail, the rivers flooded it, and most of the time it remained impossibly marshy. The meadows produced one thing—hay. Thus the levels round the town underwent three transformations in the course of the year. In the spring, and sometimes in the autumn, the meadows were covered with water; then Svislovitz was a tiny island in the midst of a tremendous sea. In the summertime the townlet was surrounded by an ocean of green. In the winter the stretches on all sides were covered with one vast mantle of white, smooth as a bedsheet and dotted here and there with tiny pyramids—the frozen haystacks. In the late summer it was not infrequent for one of these pyramids to burst into flames that reached like tongues to the dark sky. The townlet knew that these tongues spoke the language of revenge: someone had set fire to the haystack of an enemy. The government punished such crimes with great severity—but the culprits were seldom caught.

Far beyond the meadows the forests began, but between them lay the wheatfields of the peasants. They were fat, rich fields, soft to the foot, breathing an odor of fruitfulness and sustenance. That odor interpreted the Russian phrase *Matyushka Zemlya*, Mother Earth, a mother giving suck from bountiful breasts to countless children. When the peasants spoke of *Matyushka Zemlya* their eyes, usually dull and expressionless, were flooded with love, like the eyes of children who see their mother at a distance.

The forests belonged in part to the local Polish nobility and in part to the crown. They were scores of miles deep; in fact, no one knew where they really ended. The nobles, making their homes in Warsaw, lived the life of spoilers, denuding their forests stretch by stretch, cutting down the young trees together with the old. It was only in the eighties that the government began to control the ruthless destruction.

Jews and gentiles alike lived on terms of intimacy with the forest, their best friend. It provided them gratis with countless fruits and plants, with berries, mushrooms, wild apples (these we used to lay on straw and wait till they began to rot; then we ate them with great relish), wild pears, nuts of all kinds, and guelder roses. In the things that grew in the soil Jew and gentile shared, but the gentile had to himself the hunt: hare, marten, mink, and occasionally even a bear. The Jews had nothing to do with the animals; that is, they would not shoot them. But they would buy the carcasses from the peasants for the furs. However, as against this, the Jews had two exclusive benefits from the forest. They got from it their willow withes for the fifth day of the festival of Tabernacles, and the fir branches to cover their booths.

But something more bound the inhabitants of Svislovitz to the forest: they were dependent on it for their daily bread. If the winter was a good one, that is, with plenty of snow and frost, and many rafts were lashed together and floated down the river, there was prosperity in Svislovitz. But if the winter was mild, and there was not time enough to carry the felled trees to the river bank, Svislovitz hungered. The forests were primeval, virgin, thickly tangled; their owners neglected them and let them run wild. More than once a fearful storm would burst through the forest, leaving in its wake little hillocks of broken branches and overturned roots. In the winter, when the snow lay deep on the ground, and a powerful frost held it firmly packed, it was possible to drag the logs down to the river on sleds. But in the summer it would have been necessary to cut a path through the tangle and roll the logs down on wheels; and prices being what they were in those days, this did not pay.

Thanks to its topography—a long elevated strip between two rivers—the townlet of Svislovitz was well planned. It had no crooked and broken streets. It lay as on a chess board (chess being unknown among us then, our simile was: "straight as a kneading board"), six long streets parallel with the rivers and ten short ones at right angles. Only one street had achieved the dignity of a proper name: the Beresina Street. All the others were referred to by the names of their most prominent residents. But as degrees of prominence were not fixed, any more than its causes, a street might be known by two or more names. One and the same street might be indicated as Pessye the candlemaker's street, or Joseph the chicken-slaughterer's street, or simply as Stepan Harnai's street. Everyone was free to express his taste and preferences through the medium of the streets. As a matter of fact, street names were quite unnecessary; in Svislovitz everybody knew who everybody was and where everybody lived.

The dignified Beresina Street was the artery of Svislovitz. It was very broad. It began at the Svislo, climbed uphill, passed through the marketplace with its public well, and then split north and south. It was impossible to leave or enter Svislovitz without passing along Beresina Street. It was our link with the great outside world. But if you had asked me what on earth we needed such a broad, luxurious street for, I could not have told you. Nor could any other townsman. But it would be quite wrong to imagine that the modest Svislovitzers ever used the whole of that boulevard. Trodden paths ran only down the sides of it. The middle was taken up by patches of wild grass and innumerable puddles which were knee-deep in the summer. On weekdays the children would play in the grass, but on Sabbath afternoons the burghers themselves would lie there, face downward, enjoying life. The mud puddles were the happy meeting-ground of all the pigs of our gentile neighbors on the side-streets. But for that matter the "Jewish" animals, too, were fond of the puddles. It was a homelike place. They sprawled their bulk cosily in the ooze and were happy. More than once they settled so thickly on the street that it was impossible to drive through. But despite the familiarity with which it was treated, Beresina Street was the residence of the most important burghers, most of whom owned their own homes, and also housed the whole of the local administration, the representatives of the powers that were: the *stanovoy*, or district commissioner, the postmaster, the village healer, the *volostnoy*, or community clerk, the public-school teacher, and the clergy—whom we instinctively looked on as part of the administration—which consisted of two priests and a reader.

The grandest buildings in Svislovitz were the synagogue,

the two Greek Orthodox churches in Byzantine style, and a Catholic cloister in Gothic style. The last was dilapidated, almost on the point of collapse, but the government would not permit the Catholics to build a new cloister. Nor did Svislovitz possess a Catholic priest of its own, though it may have at one time, for I remember as in a dream a house opposite the cloister, and a white-robed figure issuing from it.

In addition to the above there were the police headquarters and the public school. All these buildings were of wood, the great logs lying horizontally, except in the case of the churches and cloister, the logs of which stood up perpendicularly.

At the end of the southern spur of Beresina Street was "Castle Hill," topped by the only real structure in town, five stories high and built of crude cut stones. To be exact, only the first two stories were built of stone: the upper three, in the form of a hexagon, were of wood, and out of them four gigantic wings, ruined and motionless, extended. For the building had originally been intended as a windmill, and had been put up by a half-mad magnate of the locality. There was a rumor that at one time the mill had actually worked, and had ground out flour, but I remember it only as a ruin. On the hillock also stood an empty house—for the manager—and next to the house stood the tumbledown stables, as empty as the house.

The only guardians of the ruin were four old birches in the foreground, at the foot of the hillock, with wooden benches in their shade. Sabbath afternoons we used to take a walk to the ruin and ascend Castle Hill. The prospect was beautiful: the two rivers running parallel, one on each side of the town, then a graceful bend in one of the rivers where it turned to pour itself into the other; beyond the rivers the soft green meadows, and beyond the meadows, the dark forests. At night no one went near the ruin, for then it was full of doleful creatures; owls dwelt there, and satyrs danced there. It was said that in the dead of the night, when the town lay wrapped in sleep, lights had been seen moving through the rooms, the vast wings had begun to revolve and the millstones to grind. . . . In later years, however, I learned that there were boys and girls of spirit in our town, whom stories of ghouls and satyrs could not frighten away; they spent many a happy hour in the late evenings among the ruins on the hill—astonishingly enough, always in the darkest and most terrifying corners.

I come now to the last point in our townlet—the cemetery, the *Beth Olam,* or House of Eternity, which strictly speaking was not in the townlet at all, for it lay at a remove of two kilometers, beyond the fields of the peasants, on the road to Minsk. The cemetery of the gentiles lay closer to town, but in the opposite direction, on the way to Bobruisk. As children we were taken to visit the cemetery on Tisha b'Av, the ninth day of the month of Av, the day of the Black Fast, when we mourn for the destruction of both Temples, the first and the second. For the children, however, the day of mourning was a joyous festival. The very young ones did not fast; for them the outing was a marvelous affair. We ran about the cemetery in our stockinged feet; we made ourselves little wooden swords, painted them in gay colors, and girded them on like warriors of old. And then there was the pilgrimage itself to the cemetery and back, with stops on the road, when we dived into the woods in search of nuts, already half-ripe at that time of the year, and black apples, which we did not dare to eat, but which could be squeezed out for their juice to make the best kind of ink—as good as any you could buy in a shop. There were also blackberries, raspberries, wimberries and other fruits, some of which were forbidden but which it was a pleasure to pluck and throw around.

During the rest of the year we might see a Jew being conducted amid lamentations to his last rest, but we children were forbidden to accompany the funeral. Besides, despite our gaiety there on Tisha b'Av, we were mortally afraid of the Jewish cemetery. But with the gentile cemetery we were on the most familiar terms. It lay on the Svislovitz side of the woods, and on pleasant summer afternoons, just before evening prayers, we used to climb onto its fence and sit there telling stories, not a whit frightened either by the monuments or the crosses. The explanation for this difference in our attitudes may lie in the ideas which were planted in our young minds with regard to death and the soul and the beyond. In our little world it was an accepted fact that gentiles have no souls: they have only a spirit. If I were asked today what precisely was the difference between a "soul" and a "spirit" I could not answer. But as a little boy it was quite clear to me that a soul lives after death, and a spirit does not. And since the gentiles had no souls, what was there to be afraid of?

Svislovitz, on top of its "mountain," was always safe from the danger which threatened so many villages in our vicinity —the overflowing of the rivers. It was a bad business, being cut off from the rest of the world when the Svislo and the Beresina rose above their banks and flooded the countryside, but at least we were safe. When the other villages were inundated, we felt like Noah in his ark, saved from the waters which covered the rest of the earth.

But this grant of grace was the source of another danger: lifted up as we were, we were exposed completely to the fury of the winds. There was nothing to break the impact. The lighter winds, though they brought much discomfort, were welcomed eagerly: they were the only street cleaning department we knew anything about, and when one of them had blown through the town and carried off the rubbish accumulated in the streets, the place looked astonishingly neat. But the real storm winds—and they came not infrequently—were another matter. The houses, or rather hovels, of the poor were not firmly built, and the roof sat on them like a cap slipped over the head. I use this figure advisedly: most of the Jews of Svislovitz used to wear skullcaps under their hats to be safe from the sin of ever being bareheaded even for an instant; and under the flimsy roofs of their houses some of them used to build "skullcaps"—a defense against the storm winds which might whip the regular hats off the houses. But some of them had not this reserve, and a strong wind would leave their houses roofless, just like a booth in the Feast of Tabernacles, but without the covering of branches.

The hot summer winds, too, brought a great deal of discomfort, but they were tolerable compared with the mad rage of the winter blasts. When one of these storms descended on the town, the doors were sealed and no one dared venture into the street. On such days life was suspended, congealed. Then Svislovitz looked like a town of the dead, half-buried under the snow, with the wind howling a furious dirge over it. Within the howling of the winds we heard the howling of hungry wolves, and the covered city was hidden from the heavens in the whirl of millions of snowflakes. No work was done. All we could do was wait for the storm to die down. And if the reader bears in mind the sanitary arrangements in the houses of Svislovitz, he can form some idea of the kind of life we were reduced to during those winter storms.

They would come several times during the winter, raging for anything between twenty-four hours and several days. The little ones trembled in every limb, and in order to reassure us, the older folk would tell us that the wild dance outside was the dance of witches and evil spirits, who could not hold out very long. Another purpose of this explanation was to give us some insight into the nature of things, so that we might not be altogether ignorant of the laws which governed the world. As to the first purpose, at least, the explanation was quite unsuccessful, because to the terror which the winds inspired in us was added the terror of the witches and the evil spirits.

They haunted me in the night and entered my dreams. While I lay awake I used to repeat the *Hear O Israel* prayer, which drives evil spirits away, and I used to pack myself close into my covers. But I was still afraid.

CHAPTER TWO

The Family

WHENEVER I sit down with closed eyes and turn my gaze inward in an effort to recall the past, the skein of my life unwinds with the swiftness of a spool on a loom: and always at the last point, which is the first point of my memory, one figure emerges—my mother. In that image, clear and sharp as if she were still before me, moving about the house or bending over the cradle of her newest-born in silent prayer—an unofficial addition to her daily religious services—in that image I recognize the beginning of my life and feel the first pulsebeat of my being.

Hers is the first memory, and next to hers is that of my father, with his grave, severe, intellectual face. The next places are taken by my two grandfathers and my grandmother (the other grandmother, on my mother's side, I never knew), and around them are grouped uncles and aunts, cousins and second cousins, the young and the old, relatives of all degrees. A characteristic image springs out of the groups: my mother and my father, my grandfathers and my grandmother, are like a colonnade of trees planted at equal distances, each in its own destined place. The relatives are like an irregular grove scattered about the colonnade, one tree eagerly elbowing its neighbor, a second standing darkly aside, the complete knoll serving as a background to the stately colonnade.

Beyond the farther end of the colonnade, in the shadow of which I press close to my mother's side, I see the last glimmer of the sunset. The night rises slowly and covers with her dark mantle the men and women and incidents that were before me. The past sleeps there, in the House of Eternity: the hard memorial stones serve for cushions, and over the unknown figures a sheet is drawn, sparkling with golden stars. But between me and the House of Eternity there is some sort of relationship, dark and obscure, but authentic. Beyond my living parents and grandparents (living because I still evoke them as living beings) stretches the long line of my great-grandfathers and great-great-grandfathers. I see the beginning of the line near me, but not the end of it; I try to run toward it, I try to overtake the vanished generations, but the more urgently I pursue them the more swiftly they withdraw. And at last my strength gives out, my young feet fail under me; the line curves over and disappears like the trail of a meteor on the farther side of the sea, or like a thunderclap which loses itself among distant mountains.

The image which haunted my childhood acquired a singular meaning for me in later years. In measure as I grew older and entered into more intimate contacts with life, in like measure did the colonnade of the dead unveil itself before me, as though fragment after fragment were coming up for resurrection. I know well that this is only the play of my fancy. But it is in this manner that I perceive my life, and I do not believe myself to be an exception. On the contrary, I believe with all my strength that we carry within ourselves more of a "living" past than we suspect; and if we gave the right degree of attention to this truth, and exerted ourselves to create some sort of harmony between our present and our past, we should avoid many of the spiritual conflicts which torment us.

My mother, Elke, the daughter of Mendel, of the family Astrakhan, was exactly fourteen years old when she was married to my father, Samuel Chayim, son of Solomon Salkind Ha-Levi, of the family Levin; and my father was just one year older than my mother. I have often heard my mother tell that she suffered a great deal during the first year of her marriage. Not, God forbid, because the match did not please her, but because for a whole year she was ashamed to look my father straight in the face. Whether my father suffered likewise I do not know. My mother used to add to these memories that it was wrong to marry children off so early. It was pitiful, she said. After all, we were no longer living in the days of the Terror, when the agents of the czar might descend at any moment on the unmarried boys of a Jewish family and send them off to distant military service for twenty-five years or more. One ought to wait, my mother said, until the brides were at least fifteen and the bridegrooms sixteen years of age. My mother was never a shrewd bargainer, and she was content to nibble off one year.

The meaning of the Terror, the *Boholoh,* about which I shall write again, was already known to me in my childhood; and the epoch was still fresh in the memory of the living. In those days there would be marriages between children of twelve years of age, for the horror of the military schools, which were chosen at the most distant points from the homes of the child-recruit (they would be sent as far as Orenburg in Siberia), hung over every Jewish family. Even Nicholas I would not go so far as to take married boys. That word *Boholoh* has a fearful ring in Jewish ears; more powerfully than volumes of description, it conjures up a world of agony and fear. But a people does not describe, it creates a primitive song, a word—and that suffices.

On my mother's side I belong to the mystic and passionate sect of the Chassidim; on my father's side I am a cool, logical Misnaged, or opponent of Chassidism. My grandfather Mendel Astrakhan, my mother's father, was a fiery adherent of the Lubavich dynasty of wonder-working rabbis; he did not let a single High Holy Day pass without a visit to the "court," nor a year without the payment of tithes. My grandfather Solomon Salkind was a dry, cool Misnaged, an eternal student of our sacred books. He made it a point to surround himself with the wandering preachers and rabbis and emissaries sojourning in our little town. Naturally our house was as such typically Misnaged, and my education was planned and carried out under the direction of my father. But the Chassidic stories and legends which my mother would recount to us had a profound influence on me; and even more powerful than the lore of the Chassidim was the manner of her life, her individual style.

Toward my father my attitude was one of the deepest respect, but in that respect there was not lacking an element of fear. Toward my mother my relationship was one of pure love. She was in my eyes the personification of all that is loveliest and most lovable. She was widely known as a gentle, charitable, God-fearing woman. In my eyes she was a saint.

There were thus two distinct and opposed influences in my life: the severe intellectual influence on my father's side, and the gentle and mystic Chassidic influence on my mother's side.

My father had, as the phrase goes, "a good head on him." He was especially clever at figuring, and in later years, when I was a student in the upper classes of the *Realschule*, or Secondary School in Minsk, I convinced myself that my father had a real grasp of the elements of algebra and geometry, subjects he had never studied. He frequently astounded me by the manner in which he approached a problem in either subject; the problem, it is true, would not be a very advanced one, but he had an extraordinary way of resolving it into its first elements by sheer dint of business acumen or, I am tempted to say, by a sort of instinct for what was logical and just. It was from my father that I inherited a gift for mathematics which in later years was to enable me to overcome some of the heaviest obstacles placed in the way of my education. My mother was, in every fiber of her being, a woman of mood and intuition. In all that she said or did—even if the matter was some daily commonplace—she made evident such a depth of soul, such fineness of feeling, such sympathy and compassion, that she drew me to her with magic power. To put it roughly, I would say that my father's influence was to intellectualize me, my mother's to inspire me; from my father streamed a cool, clear light, from mother, warmth and emotion. My head was drawn toward my father, my heart toward my mother, and I was forever swinging like a pendulum between the two. Which of these forces finally came to dominate? Did I finally emerge a Chassid, with a Misnaged background, or was the contrary the case? The answer will have to be given by others than myself. For my part I can only say that both of my parents played a great part in my life.

But the mere fact that a Chassidic and a Misnagdic family had entered into an alliance by marriage showed that the crest of the enmity between the two elements in Jewry had already passed. I do not believe that the difference in character between my father and mother created actual inner conflicts along the path of my development.

It was not, however, by virtue of their religious adherences that my grandfathers Mendel and Solomon belonged to different groups. Their social standing was about the same; they were both of the upper-middle class, but Grandfather Solomon's status was somewhat the higher. The reason was to be found in the characters of the two townlets from which they came. Grandfather Mendel lived in the town of Beresin, not far from Borisov, where the great Napoleon met disaster; grandfather Solomon belonged to Svislovitz. A matter of fifty kilometers separated Beresin from Svislovitz, yet the Jewish communities differed radically in structure and quality. Beresin prided itself on its metropolitan—almost its megalopolitan—standing, and looked down with tolerance on provincial Svislovitz. Eight hundred Jewish families and as many non-Jewish made up the population of the latter. There were no magnates in Svislovitz, and only a handful of comparatively rich men. Below these, in descending order, were a few score shopkeepers and small merchants, and two or three hundred artisans and laborers. These last were mostly trained in the special craft of raft-building, and were generally regarded as the most skillful in their line. The fact that there were no magnates in Svislovitz contributed a great deal to the democratic character of the community. The distinction between the merely "rich" Jew and the magnate was enormous; it was at least as great—to borrow a parallel from the British aristocratic hierarchy—as that between the baronet and the ordinary knight.

Thus Svislovitz was a healthy middle class, democratic Jewish community, organically bound up through all its parts by family alliances. The place of honor in the synagogue, the eastern wall, did not necessarily coincide with the place of honor in our social life. Wherever a birth or marriage was celebrated, the invitation went out tacitly to every Jew in the townlet. And every Jew came to a funeral, whosesoever it might be.

Now Beresin was a much larger community in point of numbers, and it was completely dominated by a family of magnates, the Seldoviches. This was the family which ordered, regulated and supervised its social and communal life. Not a step was taken without the knowledge and permission of the Seldoviches; no man dared utter a word in their presence, much less express a strong opinion. In brief, Beresin represented a small, absolute oligarchy with the Seldoviches as rulers.

There were two Seldovich patriarchs, Wolf and David, both large timber merchants, who bought up the forests of the Polish nobility, cut down the trees, and floated the rafts down to Odessa on the Black Sea and up to Danzig on the Baltic. Each of the patriarchs had a synagogue of his own, and whenever, during the services, a relative of theirs was called up for a reading of a portion of the Law, he was invited by the honorific title of "*Rav*," while everyone else was plain "Mister." Immediately after the Seldoviches came their agents and other employees. Third on the list were the independent burghers and shopkeepers. Last came the artisans and laborers. The intellectual life of the community was supplied by the doctor, the pharmacist, two lawyers, and a few teachers.

By rights the independent burghers should have taken precedence over the agents of the Seldoviches; but so powerful was the pressure of the family that this little world was divided into two parts, the Seldoviches and the non-Seldoviches, and woe to him who attempted to upset this natural order.

Learning and family status, those two controls of our traditional Jewish aristocracy, played no part in social structure of Beresin. The genealogy of the Seldoviches was of the humblest, and they never achieved the slightest distinction in the world of learning. David Seldovich was, indeed, widely celebrated as an almost complete illiterate. He was unable to read from the Hebrew prayer book; he had to have someone read out to him, while he repeated the words. Even this he did so badly, twisting words and phrases into such grotesque combinations, that the howlers of David Seldovich became classics in the region, travelling as far as Minsk in one direction and Mohilev in the other.

My grandfather Mendel was agent for one of the Seldoviches —I no longer remember which. It was his task to make the rounds of the forests put up for sale, and estimate the value of the timber. The work was exacting and responsible. The

Polish nobles had not yet acquired the Russian governmental system of fixing the price according to the number, height and girth of the trees. They sold forests in the lump. In making purchases from the Polish nobles it was therefore necessary to employ a man who was both level-headed and honest. He had to have the feel of the quantity of timber in a forest, and he had to be free from the temptation to make deals either with competitors or the nobles.

My grandfather Mendel qualified on both counts. He was a first-class expert on forests, and his honesty was above suspicion. As I first remember him he was already an old man, tall, well built, with a handsome, snow-white beard and with unusually heavy eyebrows, which stood out like rustic hedges above his deep eyes. Something in him spoke of the countless trees he had felt and appraised for so many years; he was himself like a powerful old oak planted in the center of a winter landscape. I looked upon him with awe, and I resented his inferior status in Beresin—a mere agent of the Seldoviches!

In this respect, however, Grandfather Salkind, on my father's side, wholly satisfied my pride. He was not as imposing as Grandfather Mendel, but he did not have to submit to the name of "agent." He was an independent man, also in the timber trade, though on a smaller scale. His was the monopoly on supplying the material for binding the rafts. Instead of ropes, willow withes were used, after having been softened in fire. This monopoly provided my grandfather with a decent income.

The work was seasonal; it began with the festival of Purim, in the early spring, when the rivers thawed out, and lasted until the Pentecost, at the beginning of summer. But even during the season my grandfather occupied himself little with his trade. He had turned over the management to my uncle Meyer, a plain, simple Jew who by long intercourse with the peasants had become something of the earthy peasant type. My grandfather spent the days of his life in study and prayer. He gave his nights to those midnight vigils of lamentation which we call *chtzot*—mourning for the exile of the Divine Glory from the Holy Land, and for the destruction of the Temple. Across all these years there comes to me the sound of the old man weeping in his lonely room, and I still remember the tears which, with childish terror, I sometimes saw rolling down his cheeks. He carried on his studies in the night by the light of a special candle—a long woolen wick passed through a ball of wax. Every two or three minutes he would suspend his studies, draw the woolen wick a little further through the wax, and then return to his sacred books.

My grandfather was more the pietist than the scholar. His favorite books were those of the wise sayings and moral disquistions of our sages. If, during the day, he left his studies, it was mostly to engage in charitable work. He gave to the limit of his means and persuaded others to give. Himself no scholar, it was with him a point of pride to place himself at the service of scholars. He observed with special passion the laws of hospitality to the stranger, and took it as a personal affront if someone in the town snatched from his friendly clutches a traveller of importance. His house, a large one with two wings, was always full of guests, and on the verandah which faced the street one would see on summer days travellers, wandering scholars, itinerant rabbis and preachers discussing this world and the next with the worthies of our town.

The youngsters saw Grandfather Mendel's house through their own eyes. It had the largest courtyard in town, stables, a private well and—unique possession in Svislovitz—an ice cellar. There were no trees at all in my grandfather's yard, but the adjoining yard, belonging to a gentile, was well provided, chiefly with pear trees. The nearest of these was well within reach from the stable roof, with the result that the grandchildren of the family became as agile as cats. More than once, however, the neighbor caught us red-handed, with disastrous consequences. The value of our booty may be gauged from the fact that a basket holding forty pounds of these pears sold for between five and ten kopeks. Of course we had to do all our pilfering before the fruit became ripe and was shaken down by the owner. However, if my grandfather's courtyard had no trees, it held another treasure: right in the center of it there was a muddy pool. In the summer we sailed paper boats on it or took off our shoes and stockings and waded in it. But it was in the winter, when the pool was frozen over, that the full value of it was made manifest. It became then an inexhaustible source of joy. We spent every moment of freedom sliding on the ice: not plain sliding, of course, but the highly ornamented performance of the virtuoso, in postures and gestures borrowed from the doings of our elders; with eyes closed and hands stretched before us, like Mother standing before the Sabbath candles; in an almost kneeling position, like Father when he bowed himself down in the synagogue; while making complicated circles with the right hand round the left, like Father binding on the phylacteries. Finally, most difficult and most dangerous, sliding seated.

I have left to the end, because she occupies a special place in my memory, my grandmother Toibeh, the wife of Grandfather Solomon. She was his first and only wife, lived out her years with him and bore him many children, the last three at a single birth. She was a mother and a grandmother in a widely ramified family, but for all her earthly bonds she always made the impression of a thing apart. We respected her and to a certain degree even loved her, but there was never the feeling of intimacy. It seemed to us that our love and respect were being offered to some far-off being, some shadow of a grandmother. I remember the poet Bialik once speaking in New York of the Bible in translation as compared with the original Hebrew, and he compared it to the kiss which a son might receive from his mother through the thickness of a veil. Automatically I thought of my grandmother Toibeh.

Physically she was an exception in our family. She was small and lean, and her parchment face was covered with innumerable wrinkles. Yet, as I remember her, she was barely sixty years of age. Hers was the face of one who had suffered much and borne much. From one point of view her detachment was easily intelligible. It was enough that a woman so frailly built should have brought so many children into the world, all of them ten times as strong as herself. But I do not know what other sorrows there were in her life. I have never heard even a hint of ill-treatment on the part of her husband, or lack of respect on the part of her children. Her motions were timid, almost furtive, as if she were afraid of being in someone's way. Her eyes had a submissive look, begging for something she could not formulate. In brief, she was one of those human beings upon whose forehead are clearly written the words: "Good people, merciful people, forgive me for taking up room in this world."

In my time my grandfather and grandmother already lived separately in the two wings of the house. Grandmother suffered from chronic headaches and kept to her bed a great deal. Grandfather used to snatch a few hours of sleep in the day and would pass most of the nights in vigils of lamentation and prayer. They seemed to have realized that headaches and vigils of lamentation do not go together, so they divided the house between them. My grandmother's respect for her husband was boundless. Just before she died she called him to her bedside and asked him for a fraction of the glory set aside for him in Paradise. My grandfather promised it to her and gave her his hand, perhaps—who knows—for the first time in his life.

CHAPTER THREE

Jews and Gentiles

THE JEWISH population of Svislovitz lived in the upper part of the town, near the ruined windmill, and the gentile population in the lower half, in the direction of the Minsk road. But the division was not exact, for right in the midst of the Jewish quarter were the homes of the gentile "aristocracy," and more than one Jewish family took rooms in the gentile section.

As far as I remember, relations between Jews and gentiles in our town were friendly enough. Until the death of Alexander II (1881) I do not think we knew what it was to be afraid of a gentile. True, we lived in two distinct worlds, but it never occurred to us that *their* world was the secure one, while the foundations of *ours* were shaky. On the contrary, we accounted our world the nobler, the finer, the higher. Of course we learned even as children that we Jews were a people in exile, such being the divine decree, but that had nothing to do with the details of our daily life. The exile would come to an end when the Messiah would appear riding on a white ass: but in the interim we did not stand on a lower level than the gentiles.

We had a country in common, and we also had in common an Emperor who, seated on his throne, stretched his protecting hand over Jew and gentile alike. To be sure, we were afraid of the commissioner and the sergeant, but so were the gentiles.

The rabbi of our town never alluded to the country and to the Emperor except as "our" country and "our" Emperor. As evidence of the fact that the Emperor was good and wise, dispensing justice to all, we were told that under his outer garment he wore the *arba kanfot*—the Jewish four-fringed ritualistic undergarment. In the Emperor's case, however, the two fringes which fell behind were in perfect order, meeting all the religious prescriptions of the orthodox Jew, while the two fringes which fell in front were torn. One half of the garment was therefore valid, the other half void. With the valid half the Emperor reigned over the Jews, with the other half over the gentiles.

The district commissioner was the local emperor, and the entire population, Jew and gentile, trembled in his presence. All adults would rise from their seats and remain standing when he passed down the street, and the children would scatter at his approach. "Look out! Here comes the *stanovoy!*" At this cry they disappeared as if by magic, to emerge only when he had passed out of sight. He seldom ventured forth alone. Nearly always he was accompanied by his retinue—his clerk, the sergeant, and two policemen. His rule was stern and severe. In his private office or chancellery no one dared to sit down without special permission, and this permission he was seldom gracious enough to extend. He addressed nearly everyone in the familiar and contemptuous second person singular. Marvelously enough, it was an open secret that he thirsted after every kopek he could lay his hands on and could be bought body and soul for a five ruble note. Yet this did not seem to trouble him in his pose of the stern, incorruptible guardian of the law.

Of a commissioner of the same stripe in our neighborhood a

curious story was told. He, like his colleague in Svislovitz, was so eager for bribes that whatever came up before him in the course of his duties he saw only in the form of coin. On a certain day the body of a murdered peasant was found in the woods near his village. Upon receiving the information the commissioner at once proceeded to the scene and prepared his report. "On the murdered man," he wrote, "were five wounds, of which two were on his head. Of these one was the size of a copper ten kopek piece, the other the size of a silver half-ruble." He thus listed all the wounds with their sizes in terms of coins in a separate column. Under the column he drew a line, added the total, and reported that the murdered man had died of wounds amounting to one ruble and sixty-five kopeks.

The community clerk had little to do with the Jewish population, for the Jews were not peasants but of the *petite bourgeosie* and had a separate administration and a clerk of their own, who used to get their passports for them and act as their representative before the government. We therefore knew very little at first hand of the evil ways of our village clerk and of his fellows in neighboring townlets. Of one such official it was told that he was inordinately fond of beer, and whenever he had to set down the personal description of a peasant who came to him for a travel document, he would invariably enter, opposite "Eyes"—"Beer-colored." More than one peasant got into unexpected difficulties as a consequence.

The official village healer gave medical attention only to the gentiles. It was not his duty to cure Jews, but he would visit a Jewish home professionally for a fee. There was a "Jewish" doctor, Schwartz by name, who, however, did not happen to be a Jew; he was looked upon as a medical man of higher standing. But if the village healer served no useful purpose to the Jews in his official capacity, there was another which he placed freely at their disposal. He was an inveterate card player, and among the pupils whom he initiated into his favorite game, *préférence*, were a few of the young Jewish bloods of Svislovitz. *Préférence* was regarded as the chic game, outclassing our favorite, sixty-six, much as bridge out-classes poker. As *préférence* players some of our young men actually broke into the "aristocratic" society of Svislovitz, and were finally admitted to the house of one of the priests and even of the commissioner.

The two town priests, Yuremitch and Matzkevitch, lived on pretty much the same terms as two rabbis in a Jewish community about large enough for the services of half a rabbi—that is to say, like two cats in one sack. They were already elderly men in my time. Matzkevitch was a simple priest of low rank; Yuremitch stood somewhat higher in the ecclesiastical hierarchy. Matzkevitch was long and lean, and resembled an Egyptian mummy; Yuremitch was plump, with an imposing head of hair, black and silver, drawn into a pigtail behind, and an Assyrian beard. Above all, he had a splendid face, the face of a true prelate.

Matzkevitch's parish was the poorer one, and he lived the life of a peasant laborer, worked in the field, ploughed, harvested and threshed, fished, gathered berries and mushrooms. Yuremitch, with the richer parish, lived the life of a nobleman, was addicted to card-playing, drank the rarest wines, and used to arrange great receptions and even dances. Matzkevitch was ascetic, rigorously orthodox, severe in his interpretation of religious duty; Yuremitch was liberal, easy-going, with a happy-go-lucky relationship toward his Church. But his cheerful looks and his graceful gestures carried him farther than his embittered colleague. I remember that even we Jewish children were fond of Yuremitch, and even though he was a priest of the Greek Orthodox Church we often went up to him shyly and kissed his hand: it was a plump and pretty hand, which seemed to invite the kisses of the faithful. But we were afraid of Matzkevitch; there was not a glimmer of friendliness in his features. The older Jews, however, reserved their respect for Matzkevitch. True, a Greek Orthodox priest, a superstitious "remitter of sins," but an honest servant of God.

I must confess that in my earliest years, even before I went to *cheder* (elementary Hebrew school) I used to love to pass by the Orthodox church and, on the rare occasions when it was in use, the Catholic cloister, too, and listen to the services from the outside. The doors of the churches were kept open; I could look in and see the golden altar, the pictures framed in gold and the innumerable candles, also set in gold. Above the altar stood the priest, in a mantle which shimmered silver and gold. In vain did my mother explain to me that the gentiles worshipped false gods and that their services were not even worth looking at. In this respect my mother did not exercise complete discretion. In order to alienate us from the faith and church of others, she used to tell us of the marvelous raiment, the silver bells and pomegranates, which adorned our priests in the days of the Temple; and she also told us that the gentiles parodied in their services the vanished glories of our past. She did not understand that in telling us these stories she was not alienating us from the worshippers of "false gods." On the contrary, she made us all the more curious about them. I knew it was a sin to go by and look upon the altar and the forbidden pictures and raiment; but in the struggle between duty and curiosity, the latter always won. I used to say to myself: "I am not looking at the worship of false gods. I am only looking at that part of the service which was stolen from us." Something mysterious drew me to that alien altar, to the twinkling lights and the gilded images. In the sweet singing of the choir I heard the invitation: "Do not be afraid. Come to us, little Jewish child, see how beautiful, how pleasant is our service."

I remember watching from a distance, on cold winter days, the *Krishchenye*, the Pravoslav Christening of Jesus, the holiest day in the calendar of the Church.

A broad path was cleared through the snow from the portals of each church—Yuremitch's and Matzkevitch's—down to the bank of the frozen Beresina. Then, on the ice which covered the Beresina, a large circle was cleared of snow and marked off with young fir trees. In the center of the circle a cross was cut into the ice, and in the center of the cross a hole was bored through to the dark waters beneath. These were the preparations for the festival.

In the early morning the frozen air was translucent, biting, and bluish, as if a breath of steel had gone through it. The bells of both churches rang out, the big bells and the small, the big stately and golden, the little hurried and silvery; and in the air gold and silver and steel were mingled in a cold, clear harmony penetrating all the senses.

Along the center of the broad street came the sleds, dozens and dozens of them, bringing in the peasants of forlorn and scattered hamlets. The men wore brand new leggings, and on their heads were new bearskins, covering their ears. Round their waists they wore many-colored girdles. The women were dressed in gay, brilliant holiday attire, the throat and bosom flashing with beads, the head covered with a nun's wimple of white linen slashed with red. Instead of leggings the wealthier peasants wore long, polished boots, and instead of felt mantles, sheepskin coats.

The churches were packed to overflowing. As in all Greek Orthodox cloisters, there were no seats for the congregants, so that the peasants crowded in until every inch of space was filled. Even so there was not room enough for all; crowds of young peasants remained standing outside, and a wooden fence encircling them made them part of the congregation. The numbers of those who had to stand outside ran into the hundreds. They pressed closely together against the bitter cold while they listened to the chants inside; they stamped their feet and clapped their hands in rhythm to keep their limbs from freezing. The men stood with heads bared but the women kept their white and red wimples on. Outside of that crowd, stamping rhythmically, not a soul was to be seen on the streets. Every now and again the heads were bent in prayer and then were raised again; it was as if a wind were passing over a field of poppies.

When the prayers were over, the congregations streamed simultaneously out of both churches. First came the bearers of the holy banners, radiant pictures painted on silk and borne aloft on gilded standards. There were pictures of the Father, the Son, the Mother and Son and the apostles, and pictures of the later saints in which the Orthodox Church is particularly rich. Some of the banners depicted whole groups of figures and scenes that told the story of the Church.

After the banner-bearers came a group of very young girls carrying the image of the Virgin Mother of God. Not everyone was permitted to touch the gold frame round the image; this privilege was reserved for unstained girls, for which reason the carriers were chosen from among the very young, such as could not have had even a foretaste of sin.

After the image of the Virgin came the priest Yuremitch. He wore his costliest robes of gold, velvet and sky-blue silk. Over the robes he wore an "imitation" ephod, worked in gold and silver and decorated with crosses and images of flowers. A velvet miter towered on his head, and he was flanked on either side by the deacon and the reader. In one hand Yuremitch carried a prayer book, and from the other a silver censer swung on silver chains, and while the incense rose into the air he chanted the prayers in his deep, ringing voice. With his majestic figure, his long black and silver beard, his pigtail and his robes, Yuremitch looked an ancient elder of the Church who had stepped out of one of the banners in front of him.

At the top of the hill, where the cleared road began its descent toward the Beresina, the two congregations met, two processions alike in all respects save that the one from Matzkevitch's church looked poorer. Matzkevitch went, like the members of his flock, bareheaded—he was not entitled to a miter. Step by step the two processions went down to the Beresina, and on the ice the priests, the banner-bearers and the carriers of the images entered the cleared circle, while the crowd of worshippers formed in ranks around them.

Those of us who watched the processions from afar knew that "down there" they were baptizing some of the images in the icy water through the hole which had been bored in the ice. But this intimate ceremony was hidden from us. None of the elder Jews ever went out on the street to watch even from a distance; only a few of the younger ones were tempted out by the colors and the numbers. There was many a quarrel in Jewish homes before the more obstinate youngsters were permitted to go out. Our elders told us contemptuously that there was nothing to see, but not all their arguments—not even the warning that some of the younger peasants might drive us away with stones—could prevail. We had a powerful counterargument: "Don't some of them come to watch our processions round the pulpit on the Day of the Rejoicing of the Law? And if they can look at us, why can't we look at them?"

So as a child I had already looked upon their God and upon the Mother of God, and even then I knew that between us, between the gentiles and the Jews, ran a deep stream which separated two worlds. No bridge or ferry could carry us across the waters. I knew that, and yet, like a child which breaks its toy to see how it works, I lingered round their church and their processions, driven by a painful hunger to penetrate the secret of their faith. Were they really idol-worshippers, worshippers of images and false gods, as my mother said? Or was our God common to them and to us, as Stepan Harnai, a neighbor of ours, the chief trustee of Matzkevitch's congregation, used to argue?

Stepan Harnai was generally regarded as something of a scholar. He knew all the commandments of the Greek Orthodox Church and all of its long prayers by heart. He also knew a great many of the Bible stories. The gentiles of Svislovitz were very proud of him and used to say to us: "You're not the only scholars. We have our Stepan Harnai." The Jews, too, treated him with respect as a fine type of gentile, a man who was learned in the details of the faith of the gentiles. Our respect was increased by the fact that Stepan was a pious man, fond of religious discussion. The words "so God commands," "so the angels command" were frequently on his lips. He used to spend long evenings in our house, and as he had no business relations with my father, his visits were devoted to higher purposes, the discussion, with other visitors, of "the worthwhile things of life." Above all he liked to talk to my mother, who was greatly loved among the gentiles for her piety and for the goodness of her heart.

Slowly, carefully, he used to steer the conversation toward his religion, praising it to the skies and telling stories out of the New Testament and later sacred books. With these he used to mingle stories from the Old Testament, to show how tolerant he was and with what respect he treated the faith of others. "The main thing is," he used to wind up, "you have to believe in God and in His angels. If you do that you are certain of your place in the next world—Jews, Christians and even Tartars. But not the Turks and the Bashibazouks." These last two he excluded categorically from heaven in deference to the national politics of the times. The concession to the Tartars he made on local political grounds, the district commissioner being a Tartar by blood. Faith in God and the angels went hand in hand with a proper respect for the representatives of the government.

Stepan Harnai used to speak slowly, carefully, counting his words like coins. His face was calm, his bearing restrained; he never became excited. Yet there was something of the eternal missionary in the man. His religious faith was deep, and he sought to infect others with it. He chose for his endeavors the pious Jews, in the belief that where piety of one sort or another existed he stood the best chance. I recognized in later years that Stepan Harnai was not an ordinary man; he had a life philosophy of his own in which there was no room for doubts. He was a true seeker after God, one of those types that haunt the pages of Dostoevsky, types which belonged to old Russia and which were to be found among the simple folk of that land in greater numbers than elsewhere.

With my mother, faith was something deeper than passive conviction; she wanted to do more than merely believe; she wanted to be one of the defenders of God and the faith. But what was the good of arguing with Stepan Harnai? To begin with, she could not keep pace with him, quote chapter and verse for every assertion, as he did. Second, it was a dangerous matter; we, the Jews, were the people in exile, not the Russians. An unwary word might fall from her lips, and she would never be able to take it back. So my mother would remain silent most of the time, and now and again venture a cautious remark. But she suffered under the restraint.

Only when the company had dispersed and we, the family, remained alone, were the floods unloosed. "God in heaven! Why hast Thou given so little sense to the gentiles that they cannot see how vain their faith is, how foolishly they bend the knee before idols and images?" Then, turning to me, she told me the story of Abraham and his father Terah: how Abraham the child, left in charge of the shopful of idols, destroyed with an axe all but one, and placed the axe in the hand of the one that remained; and how, when his father returned, he blamed the remaining idol for the general destruction, thereby forcing from his foolish father the assertion that this was impossible, because the idol could not so much as lift a finger. She also told me the story of Nimrod and Abraham and the fiery furnace. "Let *them* show us miracles like that," she would wind up, stormily. "With their wooden images and their gilded picture and all their rubbish."

My mother told *me* the story but she was talking at the absent Stepan. She was pouring out her heart, strengthening herself in the faith, and carrying on a one-sided debate with the adversary who had gone home.

My father would never take part in these discussions. Evenings he would either be talking with his employees or going over his accounts. He was a severely practical man, with no use for idle talk; and when my mother became excited, he would interrupt with: "Elke, aren't you ashamed of yourself, letting such a silly business upset you? Who is Stepan Harnai? And why do you take his words to heart?" But how beautiful my mother was in such moments! In my eyes she was nothing less than a saint.

All evening the samovar stood on the table. When the water ran low we filled it again—it was never allowed to run dry. And when the fire at the bottom began to grow faint, and the samovar began to sing a hoarse chant, like the cantor at the end of a long day of prayer, we piled on the coal. Tea was not regarded as a special delicacy; anyone who wanted it was entitled to it.

This was the atmosphere in which I passed the winter evenings of my childhood. Toys were quite unknown. Little girls might be allowed their dolls, but boys, belonging to the sterner sex, had nothing to correspond. I could not go to bed early; my inmost nature rebelled against it, and all the threats and blandishments of my parents were of no avail. In the end I was permitted, by tacit understanding, to stay up with the others. I sat there, breathing in a psychic atmosphere in which mingled talk of forests and logs, business accounts, stories of God and the angels, and the rumblings of war among the nations.

CHAPTER FOUR

"Enough of This Freedom"

I CANNOT REMEMBER the first touches of the fingers of life waking me in the dawn of memory. More than once I have exerted myself to the limit of my powers trying to pierce the mist beyond a certain point, to carry the thread of recollection one inch father back. All my efforts have been in vain. Sometimes I have felt that nature sets as definite a term to our conscious beginning as to our end, and just as we cannot hold open the book when the hands of death begin to close it, so we cannot open it as long as the hands of life are determined to keep it closed.

Out of my pre-*cheder* years I have rescued only three incidents, but one general memory is strong with me: I was a merry child, I liked to play, to joke, to tease, with older people not less than with children of my own age. My mother told me that in the cradle I was the merriest of all her children, always in good humor and full of life. In one respect only I caused her much trouble. I would resist with stubborn energy her efforts to rock me to sleep, and I would close my eyes only when I had completely exhausted myself. So much my mother told me. What I myself remember is that I took full advantage of my healthy and powerful young frame and saw to it that my playmates should treat me with the right degree of respect. Not that I actually wanted to hit them till it hurt, such was not my nature. But I did like to hand out a punch, or a thump, playfully, *en passant*, as it were. As against this, however, my friends knew that I could be very useful to them. Whenever a quarrel broke out I was always on the side of the weaker; and this role of the elder administering justice tickled me mightily.

I have to confess that what pleased me was not so much the opportunity to dispense justice in a wicked world as the simple fact that my playmates obeyed me. A feeling of pride came over me very early and I began to look upon myself as one who stood on a higher level. Fortunately there was, as a counterweight to this dangerous tendency, the democratic influence of my home. My mother would tell me repeatedly that pride was a great fault, and that one ought to play with all children as equals. But something stronger than my mother's admonitions contributed to keep me in balance: I was exceedingly fond of company; I could not play alone. Now, the first requisite of a truly haughty spirit is to be able to do without those it holds in contempt, and as I could not do without my friends I had to treat them in a way which kept them at my side. I was in my element only when surrounded by a small army of playmates.

I was almost as happy with the older folk as in the company of my own kind. Among them, of course, my physical prowess counted for nothing; I therefore had to create a place for myself by means of something else—my tongue. There was company in the house at almost every hour of the day, neighbors who dropped in for a chat, for some business matter, or just for a glass of tea. I knew every one of them almost as well as I knew the members of my own family, and I listened to their stories with delight. Unlike the stories which were the diversion of the peasants, those I heard in my home had little to do with robbers, murderers, thieves and bandits. They dealt instead with the deeds of pious Jews, the prodigies of famous scholars, the achievements of saints and sages, their sayings and their sufferings. Whatever I heard I translated into my own language and gave it forth again as my own. It was my special way of finding myself at home among the older people, a participant in their conversations.

And my memory, which fails me in detail, still reproduces the wonder and the freedom and the joy of those first years before I achieved the status of a *cheder* boy. Father and Mother were both busy. The idea of a governess was quite unknown in Svislovitz, and the very suggestion would have been scorned as a sign of decadence and extravagance. The fact is that at the age of four I was already treated like a big boy. Whenever I forgot to put on the *arba kanfot*, my mother would speak seriously to me, as to a grown-up, and tell me how shameful it was for an adult Jew to be running about like a heathen without the reminder of his Jewishness hung about his body. There seemed, indeed, to be grounds for the fear that I would grow up into a wild reprobate, a discredit to a pious Jewish home, the chief ground being that I had too sharp a head and too quick a tongue. These sources of worry were, however, also a source of family pride. My particular forte was arithmetic, and my father taught me a trick—I have long since forgotten it—of putting the fingers together in some special way to facilitate multiplication. His pride frequently got the better of his common sense, and he used to show me off before our friends.

Of the three specific incidents which remain with me out of my pre-*cheder* years one was the death of a little sister, the second the marriage of a big one, the third a rebellion against Father.

Concerning the first I remember that it occurred before I

was enrolled in *cheder*, that is, before I was four years old. But how I remember this circumstance I cannot tell. Of the second I remember only the great reception arranged for the auspicious afternoon when the bridegroom came over from Bobruisk in the company of a grand retinue of parents, relatives and friends of the family. All the rest I must rebuild from my own fancy: the bridal canopy, under which the young couple became man and wife, lifted on its four posts in the courtyard of the synagogue; the music that went with pomp and parade through the streets of Svislovitz, and all the other appurtenances of a "wealthy" wedding. I do not at all remember my younger sister; but I do remember the terror which seized me when they uttered the word "dead!"; I remember the burning tears that ran down my cheeks. I do not, of course, remember how my parents bore the death of their baby; I suppose they bore it as all good, pious Jews bear similar bereavements. It is forbidden to mourn too deeply and to weep too long, and if the tears still persist in rising from the heart, they must be choked back before they reach the eyes and brim over.

The third incident, however, is quite clear in my mind; it stands as it were with feet planted firm on the threshold of memory, on this side of the mists.

My father had made preparations for a journey to the vast, tumultuous city of Bobruisk. He had already packed his portmanteau and had put on his wide travelling mantle. All this time I had stood to one side, watching closely and silently. But no sooner did Arey, the drayman, come driving up with his cart, than I shot like an arrow from the house, wound myself into the spokes of one of the wheels and began to scream at the top of my voice that I wanted to go with Father to Bobruisk.

My father was usually a stern man, but the hunger in me to see the city of Bobruisk, concerning which we little ones had heard so many marvelous and incredible things, overcame my fear of him. Neither his angry reproaches nor his promises to bring back for me a wonderful present were of any avail. I refused to be intimidated or comforted, and continued screaming that I wanted to go with him.

This was my first serious battle with my father: "You are a big, strong man, but I can cry. Let's see who'll win." Since that time Freud has explained on quite different grounds the conflict between father and son. I remember that this particular battle was long and obstinately contested; for some reason my father, with all his sternness and severity, could not bring himself to leave me in tears. Seeing that he was powerless, he sent for my grandfather, and when I saw the latter approaching, a sweet feeling of revenge and satisfaction welled up in me. "Ha! Big and strong as you are, you could not conquer me alone. You had to call Grandfather."

My grandfather took me in his arms and began to tell me seriously that little children dared not travel to Bobruisk. There were big forests on the way, full of wild beasts; and there was only one protection against them, to repeat a certain secret, sacred verse which children did not know. He therefore proposed something else; he would have another drayman harness a wagon and drive me, not, God forbid, to Bobruisk, through those terrible forests, but to the Count's estate, which lay at a distance of only one kilometer from the town, and which was reached through open fields where there was nothing to fear. There, he promised me, he would let me play in the nobleman's own garden, where all sorts of trees grew, pears and apples of every size, and even grapes under glass covers.

The picture that my grandfather drew was so charming, so enticing, that all of a sudden I was flooded with a feeling of pity for my father, who had to journey to Bobruisk through forests infested with fierce creatures. So I begged my father not to go on this dangerous journey, but instead to come with me to the Count's estate; and finally we arrived at a clever compromise. My father was to go to Bobruisk, and I with my grandfather to the estate. I accepted everything in good faith, and even gave my father permission to set out at once on his journey. But my father would not have it so. He waited till a second drayman had appeared, had harnessed the horse, and made all the preparations for my own unpremeditated journey. Then, sitting at my grandfather's side in the wagon, I called out to my father to start, and above all not to forget the magic verse which alone could conquer the wild beasts. My grandfather pinched my cheek, commended me to the bystanders as a clever little rascal—and we set off for the Count's estate.

This was my first, my very first journey. The wings of fancy carried me a thousand times faster than the plodding nag. I had the feeling that I was sweeping through the air. Every two or three minutes I turned round and observed, to my amazement and disgust, that the town of Svislovitz was still visible. I wanted it to disappear. I wanted to find myself at the point where heaven and earth meet, where, according to the accounts of playmates, a window opens into the skies. This is the window through which the tired sun crawls at night and lies down to sleep.

When at last we did reach the gardens, the houses of Svislovitz were no longer to be seen, and I was a happy child. On every side of me were countless fruit trees, with the first fruit of the year upon them. My grandfather told me that I could pluck all the pears and apples I wanted, but something in me, a mingling of happiness and a tender regard for the young, innocent fruit, kept me back. I was satisfied with the fruits which had fallen prematurely from the twigs. My grandfather kept his second promise, too. He led me to a house that was covered all over with glass, and there I saw, for the first time in my life, grapes, real grapes, the kind we got only in the late summer at home, growing on thin, tangled bushes. I did not dare to pluck any of them. Who would dare to pluck so rare a fruit?

The days of my freedom, my unrestricted happiness, drew

to a close. I remember clearly the evening which was the overture to the second drama of my life. At the close of one Sabbath, when the farewell prayer to the sacred day had already been intoned and we sat with friends round the samovar, my father drew me over to him and said: "My son: most children begin their *cheder* at the age of five. I think yours is a better head than most, and we'll start you a year earlier. From tomorrow on you will be a *cheder* boy. Enough of this wild freedom. It's time for you to begin learning Torah."

The news, coming so unexpectedly, was like a light that broke on my soul. At a single bound I changed in my own eyes, dropped the status of the carefree young scamp, and took on the dignity of a *cheder* boy. I would begin learning Torah the next day, the Torah concerning which my mother had told me so much that was dear and marvelous, the Torah which recurred in the refrains of so many of the songs she hummed in the late afternoon, before the evening prayer. The world opened before me and I saw myself a famous Jewish scholar, a prodigy, a saint; the gates of the world to come opened, too, Paradise, the golden thrones, words that were intimately woven into the texture of our home life, more familiar to me, by the frequency of their repetition, than a thousand physical objects.

CHAPTER FIVE

Early *Cheder* Years

"Two things it's never too late to do; to die, and to become a *melamed* [teacher] in a *cheder*." Only those Jews who have known the old life can understand the bitterness of that folk saying. To become a *melamed* was the last resort of every failure. If a young husband who, following the ancient custom, had been living with his in-laws while he studied the sacred books was suddenly compelled to earn a living; if a merchant met with disaster and was thrown on the street; if a respectable paterfamilias saw his house burn down and found himself without a roof over his head, the first thing he would turn to until his luck changed would be a *cheder*. This was one of the most melancholy phenomena in the Jewish life of the last century, for its shows clearly how low the concept of child education had fallen among us. Parents sent their children to *cheder* in obedience to tradition, but they paid little attention to the accomplishments or character of the *melamed*.

It should be remembered that the *melamed* was not merely a teacher in the technical sense, but also a mentor and trainer and complete educator. The majority of Jewish homes were wretchedly poor; the father was away from home from early morning till late at night; either he had a regular occupation and toiled at it twelve and fourteen and sixteen hours a day, or else he was a *Luftmensch* living from hand to mouth, petty merchant, broker, commission-man all rolled into one, running from client to client, from shop to shop, like a wild animal hunting for a bite of food. But not the father alone was thus enslaved; the mother, too, had her share of it. With few exceptions the Jewish mother not only kept her house going, but went out too, took in washing, labored in the gardens of others. She found work as a berry-gatherer, she went looking for feathers in the meadows where the geese were fed, or plucked the feathers of slaughtered fowl to stuff cushions—this last an occupation which was reserved for the late night, when the little ones were asleep and the lamp was turned down very low. Such was the lot of the average housewife. Still worse was that of the shopkeeper, chained to her store from early dawn till late at night, perspiring in the suffocating heat of summer, or shivering in the bitter cold of winter over the little earthen stove. So poverty stood with lifted whip over Jewish parents, driving them in a blind circle all day and separating them from their children.

And children were never lacking; they seemed to come in droves. Every house was a pyramid, with father and mother as base and the little ones building it up to the apex. Girls were not so bad; they were quieter at play and more obedient. But when it came to boys there was only one refuge for the parents; to turn them over for the entire length of the day into the hands of a severe *melamed*. And thus the whole point of the *cheder* was lost; it might have been a salvation for the child from the wretched environment of the home; but its real purpose was to save the unhappy parents from their own children. Thus the *melamed* became the lord and master of the Jewish child and brought ruin and misery on its tenderest years. From a folk school the *cheder* had been transformed into a sort of reformatory, in which every inmate was regarded as a young criminal. Only the very few, the chosen ones of fortune, escaped from those years of oppression more or less unharmed, with mind and body unruined.

I was one of those happy few. But it was only in later years that I understood how fearful had been the danger, and to whom I was indebted for my escape from it.

It was a happy Sunday morning in the early spring, soon after the Passover. My body still had on it the taste of the new suit, with real pockets. That morning my mother woke me early, gave me a bite to eat—I was still considered young enough to eat before prayers—and sent me off with Father to synagogue. There I sat down right next to him—a privilege seldom accorded me—and he bade me follow the prayer-reader with the closest attention. Some of the responses I already knew by heart. When prayers were over my father led me up to Mottye the *melamed* and said: "Mottye, this is your youngest pupil. Shmerel, this is your *melamed*."

Of course I already knew Mottye, the terror of the small boys of Svislovitz. "Never tell tales out of school" is an admonition as current in Jewish life as elsewhere, and it was followed there as little as everywhere else. In our youthful world the day's news bulletins never omitted to mention which boy had been laid across the bench, who had yelled during the punishment and who had borne his stripes in grim silence like a hero, refusing to give the *melamed* the satisfaction of a single yell. Mottye was accounted the cruellest of all when it came to whipping or pinching. He was known as Mottye the whipper, and Mottye the pincher, and Mottye the bean, this last because of his diminutive size—he was half the size of his wife—and his rolling walk.

At the bottom of Mottye's face there was a little sparse beard which, instead of imparting some dignity to him, made him look like a boy with a false beard on. He seemed to have understood that his appearance would not inspire discipline, and what his goatee could not do he entrusted with more assurance to the leathern thongs of his cat-o'-three-tails.

Immediately after *melamed* and pupil and been formally presented to each other, the entire company of relatives and friends, headed by Grandfather Solomon, repaired to our house. There a fine table had been prepared, with sweetmeats and drinks. I was seated in the place of honor, and a toast was drunk. My mother herself served the guests. To me was handed a prayer book. Two of the pages had been smeared with honey, and I was told to lick the honey off. When I bent my head to obey, a rain of copper and silver coins descended about me. They had been thrown down, my grandfather told me, by the angels; for the angels, he said, already believed in me, knew that I would be a diligent pupil, and were therefore prepared to pay me something in advance. I was immensely pleased to learn that my credit with the angels was good.

When the ceremony was over, my father wrapped me from head to foot in a silken *tallith* and carried me in his arms all the way to the *cheder*. My mother could not come along—this was man's business. Such was the custom among us. The child was carried in the arms of his father all the way to the *cheder*. It was as if some dark idea stirred in their minds that this child was a sacrifice, delivered over to the *cheder:* a sacrifice must be carried all the way.

Mottye the *melamed* had his own house, standing on a little hill. The house seems to have been modelled after Mottye rather than his wife; it was small, dilapidated and overgrown with moss: the moss was the counterpart of his sparse goatbeard. The door was low, and Mottye entered without stooping, but my father, when he carried me in, had to bend low.

Inside, he sat me down without further ceremony, gathered up the prayer shawl, and left. There I was, on a small, hard, wooden bench, with nine other children, two of them my first cousins, Gershon the son of Uncle Meyer, and Areh the son of Uncle Shmerel, both of them a year older than I, but beginners like myself.

The table in front of the bench consisted of rough, unplaned planks, with the heads of big nails sticking out. The children sat on two benches, one on either side of the table, and Mottye sat at one end. He had taken off his topcoat, and had replaced his hat with a pointed skullcap; thus his face lay between two points, the upper point of the skullcap and the lower point of his goatee. In one hand he held a wooden indicator. He did not sit still, but as he taught swayed back and forth. He bade us keep our hands above the table, watch out for the nails, and sit respectfully.

Mottye's wife supplemented his earnings by baking big corn loaves, and he occasionally helped her, for which reason he was sometimes called Mottye the baker. The oven stood in the room where he taught, so that an odor of fresh-baked bread always filled the room. On one wall hung the leather thongs, toward one side was a small bench, just large enough for the boy whom evil fortune should befall.

As soon as my father had withdrawn, Mottye made the round of the table, administered a friendly pinch to the cheek of every boy, seated himself at the head, and began the singsong lesson. And this was my induction into the immortal temple of the Jewish Torah, which is wider than all the earth and deeper than the sea.

Even before I became a *cheder* boy—I think it was from the age of three on—not a day passed but what I went to synagogue regularly for morning, afternoon and evening prayers, but like others of my age I was merely in attendance. There were only two responses we had to make like the grown-ups, the rest of the time we played outside, ducks and drakes, prisoner's base and heaven knows what else. One of us, however, was always stationed at the synagogue door, to warn us of the approaching moment when we would have to be present for the responses. But since we were too young to follow the long prayers in detail, our sentinel had to rely on instinct rather than knowledge. The moment he called out: "Hey, the response!" we left our play, even though it was at a most passionate climax, and tumbled into the synagogue.

It was round the synagogue game that my first clash with Mottye the bean occurred, and that with little delay. I do not know whether it was on the day following my induction, or the day after, but it came about in this wise: Among my little group I was the commanding general and issued regular instructions as to the order of the games. Apparently I did not quite realize the extent of the change which had come into my life, for on the morning in question I no sooner arrived at the synagogue than I gathered my army together, trooped out with it, and decided on the game. I did not even bother to appoint a sentinel, for it was much too early, and the cantor had not yet begun. We had been playing for only a few minutes, and the first response was still a long way off, when suddenly there appeared, silently, as if he had shot up out of the earth, Mottye the bean, wrapped in his prayer shawl, and with phylacteries on arm and forehead. I remember that on one side of the head phylactery the letter *shin* (for *Shaddai*, or Almighty) had its usual three stems, but on the other side there was a letter *shin* which in an ecstacy of piety blossomed into four stems. There Mottye stood, immobile, suspicious. The children fell into a panic; like soldiers caught larking by an officer in a serious situation, they stood, wordless, trembling, at attention. I was less frightened than astonished. What was Mottye the bean doing here?

If at least he would say something! What was it he wanted, sneaking up furtively on us like this, in the midst of our play?

There he waited, silent as a ghost, looking us over with his green, catlike eyes, looking us over first as a group, then each one of us separately; and we looked back at him. It lasted a whole minute. Meanwhile we saw something kindling in his eyes; he was planning something, choosing someone. And then, sure enough, he decided on his victim. Carefully, softly, deliberately, he went up to one of my playmates, took him by the right ear with two fingers of his left hand, and with all five fingers of his right hand delivered a tremendous slap on his left cheek. "*Cheder* boys don't play during prayers! When everyone is praying, *cheder* boys remain standing near their *rebbi*. Back inside, you little heathens!"

Thunderstruck, humiliated, we crawled after him into the synagogue. None of us had the courage to defend himself, or at least to protest, demand an explanation. We followed him as though we had really committed a crime, but within me my blood was boiling. First of all, how were we supposed to know? Only yesterday, or the day before, the games had been permitted; nobody had said a word. Secondly, why had he picked out one of us and thrown all the guilt on him? The longer I brooded on the injustice of it the greater it became, till I made up my mind that this thing could not be permitted to pass just so. I would lodge a complaint against my *rebbi* before my father and mother.

As soon as prayers were over I fled from the synagogue and got home before my parents. I did not wait for them, but rehearsed my story to whomever I found. Then, when my parents arrived, all my pent-up rage burst forth, so that it took me some time before I could tell the story coherently. And there was no doubt in my mind as to the verdict.

But this incident was fated to be the first great disillusionment of my life.

My father heard me to the end—and refused to enter into any sort of discussion. "The *rebbi* is right and you are behaving like a fool." Those were his words, sharply uttered, final. I tried to begin all over again, but my father interrupted me and refused to let me finish.

I turned with imploring eyes to my mother, my last court of appeal. Now, after such a signal failure with my father, I was no longer so sure of myself; and it was here that the real disillusionment came. For my mother, my own mother, was not on my side. She was, to be sure, softer than my father, and her sentence was delivered more mildly, but she too said: "My child, you must know that a *rebbi* can do no wrong." I repeated my unanswerable thesis: "What right had he to choose just one of us and slap only him?" My mother answered: "That is the way things are, my child. You can't slap everybody, so today you slap one, tomorrow you slap another, and in the meantime all the others are afraid and learn to obey."

I should explain that the slap in and for itself did not astonish me, for I knew that *rebbis* slapped. I had already seen boys slapped by their *rebbi;* but those slaps had had something remote about them. Here was a slap which had fallen very close to me; and as my mother said: "Today you slap one, tomorrow another . . . ." I perceived that the grown-ups had entered into a conspiracy, and a hunger for revenge awoke in me. I alone, without the help of a single grown-up, would have to take vengeance on Mottye the bean . . . . I had no plan, and I took counsel with no one, young or old. I buried my rage deep in my heart and waited for the opportune moment.

That day I sat in *cheder* plunged in sadness. I enjoyed nothing, neither the lessons nor the games outside the house. I had hoped that at least Mottye would not be himself that day, that he would be depressed and absent-minded, brooding on the injustice he had committed. Nothing of the sort! He sat there, collected, swaying back and forth, as much at his ease as on other days, his little face enclosed between the two points. And not only the *rebbi*, but the boys, too, were the same as ever! The entire incident had passed without leaving a mark on any of them. "If that be so," I decided silently, "there is no one to talk to. I too will pretend that I have forgotten." But I could not forget, and for many days my happiness was marred by the protests which I had to choke back.

That afternoon we came out of the *cheder* as usual, but I did not join in the singing. The spring afternoons in Svislovitz were always beautiful, and most beautiful of all was the hour before sunset. Everyone came out then for a breath of fresh air, the entire population was seated on the porches and balconies before the houses. Along the broad street the shepherd drives home the flocks: the goats lead, themselves led by a guide, and after them come the cattle, some with young. The housewives leave their places on the porches, each one to seek out her cow or goat, to drag it home and get a glass of warm milk for the youngest children. Some of the animals have special names. One of them, a large, quiet cow, slow and stately of motion, is called the *rebbitzin*, the rabbi's wife. From the far-off meadows and woods the fresh odor of springing earth is carried across the town, and a spirit of peace and rest descends upon the houses, upon the watchers on the balconies, upon the shepherds and the flocks.

I cannot remember what became of my plans for vengeance on Mottye the bean. I imagine they came to nothing, but my relations with my first *rebbi* remained cold and formal. There never woke in me the faintest spark of love or respect for him. However, I do remember that in later years, when I had become a student of Talmud and was popular in the town, Mottye the bean would often come up to me, stroke my cheek and declare fondly that he had always liked me and that he had been my best friend.

One day he came to our house before evening prayers and

told us a story. The story was for the older people, its moral was for me. "It is well known," said Mottye, "that one ought to respect one's *rebbi* just as much as one respects one's parents —if not more. So it is written in all the sacred books. But the question arises, *which rebbi?* For the child passes in time through the hands of several *rebbis*, the elementary ones, the middle ones, the advanced ones. Now this question was once brought up in the very highest place, namely, before the Divine Tribunal above. And there the answer was given that the place of honor belongs to the *rebbi* who taught the child the alphabet. The reason is plain enough. The later *rebbis*, they who taught you the Pentateuch, the Bible, the Mishnah and the Talmud, could have erred. Wittingly or unwittingly, they may have misled you. But the *rebbi* who taught you how to read could not have erred; he would not confuse a *gimmel* with a *nun*, a *shin* with a *samech*. And does not the whole Torah consist of letters, single letters in combination? The *rebbi* who teaches you the letters lays a sure foundation, but those that come after him build walls which may be straight and may be crooked." The sledgehammer hint had no effect on me; I remained as cold toward him as I had always been.

Apart from that famous slap I have no memories of my first month in *cheder*. I have a simple check: I cannot remember the names of the boys who got whipped that month, and that a month should have passed without whippings is impossible. Naturally, I did not understand it then, but the picture has since become quite clear in my mind. Mottye the bean was simply a sadist; his whippings had no educational purpose; they were an end in themselves. He derived an intense joy from the agonies of the little victims trembling and shivering on the bench. He used to administer the whippings coldly and slowly, without ever betraying a glimmer of rage. This only increased the terror and anguish of the child, which in turn increased the joy of the *rebbi*. All the entreaties in the world, all the promises to behave in the future, were wasted. Mottye the bean did not budge; he asked the boy to let down his clothes, lie down across the bench and get what was coming to him.

Some of my playmates were weak and would submit at once, get their portion of stripes, and then go into a corner to weep away the pain rather than the shame; for the truth is that, with all of us in the same boat, no one was ashamed before his fellows. Others, stronger and prouder, did not give in so readily. They fought, struggled, defended themselves tooth and nail, until they were exhausted. In those cases too the *rebbi* betrayed no anger. Calmly, silently, he wore the victim out, and when no spark of resistance remained, he put the boy quietly across the bench and pitched in with the leather thongs.

These he used with the same cruel joy for a slip of memory as for a misdemeanor. He was careful to explain why it was necessary to whip a boy who did not study well. "You must understand," he said, "that in every person there is a Good Spirit and an Evil Spirit. The Good Spirit has its own dwelling-place, which is the head. So has the Evil Spirit—and that is the place where you get the whipping. But the Good Spirit always remains at home, whereas the Evil Spirit is forever creeping out of its den and pushing its way into the home of the Good Spirit. Now when both Spirits are in the head, the head gets stuffed up and there is no room for new ideas—the little boy can't learn. There's only one thing to be done: put the little boy across the bench and let him have it. Then the Evil Spirit hears someone knocking at his door, gets frightened, and runs back. That leaves the head free again. And so, children," he wound up, "I do you a service when I punish you."

Until this day a shudder runs through my body when I think of the horrible world in which we passed our tenderest years. If the famous Joshua ben Gamala, the founder of the *cheder*, could have risen from his grave to see what had become of his idea of the folk school, he would have hastened back in an agony of shame. I would not be wrong in saying that one-third of the *cheder* hours were taken up by the stupid, ugly squabbles between *rebbi* and pupils, and the remaining two-thirds were poisoned by them. I am speaking now of the elementary *cheder*, for the youngest children. The teachers of the higher grade were a trifle more restrained, and the Talmud teachers used corporal punishment very rarely.

During the first term the children studied only half a day —actually from nine to four. With the second term they entered on full day studies. The poorer boys seldom used to go home for their midday meals; they brought their lunches with them, consisting usually of a piece of unbuttered bread, the tail of a salt herring, and perhaps a bagel for dessert. If the bread was buttered, or smeared with chicken fat, the dessert was off. I remember well that during the whole week none of my poorer playmates ever brought to *cheder* a piece of meat or of fish other than herring. Nor did they have milk to drink. Milk was either for the very little ones, or to be sold. When we recall that food was ridiculously cheap in those days, we get some idea of the poverty which reigned among the vast majority of the Jews of Svislovitz. But for that matter even the children of the well-to-do were brought up on a Spartan regime. Our clothes were less patched, our food a little better, but we knew nothing of luxuries. This did not arise from a spirit of miserliness, for our budget was a generous one, even by modern standards; but our parents were afraid of spoiling us. My mother was surely goodhearted and kindly, but whenever I asked for something she considered a little out of the way, she would answer: "Don't look up, look down. See how your poorer playmates live."

The discipline of our early upbringing was reflected in more than our food and clothing; it affected our entire bearing. My poorer playmates had to become "independent" at an early age, for the simple reason that there was no one to look after them.

At the age of five, or six, they were already little men. They went to synagogue alone, each with his prayer book clutched under his arm. They went alone to *cheder*, through the darkness, the rain and the frost. They had to look out for the dogs, and for the horses wandering on the footpath. In larger, wealthier communities, there were ushers to take the children to *cheder* and bring them home. In Svislovitz the usher was unknown. The only help the child got was a lamp made of writing paper and fashioned in the manner of a Chinese lantern.

I cannot stress too strongly the dominating, the exclusive role which the *cheder* played in the life of the young Jewish boy. He saw his parents only for half an hour in the morning —before first prayers—and then for an hour in the evening, before he went to sleep. The *rebbi*, who thus became the complete master of the child, did not, however, pay any attention to matters of physical cleanliness. When the mother complained that the child came home in the evening altogether too dirty for a single day's study and play, the *rebbi* would retort sarcastically that he was not a wet nurse.

Thus it came about that there was little intimacy between parents and children, or even between brothers if they happened to attend different *cheders*. Between brother and sister there was even less opportunity for the ripening of friendship and affection. A wall stood between boys and girls—the latter did not go to *cheder* and had nothing to do with studies. The brother looked upon his sister as another kind of creature, belonging to another world. When my youngest brother grew old enough to distinguish between those grown-ups whom he might address with the familiar *du* and those who had to be addressed formally with *ihr*, he placed in the second class even his older sisters, and had to be told that he was permitted to classify them with the other members of his family.

CHAPTER SIX

Festivals and Fasts (1)

The first festival I observed as a *cheder* boy was the Lag b'Omer ("the thirty-third day of the Omer," the "Omer" being the seven week period between the Passover and the Pentecost). It commemorates the suspension of the plague among the pupils of Rabbi Akiba in the time of bar Kochba, the mighty rebel who for three years carried on a war against the Emperor Hadrian. We still had to study half the day, but the atmosphere was festive. We would bring boiled, colored eggs to *cheder*. The poor boys brought two, one for the *rebbi*, one for themselves; the richer boys brought more. The eggs were colored by being boiled together with onion skins or nettle leaves or other plants.

The game of "colored eggs" we learned from the gentiles, who used to play it at Easter time. It was simple enough. Each of the opponents held his egg at the broad end and the narrow ends were tapped together. The first egg to crack lost, and at the end of the games one veteran egg, unconquered and unbroken, was master of the field and owner of all the other eggs.

One other game belonged to Lag b'Omer—bows and arrows,

a memory of the struggle between the insurgent Jews and the Roman legions. We made the bows out of bent twigs and the *rebbi* himself taught us this game because it was part of sacred history. He told us how Rabbi Akiba had held war with the enemy. "Who knows," he said, narrowing down his little eyes, "but that some day you might find the art useful." His ideas of warfare were drawn from sacred history. But he bade us be careful and not shoot at each other, for fear of putting out an eye. His caution was excessive; our bows never carried the arrows more than a couple of feet.

Equally clear in my memory is the first Pentecost (Shevuoth) of my *cheder* years and the preparations for it. My mother told me for the first time of the giving of the Torah to the Children of Israel: of Mount Sinai, wrapped in sheets of fire and clouds of smoke; of the tablets of the Law, engraved with exactly the same letters as I was learning to read in *cheder*, telling the Jews forever and ever what they might and what they might not do. Her voice was proudest and happiest when she told me of that *rebbi* of old, the teacher of the whole Jewish people, Moses: how he delivered us from the hands of the gentile, how he divided the sea for us, so that the waters stood up on either side like the fir trees on the royal road that led from Svislovitz to Pinsk and Bobruisk. So dry was the passage left between, that the Children of Israel did not even have to take their shoes off. Then she told me how Moses had led us through a wilderness abounding in scorpions and snakes, with the pillar of fire before us on the march. She explained the incident of the wilderness very simply: Moses wanted to teach us, during those years, all of his Five Books, the Pentateuch, just the ones I was learning in *cheder*. And the wilderness was good because no gentiles were there to interrupt the lessons.

Mottye the bean told us the same story, but Mother's way of telling it was better, heartier, tenderer. When the *rebbi* told the story I just listened; when Mother told it my heart began to beat, and my imagination to burn with bright fires of its own. I looked before me, not at the walls of the room, but at scenes so distant that my eyes hurt. I dreamed: perhaps some day the Svislo would rear into walls, and sheets of flame and billows of smoke would encircle Castle Hill. There, on the highest story, Moses would appear, and the letters of the Law would be engraved on the four wings of the mill, telling us again of the things we might do and the things we might not do.

Three days of preparation—half-holidays for the children—preceded the Pentecost, and all the restlessness and curiosity that we had repressed for weeks broke out. There were a hundred things to do, but the most important was to run off to the banks of the Svislo and the Beresina, to watch the raft-binders at work. My father's rafts that year were among the late ones, and every day he was on the river urging the workers on. The actual binding of the rafts was done by Jewish workers, all belonging to a widely ramified family, the Poliessuks, which had monopolized this branch of the work for many generations. During the winter they were peddlers, wandering, sometimes in the most fearful weather, from village to village. They lived an extraordinarily clannish life, like some Arab tribe with the sheikh at its head. All of them were hardened by labor and exposure, of magnificent build and with muscles like the roots of old trees. They lived the simple, penurious life of peasants, adding to their savings kopek by kopek. I remember how one of them, a young man by the name of Ari Vol, came before Passover into the store of my older sister, to buy wheat flour for the festival: he asked for a sack of flour weighing five *pud*—two hundred pounds. The bystanders burst into a shout of laughter, whereupon the young giant blushed, and stammered: "It's very hard, you know, to fill yourself up on wheat." I do not believe that any member of the Poliessuk family had ever eaten his fill of wheat flour, which they regarded as an extraordinary luxury. Even the loaf which ornamented the table for the Sabbath eve was baked of corn.

After the Pentecost came a long stretch of monotonous days to be broken, not by a festival but by the "Three Weeks" which lie between the seventeenth day of Tammuz and the ninth day of Av. The period is in the summer. On the seventeenth day of Tammuz the enemy besieging Jerusalem broke through its walls, and on the ninth day of Av, having fought his way through the city, he set fire to the Temple. The seventeenth day of Tammuz is a minor fast, the ninth day of Av is the "Black Fast." For those three weeks it was our *duty* to be mournful, in *cheder* and everywhere else, and to walk about with heads down and eyes fixed on the ground. We were not permitted to bathe in the Svislo except on Friday afternoons, and that not so much for the body's well-being as for the sake of the Sabbath, which is so sacred that it thrusts aside all mourning. In the last nine days of the Three Weeks the mourning was intensified. We were forbidden then to eat meat, again with the exception of the Holy Sabbath. With regard to this last law, the prohibition of meat during the last days of the Three Weeks, most of the Jews of Svislovitz registered a clear gain in their heavenly accounts: they did not have a piece of meat to look at during the other weekdays of the year either. The privation which ordinarily was the result of their poverty could during this period be credited in heaven to their piety.

I do not remember whether I was really sad during the whole of the Three Weeks, but the last nine days did have their effect on me. There was little change in my father's customary bearing, but my mother went about the house pale and subdued, and more than once there were on her cheeks the signs of weeping. Round her an atmosphere of real suffering and sadness formed, and spilled through the house.

My mother was the first to recount to us the horrors of the destruction of the Temple, and she laid the colors on thick. She told us about Nebuchadnezzar and Nebuzaradon, and about

Nero and Titus the wicked. It was on the last, perhaps because he was the nearest in retrospect, that she poured out all the bitterness of her repressed and tormented soul. In her telling of the story there was so much freshness, so much passion, and so much personal protest, that the sense of time disappeared. It was as though she had been a participant in the calamities of our forefathers. It was not the history of a national destruction but the recital of a personal disaster. She carried us from Svislovitz back to Jerusalem, up to the summit of the hill of the Sacred House shining in its glory, and she showed us the ark and its cherubim, the altar of brightest gold, the High Priest in the splendor of his robes and the Levites with their gorgeous instruments—viols and harps and trumpets and drums.

Then followed the story of the Destruction. My mother always used the words "we," "us," "our," but not as a rhetorical trick. *Us* the cruel enemy cut down, *ours* was the house he brutally destroyed. I felt then as though only yesterday, we, our family, our relatives and friends, had been living in Jerusalem the Marvelous, and only yesterday Titus the wicked had driven us out to Svislovitz, so that instead of the golden Temple and the High Priest we had the wooden synagogue and Mottye the bean.

And just as seriously as she told us of Nebuchadnezzar and Titus the wicked, she told us of the hateful role played during the Destruction by the spiders and swallows. These two creatures were on the side of the enemy. When the latter laid siege to the city they poured in from all sides, carrying fire in their mouths. The sparrows, however, were on our side, and they came in carrying water in their mouths, but they could not prevail against the spiders and the swallows. Regarding the swallows, moreover, she told us that to this day they had the mark of their treachery stamped on them: under their throats there is a speck of red which commemorates forever their incendiary role.

It occurred to none of us to ask mother how the swallows

and spiders could carry fire in their mouths without being burned up. Whatever mother told us was sacred, so that even if the question had occurred to us we would have stifled it. Apart from its immediate effect on us, the story made us change our attitude toward swallows. We had always hated spiders anyway, but until we heard of their unspeakable treachery we had rather liked swallows, because of their black wings, their graceful flight and, indeed, for that little red mark under their throats. But from now on they were on the list of accursed things. Later on, when we went nesting, we always spared the nests of the sparrows, but we destroyed without mercy the eggs of the swallows.

I have often wondered where this strange folk legend came from, and why the hatred of a people has been directed against that innocent and charming bird, the swallow; but I have never been able to trace it to its origin.

Before the Black Fast came the Sabbath *Chazon*, the Sabbath of Vision, and it was truly a black Sabbath. On this one occasion the joy and contentment which the Jew is commanded to feel on the day of rest were overshadowed by the huge wings of our unforgettable disaster. That Sabbath a black curtain was drawn across the ark in the synagogue and all the worshippers, including the most important citizens, those that sat in the places of honor along the eastern wall, came in their workaday clothes. Judah, the president of the synagogue, came almost in rags, with buttons missing on his coat, his shirt visible in front, his earlocks hanging in neglect over his ears. Judah became in himself the total symbol of the Destruction. Close to the cantor's desk, apart from the rest, sat his older brother, Ziskind, competing with Judah for the palm of desolation. But his thin face, instead of expressing wretchedness and sorrow, bore on it a cruel and angry look; I always thought that it belonged more to the triumphant army of Titus the wicked than to the fleeing hordes of the vanquished and ravaged Jews.

In the right hand corner, in the shadow of the ark, sat the *Rav* himself, Rabbi Wolf, who was both a scholar and a saint. From his wrinkled face shone piety and learning. He had put on no outward symbols of mourning, but when they called him up to read aloud from the Torah, he walked with slow, quiet steps, like a man deep sunk in thought, and over us came the feeling: "This is the bearing of a man who remains noble and dignified even in sorrow." In later years, when I read how the elders of the Sanhedrin had followed in chains the gilded chariot of Titus the wicked, I saw them walking with the same slow pace, the same silent sadness, as old Rabbi Wolf.

The mood in the synagogue was not only mournful; it was eerie. The usual Sabbath melodies were replaced by doleful threnodies, and the portion of the Prophets intoned after the usual reading of the weekly portion of the Pentateuch was taken from the Lamentations of Jeremiah. The congregants moved about the synagogue like shadows. And though I know —and felt even then—that much of this was artificial and forced, yet there were sensitive faces on which was written the reflex of a great sorrow and a great loss.

In the house, too, the Sabbath of Vision extinguished the usual happiness of the sacred day. True, the Sabbath was always sacred, but now it was like a beloved visitor who comes into a house where some bereavement has just occurred. The honor of the visit cannot be ignored, but all the ceremonies are grave and stately, without the usual intimacy and affection.

A strange scene would be enacted that afternoon in the house. There came, on their regular Sabbath visit to my mother, her friends and neighbors, all the wives of the well-to-do Jews of Svislovitz. They wore clothes neither of the Sabbath nor yet of the weekday, a compromise between duty and pride. On the table, instead of the usual tea, there was nothing but the big, leather-bound Yiddish translation of the Pentateuch in use among women. Without greeting, without preliminaries, the women sat down around the table and my mother began to read aloud the passage from Jeremiah attached to that week's portion. The original text is oppressive enough, but the Yiddish text was accompanied by a commentary. On every verse, as on a foundation, was reared a superstructure of gruesome stories and legends taken from the books of the ancient writers and the later ones of the Middle Ages. My mother had not read very far when there arose round the table not a weeping, but a sort of wailing, the wailing which goes up from a city given up to the sword. It was as though all the cruelties and miseries of the Destruction were being reenacted in that room.

I sat next to my mother and mingled my tears with hers. Most of all I was shaken by the story of Hannah and her seven sons, which I heard for the first time in that setting. Even while I wept I felt in myself an overwhelming pride in that youngest son, a child, perhaps of my age, perhaps a *cheder* boy too, who stood like a hero before the oppressor and would not bend the knee to an earthly god. And I swore, too, that never, never, would I bend the knee to idols.

It was on the eve of the Black Fast that I learned that human beings could eat bread dipped in ashes. I was astounded by the ceremony. I stared with bulging eyes at the older people who swallowed the horrible mouthfuls, but I did not dare to emulate them.

In the synagogue we sat in stockinged feet, as one sits in the house of a mourner. The lamps were unlit; in their place tallow candles were fastened into lecterns laid flat on the floor; and after the evening prayer the congregation, too, sat on the floor, and the saying of Jeremiah's Lamentations began. The half-darkness in the synagogue, the lecterns strewn about, the naked ark stripped of its gilded curtain, the oppressive chanting —all threw terror into my soul. Everyone and everything wept. The stifled sobs of the men were like a bass accompaniment to the shriller sound of weeping that came from the women's section. The naked ark wept, and a weeping came from the shadowed walls. And the candles fastened into the overthrown lecterns wept tallow tears that ran down their sides.

In our house, that night, the children were not permitted to swallow anything after the evening meal, not even a glass of water. And that night, of course, we always felt thirsty.

The next morning, however, the effect was somewhat dissipated. On the first Tisha b'Av of my *cheder* years the sun came out bright and clear. It threw its rays with a prodigal hand into the synagogue, and disturbed the mood. Besides, we children began to be absorbed in the mechanics of the thing, and we looked with more curiosity into the faces of our elders. We observed that those who were chanting the Lamentations with the loudest and most terrifying voices had no tears at all upon their cheeks, and the kind of weeping which is not accompanied by tears could not impose on us. For we knew all the degrees of weeping: the weeping that is genuine and goes with tears, the weeping that is forced and squeezes out the tears, and the weeping which cannot even get as far as a tear —weeping to order. Then a doubt stole into my mind, and I wondered whether the night before, when their faces had been shrouded in darkness, the older people had not put upon me. We noticed also that some of the older people were amusing themselves by throwing burrs into one another's heads and beards; at least it seemed to us as if they were amusing themselves; and if the older people were making a game of it, we younger ones were surely permitted to do it.

Thus it came about that for the children of the Day of the Destruction, as contrasted with the foregoing eve, was really interesting and pleasant. Of the visit to the cemetery, traditional on Tisha b'Av, I have already told—a gay outing for the very young, with nut-gathering and berry- and apple-picking. We went through the woods, and through the open fields, ripe with the harvests of corn and wheat and oats. The ears twinkled innumerably in the sunlight, and in this golden sea were the peasant girls in red dresses, with red kerchiefs on their heads. With their sharp scythes, which flashed silver in the sun, they mowed their way through the fields. Out of their healthy, powerful throats the harvest songs floated into the sunlight. And here we went in Indian file, the children of a defeated people . . . . Need I confess that all my heart was drawn from the ruins of the past to the living fields of the workers?

CHAPTER SEVEN

Festivals and Fasts (2)

We got little joy out of the summer. While the sun was shining outside, and woods and fields were blossoming, we sat imprisoned in the dark, narrow *cheder* from morning till night. We seldom saw the happy world, and in our young minds an idea was born and grew stronger from week to week: God had made the town and the houses, the shops and the *cheder*, for *us;* the fields and the woods he had created for the gentiles. It angered me that none of the earth belonged to the Jews. I argued the question frequently with my mother, but she had an eternal answer: "Wait, my child; the Messiah will come and we shall have both forests and fields."

The week before New Year we were told not to be terrified if, in the middle of the night, we heard a knocking at the window. It would be the wakers for the night prayers which usher in the New Year. These prayers were only for the grown-ups, but I had scarcely become a *cheder* boy before I begged to be taken along, and my wish was granted. That night I did not close my eyes for fear of sleeping through the call. I heard it, leaped into my clothes, and went into the living room. The samovar already stood on the table, and my father, my mother, my older brother and I took glasses of tea before going to the synagogue.

The night was cool and clear, and in the deep blue heavens the stars shone, countless and bright. In my mind, as in the mind of every other Jewish child with my upbringing, there was not the slightest doubt that there, above, behind the stars, God sat. Our God, of course, for there was no other. He looked down between the stars and watched the Jews rising so early to go to night prayers. I was happy that I was there among the older people passing in review before Him.

The *Slichoth*, or Penitential Prayers, made an even deeper impression on me than the Lamentations of Tisha b'Av. I saw a synagogue packed in the dead of night; no Nebuchadnezzar or Titus the wicked was mentioned. There was only God enthroned above the stars and toward Him our prayers streamed; and all that was mystic in me woke in response.

On Rosh Hashanah, New Year's day, the *yishuvniks* came to town. There is no word for *yishuvnik* in English, for the type is known only to us. The *yishuvniks* were the Jews who lived abandoned in the midst of some gentile village or settlement, alien figures in a world not their own. Months might pass without their seeing the face of another Jew. We did our best to make them feel at home, gave up to them our nicest rooms, and in the synagogue assigned to them the places of honor. We children received the children from the backwoods with all friendliness. Some of them were wild creatures, terrified by the vast crowds of Svislovitz. The elders took special pains with them; my father would take some of them on his knee, caress and comfort them, and we would teach them some of our games.

Thus the New Year would have been a jolly festival if it had not been drummed into us that the Day of Judgment was at hand. God sat enthroned in the midst of His cohorts of angels, and one after another the tremendous account books were laid before Him, with their debit and credit columns of bad and good deeds; and God decided who should live out the next year and who should die, who among the living should be sick, and who well; and the prayers went into such details that my soul trembled. Young as we were, our elders already had breathed into us the terrors of death and had broken up the pure peace that had been in our minds. We were spiritually careworn in days which should have been utterly carefree. I was scarcely more than a baby when I lay awake the night of the New Year and implored God for mercy on my father and mother.

There was something of a relief in the *Tashlich* ceremony, when we went down to the river to shake our sins into it. The place we chose was the spot behind Castle Hill, where the Svislo falls into the Beresina. It seemed to me like a first-class idea. The usual ceremony was to flap the skirts of our garments over the water; but in an excess of piety many of us turned our pockets inside out. I do not know what my sins were, but I shook my coattails and my pockets mightily, and when I left the river brink with my father I felt I had been relieved of a great weight.

The eve of Yom Kippur was the holiday of the *yishuvniks*. On New Year's day and on the day of Yom Kippur, the White Fast, we were absorbed by our prayers, but Yom Kippur eve was free, and then the *yishuvniks* found a little consolation for the lonely days they passed in alien worlds far from their own kind.

Little has been written in Jewish literature concerning the life and the spiritual tragedies of the *yishuvnik*, and that little has made of him a purely comic figure. Nothing has been written of his deep suffering, his loneliness, the pain of his uprooting. He lived forgotten in an environment to which he had to look for his daily bread but to which he could not belong. While the father worried about his meager livelihood, the mother worried about the little ones growing up wild, untutored, taking on, perhaps, the worst habits of the peasants. Little wonder that the *yishuvniks* waited with longing for the coming of the New Year.

The door of our house was never closed during the eve of the Day of Atonement, and not one of the *yishuvniks* failed to come and pay his respects. Many of them had brought with them quantities of cakes and sweemeats to distribute in the synagogue—a custom which we townsmen set great store by. There was a curious belief that if God intended to make a beggar of you in the forthcoming year, you could perhaps fulfill that part of your destiny by accepting a piece of cake from a stranger. Meanwhile there would be much talk about the marvels of our Jewish laws and commandments: how wonderful it was that feasting on the eve of Yom Kippur should be as meritorious as fasting the next day. The *yishuvniks* rejoiced particularly in the first of these commandments and made the most of it.

A ceremony which took my breath away the first time I saw it was performed during the afternoon before Yom Kippur. One after another grown-up Jews stretched themselves on the floor of the synagogue vestibule while Lazar the psalm-sayer, who was also Lazar the bath-attendant, stood over them with leather thongs and whipped them unmercifully. I knew, of course, that this was the ceremony of *malkoth*, or stripes, but the actuality was altogether too reminiscent of the *cheder*. What capped my astonishment was the behavior of the victim when he rose to his feet; for he invariably threw a few coins into the plate held out by Lazar. It was surely a marvelous thing to pay for being whipped.

Immediately after the feast of the eve of Yom Kippur, my father put on a white robe, and a prayer shawl over that. My mother, too, clad herself in white. Then the children were led before them one by one. My father laid his hands on us and gave us his blessing. Then, steeped in the atmosphere of the Days of Awe, we went to my grandfather's house. There the entire family was assembled—four generations of us when my sister had married and borne children. The ceremony of the blessings was repeated, and we received a double benediction from the grandfather and grandmother.

As often as my mother told me about the Temple and the High Priest, my childish fantasy was awakened and I saw pictures. I knew they were the false pictures on which I had furtively looked from the door of the churches, and I tried to chase them from my mind. I tried instead to associate the Temple of ancient days with our synagogue, and the High Priest with our cantor. I carried on an internal struggle against the pictures of the worshippers of idols, and it was only on Yom Kippur that I was satisfied with the result. The later morning prayers of that day were particularly beloved by the children, for they touched the mystic places in our souls. At the proper moment I too fell prostrate, just like the older folk, and at that moment I could think of our High Priest without evoking the image of the cloister. I felt that for this moment I had been purified of evil thought.

When the congregation left the synagogue, the women went home; the men remained to greet the new moon with prayer before going home to break the fast.

I remember reading, many years ago, a Hebrew poem called "Benediction of the New Moon" by a forgotten poet, Zalman Luria, a description of a poverty-stricken Jewish home in a little Russian town. It is winter. The house is unheated. The hungry children lie on beds of straw, dozing and dreaming of food; the sick mother bundles them close to her for comfort and warmth. But outside, in the clear, freezing night, the father stands, with anxious eyes fixed on the sinking sickle of the moon, and he prays to God to fill out the missing portion of it. He prays as if no other worry existed for him than this —that God might forget to round out the incomplete moon. And if God will only take pity on the helpless moon, all will be well.

And what, indeed, did the Jews of Svislovitz lack on that night of Yom Kippur, when they issued with purified souls from their day of fasting and prayer? They had forgiven each other their sins against each other, and God had forgiven them their sins against Him. "He sprinkled them with clean water and they were purified of their sins." That was all they needed; so, with clear eyes they looked up into the heavens and a feeling of pity for the uncompleted moon overcame them and they lifted their hands toward heaven begging God to take pity on that too.

But the benediction of the new moon did not close the day. No sooner had Father come home than he took off his white robe, found a hammer and two nails, went out of the house again, and drove the nails into that part of the wall against which the *sukkah,* or booth would rest on the oncoming festival of Sukkoth. It is a sin to hurry over sacred duties. Let not the *Advocatus Diaboli* be able to plead against the Jews that after a day of prayer and fasting they rush home like gluttons to gulp down—a glass of tea. Slowly, then: fast all day, pray all day; when that is over, pray for the welfare of the moon; then go home, and take your time—doff your white garment, drive in a couple of nails for the booth; and then sit down to a glass of tea. There'll be time enough for the good things of the flesh.

During the five days between Yom Kippur and Sukkoth, the Jews of Svislovitz were preoccupied with the building of their booths. Few householders could boast the luxury of a permanent, all-year booth. The great majority put up theirs only for the duration of the festival—insecure structures of thin planks, old doors, old windows and the like. The permanent *sukkah* had its virtues, of course. It did not fear storm and wind, frequent at that time of the year; it had a roof with two leaves which could be lifted and lowered, so that it did not fear the rain. Lastly, it had firm doors which could be shut against thieves. As against this the temporary *sukkah* had an equally obvious moral superiority; its owner built it every year afresh, rejoicing in his labors; and the very insecurity of the structure, the declaration of dependence on the will of God, gave it a special touch of fineness. You defied the rain, it was your faith that "He would not empty His beaker into the face of His important guests."

Inside the *sukkah* I felt altogether wonderful. The light of the festival candle drew upward toward the roof of branches, which was not a roof but a portion of the sky let down over our heads; and among the fir branches the stars peeped down at night, crystal clear, as if they too had been washed and purified for the festival. The candlelight drew upward, the starlight came down, and between the two was born a warmth and tenderness known only to him who has dreamed the evenings away in a *sukkah*.

Here the Jew, symbol of man uprooted from his mother earth, alienated from the magic contact with nature, touched reality again. Above him was a roof of fresh, odorous branches of fir; in a corner of the *sukkah* stood, in an earthern pitcher, a slender palm branch brought a thousand miles from the Orient, and about it stood the willow withes from the fields outside. At no moment of the year did the suppressed nostalgia of these descendants of shepherds and peasants and bedouins waken more poignantly, or come nearer to a sense of satisfaction.

The half-sanctity of the four days which are interposed between the full sanctity of the first and the last two days of Sukkoth also had a special charm for the youngsters. The synagogue was illumined during the whole week as never during any other festival. The older people were more lighthearted than at any other time of the year, and not an evening passed without the distribution of cakes and candies among the children. We were allowed to stay up late, and during the day there was no *cheder*, or next to none.

Of course the high-water mark of jollity was reached on Simchath Torah, the Day of the Rejoicing of the Law. By that day the last weekly portion of the Pentateuch has been passed, and the round of readings begins again for the coming twelvemonth. On that day, Judah, who had the double distinction of being the son of the preacher and president of the synagogue, used to run from house to house followed by an army of children. A sack was slung over his shoulder and every housewife had to throw her contribution into it—cakes, apples, pears, berries . . . . These were the provisions for Judah's army. Every five minutes he would turn round to us and call out: "Sacred flock of Israel!" And we would answer in chorus: "Ba-a-a, ba-a-a."

The evenings were gayer still, and the evening of Simchath Torah was the climax of the gaiety. On this one occasion the women were permitted to come down from their enclosed gallery into the men's section, and this was the signal to the youngsters that all the regular laws had been suspended. For on this one day of the year the Torah, the Law, that stern mistress which for the three hundred and sixty-odd days of the year is an unrelenting ruler, bends a little toward her followers and shows them her gentler, tenderer side. Six hundred and thirteen commandments, precepts and prohibitions she imposes on her followers, and the breaking of any one of them is a grievous sin. She has put a fence round every action, every moment of the lives of her followers, and not a daily act, from the most important to the most trivial, is outside the scope of the Torah. All this is true enough, but she does it for the sake of her followers as a mother imposes rules on her children for their own good. But like a mother she knows her moments of sweetness and relaxation, and then her children dance round her wild with joy.

On the eve of the Day of the Rejoicing every burgher in the town, from the *Rav* himself down to the humble water-carrier, has the privilege of joining in the processions round the pulpit, carrying in his turn the great parchment scrolls in their mantles of velvet, with their ornaments of silver bells and pomegranates. The youngsters follow noisily, waving banners on which are painted lions and hares: "Be strong as a lion and swift as a hare to carry out the commandments of the Torah." The girls, too, dance and sing in the processions, and they seem to be keener than the boys on one traditional symbolic rite: the bestowing of a quick kiss on the silk and velvet mantle of the scrolls as they come round in the processions. But the boys, in whose instincts the foretaste of a girl's kiss has already awakened, have a trick of their own. They watch closely, and when a pair of girlish lips darts toward the mantle of the scroll, a boyish hand darts even more swiftly between the lips and the velvet; then, instead of the sacred scroll, the girl kisses the hand of an impudent boy. A great shout of laughter goes up through the synagogue, the face of the little girl turns fiery red. Sometimes she spits out the kiss again, and sometimes she swallows it in her embarrassment.

The Day of the Rejoicing and the eve that precedes it, the bridegroom is dancing with the bride, the Chosen People with the Law. For so it is written: The Torah is the bride and the congregation of Israel is the bridegroom; God Himself is the marriage broker, sometimes leading the bride and sometimes the bridegroom to the altar. The bride wears a robe of silk and velvet and the bridegroom puts his arms around her, and leads her in a dance around the altar; and the divine Matchmaker laughs and asks the bystanders: "A wonderful match, isn't it? Twin souls, affinities . . . ."

On the Day of the Rejoicing it is meritorious to drink; and

most Jews obeyed the law and drank. But I do not remember a single instance of a Jew getting drunk. There were many who pretended to be drunk, and went clowning through the congregation. Judah, the president of the synagogue, loved to play this role, but the joke of it was that, like some others, he never swallowed a drop of liquor. And the fact was that at the fixed moment when the cantor gave the signal for the evening prayers and the official closing of the Day of the Rejoicing, the atmosphere changed abruptly, and services were taken up as drily, as evenly, as if this were any other day of the year. The merriment died off the faces instantaneously; the old wrinkles, the old worries appeared on them as if by magic.

On that same evening, during my first *cheder* year, Mottye the bean was among the many guests gathered in our house. I was not particularly overjoyed to see him there; his mere presence spoiled the evening for me. And he made it a thoroughly miserable one when he came over and, beaming, confided in me that I was to remain his pupil for the coming term, that is, through the winter until Passover.

CHAPTER EIGHT

Purim, the Widow Cherneh, and Bencheh

PURIM, which commemorates the triumph of the Jews of Persia over Haman the Jew-hater in the days of Ahasuerus, Esther and Mordecai, is certainly not among the major festivals. There is even a folk saying which demotes it completely: "Malaria is no disease and Purim is no festival"—but that is going too far. In any case, what it lacks in status Purim makes up in merriment. With Purim is bound up the tradition of the Purim players, while with Purim in Svislovitz was bound up the tradition of the widow Cherneh.

In my first *cheder* year the Purim players of Svislovitz prepared two grand performances, *The Story of Esther* and *The Sale of Joseph.* The first was the authentic play of the festival, a sort of mystery or miracle play, given every year. It already had its trained actors, some of whom had conserved their roles for several years in succession. But *The Sale of Joseph*, also a traditional play associated with Purim performances, had never been tried before in Svislovitz; new forces had to be trained, and a tremendous hubbub arose round the distribution of the roles. There were three candidates for every role, and it was impossible to satisfy even the successful candidates. The quarrels spread from the candidates to their families and from the families to their friends, so that the whole town seethed with claims and counterclaims, ambitions and artists' passions.

The general organizer of the plays was Bencheh, the son of the widow Cherneh. He was *régisseur*, stage manager and promoter. He had a heart-breaking task before him, for no matter who got what part he alienated twice as many as he placated. But, to the honor of his memory be it said, he was a man of principle. He chose his actors without fear or favor, solely on their merits and without regard to influence and family connections. He was an artist in search of artists. He put all the candidates through their paces, testing their elocution and their memories. Perhaps he would not have been so inflexible and masterly if he had not had behind him his mother, Cherneh the widow, who deserves an important place in my chronicles.

This tall, middle-aged woman was possessed of a waistline which had no rival in the town of Svislovitz. She was equally notable for another possession, of a far more dangerous character—a restless and poisonous tongue. She talked inexhaustibly, and woe to the listener who fell into her clutches, for without something approaching physical violence it was impossible to escape from under the torrent of her words. They poured out like peas from a hole in the bottom of a barrel. Her arguments were clear, sharp and irresistible. She had a finger in every pie in town; private affairs not less than the affairs of the community engaged her attention closely. When questions like those of the *Rav's* salary, the hiring of a second ritual slaughterer, and the repair of the ritual baths or of the public lodging house came up for discussion, the widow Cherneh had much to say, and she said it. She went from house to house making propaganda for her views and preparing public opinion for her solution of every question. Within her inexhaustible general interests she also had a special field, the protection of the widows and orphans of Svislovitz; and if there was in Svislovitz a heavier tax on the wax candles of the rich than on the tallow candles of the poor, it was the work of the widow Cherneh. "If," she argued passionately, "there are luxurious homes which cannot do without wax candles, let them pay. Let not the poor, the widow and the orphan, be burdened with all the costs of the community."

And Cherneh the widow was a force to be reckoned with in Svislovitz, not because of the power of conviction which lay in her words, but because of the fear she inspired. She was the most daring person in town in the matter of interrupting the reading of the Torah during the Sabbath services in the synagogue.

This immemorial privilege of the poor and powerless was an extraordinary institution. The Forbidding of the Reading occupied the same place in the life of the small town as the strike does in the modern industrial world.

The scene must be recalled in its fullness if we are to understand the force of the action. It is a Sabbath morning in the synagogue. The congregation is deeply absorbed in its prayers; the sanctity of the day rests on all the worshippers, and in their minds there is a mingling of holy thoughts and a foretaste of the dainty Sabbath dishes which wait for them at home. They come to services early, and on empty stomachs; at home waits, as *hors d'oeuvre*, an appetizing piece of herring, surrounded by onion parings, the whole swimming in a sea of sharp vinegar. After it will come the sweet stewed fruit, with a succulent morsel of meat in it—perhaps the only meat tasted during the week. Then, most luscious of all, the *chalent*, the warm dishes kept in the oven since the previous day, because it is prohibited to light a fire or make use of one on the Sabbath.

Finally there is the crown of the meal, the *kugel*, the Sabbath pudding, majestic, filling, somniferous. There will be leisure, ease, forgetfulness of the sordid weekdays, when the midday meal is nothing but a tasteless, hurried interruption of the day's slavery. And after the meal there will be the Sabbath siesta. The mouth of the worshipper waters, and anticipation gives a sharp edge to his religious zeal. Who would not cheerfully pay the price of the morning prayers for so joyous and kingly an afternoon? He prays therefore with double fervor, secure in the knowledge of immediate as well as of heavenly reward.

The last of the regular prayers is said; the last roulade of the cantor dies away; the high officials of the synagogue make ready to bring out of the ark the scrolls of the Torah, the vast parchment copies of the Pentateuch, in order that the week's portion may be read. And suddenly . . .

Suddenly a Jew appears in the pulpit, where the scrolls are to be laid down, delivers a resounding blow on the lectern with one of the prayer books, and cries out at the top of his voice: "I forbid the Reading."

The effect is electrical. First there is a gasp of astonishment; then an angry mutter; then silence. The Jew in the pulpit waits, and when the silence is complete he voices his complaint. He knows that he is safe. He is exercising an ancient privilege which it would be blasphemy to challenge. Yet it needed a certain degree of courage. Not every challenger had a complaint that justified this last and extreme resort; nor was every challenger strong enough even if he had a case. The congregation listens for a moment, and if the man falters, or his words have no appeal, someone steps out of the mass of worshippers, approaches the ark, flings open the doors, and cries out the first words of the ceremony of the Reading. The real test of character then begins. If the complainant is strong, or if he is inspired by a deep sense of outrage, he will continue crying out. He may even blockade the way to the doors of the ark, and either by the threat of opposition or by the weight of his indignation prevent the resumption of the service.

Now the right of interruption belonged to women as well as to men, and as often as not the pulpit would suddenly be occupied by a woman who had come rushing down from the gallery. She herself would strike the blow on the lectern, or, if she was weak, she could even call on the beadle to strike it for her.

The widow Cherneh was the most effective interrupter in all of Svislovitz. She seldom exploited the privilege on her own behalf. She raised her voice for others, and the congregation knew that Cherneh was *not* a person to be intimidated or overridden. Once she had arrested the services she would keep them suspended until she had obtained satisfaction.

Cherneh would make full use of her physical bulk and her bitter tongue. She had developed a high technique in her use of the right of interruption, having little faith in abstract justice. No sooner had she attracted the attention of the congregation by a mighty thump on the pulpit than she would retire at once to the foot of the steps before the ark and block the approach effectively with her massive, immovable figure. There was no way of outflanking her huge girth; and any attempt to push her away would have been unseemly as well as foredoomed to failure. And then there was the lash of her tongue, and anyone prepared to undertake an act which was ludicrous as well as mean, shrank from the verbal counter-assault. In abuse she was completely fearless, sparing no one, from the *Rav* to the bath-attendant. If in addition to these advantages she was armed with a just cause, she was terrific. She did not content herself, either, with pleading the case at issue, but would pour out the venom of her resentment on all the evils ever perpetrated by the Jews of Svislovitz. Nor would she step down until the elders of the city had given their assurance that the wrong would be righted the very next day.

By profession Cherneh was a baker of pancakes, but she had a number of supplementary occupations. She knitted socks to order, plucked feathers for pillows, chopped cabbages, kneaded and spread the dough for *matzoth*, served at weddings and sat up with the dead. But pancakes were her specialty. Whoever wanted fresh pancakes, crisp, right off the pan, had to go to Cherneh early in the morning. Later she was distributing them from house to house. The pancakes were big enough to cover a whole plate, and the price was two for a kopek.

It was a difficult and thankless trade, but Cherneh could not raise the price for fear of competition on the part of the bagel-bakers. It was generally conceded that though the pancake was heavier and more satisfying, bagels were daintier and sweeter; it was therefore impossible to yield them the additional advantage of price. Cherneh used to complain bitterly: "Would to God that I had begun with bagels instead of pancakes. Now it is too late. I am known as Cherneh the pancake-maker, and I daren't experiment." And the truth was that her pancakes were known all over the town for their crispness and flavor.

Such was the widow Cherneh, the mother of Bencheh the *régisseur*, who undertook, that Purim of my first *cheder* year, to present the community of Svislovitz with two full-length performances in honor of the festival.

Bencheh was an old bachelor in the neighborhood—"old bachelor" being the designation for any Jew who had not taken a wife unto himself before he had passed out of the early twenties. Physically he presented a strange contrast to his mother, for he was short and lean. He wore a beard *à la* Napoleon III. He must have inherited his build from his father, a teacher and—if Cherneh was to be believed—a scholar. From his mother he inherited his quick and gifted tongue. If his mother's speech suggested a barrel of peas emptying through a hole in the bottom, his suggested a thin paper bag of rice emptying similarly; and when he became excited his words beat on the listener's ears with the rattling impact of birdshot.

Bencheh was by instinct a vagabond. Svislovitz was too narrow for him, and from childhood on he was tormented by the wanderlust of the gypsies. He brought his mother little joy, and long and bitter were the plaints she poured out to the housewives of Svislovitz. When he was nine years old she apprenticed him to a tailor, but at the age of twelve he ran away, dreaming of the great outside world. He thought of going down the river, to Kiev, to Kremenchug, or perhaps even farther. But finding his adventure unpleasant he stopped short in Choloi. He came home, tailored another year, and ran away again.

All his youth passed in this way—intervals of respectability alternating with intervals of futile vagabondage.

For the Purim I am speaking of he had returned from Kiev after an absence of some months. In that metropolis he had picked up a more modish pronunciation of Yiddish, and he made fun of our peasant thickness of speech. He expressed his superior culture in other ways, too. He was the only one in town to wear a short coat instead of the universal long capote; he wore a derby instead of a cap, and his trousers had cuffs at the bottom—the only trouser-cuffs in Svislovitz. He walked apart, like an artist whom a malignant fate had marooned among boors and savages. But in spite of his contempt for us, he loved to gather crowds about him and recount the marvels of the great world he had sojourned in.

Life in Kiev, he said, was glorious. You lived there like "*Gott in Frankreich*." The poorest eat rolls and butter every day, and in the evening everyone goes out to stroll on the principal street, the Kreshchatik. The houses are built of a kind of crystal, and the streets are paved with colored stones. A district commissioner such as made us tremble in Svislovitz was of no account in Kiev; as for a police sergeant, he was just dirt. No one below a general counted for anything. And then, the theaters! "But what's the good of telling you, you'd never understand. The actors wear coats of real gold and silver, and crowns on their heads with real diamonds in them. Their feet are shod in full-length boots of red morocco leather, with silver spurs on the heels, and in their hands they carry little whips with golden bells. When they walk about the stage the silver spurs ring, the golden bells tinkle, the crowns flash on their heads, and you see a million rainbows of diamonds and emeralds. As for the curtain, it's a million times lovelier than the curtain on our ark of the Torah, and big enough to cover all the eastern wall of the synagogue. And when the curtain rises, there they all stand, in their crowns and their spurs and their diamonds, and the audience applauds like mad. That's what Kiev is! And that's what life is!"

Whenever I think back on Bencheh, with his lean figure, his gestures, his wild tricks, I am reminded of Charlie Chaplin. I am convinced till this day that Bencheh was a man of genuine gifts, a born artist. His wanderlust was the expression of his thwarted hunger to live himself out; and he had to satisfy his artistic longings by organizing the Purim plays of the town. He would show us what he knew; one day in the year he would lift the inhabitants of Svislovitz to the level of the happy Kievans.

No easy enterprise, this. Where were the men, the means, the interest to come from? But Bencheh was not only an artist, he was also a man of restless, enterprising spirit. The first thing he did was to create a fund. He asked nothing for himself; true artist that he was, he donated his gifts and his labor. But there were many things to be bought and neither he nor his mother, who supported him in his high annual endeavor with all her moral force, had money of their own to spend. Bencheh's first step, therefore, was to levy a tax on each of the actors. After all, he argued unanswerably, they were not real artists, and they were receiving instruction from the incomparable Bencheh.

The tax was graduated according to the importance of the role and the number of lines assigned to it.

The heaviest taxes were laid on Pharaoh and Ahasuerus; next came Haman and Mordecai and Joseph. Vaizoso, the clown of the Esther stories, got off scot-free. Another factor in the computation of the tax was the cost of the role. The kings were ruinously expensive, and their ministers only slightly less so. Fortunately Jacob and Mordecai were only two old-type Jews, and clothes for the Patriarch might be borrowed from the *Rav*, while Mordecai, who had to appear at first as a beggar, could be outfitted by the water-carrier. Toward the end of the play, Mordecai did of course become a grand figure, being elevated to Haman's place; but Haman having by then been hanged, his clothes could be used for Mordecai—an economic coup and a fine symbolic gesture in one. The levies from the actors did not cover the costs, and here the widow Cherneh threw herself into the breach. She advanced her own money against the receipts from the two performances—it was at least as good an investment as selling pancakes on credit to hungry *cheder* boys.

The largest single item of expenditure was paper. Great quantities of gold and silver paper were needed to cover the crowns and robes of the kings and ministers. Gold and silver paper was not obtainable in Svislovitz; it was ordered from Bobruisk through one of the draymen. Then there were swords, and Bencheh insisted that they at least look like swords, and not like the wooden toys the children wore on the Black Fast. The blades had to be covered with silver paper, the hilts with gold. Then flax and hemp were needed, the first for Jacob's beard, the second for Mordecai's. Flax is smooth and with the comb can be made to flow gracefully, as was fitting for Jacob; hemp is rough and knotted, and therefore did well as the beard of Mordecai in the role of beggar.

Having attended to all this with loving care, Bencheh set

about the training of the actors. For himself he reserved the role of Haman the wicked. True, the role of that tyrant and Jew-hater was not a grateful one; but Bencheh was an artist, and wanted plenty of action. Besides, the more hateful the role, the more room there was for skill and subtlety.

The severest test of his managerial ability came in the choosing of Vashti and Esther. If it had been up to Bencheh he would have stopped at nothing and actually invited girls into the production. But modern realism was beyond the taste—not to mention the moral outlook—of Svislovitz; it would not have been tolerated. Bencheh had to use boys.

Esther was the easiest to impersonate; a good-looking boy and some women's clothes did the trick; but in the case of Vashti a fearful historical complication intruded. According to the biblical narrative, the incident that triggered the dramatic Purim episode was the refusal of Vashti to appear in all her beauty before the assembled guests of the tipsy monarch, and tradition has it that this incident had a ludicrous and pitiful explanation. It was not the modesty of Vashti that prompted her refusal, for she was as vicious as her husband was foolish. *But*—on the day when she was summoned to unveil her beauty to the banqueters, an exceedingly offensive growth had suddenly appeared on her forehead; and the modesty which prevents me from saying exactly what this growth was also prevented the realistic impersonation of the historic Vashti. Yet how could all reference to this providential if indelicate contretemps be entirely avoided? For if Vashti had been as good-looking on that day as on all others she would have been proud to respond to the King's coarse demand. And if she had so displayed herself, the King would not have divorced her; and if the King had not divorced her, he would never have married Esther; and if he had never married Esther, Haman would have triumphed and the Jews of Persia would have been massacred down to the last child.

As might be expected, every *cheder* boy in Svislovitz knew what had happened to Queen Vashti and what the biblical account does not mention. Who it was that told *me*, I cannot remember, but it was certainly not the *rebbi* or my parents. For that matter I cannot imagine who told whom; but all of us boys just knew, and when we asked each other: "Do you know what grew out of Vashti's forehead?" it was a purely rhetorical question. Therefore neither historical accuracy nor the public demand would have been satisfied unless Vashti was somehow or other true to her part. Bencheh could of course have wriggled out of the difficulty, as most Purim players did, by keeping Vashti offstage and giving a few allusive lines to another character. But Bencheh was not the man to stoop to such intellectual dishonesty. He had, after much inner torment, found a solution. Vashti would appear onstage, but besides her crown she would wear a veil to cover the upper half of her face. What was under the veil could be left to the imagination.

Other inspirations came to Bencheh in the course of his preparations. He who had looked upon the Kiev actors in all their glory could not appear on the stage in the same village style of makeup as the amateurs of Svislovitz. Moreover, the King's first minister, the overlord *de facto* of one hundred and twenty-seven provinces stretching from India to Ethiopia, had to look like what he was, not like a ridiculous bucolic. By devious ways, perhaps with the help of a bribe, he obtained the cast-off uniform of the district commissioner. The epaulettes were missing, but Bencheh supplied his own variety. By a similarly obscure and circuitous route he obtained an ancient sword discarded by the town sergeant, and polished it up. And he had a regular crown made for himself by the town cooper, so that he towered above his fellow-actors not only by virtue of his superior talents, but by virtue of accoutrements never before seen among Purim players of Svislovitz.

In the second play, *The Sale of Joseph*, he took the role of the hero, and had his brother-in-law, Mottye, the best ladies' tailor in Svislovitz, make him the famous coat of many colors. But *The Sale of Joseph* was only dessert to the banquet; it was in the authentic Purim play that Bencheh took the town by storm.

The preparations for the Great Show lasted about a month. The actors—*cheder* boys and apprentices to various trades—were occupied during the day, and Bencheh himself had been driven by need to take up again the despised needle. The training therefore had to be intensive. Cherneh's home, a two-room cottage, became for that one month a dramatic school with Bencheh as director.

In this capacity Bencheh, snobbish enough in a general way, became so inflated with importance that one could not hold sensible converse with him. Svislovitz could believe what it liked about what he had seen in the great world, but here was no room for doubt, and he said so. "I take dolts, village idiots, and I make actors of them. Say what you want about Kiev—but about my talents . . . ."

Bencheh's family acquired, for that brief period, some of the haughtiness radiating from the central figure. Cherneh had more than once bewailed her fate and her son's: "An old bachelor, a dead loss . . . . A fine head on him, could have been a great scholar, and there he sits, when he does sit, with the needle in his fingers. What can I hope for from him?" But during the time of the Purim plays Cherneh forgot her blasted hopes and shone with happiness. "You'll see him in the role of Haman. I tell you not a hundred district commissioners and not a thousand police sergeants are a patch on him. I tell you, not the governor himself could be half as terrifying. When he opens his mouth the walls and windows tremble."

Poor Cherneh! It didn't need much of a voice to make the walls and windows of her hovel tremble. And who would have cared to contradict the widow Cherneh when she sought consolation for the sorrows of her life in the talents of her wayward son?

No spectators were permitted at rehearsals. To begin with, Bencheh's home was scarcely large enough for the actors; but apart from this his instincts revolted against a display of talent in the making. Close relatives of Cherneh's and one or two chosen friends were excepted. But it was impossible to keep away the crowds which gathered at the windows and looked on from the outside, for the winter had relaxed its grip and the curiosity was immense. I, because of the friendship between Cherneh and my mother, was once admitted to the sanctum, to my immense pride and the envy of my playmates.

Parallel with these formidable preparations for the play were minor ones which were related to the traditional observance of this not too important festival. Such was the procurement of the *graggers* for the young people. This traditional appurtenance of Purim is a simple instrument, a kind of rattle, with which the children are permitted, and even encouraged, to express their contempt for Haman whenever his name is mentioned during the reading of the Scroll of Esther. It consists of a toothed wooden disk, circular in shape, attached to a handle. A rotating framework pulls it against an elastic wooden prong, with earsplitting results. This was the sole weapon allowed us in our war against "Haman, the son of Hamidatha, the persecutor of the Jews."

Immediately preceding Purim a general fast commemorates the individual fast observed by Queen Esther before she ventured to present herself, unbidden, to King Ahasuerus. The much-loved little cakes, stuffed with nuts and poppyseed, which are called "Haman's ears"—sometimes "Haman's pockets"—had been prepared for us in vast numbers. Their shape alone was a joy. They were neither round, like rolls, nor long, like the loaf; with their triangular shape they were like nothing else that we ate during the year. The stuffing was made of poppyseeds fried in honey, but there was not enough of it, so we used to eat the cake cagily, in such wise that with every mouthful we got at least a nibble of honeyed poppyseed.

The older people fasted on that day. It was not one of the important fasts, but my mother fasted with special pleasure, for here was a fast day in honor of a woman. But while she fasted, she was occupied from morning until evening with the preparation of the Purim dishes, and I loitered about to catch the droppings.

The joyous reading of the Scroll of Esther during the Purim service was by tradition the right of Judah, the president of the synagogue. It was he, we may recall, who on the Day of the Rejoicing of the Law, organized the children for the raiding of the town pantries. On Purim he organized no army, but he was heart and soul with the youngsters in their anti-Haman demonstrations. We waited, breathless with impatience, for the third chapter of the Scroll, where the name of Haman is mentioned for the first time. Throughout the preceding two chapters we sat like soldiers awaiting the word of command, our rattles held tight, our muscles tense. And then, when the word "Haman" rolled off Judah's tongue, a deafening roar shook the walls of the synagogue, the tumult of several hundred rattles whirled vigorously by as many youthful hands. Some of the older people, too dignified for rattles, but too human to be kept entirely out of the fun, brought along sticks and contributed to the uproar by beating the floor and the desks. For several minutes the reader was unable to proceed. But this was not enough. The full name of the Archenemy reads "Haman, the son of Hamidatha the Gagite." When the reader resumed and proceeded to the genealogy, the tumult broke out again. Judah, who loved children, waited it out good-humoredly, giving no sign of impatience.

Judah had an older brother, the lean and bitter Ziskind, who was a *rebbi* of the same type as Mottye the bean, perhaps a shade more obnoxious. A terrible story was told about him and my uncle Meyer, the oldest son of my grandfather Solomon. Because he was a slow learner Meyer was kept in Ziskind's *cheder* even after his marriage at the age of fifteen. When the famous incident took place my uncle Meyer may have been sixteen years of age—probably on the younger side. During *cheder* hours news was suddenly brought to him that his wife had borne him his first child. But the messenger of the happy tidings found the new father, his nether garments down, lying across the bench receiving the ministrations of his *rebbi.* He was asked at once to dress himself and hurry home to his wife; but Ziskind met the situation coolly. He gravely requested the messenger to wait. "Time enough," he said. "I'm not through yet." Now this same Ziskind could not tolerate the merriment of the youngsters at the Purim services. In his opinion two or three turns of the rattle sufficed; he begrudged us the pleasure of a longer and fuller expression of opinion. We ignored Ziskind's protests, and we had the encouragement of Judah, who deliberately paused before every mention of Haman—paused, hung in the air for a moment, then flung the syllables at us as an open signal, in defiance of his brother and our ancient enemy alike.

Children though we were, we knew well enough that Haman was not in the synagogue, but we understood the symbolism of our demonstration. There were Hamans living in the world everywhere, great and little enemies of the Jews. We took revenge for the wrongs they had done us, and the wrongs they contemplated. If noise could kill, the Hamans of the world would never rise for the resurrection.

Such was the eve of Purim. On the day of Purim we read the Scroll a second time, again with hostile demonstrations at the mention of Haman's name; but like the second reading of Jeremiah's Lamentations on the Black Fast, the repeat performance was a failure. We demonstrated passionately on the eve of Purim, dutifully on Purim day; and when we left the synagogue, whatever holiday feelings we had were dissipated by the sight of the open shops. It was only in the afternoon, when the shops began to close and the preparations for the Purim banquet reached their final stage, that the festive mood returned.

Between the closing of the shops and the opening of the celebrations the Sending of the Gifts took place, an ancient tradition connected with this festival. For several hours the carriers of the gifts were seen hurrying from house to house, bearing plates covered with napkins. Carrier after carrier came into our house with the gifts of relatives and friends. There were two kinds of gifts, those of private individuals and those of officials, the cantor, the beadle, the bath-attendant, the water-carriers. And there were some "officials" by courtesy, certain widows, the Sabbath *goy* (the gentile hired to attend to the fire on that day). The *Rav* of the community, though he received Purim gifts, never sent any. The gifts of officials, real and honorary, had a significance of their own. We did not examine them, we took no part of them; we put a few coins in the plate and returned the gift with our compliments, not forgetting the little fee for the messenger.

Very different was the social or personal Purim gift. This was not only examined, it was weighed in the balance of social standing, it was counted, scrutinized, appraised from every angle. And it was a point of honor to make the return gift a little finer and more original. There was infinite care and forethought to make the return gift expressive of the exact degree of affection or esteem which the receiver was to deduce. My mother took the whole business very seriously. So, for that matter, did everyone else. But when my mother had gone through the entire list and when, just before we sat down to the Purim feast, she despatched the last of the carriers, she sat down with a sigh of relief, the anxious look died off her face, and she sighed: "Thank God! The last plate sent out. I only hope I've offended nobody, and that everybody will feel satisfied."

And what was all the worry and excitement about? Another piece of cake, another piece of candy, another package of honeyed poppyseed . . . . But against the background of that small, pitiful life of Svislovitz, those trifles took on vast importance. There was a sort of gift language for Purim, a language as expressive in subtle shades of meaning as the language of flowers in Spain; for every degree of respect there was a different combination of goodies, a larger or a smaller plate. And on more than one occasion a gift which seemed to the recipient to fall short of the respect it should have conveyed occasioned a minor feud which lasted for months.

At long last, after the Purim banquet, came the sublime moment, the Purim plays, which were performed in our house. The door was flung open, and the Purim players, accompanied by a host of children and grown-ups, poured into the house. Our dining room was probably the largest in Svislovitz, but for this occasion it was too small, and protesting voices began to rise: "Let me in, I'm Haman's brother. Let me in, I'm the queen's first cousin . . . ." Then, when order of a kind had been established in the crowded room, the players began. Of course I knew every one of them personally, and could have told you to a man who was hidden behind that flaxen beard or got up in those girl's clothes. But the hunger for illusion was strong, and I felt that these boys were the same and not the same.

And when Vashti, a young yeshivah student, dressed in women's clothes, with a little crown on his head and a veil covering the upper part of his face, piped the first lines: "Would that I were a little bird, would that I were a little flower, nay, even a little worm," my heart melted for the unhappy queen. Ahasuerus sat in glory, sullen, gross, almost wordless, as befitted his royal stupidity. Then the word of the chamberlain, Mehuman, was heard: "Come forth, come forth, O Haman, thou prince," and Bencheh strode into the center of the room, magnificently caparisoned, and taking up a haughty pose, glared upon the players and spectators with the look of an outraged general—what am I saying?—a field marshall. The Jews of Svislovitz had never seen the inside of a theater, but instinct told them that here was no ordinary village Purim player: here was a master of makeup and histrionics, and before he had spoken a word a shudder ran through the room. It was Haman himself, an enemy as resourceful as he was implacable. His furious glances, his bitter gestures, his intolerant bearing declared: "Before you stands the Eternal Persecutor, who will pursue you to the Gates of Destruction."

The play took up half an hour, and was followed immediately by *The Sale of Joseph*. But the addition to the program was not a success. Haman suddenly became Joseph the sacrifice; Vashti the Queen became Reuben; Mordecai, Joseph. In the center of the room a barrel was placed to represent the pit into which the older brothers threw the spoiled darling of their father.

A second banquet followed the close of the performance, and for the remainder of the evening Bencheh was the hero of Svislovitz. He told again the story of his wanderings, the marvels of Kiev, and the glories of the theater. The older people were sleepy, and I could scarcely keep my eyes open. My thoughts became confused: Haman's ears, the Scroll of Esther, rattlers, drama, banquet, beards flowed together and the tumult moved slowly, dimly, into the darker spaces of my mind. At last everything sank into a dream, the misty and eternal dream of a people forever at war with an invisible enemy.

CHAPTER NINE

The Grandest Festival of All

PASSOVER was approaching, the grandest and most splendid of the festivals, with new clothes for everybody, everything brand new from head to foot. So there were visits to Hershel the tailor, who spent half his time working and half running down his competitor Yenkel. There were visits to Isar the shoemaker, Isar with the red nose, whom everybody in the town feared, from the president of the synagogue to the water-carrier, because of his fiery advocacy of absolute justice. First came the visits considered necessary by Hershel and Isar and me; then came the visits which I alone considered necessary. How, I asked, was it possible for Hershel to sew pockets into my suit, or for Isar to put a strip of raw leather into my shoes to make them squeak with newness, unless I was present to watch? My visits to Hershel took place in the day; to Isar I went in the evening. I had a friend in Isar's best apprentice, a certain Shaikin, who taught me how to braid a shoemaker's thread and even let me hammer a few nails into the sole of a shoe. But Shaikin exploited me. He made me bring him a pound of sugar and a quart of whisky. Not in payment for my privileges, he explained, but because he needed them to make the leather strip without which the new shoes would not squeak. And how could I wear new shoes that did not squeak?

Last, and certainly not least, there were the *matzoh* bakeries of which the most distinguished was that of Mottye Kailes. His *matzoth* were delicate, thin as paper and neatly holed in straight lines, as if with the best machine. I used to go from bakery to bakery to watch them punch the holes in the *matzoth*. I had pull with Mottye Kailes, for we bought our *matzoth* from him, and the chief "holer" was a Talmud student who had his Friday and Saturday meals in our house. The widow Cherneh was Mottye Kaile's chief dough-kneader; she instructed me in the details of the work, the pouring of the dough in equal quantities and the flattening of them into *matzoh* cakes. I reached the peak of joy when the Talmud student let me take the holer in my hand, pass it across the dough, and produce the line of neat punctures.

What pity it is that the vast majority of grown-ups have never learned to understand the powers of direct and honest observation which belong to the child before life has distorted its intelligence. The child not only observes every detail in the behavior of grown-ups, but is quick to sift the false from the genuine, pretense from unaffected truth. In my own childhood I learned that older people, careless in this respect, can do much damage to the pure souls of the young.

On a moonlit evening not long before the Passover, I sat with my mother at the window of the living room, and watched the procession of the Greek Orthodox worshippers round the church. They were carrying images and banners, and they chanted as they walked. And suddenly my mother broke into laughter and said: "See, they are making preparation for their Paschal festival. They take their God and hide him in a certain place, and then they pretend that they have found him again."

On the night preceding the Passover eve, my father went through the ritual of removing from the house the last traces of leaven. With a lighted candle in one hand, and a goosefeather and wooden spoon in the other, he searched from room to room. This was the preparation for *our* Passover. But I knew that he was only pretending to search. Those little crumbs and fragments—the last traces of leaven—which he "found" he had himself hidden away. And I noted that my mother did not laugh at the pretense, and I was hurt.

There was, however, something that cut me even deeper. The next morning my father made a fire in the backyard and burned the last fragments of leaven, together with the feather and the wooden spoon. The fire was lit not far from the barn which was full of leavened food for the peasants working on the rafts.

I asked my father: "But why don't you burn the barn too? It's full of leaven." My father replied: "That isn't necessary, it no longer is ours. We've sold it to the gentile water-carrier."

Then I put a second question to my father. "The water-carrier is very poor, isn't he? I know because he goes from house to house and begs pieces of bread. So how can he buy that big barn from you?"

My father answered: "We sold it to him for one ruble."

My mind would not rest. I began again: "But what are we going to do without all that food? How are we going to feed all the peasants?" Whereupon the answer came that we had sold the barn and its contents to the water-carrier under a special arrangement; as soon as the Passover ended, and Jews were again permitted to possess leavened food, he would return the barn to us.

I asked no more questions after that; but I remember that a feeling of shame stole over me. I thought to myself: "They're fooling me; they're fooling the water-carrier, too."

By ten o'clock on the morning of that day the house had been wholly purified of its leaven, and the only food given us was Passover food, but not *matzoth*, for it is forbidden to taste those up to the moment the festival begins in the evening. So we waited for the first bite of *matzoh* as the bridegroom waits for the bride. Even the mention of bread was forbidden; it had to be alluded to as "leaven." The sole food, apart from meat, consisted therefore of potatoes in various forms, and Talmud students who got their meals at our house complained that without bread there was no filling the stomach.

There were, I remember, three or four of these students coming to our house, and in the whole of Svislovitz there was a dozen of them. They were called *yeshivah bochurim*—yeshivah boys—though in actual fact Svislovitz was too small to maintain a yeshivah, or talmudical academy. Our yeshivah boys were quartered in the study house of the synagogue, and in the women's division of the synagogue. A regular pillow stuffed with feathers was rarely to be seen among them. They slept mostly on sacks stuffed with straw, and blankets were unknown, topcoats being used in their place. In the winter they used to lie down round the two big stoves at the entrance to the synagogue. For food they "ate days"—that is, they were assigned to different families on different days of the week; and when they were short they complained: "I haven't got a Wednesday—or a Thursday."

In the study house they passed the best years of their life, under a regime which to the modern student must sound incredible. Five or six hours of sleep was all that was permitted them; two hours were given to meals and prayers, the remaining sixteen or seventeen to study. Not all of them were able to endure this grinding discipline and maintain themselves during all their waking hours in a condition of intellectual tenseness; but whether they could endure it or not they were ashamed to display weakness before one another. The weaker ones would become tired and drone through their studies in a state between waking and sleeping, but there were to be found real giants of the spirit, too. They glued themselves to the Talmud as the Cossack glues himself to his horse in time of war: only death can dislodge him. Most of their attention was given to the *halachah*, or legalistic side of the Talmud; the *aggadah*, or folklore and humanistic side of the Talmud, as well as the moralistic books of later epochs, were regarded as of a lower intellectual order, while the Bible occupied the last place—something to take snatches from at off moments.

On the day ushering in the Passover these Talmud students stayed away from their studies—at least those of them who ate in our house—and made themselves useful. This practice of putting the students to work on the day before Passover had been introduced by my grandfather on the following grounds: "Passover is the festival of freedom, and during the Passover every man must feel himself free. Now these Talmud students eat in your house without payment. How, then, can they feel themselves freemen? There is only one way: let them work for their meals that one day, and not be beholden to you for their food." But the work they were put to was of the lightest. They ran errands, carried small parcels, went to Hershel the tailor and Isar the shoemaker to bid them hurry up with the new clothes and shoes lest we should be forced to sit down to the *seder* ceremonies unbefittingly clad. They also prepared the bitter herbs for the ceremonies, checked up on the number of Passover prayer books, and so on.

Evening comes on, and the last sunlight is spilled on the roofs and walls of Svislovitz. Every Jewish home shines, renewed and purified, and on every table the largest and whitest cloth is spread. The children are dressed in new clothes; even the street has been newly swept and the entrance to the house strewn with clean yellow sand. Through those quiet streets, with their trees in first blossom, we go, young and old, to the synagogue. There is contentment in the air, peace and the feeling of plenty; for at what other season of the year can every Jewish family in Svislovitz boast that it is provided with food for every one of eight days ahead—the duration of the festival? The poorest household, haunted by hunger fifty-one weeks in the year, is stocked up till the last day of Passover: such is the law. And when else in the course of the year can the Jews of Svislovitz lay aside their pitiful cares and rejoice in the festival and in the spring? At the *seder* table the poorest householder in Svislovitz could repeat with generous sincerity the passage which opens the ceremonies: "Let every man that is hungry enter and eat, let every man that is thirsty enter and drink." And the sages of the town argued knowingly: "Could God have chosen a lovelier festival than the Passover on which to liberate the Jews from Egypt?"

We have returned from the synagogue; we are at home. Nothing, in all the memories of my childhood years, shines so clearly and lovingly as this evening of the Passover. Its luminous shadows have been thrown forever across my life, and the magic does not diminish with the years. For on that evening the house was a palace, my father was a king, and all of us were members of a royal family, queen and princes and princesses. Even the poorest guest that sat at table with us was an ambassador. My joy was too full to be contained; it spilled over and poured itself through the room and upon the people in it. I wanted the older people to tell me wonderful stories, and I wanted to tell others in return. I was full of the glorious Exodus from the land of Egypt and I lived, in my own way, through all the acts of that greatest of world dramas.

The tables had been stretched and filled in with extra boards, to accommodate the guests. At the head sat my father, leaning upon pillows at his right hand—a symbol of his freedom, majesty and rule. My mother sat by his side. Near them, in the places of honor, were the guests, and after them came the members of the family. Countless beakers and glasses of wine sparkled on the table, flanked by glowing carafes. My father conducted the *seder* ceremonies with royal dignity, without haste, without impatience. I was chagrined that I should have only so simple a part as the asking of the "four questions," for I understood nearly the whole of the ritual. But I repeated the four questions in Hebrew, with their Yiddish translation, like one who obeys a command. After the questions came the reading of the answer. Great was my glee when we reached the counting of the plagues that were inflicted on the Egyptians, greater still when we repeated the complicated calculations of certain sages who proved by a logic all their own that the Egyptians were smitten not with ten, but with every bit of two hundred and fifty plagues. Serves them right, I thought; that'll teach them to leave the Jews alone.

A certain tradition is attached to the *seder* ceremony—the stealing of the *afikomon*, a specially dedicated *matzoh*, from under the pillows on which the father is leaning. It must of course be stolen between the time it is tucked away, near the beginning of the service, and the end, when it has to be distributed and eaten. My brother wanted to help me in the theft on condition that we divided the reward with which the *afikomon* must be redeemed; but I had an excellent idea. I went up to my father and asked him what he would give me if I did *not* steal the *afikomon*. The idea pleased him mightily, and he promised me more than I would have expected as a reward for a successful theft. I got my reward and remained honest into the bargain. Not only did I make no attempt to steal the *afikomon;* I even watched my brothers to prevent them from stealing it.

In the center of the table stood the beaker of wine set apart for Elijah the Prophet. None may drink from it but he when he approaches invisibly at the right moment; and I watched it closely for a sign of diminution in its brimming contents. Of course none of us doubted that Elijah appeared that evening in every Jewish home. But we also knew that it was quite impossible for him to drink up those thousands and thousands of beakers of wine set apart for him. A tiny drop he *might* take from every cup, and I watched, fascinated, for the minute shrinkage. When the moment came we stood up, my father flung open the door and repeated the tremendous words: "Pour forth Thy wrath on the nations that know Thee not . . . ." I held my breath and looked and listened. Oh, I knew very well that Elijah would not enter like a common mortal, grossly visible and audible! But I waited for a shadow, a ghost of a sound, a whisper of footsteps. The invocation ended, the door was closed, and I could not tell. Had I heard something? Had I felt something pass? I looked back at the table, and scrutinized the beaker of the Prophet. But again my own intensity had defeated me, and I could not remember exactly where the wine had stood before. Perhaps the lips of the Prophet had touched the wine, invisibly, faintly. And all that evening I wondered, and, wondering, slipped into a half-sleep, till my father woke me up and bade me sing with everyone else the last of the songs of that evening: "*Chad gadya, chad gadya,* an only kid, an only kid, which my father bought for two *zuzim, chad gadya, chad gadya.*"

We children were not the only ones who believed that Elijah the Prophet was going to appear, and that he was compelled, by elementary considerations of courtesy, at least to touch the wineglass with his lips: for millions of Jews had prepared it for him, and millions of Jews had shown their faith in him. There were adults, bearded Jews, who expected his momentary appearance, who would not have been at all surprised if the stern Tishbite had suddenly swept in through the open door. Far from regarding it as supernatural, they would have said that even a prophet should not let himself be asked too often. And after all, it would not have put the

Prophet much out of the way. Saints—less illustrious beings than he—had achieved the magic "conquest of distance," and could fly over hundreds of miles in the twinkling of an eye; and faithful believers were bitterly disappointed when, year after year, Elijah failed to put in an appearance when the door was thrown open on the Passover night.

There was only one man, the most illiterate among the Jews of Svislovitz, namely Asher Pakess, public water-carrier and keeper of the free lodging house, who had been honored by a glimpse of the Prophet, and that not only once, but twice. He was a man of extreme simplicity; he had carried over into his manhood the naïveté of his childhood and understood all things literally. He was as honest as a child; his mind did not turn to the right or the left by a hair's breadth. No one ever had to watch Asher Pakess; and in this he differed greatly from Pala-hey, the peasant woman, another water-carrier, who could not be trusted in the kitchen if a wooden spoon were lying around. Asher Pakess could be trusted alone in the kitchen with a fistful of gold coins on the table. He spoke like a child, too, short phrases, six or seven words at a time and no more. At the seventh word he stopped and panted, as if the full load of a completed sentence tried him more than the full buckets he dragged uphill from the Beresina.

Such was Asher Pakess, to whom was granted the privilege of looking twice on Elijah the Prophet, in person. During the Passover the free lodging house, or *hekdesh,* was empty, for even wandering beggars found some sort of home for those eight days. So Asher and his wife Pakicha remained there alone, and the two of them went through the ritual. Asher's wife, somewhat more intelligent than he, knew all the details. She knew, therefore, that among the beakers on the table, the largest was set aside for Elijah. She also knew that when the passage, "Pour forth Thy wrath," was reached, the door had to be opened wide. Right enough on a certain Passover night, when the moment came, Pakicha flung open the door, and a goat entered at once. Neither Asher nor his wife thought of driving the goat out. They knew who the goat was. This was Elijah the Prophet himself, in one of those disguises that are told of so often in the folk stories. The goat, encouraged by this friendly welcome, advanced to the center of the room, leaped up, placed two forefeet on the table and mouthed one of the *matzoth*, as if saying a prayer over it, and upset the beaker of the Prophet.

And at this point, Asher Pakess could not contain himself. "Rabbi, Prophet!" he exclaimed breathlessly. "Don't be angry, please. Eat as much as you like, drink as much as you like, but oh, please, don't break anything!"

On the second night of that Passover, when the same ceremony was repeated in detail, a second visitor appeared at the door, a man in a long white gown; he entered, and strode up to the table. This time Asher cried out in terror. But all the visitor did was to lift up the cup of the Prophet, drain it, and disappear. It became known that the visitor had been Israel, the son of Joseph Bear, the cantor. But Asher Pakess was convinced that none other than Elijah the Prophet had appeared again, in another disguise, to empty the beaker of wine.

These two stories were very popular in Svislovitz, and Asher was frequently asked to repeat them, which he did readily, to the vast amusement of his auditors. He recounted the incidents simply, straightforwardly, as a child might. But there were some who did not laugh. They would ask themselves: Who knew who the goat was? And the visitor in the long white gown? It was all very well for Israel, the son of Joseph Bear, to claim that it had been he; but who had it really been? And above all, did anyone know who Asher Pakess was? Had it not often turned out that the woodchopper was no woodchopper, the water-carrier no water-carrier? And what of the "Thirty-Six," those hidden saints, the modest, silent spirits who haunt the earth in humble guise and whose merit keeps the world going? Who could tell if he had not met, in the guise of some pious, honest simpleton, one of these?

Between the first two high festival days of Passover and the last two are four days of half-festival. It is still Passover, all leavened things are forbidden, but you may work, you may carry on in the ordinary way. But during the full festival days at the beginning and at the end we youngsters lived a happy life. Nothing to do after synagogue services but visit and be received in style. Cakes, cookies, ginger candies, special delicacies made of *matzoh* flour and filled with baked parings of beef and carrots . . . and then chicken necks and chicken guts, roasted and stuffed, and jams and fruits of all kinds. And on top of all that, they gave us wine and mead to sip—as much as we wanted. We could drink a great deal of it, for it was homemade wine and mead, on which it was difficult to get drunk.

Much of the Passover centered on the children, just like Chanukah, in the winter, with its *dredlach,* or tiny, four-faced spinning tops. But Chanukah was not then, in my childhood of the eighteen-seventies, regarded as one of the important festivals. The miracle of the inexhaustible oil did not seem to grip the imagination of the Jews, who had become accustomed to miracles on a larger scale. And for some reason or other they told us little about the heroic ways of the Maccabees. But Passover was a very great occasion, perhaps the greatest of the year. And it was a marvelous time for the children.

The traditional games for Passover are played with nuts—little Brazil nuts and big walnuts. With the latter the game was difficult. Five or six nuts were placed in a row; the challenger stood at a distance of twenty paces and tried to hit them with a small steel pellet. The favorite game, however, was odds and evens, played with Brazil nuts. All you had to do was guess whether your opponent had an odd or an even number of nuts in his clenched hand. But there were sharks and swindlers among us. Jakey, the son of Reuben the bath-attendant, was one of them. He introduced a variant of the game which baffled all of us. Anyone who wanted to play with him had to place one nut on the table for the privilege of guessing odd, two nuts for the privilege of guessing even. Jakey then held his hand, with the nuts clenched in it, over the table, and emptied it when we had made our guess. And he always won! We played with him all of one day, and most of a second day, and he did not lose once. We were stripped of our hoards, while Jakey had not once lost a fistful of nuts.

I was amazed. How could a man be so consistently lucky, always show even when the challenger said odd, and vice versa. I complained to my father. Having listened carefully, he smiled and said. "Stupid! Don't you see that Jakey always puts an odd number of nuts in his hand? When you guess odd and pay one nut for guessing, he adds the nut to the odd number in his hand and that makes it even. When you say even, and pay two nuts for guessing, he adds the two nuts to the number in his hand, and that leaves it odd."

Burning with rage, I ran out to my playmates and explained the con game. We did not speak to Jakey for nearly a year.

On the afternoon of the eighth day of Passover we were given *matzoth* folded in two, a sign that Passover was closing. With that particular Passover my first *cheder* year, too, closed. I was still a child, but with something of the adult. I already knew much about our people and the lore of our people. I understood something of the meaning of that dark word *golus*, exile, which recurs so frequently in our talk, and I understood why the Jews pray for the coming of the Messiah. The child in me was still happy, carefree, merry; but now and again a sigh escaped from my lips—a sigh which I could not account for.

CHAPTER TEN

Rescue

My year with Mottye the bean was an unhappy one, but the second half, or term, was easier to bear than the first. I, together with most of those who had entered *cheder* with me, had moved up; we had become *Chumash* or Pentateuch boys. We could now read the text fluently, and we began to translate by rote. Mottye treated us with somewhat more consideration; actually, he used the newcomers as his primary scapegoats, leaving less of his ill-humor to be vented on us.

The automatic translation of the Pentateuch was as far as Mottye could take us, but that little advance made us vastly proud of ourselves. Even so, we were not content; I certainly was not. Mottye's way of explaining things left us unsatisfied. He had a materialistic outlook on life, perhaps the result of his secondary occupation as a baker. He told us about Leviathan, the monster fish who lies at the bottom of the sea and, with his tail in his mouth, encircles the globe. God, Mottye told us, plays with Leviathan daily, as he does with the Torah. When the end of the world will come God will slay Leviathan and roast him, and those who have been careful to observe all the laws of the Torah will eat roast Leviathan in the world to come. "Nothing for nothing," said Mottye the bean. "Everything must be earned. If you want to eat first-class fish in the world to come, you must study Torah in this world."

Another story that Mottye told us—and I still do not see the point of it—was about the argument between two teachers in the Talmud. One said that the world was created in the month of Nissan, in the spring, the other that it was created in the fall, in the month of Tishri. The details of the controversy escape me, I can only remember that it served to confuse me completely, for it fitted in with the facts neither way. Now there was no question about it to me that Adam, the first man, was a Jew, for it was unthinkable that God would first produce a gentile. Well, if the world was created in the month of Nissan, where did Adam get his *matzoth* for Passover? And if the world was created in the month of Tishri, where did Adam get a man to blow the ram's horn on the Day of Atonement?

Every story that Mottye the bean told us awakened in me a thousand questions with which I pelted him from morning to evening. I was impulsive by nature, in thought as in word, and no sooner did a doubt occur to me than I expressed it. Mottye, on the other hand, was cool and phlegmatic; a duel developed between *rebbi* and pupil. I hardly gave him time to collect material for one answer than I sprang another question; in the end, exhausted, he responded with the stereotyped warning: "That's enough; if you learn too fast you'll grow old too soon." After I had heard this from him several times my questions died out; but that did not put my imagination to rest. The material for my fantasies came from my studies; I swam in other worlds; I dreamed of God, the Torah, Leviathan, angels, Adam, the first Passover, the first New Year—a fearful mixture of reflections, inspirations and doubts which ran riot in my mind, so that I frequently went about like a child bereft of its senses.

I remember well, however, that the opening section of the Pentateuch, with its description of God's creation of heaven and earth, the plants and animals and man, gave me a sense of satisfaction unattended by doubts and questions. There I seemed to have found an anchor in the midst of a stormy sea. I can think of only one explanation—the supreme artistic form of the first chapters of the Bible. The story is told with such simplicity, such elementary power and conviction, so harmoniously, that it carried me along, filling me with a great contentment. The telling of the story sufficed. "And the earth was without form and void, and the spirit of God moved upon the surface of the waters." So thrilled was I by this description that all questions of accuracy and historicity simply disappeared.

In the town of Svislovitz electric lighting was of course unknown, and we children had never seen anyone press a button and flood a room with light instantaneously. But I remember that when I first saw the marvel—this was years later, in the town of Minsk—my mind flew back to my *cheder* days, and to my lips rose the words: "*Vayomer*, and said; *Elohim*, God; *yehi*, let there be; *or*, light; *vaihi*, and there was; *or*, light." The foundations of Genesis were laid in my mind like six gigantic stones, one stone for each day; I still see them, concretely. But the Sabbath never produced a concrete image in my mind; it remained abstracted and nebulous, thin and translucent, hanging like a vague cloud over the six vast stones. So it happens that till this day, when I think of a week, I picture only six days, and the Sabbath is a sort of addition to the six, not an integral part of the week. It is still the effect of those first lessons: "*Vayecholo*, and He finished; *hashomayim*, the heavens. . . ."

As soon as I knew the first portion of Genesis, most of it by heart and all of it with the translation, Mottye the bean persuaded my father to conduct the first official examination at home. The ceremony took place on the Sabbath afternoon, immediately after my father had risen from the ceremonial siesta. The table was decked with the Sabbath cloth; on it stood the big-bellied copper samovar—no fire in it, of course, on the Sabbath—holding the oven-warmed tea, and all of us drank. My father sat at my side, Mottye the bean opposite me. Then my father gave me the signal. I stood up for the recitation, but my father told me I could sit down this time. I began—and got stuck at the second verse. I began again, and fared no better. I became nervous, and everything went out of my head. Mottye the bean turned as red as a beet, for these examinations were aimed at the *rebbi* as well as at the pupil. Suddenly an instinct told me to stand up in spite of the permission to be seated. No sooner was I on my feet than everything rolled back on me like a flood. The Hebrew words and their translation flowed out of me so smoothly, so easily, that Mottye's face began to shine. My father looked proudly at me and I, with confidence restored, carried on without one mistake and without one stop right to the very end.

Of my second *rebbi* I shall have little to say, for he was more or less a repetition of Mottye the bean, though in some respects worse. His name was Abraham Berchifonda, and how a Jew of Svislovitz came by such a sonorous family name is quite beyond me. But it was seldom if ever used. We called him, instead, Abraham Kazar, out of contempt. Kazar is a contraction of the Russian words *Kazyonne Rabin*, State Rabbi, an institution to which I shall return at some length further on in this narrative. Here it is enough to say that the *Kazyonne Rabin* was the mirror and symbol of the political bondage and the general degradation of the Jews of Russia. From my earliest childhood I learned to hate this institution with a deep and burning hatred, and in my manhood I dedicated much of my life to the struggle for its eradication. So bitter was my hatred of it that I did not draw back from the most painful sacrifices.

I myself became a *Kazyonne Rabin*, taking upon myself the name and title which I had always regarded as the sign manual of our shame and slavery. It was my dream then to fight against the evils of the institution from within. In this struggle I achieved some success, but I could not endure the life for long.

The origins of my hatred for the institution of the State Rabbinate are rooted in my memories of Abraham Kazar. He was, in my eyes, a mean and contemptible person. I was of course too young to understand the profound irony which lies in the yoking together of those two words *Kazyonne* and *Rabin*. But instinct told me that there was something base and false in it. More than once I saw Abraham Kazar tremble like a leaf not only in the presence of the district commissioner, but even before the sergeant, or the village policeman, the humblest official in Svislovitz. What kind of government or state did he represent? And on the other hand I perceived that he was just an ordinary *melamed*, or teacher of the lower grade, to whom no Talmud student would be entrusted for instruction. What kind of rabbi was he then?

I must add, however, that Abraham Kazar was, in spite of the full title which we had conferred on him, only an underling of the real State Rabbi, who lived in Bobruisk. Svislovitz was too small to rate a State Rabbi of its own. Abraham Kazar's duty was to keep the register of the Jewish population for births, deaths, marriages and divorces, and the manner in which he performed this duty defies description. The forms were sent to him from district headquarters in Bobruisk, every form numbered and bound into a small volume. But Abraham had a wild system of his own. To begin with he completely ignored the Russian rubrics at the head of each column, and made all his entries in Hebrew. Then he made it a principle to ignore marriages and divorces and the birth of girls. He concentrated on funerals and the birth of boys; but even here he was shockingly careless, so that dates, names, births and deaths were jotted down at random, and in the wildest confusion. The register should, according to law, have been kept in the synagogue, under lock and key, but the volumes lay around in Abraham Kazar's home, among pots and pans and comestibles.

The register kept by Abraham Kazar was the only one recognized by the courts in all disputes regarding inheritance, military duties, etc., and the miseries which frequently resulted from the stupid and disorganized entries can hardly be imagined. In thousands of townlets the same disorder prevailed, and the Jews of Russia, disfranchised and half-outlawed as they were, saw their few recognized rights swept away through their own negligence and incompetence. One instance will suffice. It often happened that a State Rabbi of the type of Abraham Kazar would, through sheer ignorance, enter the birth of a girl under the rubric for males. He would then go on to a complete description of the child, adding the date of the circumcision. Twenty years later the government would turn up and demand a conscript, and failing his appearance would impose a fine of three hundred rubles. And there was no getting out of it. A widely held belief among the Jews was that many a Russian church had been built with the moneys collected for the failure to report of these young men who were actually young women.

In appearance Abraham Kazar resembled Mottye the bean; he had the same lean, hungry frame, the same sparse goatee; but he was much taller than Mottye and his beard was reddish in color. He differed from Mottye in another respect: he used his hands instead of a leather cat-o'-three-tails. He did this out of laziness, finding it easier to hand out a few slaps right and left than to go through the formalities of a regular whipping; it was easier for him because he was tall and his hands were long and elastic. He just had to stand where he was, lean over the table and make the round of his class with his merciless hands. His fingers were bony, and hard as nails, and every slap left its mark, sometimes in five distinct red patches. If there were sometimes fewer than five this was due less to his want of markmanship than to the want of area in a young cheek. Some of the pupils complained bitterly that the slaps of Abraham Kazar were worse than the whippings of Mottye the bean. First, they hurt more; second, they left signs on a visible section of the anatomy, whereas the signs of Mottye's whippings could be covered up, and nobody at home needed to know. They were miserable because they could not wear a pair of pants over their faces to conceal their disgrace and—what was not less important—to avoid the inquisition at home on the part of the parents: "What have you been up to *now?*" Indeed, the reception at home was often more unhappy than the original punishment.

This is about all that I can remember of my second *rebbi.* Not a thing of what he taught me remains in my memory as having come from him. I cannot even recall whether I stayed with him for one term or for two. It is a blank in my life, a lacuna between two written passages, a sandy strip unsown and uncovered running across a planted field.

When I examine my past carefully, and trace the devious and accidental paths along which I wandered blindly before I made contact with the culture of Europe, I am driven to the conclusion that mine was not among those powerful spirits—powerful either in talents or in impulse—which could break their own way through the walls of the dark labyrinth which the old *cheder* represented. It is clear to me that I might easily have gone down with those of my schoolmates—their name is legion—who were asphyxiated in that repulsive, pent atmosphere. A miracle was needed to save me.

I look upon my life as one in which many miracles have occurred, but the greatest of them all was the one which came to my rescue when I was a child of six; and the angel who was the instrument of the miracle was my uncle Meyer, not the one whom the *rebbi* Ziskind had laid across the bench after he was married, but the husband of my grandfather Solomon's only daughter, Lyube Henye. His family name, Vendrov, had a lofty and heroic ring about it.

Meyer Vendrov came from somewhere around Slutzk. He had received his education in the city of Slutzk itself, that is, in the very cradle of the secular Hebrew renaissance of that time. He was generally regarded as the handsomest man in Svislovitz, and it is as such that he has remained in my memory. He was a man of medium height, well-proportioned, with a fine black beard. In later years, when I saw Theodore Herzl for the first time, his beard put me in mind of my uncle Meyer Vendrov. But my uncle was respected for something more than his looks; he was considered the foremost Hebrew scholar in Svislovitz. His letters were the wonder of the town, and were carried around by their recipients and displayed to anyone who had the slightest understanding of such matters. He was extraordinarily skillful in the art of piecing together half-verses and fragments of verses from the Bible in order to reproduce a complete thought of his own, an art which was considered the supreme form of expression among the "stylists" of that time. He knew the entire Bible by heart, and was a great believer in the commentaries of Moses Mendelssohn and his followers. Moreover, he could speak, read and write Russian well. His character, in contrast to that of the Levins, was gentle and dispassionate. He was slow and careful of speech, always finding the right word to put in the right place.

His outward appearance corresponded to his character. He was always well-dressed, sometimes to the point of foppishness. He affected the mode, but with a slight compromise; that is to say, his coat was short, in contrast with our long capotes, but not quite as short as the coat of the city dandy. His vest was cut out at the throat, but not too deeply. Had any other man in Svislovitz concentrated on Bible study in preference to the

Talmud, studied the modern commentators and understood the secular, worldly subject, grammar; had he in addition worn a short coat and cut-out vest; and on top of all this had he spoken Russian—he would have been regarded as next door to an atheist. But Meyer Vendrov was held in deep respect. Even the *Rav* of Svislovitz, a great scholar and a greater saint, treated him with high consideration, frequently drew him into conversation after prayers and went for walks with him under the colonnades of trees on the great road. Their conversations revolved round the affairs of the world, for in talmudic studies —the specialty, of course, of our *Rav*—my uncle was not beyond the stage of the decently educated Jew of the middle classes. In Bible studies, as well as in grammar, our *Rav* was a comparative novice: and he did not have much use for them. The Talmud was his element, and if he happened to need a biblical verse he would look for it not in the original sources, but in a quotation in one of the talmudic tractates, which he knew by heart.

In the field of learning there was, therefore, little to draw them together; yet it was the *Rav* who made the first friendly advances toward my uncle. There were, I think, two reasons for this attraction. My uncle was elegant not only in his appearance, but in his spirit and in his behavior. He conducted himself with all the carefulness of a fine, religious Jewish householder. The second reason was perhaps equally cogent: my uncle had the merit of not living in Svislovitz. Only his family lived there; he himself passed almost his entire life in Dvinsk, or as some of us called it, Dinaburg, where he was one of the leading agents of Meir and Leib Friedland, the great building contractors. Any agent of the Friedlands was looked upon with respect; but one that occupied so exalted a position, constructed armories and forts for the Russian government, dealt with generals and even with ministers of state, yet nevertheless remained a good religious Jew and comported himself as such in all details, commanded a respect that approached awe. My grandfather, like the rest of our family, was proud of uncle Meyer who, against the dull life of Svislovitz, shone like a strip of silk in a rough woolen garment.

Uncle Meyer used to come home from the faraway city with the German name once or at most twice a year, and I cannot say that he had much joy of his homecomings. My aunt Lyube Henye presented a painful contrast to him. Her looks, and particularly her huge masculine nose, were very much against her, and she paid no attention to dress. To these handicaps she added a quarrelsome nature. All year round she would boast about her Meyer, her husband, who was as handsome as a count and as clever as a cabinet minister. I do not know where she could ever have seen a count or a cabinet minister for purposes of comparison, but she never forgot to mention them in connection with her brilliant husband. But when the great man came home trouble set in at once. On the one hand, she would never let him out of sight, and would not take her eyes off him for a moment; on the other, she was perpetually tormenting him with foolish questions. She worked at it until my uncle was exhausted and irritated; the atmosphere between them became tense, and quarrels followed.

I was present more than once during such quarrels, and I was always on my uncle's side. My aesthetic instincts were stronger than my family pride, and even as a child I wondered how this Adam had chosen himself such an Eve. I did not like the match and I do not believe that my uncle liked it, either. But in those days divorces hardly ever took place among "decent" families. If a man had made a bad bargain he would stagger along silent and doubled up under his load. As I see it now, my poor aunt Lyube was jealous, and she suffered terribly from her husband's almost perpetual absence. It is true that the Jewish wives of Svislovitz were quite ignorant of jealousy as an institution; it never occurred to them to suspect their husbands of infidelities, and in their pitiful vocabulary even the word jealousy was unknown. But Nature asserted her outraged rights without regard to vocabularies, and a Svislovitz house might speak ungrammatically and yet think in naked concepts. But in respect of her loneliness my aunt was no exception. There were many Jewish wives in those days who spent their lives as grass widows. There were many agents who spent three-quarters of the year on the Niz, and teachers who passed many years laboring in some stuffy *cheder* far from their families. The wives were in effect half-divorced from their husbands, though the Jewish population did not seem to suffer as a consequence; there was a compensating factor in the universally large families brought into the world by the shopkeepers and workers and teachers whose occupations did not take them away from home.

My aunt Lyube Henye had four children, two boys and two girls, and died giving birth to her fifth child. The disaster shook our whole family. Little Toibeh, my grandmother, wept longer and more bitterly than anyone else. My uncle arrived from Dinaburg after the funeral and it was seen that he too was deeply affected. The tears that ran down his cheeks were for the mother of his children, who had now been left orphans.

Some years after the death of my aunt, my uncle founded the first *cheder metukan*, or modern and improved *cheder*, in Svislovitz. The very appellation was unknown to us. Both of uncle Meyer's sons were older than his daughters, and when the problem of their education became urgent, he put all the teachers in Svislovitz through a tactful examination. He finally chose one Judah Artzer, and, having consulted my father, included me among the pupils of this first modernized *cheder*. My uncle remained for many years the controller and inspector of this new institution; twice a year he visited us, looked into our studies, examined us, and laid down the course for the ensuing term. Four pupils made up the entire *cheder*, the two sons of uncle Meyer, one son of uncle Shmerel, and I. Thus

Judah Artzer became my new spiritual guide and mentor, and to this day my memories of him are among the happiest and most grateful of my life.

Among the twenty *melamdim*, or teachers, of Svislovitz there were perhaps three or four who were teachers by profession, which does not mean, of course, by training; it only means that they chose the profession deliberately and out of love for it, and took it seriously. The foremost among them was my new *rebbi*, Judah, and his nearest rival was an older man called Azer.

The two men made a curious contrast. Azer was known as one of the most miserly men in town. He parted with a kopek only under dire compulsion, and he ruled his house with an economic severity which kept it on the borderline of starvation. Judah was instinctively generous; he liked good tobacco and distributed his store of it right and left. Azer saved his money kopek by kopek, and with his first few rubles opened a loan office, lending out at weekly rates of interest.

In my day it was already rumored that Azer the *melamed* had a capital of four hundred rubles, which could only be explained by the terms on which he lent out money. From a loan of ten rubles he would at once deduct two rubles and forty kopeks as interest, the borrower getting only seven rubles and sixty kopeks. On this he paid twenty kopeks a week for a year's time, i.e., ten rubles and forty kopeks; and the kopeks Azer gathered in did not lie idle—they were immediately put out at interest, and so the kopek begot the ruble, the ruble the hundred. Azer might have become one of the richest men in town if things had gone right; unfortunately for him, however, there were "bankruptcies" to be reckoned with.

In the Svislovitz of those days Jews did not use the Russian courts for the settlement of disputes. The appeal was made instead to the Torah, to Jewish law, as interpreted by the *Rav*. Azer was forever hauling someone before the *Rav*, appealing to the eternal principles of the Torah and invoking, in all his arguments, his considerable knowledge of them. He forgot only one thing, that usury was forbidden by that Torah to which he appealed. Judah Artzer was in this respect at the opposite pole from Azer; he was ready to give his last kopek to a friend, and he was for that reason perpetually in debt, even though he had the best-paying *cheder* in town.

The difference between the two men also expressed itself in their respective attitudes toward Judaism. Azer guarded with embittered fidelity every one of the outer formalities, and brought his pupils up in the same spirit. During the prayer of the Eighteen Benedictions, which the worshipper must repeat while standing motionless in one place, and without interruption, Azer made it a point to remain standing longer than anyone else; and woe to the pupil who was overhasty in resuming his seat. Judah cared little for those flourishes and was much more concerned that his pupils should distribute the accents correctly on the words. Azer was the true Talmud teacher, but a stranger to the spirit of the Bible, devoid of understanding of the Prophets and their ethical-aesthetic influence. Judah, who later became the equal of Azer as a teacher of Talmud, remained to the end a man of the Bible, a lover of the Prophets. Azer and Judah could have been called the Shammai and Hillel of Svislovitz—in miniature, of course. But then, was not the entire life of Svislovitz a miniature? One day God wanted to make Himself a vest-pocket edition of the world, and He created Svislovitz.

It is hardly necessary to say that the two men were not friends. It never came to an open quarrel, but it was well known that Azer had no use for Judah's attention to the secular, even profane subject of grammar, and looked with dislike and contempt on his pedagogic methods and his general attitude toward his pupils. Judah, for his part, put little stock in Azer's piety and less in his approach to the Talmud. The pupils of the respective *cheders* felt the hostility of the teachers in their own bones, and as is always the case, the hostility of the schools was more open than the hostility of the founders. In time this developed into something like genuine hatred. At first my ardor was dampened by the fact that my older brother, Meyer, attended Azer's *cheder*, but in time I succumbed completely to the mood of my schoolmates.

For the first time I felt myself drawn to the man who had been appointed as my teacher, and I remember the happiness this brought in its wake. Nothing contents a child more than an awareness of the process of his own growth, and nothing bribes a child more than being taken seriously. I felt at once that my new teacher was genuinely interested in me, not because he was paid for it, but because he looked upon me as a little man and wanted me to become a big one.

My uncle had made Judah promise that without the consent of the parents he would not increase his pupils beyond the original number of four. In compensation he received, for every pupil, the then unheard of fee of twenty-five rubles a term, a total of two hundred rubles (one hundred dollars) a year. The average earnings of a Svislovitz *melamed*, with a much larger number of pupils, was one hundred rubles a year. In addition to the fees, Judah received fifteen rubles a year from each pupil to enable him to rent a *cheder*. This was another of the new-fangled ideas of my uncle Meyer. He could not tolerate the universal practice of turning the living room of the *rebbi* and his family into a temple of learning. He argued that when the *rebbi* was engaged in teaching he ought not to have his family around him, forever distracting his attention; nor was it good for the pupils to be forever mixed up in the family affairs of the *rebbi*. Thus, at last, we had a room to ourselves in a Jewish home which happened to have a gentile home as its neighbor. The room protruded into the garden of the gentile, with its high fence. We were alone, *rebbi* and pupils, with our books, an intimate group in a happy corner of our own.

CHAPTER ELEVEN

Studies

When Judah Artzer opened his class, his first impulse was to treat us like complete beginners. Had he been able to, he would cheerfully have erased from our memories all we had learned till then. But at least he could and did go over the ground again, teaching us the correct way of reading simple Hebrew, eradicating all the errors we had picked up from previous teachers. He complained that it tortured him to hear us read; he would start, catch his breath and pull a face every time we misplaced an accent—which was frequently. "Children," he told us, "if anyone of you should be praying aloud in the synagogue, or reading a chapter of the Pentateuch, I want every listener to know that you are one of Judah Artzer's pupils."

During the summer we spent ten hours a day in *cheder*, in the winter nearly twelve. We always began at nine in the morning, and in the summer ended with the afternoon prayers, in the winter much later. Not more than one hour was taken up by meals. We had somewhat less than eight hours for sleep. For play we had Friday afternoon, half the Sabbath, the Holy Days, and the end of each term.

Judah Artzer instituted a rigid schedule. For the first two terms the subjects were the Pentateuch, the rest of the Bible, grammar, and writing. With the Pentateuch we studied the commentary of the famous medieval scholar, Rashi, and spent more time on him than on the text proper. This introduced us to Hebrew without vowel signs and to fragments of Aramaic, so that when we reached the Talmud its language was not altogether strange to us.

Grammar was an absolutely new experience for us, and it was something new for Svislovitz. A table of verbs was handed to each one of us—an analysis of the sacred Hebrew tongue into its base mechanics; the blasphemy of it! I conceived a tremendous affection for the discipline of the conjugations, which we learned by heart in between the courses and at home. I was forever jingling the words, so that my mother begged me to stop my eternal *pokod*, *pokadti*, *pokadto.* I believe that the sense of logic developed in me very early, and I felt grammar to be the logic of speech. I realized dimly that language was no longer a random, casual sort of affair; the long lines of the conjugations became the alleys of a disciplined garden; on one side the flowers of the past, on the other those of the future, in between the line of the present, down which I strolled, myself a verb, a *poel,* a thing that works.

I look back at those days and marvel. Ten hours a day we sat glued to our places; where did we get the strength, the endurance to sustain so rigorous a regimen of study? Amazing as it must sound nowadays, it never occurred to anyone that we might be under an excessive strain—not even to my uncle Meyer, who had a modern outlook. The world in which I lived was a stranger to the idea that too much study can be bad for your health, can constitute a mental strain. The word "strain" was applied only to physical effort.

The truth is that much study seldom leads to sickness. Our greatest teachers, the Tanaim, the Amoraim, the Gaonim, all passed their entire lives in study, yet not of a single one is it recorded that he fell sick from too much study. But we did not have to go so far afield. There was the *Rav* of our town; did he not pass sixteen and sometimes twenty-four hours at a single stretch in study? It was quite true that he was sick enough from time to time, but that was because he rarely received his miserable salary in time. It was equally true that our Talmud students were pale, lean and sickly-looking; but that was because they were short of "days."

I cannot remember that I ever overstrained myself. It seemed to me that my brain was always at play and the things I learned just leaped into my mind. In grammar it was the logical faculty that took the lead, in Bible study the psychological. Back of the ability to learn and to remember much without putting myself under undue strain was my living relationship to all that surrounded me, and particularly to the world of nature in all its forms. I sought life in all things, and found it. I remember someone telling me that stones too could grow, and that all big stones had once been little; and I was happy that one more way of life had been added in this world of ours. It was always patent to me that the woods and fields lived not only in the sense of growth, but in the sense of the possession of an individual spirit; and later, when I learned the book of ben Sirah, Ecclesiasticus, I found nothing forced or unnatural in the thought that the trees had their verse of praise, the fields theirs, and so on. Often enough I went out into the woods to listen; not that, even then, I expected the trees to lift up their voices and with human tongues repeat the exact words of the Bible. But of course there was a distinct, fixed language of the trees, inaccessible to us. Why, King Solomon had understood it!

A complete break came in my inner life with my entry into Judah's *cheder*. With every new chapter of the Bible that I learned, with every new hero that I came to know, every incident that I lived through, I was drawn one step farther from the soil into which I was born and closer to the sacred soil of ancient heroes and ancient heroisms. I am certain that my *rebbi* did not quite understand what he was doing to me. Fragment by fragment a new life grew up within me, a life which began in Ur of the Chaldees, stretched through Mesopotamia, wound its way across a gigantic desert, held war with the most powerful kings, and at last found a resting place in Palestine—the first half of a world drama. I studied diligently, and became a more intimate part of this life. I forgot completely that these were stories and descriptions of a world which has been gone these thousands of years. Strange paradox! The more clearly I understood the meaning of the words *past, gone*, the more potently did I feel the presence of that world. It had captured me, I had become part of it, I could not free myself.

When the books are closed, when the *cheder* is shut, and with my *rebbi* or my companions I walk homeward, I must exert myself to return to the world of reality. I do not notice what is happening around me. I must make a deliberate effort to bridge the gulf between Abraham of old and Abraham Kazar, between Moses our Teacher and Moses the shoemaker.

Day by day I am drawn more deeply into this double existence—the tangible world of Svislovitz and the dream world issuing from the books of the Bible. In my sleep, too, there is confusion, I do not know from which of the two worlds my dreams are drawn. I can well remember seeing in a childhood dream the dividing of the Red Sea. The water rises like two walls on either hand, and in the midst is a broad path of sand with millions of smooth pebbles, like the banks of the Svislo. In the midst the Jews march along in holiday attire, the men with prayer shawls over their shoulders. Among them I recognize my grandfather, the *Rav*, and many other familiar figures, and it does not occur to me that my grandfather had nothing to do with the crossing of the Red Sea. Two worlds have mingled within me and I can no longer distinguish where the one ends and the other begins.

There is only one passage in the Bible which can describe adequately the strange state in which I lived in those years between childhood and adolescence (we were adolescents at the age of twelve)—that which tells of Jacob and Esau in the womb of Rebeccah. "And the children struggled together within her. . . . And the Lord said unto her, Two nations are in thy womb and two manner of people. . . ." Two brothers, two worlds, in the mother-womb. And when Rebeccah went past a Jewish house of prayer and study, Jacob trembled and struggled within her; and when she passed by a church, it was Esau who trembled and struggled to get out. That was what the commentator Rashi said, and that was what the *rebbi* taught us. Where churches and synagogues had sprung up in those days was a mystery, and still remains one. But I see now that our sages had the trick of my own childhood: they pulled the world which was ancient even in their days into their own lives; they too lived in a double world. At that time, within me, the struggle was not between Jacob and Esau—that was to come later, when I became acquainted with the world of Esau—but between two Jacobs. One little Jacob was the child of Svislovitz, the *cheder* boy, oppressed by the narrow life which encircled him; the other little Jacob came from a mighty and tumultuous world. For I was acquainted with many Jewish heroes of old other than Jewish. I knew the giant Og, King of Bashan, and Sihon, King of the Amorites; I knew the most wonderful magician of all times, Balaam, and the mightiest warrior, Nebuchadnezzar of Babylon. And on the threshold of the *cheder*, as I entered and left, the two twin brothers, the sons of Isaac, held war. Within the *cheder* the Jacob of the great world was completely triumphant; outside, the Jacob of Svislovitz had to ask for his place in the sun, and struggled to assert himself.

In one sense it can be said that I was receiving a classical education, for what does that mean but that the child is introduced to a world that existed a long time ago, and learns that in ancient times there was already a rich life, an organized society with its own art and knowledge, and its own ideals of justice and beauty. To most people a classical education means Latin and Greek and a knowledge of the best books in those languages. Through them civilized man may learn how the process of life stretches link by link from generation to generation, from the beginning down to his own day; and I am quite certain that the ordinary classical education, too, gives rise to a conflict within the mind of the child. I cannot, however, admit for a moment that the conflict would be of the same order as mine. Latin and Greek have remained dead languages to the most gifted of students. The life which these languages portray is alien to the student, and only the rare genius can identify himself with it. For the ordinary student the classical languages and their content are like the faint echo of a life that has uttered itself a long time ago and has died. For him there is not a conflict; he is only aware of a contact. Yet that contact has been enough to rouse a world-wide movement against classical education as such. I do not wish to enter here into the relative merits of the two sides in the dispute; I only wish to stress the fact that the Jewish *cheder* was a classical school, and that the effect on the Jewish child was infinitely more powerful than the effect of the non-Jewish classical education even where the classics were regarded as the chief, perhaps the sole substance of education.

Two considerations, one quantitative, the other qualitative, explain the difference. The actual time spent in the *cheder* on Hebrew and Hebrew subjects was between three and four times as long as the time spent on Latin and Greek in the best high schools of Europe. The *cheder* boy was simply steeped in Hebrew from morning till night. And he also learned, in passing, several important Hebrew dialects.

The qualitative element was perhaps even more important. In Hebrew the child was learning the history of his own people. These were not the stories of an alien world, but of events and individuals who had some sort of inner relation with Father and Mother. A third factor, of less importance, should be remembered. At the time of which I am writing, the Hebrew language played a much more important role in the daily life of Jews than it does today. Contemporary Hebrew literature was, it is true, very poor; the language had not yet been adapted to modern life and the efforts of writers at modern self-expression were clumsy in the extreme. But I am speaking now only of the daily life of the Jewish householder in our world. Fifty or sixty years ago (that is, in the eighteen-sixties and seventies) nearly all Jewish shopkeepers kept their accounts in Hebrew, Jewish merchants corresponded in Hebrew, and among the more cultivated classes bride and bridegroom exchanged notes in the same language. If they could not write Hebrew they would have their love letters written for them by their teachers or by special scribes; and the Song of Songs was ransacked for quotations, from "Let him kiss me with the kisses of his mouth" to "Flee, my beloved."

For me Hebrew became a completely living tongue. The transformation had already set in, I believe, with the second or third term under Judah. I have an infallible "marker" of the transformation, or rather of my having become aware of it. When a language has become real it is no longer necessary to translate it, and I remember that in my second or third term I was already reading the Bible without translating it—and my *rebbi* let it pass. It was only at the most difficult passages that he would stop me and make sure that I understood the meaning. The translation had by now become superfluous ballast which only impeded my progress. I was impatient, eager to run ahead, and the translation had been weighing me down for some time like heavy winter clothing when the spring is already here.

Finding the tempo of the studies rather slow, I had too much time on my hands, and during the actual work I was able to think things over. With Judah Artzer, as before with Mottye the bean, I had question after question. The logical faculty I had inherited from my father was manifest in my childhood, long before I knew that such a thing as logic existed. And then our *rebbi* taught us the elements of the subject from the textbook of ben Ze-ev. But even then, whenever I became confused it was my habit to reconstruct first the syllogisms of a case, just as I learned to do years later, and then to thread my way cautiously through the labyrinth of arguments. My mind moved swiftly and smoothly and always felt a quick jolt when it ran across a break in the logical path; and there are logical breaks enough in the Bible stories.

But apart from logical contradictions, there rose in me questions directed to the psychological aspects of the stories. I was interested in the ethical principles which the stories were supposed to illustrate, and whenever a struggle arose I could not remain neutral but had to become the passionate ally of one of the two sides; this was my inheritance from my mother. My schoolmate Gershon, my cousin, older than I, used to ask me, bewildered, what business was it of mine who was in the right and who in the wrong? It was only a story, and the outcome settled no point of law. But his question was in turn unintelligible to me; for the stories were living things for me, and where there is life the principle of justice is relevant. Thus I was drawn into heated arguments with my *rebbi*, defending one of the protagonists in a biblical drama, attacking another, without regard to the orthodox view.

My *rebbi* never lost his temper with me, either for my questions or for my arguments, not even when the latter made the sweat start to his brow. On the contrary I could feel that he was happy in my restlessness and excitement. Often, when he had answered a difficult question weakly, he would laugh at me with his eyes, and on his face I could read the marvelous answer which God once gave to an obstinate questioner: "My sons have conquered me!" For Judah was an honest man; he never abused his authority, never said to me: "If you know everything, you'll grow old too quickly. . . ." He treated me like a young comrade, gave my thoughts free rein and my tongue free play. His *cheder* was for me the best debating school I have ever known.

Among the countless stories in the Bible which provoke a partisan feeling for the one side or the other, I choose only three to illustrate the workings of my mind in those days. Two of them I had already heard in my first *cheder*, but I do not recall that they awoke a conflict in me then. The third story I learned during my second term with Judah. I have chosen these stories because they are in my opinion the most important and the most characteristic.

They are the stories of Sarah and Hagar; of Esau and Jacob; of Saul and David. In all three I espoused the "wrong" side. I was for Hagar and against Sarah, for Esau and against Jacob, for Saul and against David. I left the straight and narrow path and began to tread a dangerous road.

I could not bring myself to forgive Sarah for her treatment of Hagar. It is clearly written: "And Sarai said unto Abraham, 'Behold now, the Lord hath restrained me from bearing: I pray thee, go in unto my maid; it may be that I shall obtain children from her.' And Abraham hearkened unto the voice of Sarai." So who, I argued at the age of seven, was to blame but Sarah herself? It was she who had persuaded Abraham to this new marriage. What right had she, then, to vent her anger against the poor servant girl? The answer, that when Hagar saw that she had conceived, her mistress was despised in her eyes, did not content me. I could not get the meaning of the text. It was inconceivable to me that Hagar should have borne herself haughtily against Sarah. Suppose one of *our* servant girls were to try and bear herself haughtily against my mother . . . the mere idea was absurd. And all my sympathies went out to Hagar; and I conceived a love for Ishmael, the little "wild man" with black, curling locks—the rascal who never went to *cheder*, but ran around in a short smock, bow and arrow in hand, as we did on the New Year of the Trees; not a Jewish boy, and yet not a gentile boy; but gracious, charming and lovable.

What I resented, too, was that God had given us such an old grandmother as Sarah, so wrinkled and so bad-tempered. My grandmother Toibeh was much nicer. She would surely never have driven a servant girl out of the house into a wilderness without a spring. There was, for instance, Pessye the deaf, who served my grandmother for so many years; not a good servant, because she hardly ever did what she was told, first because she was as deaf as a post, and second because she was incredibly obstinate. Yet she remained thirty years with the family, and when my grandmother died, she kept house for my grandfather, and it never occurred to me that one could be angry with Pessye. After my grandfather's death she was "inherited" by my mother, and she served us for several years. My grandfathers and my grandmother always fused in my mind with the Patriarchs and the Matriarchs. I transferred the respect which I felt for the ancient fathers of our people to the oldest members of our family; and from our "Old Men" I learned to understand and to feel more intimately the lives of the Patriarchs.

The story of Jacob and Esau gave rise to a much sharper dispute, for after all, the grandmothers are not as important as the grandfathers. Granted, Sarah was not one hundred percent perfect—but then Abraham was such a saint, so hospitable to wayfarers, so lovable, so gentle a fellow, that he atoned for the sins of Sarah. But what could be done about Jacob? Was he not the last link in the chain of the Patriarchs, the last, the most active—and the most productive—of our grandfathers? Jacob should be immaculate, pure as a ritual citron—and here he was, cheating his older brother out of the birthright, and sneaking the blessing out of his father. And how did Rebeccah, the sweet, lovely girl who stood with her pitcher upon her head by the wellside, who pitied the thirsty camels and drew water for them, that same Rebeccah of whom Rashi tells that when she went into Sarah's tent soon after her marriage with Isaac, the tent was flooded with light—how did she come to be helping her son to steal the birthright? And from whom? A blind old father!

The tortuous excuses and explanations of my *rebbi* were of no avail; he quoted learned and sacred sources to the effect that Rebeccah knew, with the help of the Holy Spirit, that red-haired Esau was headed for a bad end; in the morning he never poured water over his fingertips, as all good Jews should the moment they step out of bed and before they say their first morning prayer; he went around roistering for days at a stretch; he sat down to a meal without washing his hands, and never said grace after it. A bad lot. And that was why she arranged that Jacob should get the benediction; for Jacob sat from morn to night in the house of prayer and study of Shem and Eber, learning what good Jews are supposed to learn. I replied that all this might be very true, and the Holy Spirit was not a matter to be ignored, and I too loved Jacob greatly; but a swindle was a swindle, and excuses could not wash away the blot. I refused to yield. And long after I had left *cheder* I kept turning the story over restlessly in my mind. Jacob was for me one of the most fascinating figures of that ancient world. I marvelled at his strange endurance, both in his love and in his life-struggles. I marvelled, too, at his dream, the greatest of dreams, bringing heaven and earth together. But most of all I marvelled over the story of his battle with the angel and of his victory. Still, the blot remained a blot, a disturbing element in the life of the hero. I was not less disturbed in later years when I heard Christian teachers refer to Jacob—precisely because of this blot—as a negative character; and I was more disturbed when I in turn taught the Bible to growing children and was false to myself, and choked over the first chapters of the story of Jacob.

Something of a like nature took place in me when I first read and then saw on the stage *The Merchant of Venice.* I was drawn instinctively to Shylock, the victim of merciless robbery. They stole his daughter, they stole his money; but that pound of flesh which he demanded stuck in my throat, almost literally; I could not gulp it down.

I am grateful to the men who, through their works, resolved in me the Jacob and Shylock conflicts. Vladimir Solovyov, the Russian philosopher, by his classic analysis of Jacob, in *The National Question from the Moral Viewpoint* returned my hero to me, cleansed of the blot; the poet Richard Beer Hoffman, in his play *Jacob's Dream*, helped to draw me closer to him. The Shylock conflict was resolved in me in part by Heine's essays on the Shakespeare plays, but still more by a performance of the role by Schildkraut in the Deutsches Theater in Berlin. The interpretation of Shylock given by the actor that evening was such that a number of visitors—probably bitter anti-Semites—rose in the middle of the performance and left in a rage. I mention this incident only because it was a psychological throwback to the struggles of my *cheder* days.

In the long epic narrative of David and Saul I refused again to follow the trodden path. I could not for the life of me understand wherein Saul had sinned. Samuel had bid Saul wait for him with the sacrifice, and Saul waited. But Samuel did not appear at the appointed time, whereupon Saul sacrificed without him. Was this a punishable offense? Or if Saul could not bring himself to destroy Amalek, root and branch, leaving no trace of that people, was he therefore to lose his throne? I was on the side of Saul, too, in his struggles with David. It was clear to Saul that the kingdom would pass into the hands of David; that was enough to explain why the evil spirit terrified him, so that his mind became confused. But in detached intervals of lucidity the old Saul awoke in him, and how great, how pure, was the soul that spoke from him then: "And Saul knew

David's voice, and said, 'Is this thy voice, my son David? . . . I have sinned; return, my son David; for I will no more do thee harm, because my life was precious in thine eyes this day; behold, I have played the fool, and have erred exceedingly.'" Children are sensitive; they have a feeling for the natural as against the artificial; they give themselves instinctively to that which is honest, and to me no one was as honest—as naïvely honest, perhaps—as Saul, and no one's fate was as tragic as his.

The *rebbi* was compelled, ex officio, to be on David's side. He uttered his formal verdict on the case, but in my heart there was a suspicion that in secret he too sympathized with Saul. I suspected my *rebbi* not because I had no faith in him, but because I had much faith in him and believed implicitly in his sense of justice.

I must have been seven years old, certainly not more than seven and a half when I began to learn the Talmud. I did not begin with the light anthology used in most *cheders*, but with the body of the Talmud itself, plunging at once into the tractate *Berakhoth*, or Benedictions. My *rebbi* declared that he had no fears for me; only weak and timid children must be led gently into the waters of a cold lake.

But it was not as easy for me as my *rebbi* imagined, and I was not at all happy as I floundered about in my first attempts to swim. It was not that the material was too difficult for my young—my too young—brain; the resistance was psychological. I was too closely bound to the world of the Bible, a world governed by the emotions, a world of marvelous stories and incidents with a language of their own for the tender soul of a child. The talmudic world, and especially the legalistic-theological province called *halachah*, is the complete antithesis of the Bible. It is a world as dry and logical as a square root; it is governed not by the emotions, but by a stern and somber logic. The jest, the parable, the maxim, the fiery phrase, disappeared; their place was taken by the intellectual syllogism, cold and inflexible as a bar of iron; and the transition was painful.

When my brain grew weary with the strain of logic I pleaded with my *rebbi* to close the Talmud and take me back to the Bible. He understood—but he seldom yielded. On the contrary, with the passage of each month he decreased the allotment of the Bible and increased that of the Talmud. He comforted me: "Wait a while; you will soon find out how lovable and delightful the Talmud can be." And indeed, before long the taste of it came to me—but not as my *rebbi* had meant. Several terms had to pass before I got the swing and joy of the dialectic *halachah;* but what preceded that, and what filled me with happiness, was the *aggadah*, the folklore section of the Talmud. I might almost say that the *aggadah* made complete restitution for the losses I had suffered in the *halachah*. A new world opened for me in the *aggadah*, and this time not a distant one, but a world that was intimately my own. I felt the breath of the prophetic episode borne over me again—the continuity of the first ecstasies which I had learned to know so well. Heine has defined the distinction between *halachah* and *aggadah* in an excellent simile. The *halachah*, he says, is like a fencing school where the swordsmen of Pumbedhita and Nehardea, armed with the sharp, flashing swords of logic, compete for supremacy; the *aggadah* is like the hanging gardens of Semiramis, strange and marvelous trees bending in tangled profusion, hiding among their branches the secrets of creation. And when the athletes in the arena grow weary of the contest, they leave *halachah* for *aggadah* to find refreshment and repose. But I would use another simile: the *halachah* is like the Atlantic Ocean and the *aggadah*, the Gulf Stream which cuts across it.

It did not take long before I was as intimately at home in the *aggadah* as I was in the Bible, but the *aggadah* did not represent a new phase in my development. It fused completely with my experience of the Bible. Nevertheless there was a boundary line and a new experience too. For the Bible drew toward its close with the destruction of the Temple by Nebuchadnezzar and Nebuzaradon. About what came after I knew something from the accounts of Ezra and Nehemiah and the very last of the prophets; for here the boundary line, or I would rather say the bounding area, lies. The bitter rage of the prophets has died down and no longer falls on the ears of mankind "like a hammer that shatters the rocks." In Ezra and Nehemiah the voice of the protagonists is gentle, entreating; they write diplomatic letters to foreign kings. It seemed to me that with Ezra and Nehemiah a curtain fell, and I felt that behind the curtain there must be a world as rich in storm and wonder and catastrophe as that of the Bible; and I asked my *rebbi* to tell me more, more: what happened when the Bible closed?

His answer was: "The Bible was written with the Holy Spirit, when the Prophets still lived and the word of God came from their lips. But with the death of Haggai, Zechariah and Malachi, the well was closed and sealed. No new Prophets came after them; that is why we have received no new sacred books. The Talmud is sacred, of course, but not with that first unforgettable sanctity. The voice has died away, and all we hear is the echo."

CHAPTER TWELVE

Svislovitzers

FACES crowd in on me from the far-off past. They engraved themselves in my memory during my earliest years, and they are the background to the narrative of my growth. Individually some of them may have been of no importance in my development; in the aggregate they gave me my first pictorial representation of the world. And they were vivid types; they do not lose themselves in each other. However humble they and their circumstances were, each of them stands out clearly.

Perhaps the humblest of them was that Asher Pakess of whom I have already told that he was twice privileged to have received as visitor Elijah the Prophet. Humble as he was, he was the dispenser of the town's hospitality to all the poor and humble that came our way. For our town possessed no inn or hotel. Our only public accommodation was the *hekdesh*, and there all penniless wanderers of the vagrant class were lodged free of charge. Asher, we may recall, was also the Jewish water-carrier. Between his earnings in that capacity, and the free lodgings he and his wife got in the *hekdesh*, he scraped together his livelihood—for he received no extra pay as the manager of our only communal institution. That was his voluntary contribution. But certain privileges attached to his public function. First, the synagogue and the study house were obligated to buy their water from him, and he lugged it up from the Beresina at a kopek for two buckets. He was also the purveyor of the willow withes for the festival of Tabernacles or Booths. Third, every firstling kid and calf which acquired a ritual blemish was his property. Fourth, he was permitted to buy all the meat he and his wife could eat without paying the *karobka*, the kosher meat tax which was collected by the wealthy Jew to whom it had been farmed out by the government. As Asher never had the price of a meat dinner, tax or no tax, this last privilege was purely honorific.

The *hekdesh* was the asylum of the *déclassés*—the outcasts. Mostly it was used by lonely beggars. Now and again—but this was rare—it would shelter an entire family travelling in its cart. The *hekdesh* consisted of one vast room, in the center of which stood a tremendous stove. Above the stove was a *liezanka*, or alcove, in which a dozen people could lie down comfortably on winter nights. Travellers with any sort of standing, such as the emissaries of little backwoods talmudical schools, or second-class itinerant preachers, respectable unfortunates, refugees of a fire, or such Jewish fathers as were travelling from city to city piously gathering a dowry for their unmarried daughters, were lodged not in the *hekdesh*, but in the annex to the synagogue. For the important travellers, the emissaries of great *yeshivoth*, pilgrims from the Holy Land, preachers of repute and travelling rabbis, the doors of my grandfather's house stood wide open with food, drink, lodgings and services, all gratis, of course.

Not quite as poor as Asher Pakess and his wife were the couple from which my *rebbi* rented the room which was our *cheder*, but of these two the woman was the outstanding character. Feigeh Riveh, as she was called, was a public figure among the gentiles of Svislovitz not less than among the Jews, and her reputation as an exorcist of the evil eye gave her a unique position in our parts. Her husband, Abraham the yellow, derived some benefit from his wife's public role; he was able to pick up bargains from her gentile clientele—now a young calf, now an ox, now a wagonload of hay or a sack of wheat. Sometimes he did a little business as a broker, and in between whiles he would earn an honest ruble as a matchmaker. This last profession he loved independently of its material returns; more than anything else he loved to urge a match on two young people in the presence of both. He would praise the prospective bride to the bridegroom, and the bridegroom to the bride, extravagantly, joyously, with genuine artistic feeling. And as he proceeded, his eyes narrowed contentedly, like those of a happy cat, and the freckles on his vast face would begin to glow like the faces of the young people whose praises he was singing.

Abraham the yellow had little luck with his proposed alliances, and rarely succeeded in bringing them to a consummation. Once he worked on a case for six months. He was bent on persuading a young man of Svislovitz to take a bride from Lapitz, a village some thirty Russian miles away. He would not leave Svislovitz until he had finally wrung from the young man a reluctant half-consent; and this he obtained by dinning into the ears of his family the praises of the bride, distributed among detailed descriptions of her appearance, her education, her wit and her other natural gifts. Finally Abraham left for Lapitz to begin convincing the bride's family. He returned from Lapitz the next day speechless. Not a word on the subject of the match could be wrung from him. But before long the truth leaked out. Abraham the yellow had never been in Lapitz before; he had not known the family he had been speaking of; he had been working on a rumor that a family in Laptiz was looking for a match. But when he got to Lapitz he discovered that the rumor had worked a change of sex en route. The eligible party in Lapitz was a male; and for a long, long time the Jews of Svislovitz had something to laugh about: "Abraham the yellow is the most dangerous marriage-broker in these parts; he seeks husbands for men and wives for women."

On top of his other virtues Abraham had those of a henpecked husband. This huge, lumbering body, nearly twice the height of his wife and four times her weight, used to tremble before the sharp glances of the tiny mercurial creature—a fistful of bones and nerves—that was Feigeh Riveh. A great talker, he suffered from repression in the presence of his wife; no sooner did he feel her eye fastened on him than he would stop in the middle of a sentence and turn two pitiful, cowlike eyes on her with the question: "Feigeh Riveh, do you think I am talking nonsense?" And if she made no answer, he would go on, timidly. But if she said: "You know what I think," he would collapse into silence, without ending the story.

Feigeh Riveh was in some sort an assistant to my mother, who played the role of the local wisewoman, for in addition to her pious observance of the laws of visiting the sick, she was also something of a healer. She had not a little knowledge of the names of sicknesses, and where she got them I cannot tell, for she read nothing but Yiddish. She was a great believer in the ancient, traditional folk remedies, with their admixture of superstition and occasional obscure good sense. However, she did not administer them herself; she was only the diagnostician. She would identify the disease and leave it to her "assistants" to apply the remedy. Naturally everyone in Svislovitz believed in the exorcising of demons and diseases; but every case, whether of toothache or the evil eye, had its specialist. Feigeh Riveh was reputed to be able to remove the evil eye as if she literally laid hands on it; but she was useless for toothaches; the specialist in that field was Sossye the bun-baker. My mother, as the diagnostician, was considered a superior person, and with her diagnoses there was no arguing. In fact, the regular doctor —who was no doctor at all—was only sent for after my mother had delivered her decision; and if Elke, the daughter of Mendel, said it was typhoid, typhoid it had to be, and if she said it was a cold, it had to be a cold.

As soon as morning prayers were over, my mother used to start out on the round of her patients like a qualified practitioner. We children had learned early not to wait for her with breakfast. Only father waited, and when he became impatient he used to ask, ironically: "I wonder what can be keeping the doctor this morning."

Among the strange figures in my childhood were the Dvaretzers, who did not live in Svislovitz but in a nearby village. The way to the city of Bobruisk lay over a long bridge across the Svislo. In normal times the river was narrow enough, but the bridge took a very large span because of the floods. There was no bridge across the Beresina; we went to the villages beyond it by a ferry which had been leased by the landowner to Akiba David Dvaretzer, so surnamed after the village. Dvaretz was nothing more than a hamlet on the further bank. It consisted of two houses, the inn where David lived with his large family, and the cottage of the peasant who pulled the rope of the ferry. Akiba David was a gigantic Jew, and of his two sons one was renowned for his stature, the other for his incredible strength. In our town the Dvaretzers were despised as earthy peasants; what business had Jews to be so gigantic of stature or so unbelievably strong? They must have got these physical attributes from Esau, the *goy;* not thus were the sons of Jacob. But if they were looked down on by the Jews, Akiba David and his sons were thoroughly respected by the gentiles of the neighborhood, none of whom dared to make themselves obstreperous round the ferry. They knew that on the place where Akiba or one of his sons once placed a hand, the grass never grew again.

The Dvaretzers became half-legendary figures to me, and I associated them with my first *cheder* lessons. When I learned that there had once been a place called *Aram Naharayim*, the Land of the Two Rivers (Mesopotamia), and that beyond one of the rivers had dwelt Terah, the father of Abraham, and therefore the grandfather of our people, the picture was clear to me. Terah, an ignorant man who had worshipped idols, was Akiba David Dvaretzer; Mesopotamia was our little Svislovitz, lying between two rivers; and there, sure enough, on the other side of one of the rivers, was the land of Terah.

A certain Dave the ascetic, and a young brother of his known as "the Orphan," remain imbedded in my mind associated with the winter. The first winter in my memory became legendary for its cold and for its great snowfalls. The rivers were frozen over and became invisible under the uniform sheet which turned the whole world into one blinding white plain. On our broad street the snow lay "just as when it was born," that is, in a vast drift along the center. Along the sides of the street and from door to door of facing houses paths were cut through the snow. The hand of winter lay dead and even on town and river and field and forest. Only the summits of the evergreens, the firs and the yews peeped through unconquered, like stubborn fingers thrust upward by the gnarled old forest to show the world that the winter had not bludgeoned it out of existence.

During that winter a singular incident occurred which shook the whole community.

Dave the ascetic, blessed with a large family of his own, also looked after his younger brother. Why the latter was known as "the Orphan," as though there were not other orphans in town, I cannot tell; but his given name was seldom used and if I ever knew it I have forgotten it. This one had somehow become *the* orphan, and everyone was interested in his welfare, particularly on the spiritual side. Everyone was anxious that, lacking as he did the guidance of father or mother, he should grow up into a fine God-fearing Jew. And everyone took it upon himself to correct the boy, this one with a harsh word and that one with a slap. The latter he would get in synagogue, during services, for omitting an "Amen" or failing to bow at the right moment. The slap was given out of collective affection for the poor little fellow. The pity of it! He hadn't even a father to slap him when he needed it.

One stormy morning Dave the ascetic insisted on sending the little fellow to morning services in the synagogue—and to first services at that. Dave and his own sons did not turn up until the second service. The roads were only half-cleared, and the frost was unusually severe, even for Svislovitz. When David arrived at the synagogue, the Orphan was not there, nor had anyone seen him during the first services. At once a hue and cry was raised, and angry fingers were pointed at Dave for having sent out the Orphan alone. The old people organized a search. They looked for the child on every street in Svislovitz; they beat the snow on the side of the roads, but not a sign of the Orphan was found. There was not even the trace of his footsteps. Before long a rumor spread through the town that evil spirits had carried off the Orphan. Characteristically, no one thought of looking for him among the peasants.

It is hard to say how this tragedy would have ended for Dave the ascetic if the next morning the Orphan had not returned, all alone and unharmed, to the house of his brother. It transpired that he had actually lost his way and had fallen exhausted in the snow. A peasant saw the little body and carried it off to the district commissioner's headquarters. There they rubbed it with snow and towels until the boy came to. He could not speak a word of Russian, and was therefore unable to give an account of himself. The peasants, for their part, were not unduly exercised by the fact that somewhere a family might be worrying itself to death over the missing child, so they kept him for twenty-four hours; then, the storm having abated, they let him out. Their intentions were not unfriendly; they were only playing what they thought was something of a joke on their Jewish neighbors.

And here begins the second act of the tragedy.

On the third morning the Orphan came as usual to services in the synagogue. As soon as these were over, the congregation surrounded him and began to ask him for the details of his adventure. The child naïvely told everything. He said that the gentiles had treated him ever so nicely, much better, in fact, than he was treated at home. He was kept comfortably warm and they fed him bread and "white herring."

"White herring!" There is no such thing! Like a lightning flash the truth broke on the listeners. The child had been fed bacon! A universal horror came into the faces of the crowd—horror and indescribable pain. At once the tragedy was shifted to the "white herring," and the rage of the older people against Dave the ascetic rose now not from his cruelty in exposing a child to death in the snowstorm, not from the near-murder he had committed, but from the abomination which was now recorded for ever against the Jewish community of Svislovitz. A Jew had partaken of swine-meat! In the person of the helpless Orphan the entire community was touched with uncleanness. On the Orphan himself they looked with genuine commiseration. They questioned him more closely; they tried to make him admit that he had eaten the flesh of the swine. But he looked back out of innocent eyes and repeated that he had only eaten "white herring."

When the big ones were done with the child, the youngsters got their turn. We surrounded him and submitted him to a minute and merciless cross-examination. He had to tell us ten times over what the "white herring" tasted like. And at last he found a description for it: "It tasted like fat stewed meat dipped in salt." In our subconscious we envied the Orphan. The horrible sin would not be laid to his account, but to that of Dave the ascetic. He had had this extraordinary adventure, and yet was as untainted as if it had never taken place.

The Jewish community of Svislovitz was not destined to have much joy of its Orphan—nor he of the community. Soon after the Passover of that year he disappeared a second time, and now, it seemed, for good. It was taken for granted that gypsies had spirited him away. Years later it transpired that a group of Jewish tumblers had tempted him to join them and had taught him their trade. In time, feeling certain that the child had been forgotten, they even came to Svislovitz to offer a performance. The Orphan happened by then to be their star actor, their best drawing card. Right in the middle of the performance Moses the shoemaker rose up and cried: "It's the Orphan!" The band of tumblers denied everything, and when the young acrobat was questioned he remained stubbornly silent. When he could not avoid saying something he played the idiot, making himself unintelligible. Finally Moses the shoemaker mentioned the story of the "white herring," and in spite of himself the boy burst into laughter.

A great battle ensued between the community and the actors, and the community won. Svislovitz had its Orphan again.

An old figure that still haunts me is that of Joseph Bear Schatz the cantor, but not for his services in the synagogue. I have mentioned that the Jews of Svislovitz were passionately fond of river bathing. Young and old waited for the approach of Pentecost, hoping always for an early summer, so that the bathing might begin. The gentiles were not given to the pastime, and it was the rarest thing to see one of them bathing or swimming in the river. I wonder whether this weakness on the part of the Jews had anything to do with the passage in the Talmud which bids every Jewish father train his son to a trade—or at least teach him to swim! In any case the fact remains that the

Jews of Svislovitz were excellent swimmers, and among them Joseph Bear Schatz the cantor bore away the palm.

There were two favorite local tricks in swimming. The first was to lift one arm after the other out of the water and use it like an oar; this made for speed. The second was for show; the swimmer had to keep himself afloat perpendicularly while holding both hands clear of the water. Old Joseph Bear Schatz practiced this second trick with extraordinary refinement. He kept not only both hands clear of the water, but a knee as well. While floating thus he would pare the nails of his hands and let the parings fall on a sheet of paper which he balanced on his knee. This was all the more marvelous because he did the paring according to the somewhat complicated instructions prescribed in the Talmud for the superpious.

An incident rises in my mind concerning a Svislovitzer I have already mentioned, and he not a Jew, but a pious Christian, Stepan Harnai, the God-seeker, who loved so much to discuss religious questions with my mother.

I was six or seven years old when I fell sick with typhoid, and when I recovered my mother was brought down with the same disease. My father was away, either in Minsk or Bobruisk, on business, and on his return after a week's absence he found my mother in a dangerous condition. I cannot forget what happened when my father received the sudden tidings. He wept like a child. He threw off his travelling clothes and went at once to my mother. She barely recognized him, and only with an effort could she pronounce his name. My father, unable to restrain himself, burst into a loud sobbing. There was standing on the table, I remember, a glass of tea to refresh him after his journey. He did not drink it; instead he put on phylacteries and prayer shawl and began to pray with a passion which I had never seen in him before. When he had ended his prayers he approached my mother's bed and said: "Lord of the universe!

Perhaps I have sinned and this is the punishment You have prepared for me. But I pray to You: punish me as You will, but leave my wife Elke untouched; do not punish the innocent for the sins of the guilty . . . ."

During one of those days—it was the middle of the week—the bells of both Orthodox churches began to toll over the town. It was not a festival, and a fire had not broken out. We were living at that time in our new house opposite the church of Yuremitch, and looking out of the window we saw the gentiles streaming toward the church. One of us went out and asked a passerby what had happened. The answer was: "We are going to pray to God for Elke." They did not say it boastfully, for they found it natural. Later we discovered that the man who had initiated these prayers for my mother was Stepan Harnai, the God-seeker.

My mother did not forget. Years later, when my older brother Meyer was married—the wedding took place in our home—my mother suddenly disappeared before the wedding supper and was absent for above an hour. We became worried and sent out to look for her, without success. It was not until her return that we discovered where she had been. The wife of one of the gentile water-carriers (Asher Pakess' opposite), had been brought to bed of a child. My mother, hearing of it, had taken a hen and prepared a pot of soup for the woman. She fed the woman, attended to the newborn child's needs, gave instructions to the mother, returned to the festivities, and sat down at the wedding table as if nothing had happened.

CHAPTER THIRTEEN

The Writer

I BEGAN to learn writing when I was six years old, at first half an hour and then a whole hour a day. In this branch of his duties, too, my *rebbi*, Judah, was thorough and systematic. He wanted his pupils to develop a clear and beautiful script, and he surrounded the shape of every letter, the spaces between letters and words, and the proportions of the letters, with a complete philosophy. The script, he said, was the vessel, the thoughts were the contents; it was necessary to develop, from early childhood, a beautiful script, for beautiful vessels attract beautiful contents, and by learning to write finely we would also be led to think finely. However, my *rebbi* was dead set against the practice which still survived among certain schools —a memorial of the old Oriental days—of adding flourishes and arabesques and curlicues to the letters. He thought it harmful: "You learn to twist and embellish the letters; afterward you will also twist the thought."

We used to do our writing with goose quills. Judah whittled them, and from him I learned the medieval art of transforming a feather into a pen. When we had been writing for a couple of years we graduated to steel pens. The change was uncomfortable. A goose quill pen is softer, travels more lightly over the paper, and follows more readily the commands of the fingers. Steel is hard, sharp and obstinate. The writer can fashion the goose quill to his taste and character, but the steel pen comes to him ready-made, with a will and character of its own. Thus with the appearance of the steel pen have vanished those marvelous old scripts which sometimes made letters so beautiful that they begged to be framed and exhibited.

The *cheder* assignments were not enough for me; I did a lot of writing at home, where I did not have to follow a prescribed text. I often wrote biblical verses from memory, and when the verse coincided with my own thought I set it down whole, but where it diverged I labored to find fragments of different verses with which to express myself. But even what I wrote at home I carried to *cheder* the next day for correction. My liking for writing became a passion, and on winter nights, when I returned from *cheder* after ten or twelve hours of study I would eat quickly and sit down again with my pen.

Of one thing I am certain; the first language I used in writing was Hebrew. The fact is, it never occurred to me to write Yiddish. Everybody knew Yiddish; what marvel was it, then, to write in that language? Besides I knew no ready-made verses in Yiddish; and as for Yiddish books, apart from my mother's devotionals, they were unknown in our house. Without biblical verses, too, the things you wrote would sound just like the ordinary things people say. Everybody would understand them and nobody would carry the letters around and ask their meaning and shake his head over the wonder of it. In a word, all my ambitions lay in the Hebrew language, and that alone could give me the opportunity to satisfy my pride.

But I believe there was a deeper force at work. Although everybody around me spoke Yiddish, it was Hebrew, *as a language*, that I knew better in my childhood. For a language does not consist merely of words; it is built up by pictures, by ideas which the words awaken in us. A language must possess, besides its ordinary everyday self, a holiday self, a spiritual aspect. A language is firmly rooted in the mind of a child only by the book; there is no other way of giving literary force to a language, and no other way of making it writable. The language that is not reflected in classic books is doomed to remain a language of the street. It was inevitable that Hebrew should become for me the medium of the written word. For I learned it from books, from sacred books, the contents of which had become flesh of my flesh, bone of my bone.

I remember very clearly my first essay in Hebrew, that is, the first one which my *rebbi* carried round the town to glorify his pupil.

Among the Jews of Svislovitz there were no thieves. Among the gentiles there were a few professionals—chiefly horse-thieves. All of them were known and feared, for between thefts of horses they would not turn down minor jobs. The big robberies, however, were executed not by our local craftsmen but by the masters of Bobruisk, who would pay us a visit now and then and leave ruin behind. A merchant of Svislovitz would wake one morning, go down into his store, and discover that every scrap of merchandise had been removed: nothing left but the bare shelves. More than one merchant of Svislovitz was ruined in this way. As it happened, there were Jews among the thieves of Bobruisk, and they concentrated on Jews: they were probably actuated by some obscure family feeling. (The subject would, by the way, make an interesting study. Statistics would show, I believe, that Jews prefer to rob Jews; they feel safer.)

Among the Jewish thieves of Bobruisk there was a famous ring-leader by the name of Chaim Gimelleh. More than once he would descend with his band on some drayman travelling toward Bobruisk and remove the entire contents of the cart. It never got so far as the shedding of blood, but "dry" blows were exchanged more than once. Benjamin the storekeeper, a son of my second *rebbi*, Abraham Kazar, returned one day from the Bobruisk road beaten up and with an empty cart. He had been waylaid by Chaim Gimelleh and his gang, who had taken both the merchandise which he was going to sell in Bobruisk and the cash which he and his passengers carried with them. Benjamin got badly beaten up because he had protested, had appealed to the sense of justice in the robbers, and this was Chaim Gimelleh's salutation to the other shopkeepers of Svislovitz. The extraordinary thing was that everyone knew who the chief robber was and nobody ever thought of prosecuting him. Had it been possible to get him to a *din Torah*, a rabbinical court, it would have been done. But not the gentile courts; after all, the merchant would not have got his goods back. The Jews of Svislovitz put robberies, thefts and fires in the same class of disasters.

This was the incident which was the theme of my first Hebrew essay. It ran somewhat as follows: "And Benjamin the son of Abraham rode forth in his chariot on the road which goeth by the way of Bobruisk. And he came to Brishanke and he rested there. And it came to pass that when the sun went down robbers fell upon him, and the chiefest among them was that great robber Chaim Gimelleh. And they said unto Benjamin: 'Give us all thou hast, but thy soul thou mayest keep.' And Benjamin said: 'This would be a great sin,' but they would not hearken to his voice. And they took from him all that he had, leaving not a thread nor the latchet of a shoe. And they smote him grievously. And Benjamin returned home weeping, and the city of Svislovitz was in great confusion."

The beauty of my language created an enormous impression. In particular, the scholars of Svislovitz were delighted with the inverted phrase: "Give us all thou hast, but thy soul thou mayest keep"—the very opposite of what the King of Sodom said to Abraham. It showed that I was not only capable of weaving in a biblical verse; I could also turn it upside down if need dictated.

I ought to say that the only newspaper received in our town was the Hebrew weekly *Ha-Zephirah*, edited by Chaim Slonimsky, and the majority of its correspondence stood on about the same level as my essay. It was therefore proposed to send my essay to *Ha-Zephirah*, and thereby bring honor upon the city of Svislovitz. The idea took my breath away. The possibility of being printed had not occurred to me, and when it was mooted I was thrown into such confusions of joy that I hardly knew what world I was living in. Like everybody else I pitied poor Benjamin the shopkeeper, but in my subconscious I was thoroughly happy that the incident had occurred and that I had been able to describe it so well.

By the time I was nine years old the foundations of my Hebrew education had been laid. I knew the Bible by heart, and stood up under all the weird tests that were devised for us. Here is one of them: in *cheder* we used the Letteris edition of the Hebrew Bible, issued by the London Bible Society. The book would be opened at a given page, a word would be chosen, and then a pin would be driven through the pages as far as it would go. I would then be asked what words the pin had passed through on the various pages; and with the rarest exceptions I would be able to name every one of them. I also understood well all the commentaries on the Bible, through Rashi and Mendelssohn to the later ones. As grammarian I was accounted the best in Svislovitz, and my *rebbi* treated me now not as a pupil but as a comrade. In Talmud I knew thoroughly the three tractates *Benedictions*, *The Upper Gate* and *The Middle Gate*, and could quote long passages from them. From the translations of Kalman Shulman I had already formed some idea of history and geography; but my best gift, which was for mathematics, remained dormant, for there was no one to awaken it. The foundations of my education were still one-sided and purely literary. It may be objected that I ought to say "theological-literary," but the emphasis of my education was on the literary, not the theological. This was due to the character of my teacher, which was completely worldly. The theological element was introduced only to the extent that the Bible dealt with a theocratic order of society.

It was at the age of nine that I began to learn Russian, and again it was my uncle Meyer Vendrov who intruded as a benefactor into my education. He lived in the big world, and his position brought him into close contact with leading military figures, which would have been impossible without a knowledge of Russian. It was his plan that his two sons, my *cheder*-mates, should in time continue their studies in a technical school and become agricultural engineers. Before they could take up such studies they would have to pass through a secondary school, but he wanted them to begin with a thorough Jewish education. In those days every *Maskil*, or modernist, had the same ambition for his children, a combination of Jewish and general education. Thoughts like these were far from my father; he had no plans to send any of his sons into the liberal professions. He wanted them to be able merchants, timber dealers. It was my mother's dream that I should become a rabbi, a *gaon*, a great scholar and light in Israel, in which my teacher seconded her. But my father agreed that I should learn Russian. "It's a good thing," he said, "to be able to talk to a landowner in his own language, to be able to draw up a contract or address a petition to the government." The *Rav* of Svislovitz, who was a great influence in my father's life, gave his approval.

We imported a teacher from Mohilev on the Dnieper. Some two years earlier my second sister, Frieda, had married one Asher Shafrai, of Mohilev, and it was he who recommended an acquaintance of his by the name of Krugliansky. My brother-in-law was a great Jewish scholar, but knew not a word of Russian. He assured us that Krugliansky was a first-rate teacher, spoke Russian like a Moscow aristocrat, and in addition was an observant Jew: he would not set a bad example to the young folk. This last point was the most important. It was the teacher himself who was feared as a disruptive influence rather than the Russian language; and a Jewish teacher was more feared than a gentile teacher, for the Jewish teacher could become intimate with his pupils and more easily lead them astray.

Krugliansky remained in Svislovitz two years. During the first few months he went to synagogue daily and put on phylacteries, just like everyone else. But at the end of the first year it became known that in his own lodgings he was given to all sorts of un-Jewish practices. The place finally got too hot for him and he had to leave. The fears of the parents for their young children had not been unfounded. On some of his friends and older pupils he had a decidedly negative influence as far as Jewish ways were concerned, but this could not be said of his youngest pupils. We looked upon him as a visitor from an alien world. Our contact with him was limited to one hour a day, five days in the week. His pedagogic method was in the old style: that is, he used to teach the language by translating passages from Russian into Yiddish, putting the main emphasis on grammar, making it all hopelessly dry and unattractive. I regarded my Russian studies as a duty to be discharged as rapidly as possible, with the result that my progress was retarded. But I cannot put the entire blame on the teacher; at least half of it belonged to me. Hebrew had already driven deep roots into me, and I had not the strength to tear my mind loose and absorb a strange language easily.

It was not my first Russian teacher, but the Russo-Turkish War of 1877-78, which drew me closer to the Russian world and to the living interests of the Russian state, making me conscious of the fact that the Hebrew world which I carried within me was an old, old world lying far behind me. Immediately surrounding me was a great world of reality, Russia, and it was in this world that I really breathed and had my being. Some two years before the war broke out, the Russian government, or rather the Czar, Alexander II, had decreed universal military service. The Jews naturally regarded the decree as a heavy blow. Until that time, only the children of the poor, whom there was no one to defend, had been pressed into service; and now the children of the middle classes, of the finer homes, would also have to serve in the army, and the thought was horrible. I remember that a relative of ours, Leivik, the son of Pessye the candlemaker, hid himself in our house from the military "catchers." It did not help him much. One winter night the catchers broke into our house, dragged Leivik out of bed, bound him with ropes, and led him out to the sled which was waiting to carry him off to Bobruisk. It was a ghastly scene. The catchers had the look of wild animals, and Leivik himself struggled like an ox being led to the slaughter.

There were numbers of Jews, part of them the more enlightened, part belonging to the poorer classes, who looked on the reforms of Alexander II as acts of justice. If there had to be military service, let it be borne by all, let there be no privileged classes. Poor optimists! They did not understand that though formally there might be no "privileged classes," the power of money had not been legislated away, the rich would still be able to buy their sons out of the service. For that is what happened. When war broke out there were Jews of Svislovitz, too, who went forth; but they were all poor Jews. One of them was, in fact, Leivik's brother, Pessye's second son, the breadwinner of the family.

The Jews regarded the Emperor Alexander II as a king who reigned in justice. Nicholas I, who preceded him, was a king whose name made men tremble and concerning whose cruelties there were living legends in every part of the country. But Alexander II was the czar who had freed millions from slavery, who had reformed the government and the courts. In his reign even the persecuted and oppressed Jews could breathe more easily. It was he who had decreed that the schools and universities should be opened wide to the Jews, and he had even made it possible for Jews to become officers in the Russian army. It is not to the point to remark here that with the exception of a few modern Jews the masses of our people were afraid of the Jewish benefactions of Alexander. They were afraid, instinctively, that a break would come in their lives, that the freedom they were winning would be more apt to destroy their world than had been the oppressive decrees of his father. But their attitude toward Alexander, their czar, was a positive one. His picture could be found hanging on the wall in almost every Jewish home; and when the customary prayer was said for the royal family and the name of Alexander was mentioned, the words did not convey a bitter irony, as they did in the case of his son, Alexander III and of his grandson, Nicholas II.

As far as I can remember, the Jews of Svislovitz were submerged by a wave of patriotism when the war with Turkey broke out. There were great scenes in the synagogue between afternoon and evening prayers, when *Ha-Zephirah* had arrived and was read out, or when Krugliansky read out a Russian newspaper. The majority were on the Russian side, but there were also a number of "Turks" who, feeling secure in this place, openly expressed their sympathies. One of the main factors in their reasoning was that the Turks were regarded as Arabs, for they were Mohammedans: they were therefore, by this logic, Semites, descendants of Ishmael, the son of Abraham and Hagar, which is to say that they were actually cousins of ours. It was true that it would be better for us if Russia emerged victorious from the war, but how was it possible to pray actively for the murderous defeat of so close a relative? The call of the blood rang louder than the call of self-interest.

For quite a time the national hero of Russia was the young general Skobeliov, conqueror of Plevna, the most important Turkish fortress, which had been defended by the ablest Turkish soldier, Osman Pasha. The papers were full of

Skobeliov and his heroism. They told how, on horseback, he led the army to the attack in person. The enemy marksmen singled him out and shot at him from every side; a bullet went through his hat, another killed the horse under him. He leaped onto a second horse and led the army with uncovered head. The bullets sang round him like rain, but not one of them could touch him. The Russian masses saw in him the hero of their folk legends and bowed the knee before him in religious ecstasy.

Morning and evening crowds gathered round the district commissioner's building and in the open marketplace. Jews and gentiles hotly debated the news from the front. On several occasions the priests held special services and a *Te Deum* was sung for Russian victories. At such times the Jews would gather in the synagogue and utter prayers of thanks. The *Rav* of Svislovitz stayed aloof from such matters, but the Jews did it of their own accord. It was accepted as natural that if the gentiles went to church to pray for their Emperor, the Jews should resort to the synagogue for the same purpose. Was he not the common Emperor of Jews and gentiles? And such an Emperor! One who did not shrink from the perils of war, but went to the front and exposed himself to death like any soldier. . . .

In the synagogue the "Turks" gradually lost ground and became less vocal. The series of Russian victories had raised the general enthusiasm, and in the face of a rising fervor they found their position hard to defend. A few, however, were hard-bitten and obstinate. They admitted that according to Jewish law they were compelled to pray for a Russian victory, but they could not bring themselves to pray for the defeat of the Turks. There was a conflict in their hearts, and they would have been happy for the war to end in a stalemate. And God heard their prayers; the Treaty of Berlin did reduce the Russian victory to a stalemate.

I was swept along with the tide of emotion, and my Russian

teacher did all he could to push me along. I expressed my longings for the triumph of Russian arms not in prayer, but in song, for by that time I was already writing Hebrew poetry. I suddenly became a fierce Russian patriot, and even began to take a new interest in my Russian studies. I must have written at least ten poems on Skobeliov, and one of the verses I remember to this day: "Arise, Skobeliov, and lead thy captivity captive, thou son of Dmitri." I had lifted it bodily from the song of Deborah: "Arise, Barak, and lead thy captivity captive, thou son of Abinoam. . . ."

Thus, with a verse from the oldest, finest and most powerful song of the Hebrews, a *cheder* boy of Svislovitz made a payment on his debt to the great Slav nation.

The fortress of Bobruisk was at one time ranked in the first class of those that blocked the road to Moscow from the West. With the building of the Warsaw-Moscow railroad Bobruisk lost its strategic value and Brest-Litovsk took its place. Bobruisk was thenceforth used only as an ordnance center and a base for maneuvers. For this reason it was chosen as a concentration camp for prisoners of war. But as the numbers of these kept rising almost daily, the fortress itself became too small and the military authorities began to quarter numbers of them among the civilian population; later, when Bobruisk was saturated, the surrounding towns and villages were pressed into service. In this way Svislovitz was privileged to quarter some two hundred real Turks, distributed equally among the Jews and gentiles. The Turks themselves asked to be quartered with Jews; they felt more at home there. It would be quite unjust to say that the gentiles treated them harshly, as enemies, but the attitude of the Jews was one of pity, almost of affection.

Added to the blood relationship which we imagined to exist between us, there were three elements which increased the feeling of intimacy. The Turks, as Mohammedans, were all circumcised; as Mohammedans they also refrained from swine-meat; and, again like Jews, they never took their hats off, not even in the house. The attitude of the older folk toward the Turks quickly communicated itself to the children, and we felt even more tenderly for these unhappy men whom the destiny of war had cast among strangers in a strange land. Old pictures rose in my memory. It seemed to me that our great-great-great-grandfathers must have looked thus when they were driven forth into Assyria, into Babylon, and among the Medes and Persians. But our great-great-great-grandfathers had it worse, for where they went there were no Jews to take pity on them. . . .

On summer days the Turks would go down to the Svislo to bathe, and would sit hour after hour Turkish fashion, with their feet folded under them. Then I would think of the psalm "By the waters of Babylon," and of how *we* had sat by alien waters, longing for Jerusalem. Nothing was missing but the harps and the willows to hang them on. But the waters were there and the prisoners, too, and the rest my fantasy supplied.

I remember we were told that the Turks were delicate people and were not accustomed to black bread; they ate only white bread and rice. Some of the children would often stuff their pockets with white bread and with handfuls of rice and bring them to the Turks. Conversation was of course impossible; all we could do was fill their mouths with bread and rice. And it seems they were delicate indeed: not one of them ever refused our little gifts.

The war went on, and victory was added to victory on the Russian side. It began to look as though the Slav-Byzantine dream of Constantinople was drawing nearer and nearer to realization. And who knows what turn might have been given to world history if Russia had not been thwarted in her ambitions by the European powers. The chief anti-Russian role was played by England. She it was who guarded the gates of the Mediterranean and put a curb on Russia's appetite. The British lion shouldered the Russian bear away from its prey. There came the peace of Berlin, at which the Jew Disraeli-Beaconsfield was the leading spirit; under his skillful hands the Russian victory was almost completely spirited away. Not for nothing did the entire Russian press rage more against England than against Turkey, and most of all against the insolent queen and her Jewish envoy. Not for nothing did certain of the Russian journals say that the legend of the ten tribes was no legend at all, that the English were the lost ten tribes, and that Disraeli was descended from King David. . . .

Who can fathom the ways of history? There are events that break suddenly upon us, like a bolt from the blue, unheralded, unexpected—but only because we are absorbed in our immediate affairs and cannot sense the vast preparations which usher them in. After all her victories Russia came out of the war almost empty-handed, and the chief responsibility for this rested with one man: the Jew Disraeli. Within three or four years the wave of pogroms passed over Russia.

As a Jew his name was Disraeli; as a peer he took the name of Beaconsfield. It was as Beaconsfield that he acted in Berlin, but the Jews of Russia paid for Disraeli. And in more recent history, too, the picture was repeated. As a Jew his name was Bronstein; as lord of the Russian revolution he was known as Trotsky. In the days when Trotsky was taking Russia by storm one of the leading Jews of Russia, Rabbi Jacob Mazeh of Moscow, said: "It is Trotsky who storms through the country, but we will pay the reckoning for Bronstein." When the organizer of the mighty Russian army was left with only two soldiers, who guarded him on his way into exile, he was engaged—so all the newspapers reported—on a close study of the biography of Beaconsfield. Was it Trotsky who was interested in Beaconsfield, or was it Bronstein who was interested in Disraeli?

CHAPTER FOURTEEN

Childhood Closes

THE WAR was a great influence in my life. After it I could no longer live exclusively in that ancient world which I carried about within me; I began to look for ways of entering into the vast life, with its stream of living events, which filled the newspapers. I was chagrined that I was still unable to read Russian and I returned with new vigor to the study of the language. I asked for and got two hours of tuition a day; but with all my eagerness I still found the road extraordinarily difficult. Sometimes I had the feeling that the language spoke to me: "Not so fast, stranger; I was not created for you. My doors are closed to you." But the more difficult I found it, the more obstinate I became. I wanted to take the language by storm, and a real war ensued between Russian and me, a war which lasted longer than the Russo-Turkish War. It was only years later, when I completed my studies in the *Realschule* of Minsk, that I was able to enter into the life of the language and to taste in direct contact her classic writers.

The center of gravity of my education still remained in my Jewish studies. From my tenth to my fourteenth year I gave five hours a day to the Talmud. But my *rebbi* introduced another important innovation into the curriculum. Through him my fellow students and I became acquainted with modern Hebrew prose and poetry, with Naphthali Herzl Weisl, the Luzzatis, Adam Ha-Cohen, Shulman and their like. On me, as on thousands of others, the *Ahavath Zion* (Zion's Love) of Abraham Mapu made a profound impression. It was the first novel I ever read, and this was at a time when I was ripening toward the point at which love becomes a living theme. I do not remember exactly how old I was at the time, but I do remember the impatience with which I waited every day for the hour devoted to this book. True, I was enraptured by the language and by the verbal pictures, drawn as they were from the world which was so peculiarly my own. But more than by these I was taken captive by the heroine of the romance, Tamar, and I envied her lover Amnon, for whom God had created her in her loveliness. That book was the symbol of the springtime in me; I felt on my forehead the dew of Hermon and the wind that blew over the snows of Lebanon. My delight was in the roses of Sharon and the lilies of the valley. *Ahavath Zion* was my morning star, and the Song of Songs was in my heart.

During my last *cheder* years I still loved and respected Judah Artzer, my *rebbi*, but I no longer regarded him as a universal authority. He himself boasted that I wrote the better Hebrew and that in grammar I could even be his teacher, while in the Talmud the gulf between teacher and pupil was becoming narrower every month. My bar mitzvah drew closer and with it the time for our separation, when I would pass on to other teachers. In preparation for that change Judah began to discuss earnestly with me the course of studies I would follow after leaving him. By now he believed that I ought to become a man of letters, and he advised me strongly to write not only in Hebrew, but also in Yiddish, and to this end he read with me the novel *Der Yiddel,* by Mendelle Mocher S'forim, and, if I remember aright, *Der Shvartzer Yungermantchik,* by Dinenson. Both books made a deep impression on me, and I even translated part of them into Hebrew. But the Yiddish language failed to attract me strongly enough. I began to write Yiddish only many years later; the simple fact is that Yiddish, like Russian, was never as intimate a part of me as Hebrew. Further, in my early years modern Yiddish literature was still in its swaddling clothes; its sudden and powerful development still lay in the future.

For my bar mitzvah my parents prepared a banquet fit for a wedding. I think there was hardly a householder in Svislovitz who was not invited; and all of them came, for my father's sake, and I must add, for mine. At the age of thirteen I was the favorite of the town, and more than once, both in the street and in the synagogue, I would be asked by grown-up Jews to settle a dispute.

Four rabbis came to my bar mitzvah ceremonies: our own, and three from neighboring townlets. I was seated at the head of the table, exactly where I had sat nine years earlier when they had smeared the pages of the prayerbook with honey for me before my father carried me to my first *rebbi,* Mottye the bean. My father sat at my side while my mother helped to serve the guests. When the moment came for me to deliver my address my mother took a seat at the side. My bar mitzvah discourse was a complicated treatment of a talmudic point of law, and I went through it without an error. At the close the four rabbis cross-examined me on the subject matter, and I answered on that day with unusual ease and skill. When the examination was over, they congratulated my father and expressed the pious hope that I would grow up to be a great man in Israel.

The banquet lasted until late in the afternoon. The importance of the occasion and the success of the ceremonies created a universal mood of happiness. Only one man sat quiet and thoughtful—my *rebbi*, Judah. When the guests had withdrawn, and only he and the family remained, he asked me to go for a walk with him. We went downhill out of the town to the colonnade of the state road. I felt that something was weighing heavily on my *rebbi*'s mind, but I dared not ask why he had called me out to walk with him. We walked under the shadows of the trees, each of us sunk in our own thoughts. When an hour had passed, we turned back, still wordless, and then my *rebbi*, like one who had intended to say something but had given it up, suddenly turned to me: "Come, my ex-pupil; we will go to the synagogue for afternoon prayers."

The public acknowledgment of my *rebbi* that he himself had nothing more to teach me created a problem for my parents. Among decent middle-class folk it was the custom to keep a boy in *cheder* at least until his fifteenth year. This was done with my older brother, Meyer. But Svislovitz had become too small for me. My father, strong in the idea that I should ultimately become a merchant, did not care to send me to a yeshivah. He feared that the atmosphere of unworldliness, of pure study, would turn me into a *batlan*, a learned and helpless drifter, like my brother-in-law, Asher Shafrai. Finally it was decided that for the time being I should receive private lessons from the *Rav* of the town.

As far as I can remember no one had ever been the *Rav*'s own pupil, and this new situation was a heavy yoke to me. I had dreamed that with the ending of my *cheder* years I would have a little more time to myself; I would be able to divide up the day according to my own wishes. The old passion for the rivers, the meadows, the fields and the forests of Svislovitz stirred in me; I wanted to go boating and fishing, to wander among the trees, many of which were familiar to me, for I had watched their yearly growth since my earliest days. And with these dreams were mingled others, in which swam up the faces of girl playmates, with one face more frequent and more friendly than the others. The other girls had called me "Shmerel," simply; her name for me was the more affectionate "Shmerelle." When I heard her calling, a softness flowed through my limbs, and verses of the Song of Songs rose to my lips. Now, I thought, I would be able to see her oftener, perhaps in the evenings on Castle Hill, when the sun was setting behind the tangle of the old birch trees. . . .

And suddenly I was singled out to be the only pupil of the *Rav* of Svislovitz. I would have to be more circumspect, more grown-up, than ever: always serious, tied to books the whole day and forbidden to leave the synagogue even between afternoon and evening prayers.

Actually the *Rav* was not a martinet. It was not for his sake that I would have to put on the sober bearing of the adult scholar. It was my mother who, more than anyone else, kept reminding me that I was a man, that I could no longer compare myself to my schoolmates of yesterday. Perhaps she already suspected, in her heart of hearts, that her dream would never be fulfilled, that I would never become a *rav;* and she snatched what joy she could from the passing illusion that her son would be dedicated to the Torah.

The *Rav,* as it happened, was as much given to the study of secular affairs as to purely spiritual matters. Apart from his talmudic training he was a fine Hebraist, and this helped to develop a closer friendship between us. Those who have some inkling of the spirit of those times will realize how far from a fanatic he was when I say that he used to read with me *Ha-Shachar*, the weekly edited by Perez Smolenskin, and that he would speak to me at great length about the struggle then convulsing Jewish life—the struggle between the nationalist and assimilationist forces. Himself a passionate nationalist, he never mentioned the name of Smolenskin save with deepest affection and respect; yet he well knew that in orthodox circles

Smolenskin was regarded as a dangerous freethinker, a revolutionary spirit who was corrupting the Jewish youth. *Ha-Shachar* had been banned from all *yeshivoth*, and woe to the student who was caught with a copy: his dismissal took place on the spot. Nevertheless, the influence of this periodical was perhaps greater among the students of the *yeshivoth* than among any other group. For them Smolenskin was the prophet of those stormy times; they saw in him the pillar of fire going through the wilderness, while the older folk trembled at his name.

Smolenskin fought on two fronts. On the one he stormed against all that was rotten and outlived in Jewish life; on the other he directed his fiery energies against the Mendelssohnian school. He thundered alike against the forces of conservatism, which led to petrifaction of the Jewish people, and against assimilation, which led to its death.

The quintessence of the Mendelssohnian position was expressed in a famous phrase: "Be a Jew in thine own tent and a man when thou goest out." Smolenskin was the first to expose the pitiful implication of this apparently innocent aphorism: the contrast between being a Jew and being a man. There is not a civilized man, to whatever nation he belongs, who would not regard the dichotomy as a studied insult. The phrase has only one meaning, namely, that Jewishness is not a commodity with which you can be seen in public.

To these views the *Rav* gave his passionate consent, but he would speak of them, and of the questions of literature and life at large, only during "off" hours. Within the circle of his official duties he kept close to the program of studies, which consisted mostly of the Talmud and *poskim*, the legalistic and ritualistic codes. It was his belief that I bade fair to become a great scholar, yet, astonishingly enough, he did not once try to persuade me to devote my life only to study. On the contrary, it was clear from his conversation during the free hours that he looked on the role of such a man as Smolenskin as being superior to that of a great scholar.

A picture rises in my mind: the *Rav* is sitting with me at table, directing my studies; the door to the adjoining room opens, and there my mother sits with the *Rav*'s wife. A woman enters, carrying a chicken or a pot; she has come to find out whether something or other has not made the chicken, or the pot, ritually impure. The *Rav* turns to me and gives me the honor of rendering the decision. I become grave and play to perfection the role of the *Rav*'s assistant. My mother cannot take her eyes off me. Why should she think of what may come later? Is she not in Paradise already?

But amidst all this I was not happy. Neither the codes nor the Talmud, nor the prospect of answering ritualistic questions relating to chickens and pots excited me. Instead I saw, as in a vision, the modern prophet, Smolenskin, and I heard his call to battle. I did not know what Smolenskin looked like, but I pictured him in the midst of a gathering army of followers, sending out over the increasing ranks the fiery message of the last war for liberation. The forms which the struggle would take, the nature of the liberty we sought, was veiled from me. I did not know that a great scholar had already written a book called *Shivat Zion* (The Return to Zion), nor had I heard of the thinker, the friend and colleague of Karl Marx, and of his book, *Rome and Jerusalem.* Yet the latter had appeared in 1862, and in Germany of all places, the classic country of Jewish assimilation. I did not know, either, that both the scholar and the thinker had formulated a program for the national liberation of the Jewish people, a new exodus from Egypt. The names of Zvi Hirsch Kalischer and Moses Hess were never mentioned either by the *Rav* or by my *rebbi.* I only had a dim sense of a vast process of preparation around me.

Two incidents mark my emergence from childhood into the early phases of manhood, the first a protracted one, the second brief as a lightning flash; the first a struggle within myself, transient and symptomatic, the second in the nature of a prophecy understood much later.

The first incident was connected with a young man, one of the "ascetics" in our community, who had a high reputation as a scholar and a still higher one for his religious devotion. His place in the synagogue was behind the pulpit, among the poor. He prayed with the fervor of a true saint, and in all matters his bearing was that of one who had renounced the things of this world. He fasted Mondays and Thursdays, and every night he kept vigil until after midnight and lifted up his voice in lamentation for the Destruction, so that the walls of the study house rang again. There were rumors that he had "taken exile upon himself," that he knew the lore of the Cabalah, and that he was perhaps one of the "Thirty-Six" concealed saints.

This young man took a liking to me, and made me an intimate of his. He told me many stories of the Other World, of Paradise and Hell, of the Patriarchs, of Moses, and of Elijah the Prophet; and every story ended with an allusion to the Messiah. "If the Jews only did what is right, the Messiah would have come long ago." His speech was full of vague mystic hints, half-phrases, uncompleted sentences, and I always left him tantalized and tormented, like a thirsty man to whom the beaker of water has been proffered only to be withdrawn.

I was then in my thirteenth year, and the time had come for me to think of my soul which, I perceived, was steeped in evil and honeycombed with wicked thoughts. I knew too many profane Hebrew books belonging to the secular modernistic "enlightenment"; I was altogether too intimate with Smolenskin's *Ha-Shachar*. My ascetic told me unequivocally that all this was sin. He told me further to forget about grammar, for grammar was a plaything of the Devil himself. The Devil, he said, is most effective when he puts on garments of piety and bids you learn grammar as it were for religious ends; thus he introduces the spirit of profanity in sacred things. Grammar itself, he said, was of no value; nothing mattered but the passion and the intent put into words.

I do not know whether the ascetic was moved by true piety or by the Evil One himself; for he sought to destroy the world which was dear to me. He began with grammar, but step by step he moved closer to my beloved Prophets and stretched out his destroying hand toward them. In any case, I fell for a time completely under his influence. Judah Artzer faded into the background and I became a changed person. I began to imitate the ascetic; I became fiercely religious. My morning prayers now lasted more than an hour, and I counted out the words "as one counts out money"—such is the commandment. I gave up writing and I turned away from the books of the Enlightenment. I spent every free moment in the company of the ascetic, who began to teach me the Zohar and other books of the Cabalah. I became a nuisance at home; I demanded more piety in everyone's bearing; grace after meals was to be said slowly, distinctly, loudly; idle chatter was to cease. If there was nothing to be done in the house, there were always psalms to repeat. And so on.

My *rebbi* took this to heart, and did all he could to restore me to common sense. My father, in his practical way, reproached me gently, and in very extraordinary terms: "Time enough to become so pious. You're too young to be a saint. A boy of your age must study first—must keep on studying." And the only one who was made happy by the sudden change in me was my mother. I would catch her looking at me out of eyes filled with admiration. . . . Who knew? Something great might come of this. My mother lived in a world of dreams—literally. Every other day she would ask to have her dreams interpreted. About me she dreamed in her waking hours. The old chassidic spirit blazed up in her, and she began to hope for the miraculous.

This was the most pious period in my life. I cannot remember by what method or along what path I crawled out of the labyrinth of tormenting thoughts and emotions. I only know that the feeling of liberation resembled closely my emergence from a bout of typhoid fever. The ascetic lost his hold on me, and I went back with renewed delight to my studies. I took up my pen again and plunged once more into the neo-Hebraic literature.

The second episode occurred in my fourteenth year, on the eve of Purim, in the year 1881. The Jews of Svislovitz were assembled in the synagogue, prepared for the reading of the Scroll of Esther. Suddenly the doors were flung wide open, and at the entrance stood the district commissioner and the sergeant. A shudder ran through the congregation, the hereditary terror, the memory of evil decrees. Without introduction the district commissioner read out the telegram he held in his hand: "Alexander II has fallen a victim of a revolutionary plot. Alexander III sits on the throne of all the Russias."

I remember well that I could not quite understand the meaning of the words. I looked at the faces of the grown-ups; but they were frozen, expressionless, and I found no answer. I did not dream then that on a far-off day the grandson of the murdered Czar would be compelled to open the first constitutional parliament of Russia and that, standing before me, the *cheder* boy of Svislovitz, deputy from the city of Vilna, he would have to read out the first address from the throne in the history of his country.

BOOK II

YOUTH IN REVOLT

CHAPTER FIFTEEN

Nationalists and Assimilationists

I HAVE already told how the Turkish war was the first battering ram to break through the wall of my mental ghetto. The second battering ram, infinitely more powerful and more effective, was the assassination of Alexander II. I still see before me, with the freshness of an immediate event, the petrified faces of the Jews in the synagogue; wordless, with bowed heads, they filed out and scattered to their homes. The Purim players slunk away, the Purim banquet was abandoned. The mood in Svislovitz was that of the Black Fast, not of Purim. The heart of an entire people was contracted with a nameless terror.

The reader must bear in mind that the days of Nicholas I, the father of Alexander II, were still fresh in the memory of the Jews, the days of the modern Haman, with his implacable hatreds and his inhuman decrees. Preeminent among all others for horror was the memory of *Boholoh*, the Terror, about which I had heard so much in my childhood, and of the

Cantonist schools, as they were called, the most fearful of all inquisitions—more fearful even than the infamous Spanish Inquisition, for the latter was directed against adults, and the former against children. Only Asmodeus, the Spirit of all Evil, could have inspired the invention.

Two "Cantonists," "Lazar the soldier" and "Mottye the soldier," still lived in our town. They had been snatched away at the age of ten, and they had served thirty-five years, so that when they returned they were men of forty-five. Mottye was taciturn, but Lazar loved to talk of what he had endured, and I loved to listen, fascinated and terrified; as I listened I felt the blood standing still in my veins.

No family was secure in those far-off days. Without warning, in the dead of night, the "snatchers" would break into the house and drag the child out of his bed. The father screams in terror and begs for mercy, the mother faints; but there is no help in heaven or on earth. "Farewell, dearest child, farewell for ever! From now on no father's hand will guide you, no mother's lips will kiss you. The place to which they will take you is far, far from us. If your frail body survives the long journey, they will turn you over to the care of a *diadka*—an uncle, a mentor. He will be your guide and lead you in alien and idolatrous ways. And when you have forgotten us, when you have forgotten the prayers we taught you to say in your earliest childhood, the morning prayer with which you opened your eyes, the evening prayer with which you closed them, then your new teacher will bring you a prayer shawl of metal" —in this bitter, oblique fashion did the Jews refer to the cross. "Our child, do not forget! Remember all the days of your life our God who is in heaven, and be constant to our faith."

The majority of the young victims did not survive the journey—their graves were scattered along the remote roads of eastern Russia and even in unknown corners of icy Siberia—and the majority of those who survived did not long resist the inflictions of the Cantonist schools. They soon yielded and bore witness to the everlasting glory of the mighty Orthodox Church. But among those abducted Jewish children there were also heroes in whose veins ran the blood of the martyrs of old. They did not yield. They endured, for twenty-five, or thirty, or thirty-five years, a regimen of ingenious tortures, and their spirit remained unbroken; they returned to their native villages still displaying the four-fringed ritual garment and the prayer book which their mothers had given them as "provision" for the journey. The stories they told concerning their tortures have been confirmed by a thousand recitals and by innumerable documents. It was the custom to separate in a special group the most obstinate of the children. For an entire week they would be fed herring and other salted and spiced foods. They were given just enough water to keep them from collapsing. At the end of the week they were led into the hot chamber of a Turkish bath, and when they thrust out their little tongues, tormented by a frightful thirst, the *diadka*, the uncle, would bring forward in one hand a vessel with cold, refreshing water, and in the other a cross. There was no bargaining. The price was fixed and unchangeable: a Jewish soul for a drink of water.

What wonder that after Nicholas I the Jews looked upon Alexander II as a saviour? Any ruler that followed Nicholas I could only have been an improvement; how much the more, then, Alexander II, who was known even before his accession as a man of gentle soul and good intentions. Nor did he, at least during the first half of his reign, betray the hopes he had awakened. It was not only for the Jews that he was a just and upright king; the first half of his reign was from every point of view a glorious period in Russian history. A series of great reforms began: the liberation of the Russian serf, the introduction of the jury system into the courts, the reorganization of the municipal administrations. Had these reforms been followed through, the half-European, half-Asiatic country that was

Russia would almost certainly have set its feet fifty years ago on the road of enlightenment and progress. But it seems that it was not the destiny of Russia to achieve happiness through normal and natural growth. In the second half of Alexander's reign the nobility of Russia, fearful of losing its ancient privileges, forced the hand of the monarch, and a reaction set in. The evil genius of the Russian people reasserted itself and widened the gulf between the intelligentsia and the government until it became impassable. The first act of the drama ended with the assassination of the "Reformer," Alexander II.

The Jews of Russia saw little to hope for from Alexander III. He was widely known as a bigot who looked at the Jews through the dark glasses of the Orthodox Church. It was no secret that while still crown prince he had, as a sign of special friendship, presented a ring to the notorious Jew-hater Lyutostansky for his book on the Jewish ritual use of Christian blood. The Russian press, which had seldom lost an opportunity to attack the Jews during the second half of the dead monarch's reign, now overflowed with poison. The biggest dailies of St. Petersburg, were, like those of the chief provincial cities, subsidized by the government, and were therefore properly regarded as semi-official organs. It soon became obvious that the Jews had been virtually outlawed and that no one would dare to raise a hand in their defense.

And so the pogroms came. The first broke out in Elizabetgrad on April 16, 1881, exactly six weeks after the assassination of Alexander II. These six weeks must be regarded as the period of incubation between the time when the virus of the press entered the body of the Russian people and the time when it took effect. Elizabetgrad was followed by Kiev, Kiev by Odessa. These were the scenes of the biggest pogroms; in between these major actions scores of smaller centers were sacked.

It is hard, after this interval of years, to describe the effect produced by the news of the pogroms on Jewish settlements lying at a distance from the center of action. No pogrom took place in Svislovitz, but the terror of the pogrom was suspended almost visibly above our heads. There were times when we envied the towns that had already suffered the pogrom. "Better an end with terror than a terror without end." The fear that could not be abjured, the uncertainty that haunted us in the home and in the streets, the momentary expectation of the storm that did not break—this is a species of mental torment that cannot be described. The Jews of Svislovitz went about like shadows of themselves. They could not lie down and die; they had their daily bread to earn for themselves and their families, and pitifully small as their needs were, they could not meet them without maintaining their usual contacts with the gentiles. The contacts were traditional, intimate. True, these were our own village folk—but all that belonged to yesterday. Who could tell what deadly thoughts were theirs today? The volcano, too, is peaceful just one moment before it erupts.

We read the Jewish, that is, the Hebrew papers. And if our peasants could not read, they at least knew what was written in the Russian papers. And how was it possible to foresee what effects the stories of the pogroms, always accompanied by hateful and derisive comment, might have on their minds? The most fearful of the maledictions enumerated on the Mount of Curses was visited upon us: "In the morning thou shalt say, 'Would God it were even,' and at even thou shalt say, 'Would God it were morning!' " It was the unremitting anguish of constant terror. And then, the shame and degradation of it! It is not easy to say which was the greater affliction, the terror or the shame. A Jew was ashamed to look his gentile neighbor in the face; as far as possible, he would avoid meeting his look; he feared to catch in it the first glimpse of the first fires of hatred. And he was afraid to let the gentile catch his own look because of the shame that was in it. He was ashamed of his own shame and humiliated again by his own humiliation.

That time of shame and degradation—the summer of 1881—

coincided for me with the time of my personal crystallization. I felt I was ripening quickly, and the intimate question, "What is my life to be?" was becoming earnest and urgent. To the crystallizing effect of my own growth was added the crystallizing effect of the epoch. The pogroms had opened my eyes; I understood that I was forever bound to my people, my persecuted and tormented people. Two dreams ran side by side, the dream of my own liberation and the dream of the liberation of my people. Their courses at first were parallel; then they drew together and mingled with each other.

Long before the pogroms, and long before the question, "Whither now?" blazed up on the Jewish heavens in letters of fire and blood, long before we suspected that the issues of our larger destiny would be bound up with the need of the hour, the Jewish press—exclusively in Hebrew—had begun to debate the general problem of Jewry.

"The Jewish problem" was tacitly, if not explicitly, understood to be the problem of the Jews of eastern Europe, where the overwhelming majority of our people was to be found. The Jews of western Europe, too, still had a long road before them, for their emancipation was accomplished in stages, and the governments were not in the same hurry as the Jews. The former haggled over every point, and the latter had to struggle bitterly as they advanced from position to position. For all that, the road before the Jews of western Europe was a clear one: it was the road of consistent assimilation. Jewish emancipation in France was the model—a plain, simple renunciation of Jewish folk identity in return for civic rights. This was the bargain reached between the government and the Jews. The French government had declared clearly that it could not and would not liberate its Jews—who, in passing, made up at the time of that declaration an insignificant total of forty thousand —as a national group. At best it could guarantee equality only to the individual Jew as a French citizen, and not as a constituent member of the national body to which he belonged. In other words, the Jewish national group had first to be abandoned and disintegrated, so that no organic relation existed between atom and atom. And then, one way or another, room would be found for the individual atoms in the body of the great French people; they would be used here, there, somewhere else, to fill up empty places.

These terms the Jews accepted. In a number of official declarations that allow of no two interpretations, they proclaimed that not only were they prepared to renounce their national character for the future, but that they already felt themselves completely and utterly voided of every vestige of Jewish nationalism. They were Jews only in the religious sense. From that day on, the pact ran, Jews no longer existed as a closed group, the bearers of a historic past and of a specific individuality. Long ago Esau sold his soul for a mess of pottage; now Jacob sold his soul for civic rights.

It is difficult to understand what it was that Jacob acquired with the birthright of Esau, but it is certain that the French got nothing from their bargain. True, the Jews sank lower, but France did not rise higher. It is only the extremest chauvinism that, in a distinguished people like the French, could have dictated a bargain which was shameful to both sides.

However that might be, the other Jews looked with envy on their co-religionists of France and exerted themselves to imitate their strategy. The technique, the ideological clichés, had been worked out; the changes from country to country were slight. The French Jews proclaimed that France was their Zion, Paris their Jerusalem; the German Jews had only to substitute Germany for France, Berlin for Paris. Thereafter there remained, for the expression of Jewish character and Jewish individuality, but one domain, the religious. The governments which had extended civic equality to the Jews would, as a matter of fact, have been grateful if their Jewish subjects had submitted to the heroic cure and become Frenchmen, Germans, and so on, completely, by baptizing. But this extreme demand they were ashamed to make; in any case, they believed that the religious citadel, the last remaining outpost of Jewish identity, would not long hold out of itself.

The leading Jewish spirits of the time, those who had formulated the Jewish policy, settled down to the work of introducing the assimilatory program into the everyday life of the Jews. And suddenly they became aware that the task was by no means as easy as it had seemed to be on the surface. The most intractable obstacle lay in the character of the Jewish religion, in its peculiarity and uniqueness. The center of gravity of the Jewish religion had never lain in abstract faith and specific dogma. It lay rather in its folk nature, in the relationship of the individual to the people and in the duties that proceed from such a relationship.

Ninety percent of Jewish prayers ignore the longings of the individual; they have to do with the group; they are directed to the fate of the people as a whole. They evoke the memories of the past in order to give hope for the future, and every hope is national in character. The prayers speak the language of spiritual and national independence. How, then, was it possible to reconcile this religion with a policy of assimilation in the everyday relations of Jews? What assurance was there for the success of the program of assimilation as long as the Jews were bound up with their religion in its old form? And thus, out of that inner conflict between life and religion, was born, in western Europe, the Reform movement, which is in essence more political than religious. In it religion is demoted; it ceases to be the guiding star of life and becomes instead its camp-follower, a servant of the wealthy classes, whose only dream is to be permitted to enter non-Jewish society.

During the sixties and seventies of the last century a deep-reaching assimilation had set in among the Jews of Russia.

There arose a Jewish intelligentsia reared and nourished in the culture and literature of Russia, and its views were as radical as those of the assimilatory intelligentsia of western Europe. Its goal, too, was civic equality and entry into non-Jewish society; and like the intelligentsia of western Europe it was prepared to pay the highest price that a people can pay for civic equality—its own ego. In one respect the assimilationists of Russia went even further than their west European brethren: they did not try to accommodate their religion to their social and political objective. And that not because they considered their religion too sacred, but because they simply ignored it. They wasted no time on the problem of readapting the religious side of their lives.

Thus the internal Jewish struggles in western Europe and in Russia were quite different in character. In the first it developed in the religious field—Reform Judaism versus Conservative; in the second the struggle evolved in the literary field, between the nationalists and the assimilationists. For that reason the struggle in Russia was a more honest one. The protagonists called themselves and each other by their right names: nationalists and assimilationists; while in western Europe the combatants were masked and gave themselves and each other theological names: Conservative and Reform. Actually the struggle was identical with the one taking place in Russia.

There was another difference between the parallel internal Jewish struggles in western Europe and Russia. In the former, the two contending parties used the same language, German in Germany, French in France. In Russia the camps were divided by language too: the assimilationist camp adopted Russian, and in the nationalist camp Hebrew was the written medium of expression.

In the Hebrew press the standard was set by the *Ha-Maggid* of David Gordon, the *Ha-Shachar* of Perez Smolenskin, the *Ha-Melitz* of Alexander Zederbaum and the *Ha-Zephirah* of

Slonimsky and Sokolov. The first two were explicitly nationalist; the last two not definitely so. The three Russian-Jewish weeklies, the *Russkiye Yevrei*, the *Voskhod* and the *Rassviet* presented the assimilationist view. The last named, however, changed color in 1881 and turned to the nationalist cause. The struggle between the two sides was bitter, the debates passionate. The nationalists brought to the fight the accumulation of centuries of Jewish history, the assimilationists were armed with the weapons of a new era, imported from western Europe and made mostly in Germany.

It is an historic mistake to associate as cause and effect the first pogroms in Russia and the rise of the nationalist movement. The fact is that the *Chibath Zion*, or Love of Zion movement—the proto-Zionist stirrings of the mid-nineteenth century—emerged not in Russia, but in western Europe, and not in the time of the pogroms, but some decades before. And it is well to note that the birthplace of the *Chibath Zion* movement was the land of classical assimilationism, Germany. The truth is, again, that the practical work in and for Palestine began—even if on the tiniest of scales—principally in Germany, and to some extent in France and England, some time before the Jewish world was shaken to its foundations by the events in Russia. And once again let us note that the idea of a Jewish settlement in Palestine, autonomous and even with sovereign rights, was frequently urged long before the pogroms took place, and more often by non-Jews than by Jews. It would be proper to draw attention to this error even if it were only a question of chronology; but the error was broadcast by the enemies of Jewish nationalism with a specific purpose—that of compromising the character of the movement.

In this matter I submit the testimony of an individual. I can affirm without hesitation that, as one brought up in an entirely Jewish atmosphere, remote from the currents of Russian life, I found nothing new or revolutionary in the *Chibath Zion* movement, which began to take concrete form in Russia immediately after the first pogroms. It was neither a revelation nor a surprise. On the contrary, I found the movement so natural, so logical, in such complete harmony with what I had learned and drawn into myself since my earliest childhood, that I believed myself to have been born—like every other Jew—a *Chovev Zion*. I therefore looked upon the movement as our historic heritage, brought down from generation to generation, from age to age, the cure provided by God, as the proverb has it, before He sends the disease. And this belief was my solace in the darkest hours of my life. My soul was shaken by the first news of the pogroms; that men and women had actually been killed in them came somewhat later, for the censorship did not permit the whole truth to be printed. And the victims stood forever before me and gave me no peace. In those moments of terror and despair I fled to that ancient world which I carried within me, and it was clear to me that this was the model on which we were to build our new world, where we might live in independence and freedom. And it was equally clear to me that the new world which we were setting out to create could be in no other earthly place than the old one.

It was thus that the Hebrew press inducted me into all the complicated ramifications of the Jewish problem. I now began to find the logical elements in that Jewish nationalism which I had apprehended till now only through my emotions. I took note of all the arguments of our opponents and found satisfactory answers to them. The only trouble was that in Svislovitz there was not a single enemy of Jewish nationalism. My schoolmates were average *cheder* boys with whom I did not care to discuss the questions that filled my mind. With the *Rav* and my old teacher Judah Artzer I could talk freely, but we were too much of one mind on all points. There was no room for passion, for ingenious arguments. So I suffered a great deal. I wanted an opponent on whose devoted head I might pour out all my rage and scorn, whom I might assault with all the weapons I had sharpened. I could not find him. I think that my passion for writing came from my loneliness.

The spring passed, the summer followed—a summer, if I remember rightly, exceptionally hot and dry. The last pogrom of that spring took place in Odessa, a city with a Jewish population of one hundred thousand. The papers brought the news that here, for the first time, the Jews had dared to defend themselves, and that the self-defense had been organized and led by the Jewish students. It was the first cheerful note in the chronicle of those days. I remember that even my mother thanked God. It was true that the defense helped but little, the wound was deep and painful; but the reproach of our shame was in part removed and we could again look our gentile neighbors in the face.

But in the same report was incorporated something new and significant: the police and the military had intervened to prevent the pogrom from assuming unmanageable proportions—a sign that a hint had come from someone higher up. At that time no one suspected that the government itself had instigated and assisted in the pogroms, though it was clear enough that had the government so desired it could have crushed every pogrom at its beginning or even have taken steps to prevent a beginning. When a government remains passive during a pogrom it clearly indicates its approval. This was the view taken by Jews and non-Jews alike. The news that the government had stepped in to curtail the pogrom brought a note of comfort into the Jewish camp: we had not been utterly abandoned.

Then, when several weeks passed and not a single new pogrom was reported, the Jewish population breathed freely again, and life resumed its normal course. It is thus that a people living in the shadow of a volcano forgets its disasters.

The love of life is strong, it easily creates the illusion that the same disaster cannot occur again so soon.

The interval was of short duration. Before long, dreadful reports reached us of a new epidemic of pogroms, again in southern Russia. The descriptions, as they followed one another, were so similar that it began to look as if there was now a pogrom technique. An unknown power had set up the model and the instructions, and the execution followed the given lines. For the time being Lithuania and White Russia were not delivered up to the pogroms. The Governor-General of Vilna, Todleben, had stated clearly that he would permit no pogroms, and he kept his word. It was told that he had issued his decree in the form of a German pun on his name. "Any man who destroys the second half of my name, *Leben* [life], will be visited by the first half, *Tod* [death]." The Jews were delighted almost as much by the General's wit as by his humanity. The marvel of it! A general who had the courage to declare that he would tolerate no pogroms, and did not even wait for them to break out!

But it would be wrong to imagine that the Jews of Lithuania and White Russia escaped unscathed. There began a fearful epidemic of fires. It was widely known that this was the revenge of *pogromshchiks* for the Governor-General's prohibition. The large Jewish city of Minsk was set on fire at several points, and three-quarters of it was reduced to ashes. The same fate overtook many other towns and villages, and thousands of Jewish families found themselves starving and homeless.

The Jewish papers were filled with lamentations; the Russian papers, almost without exception, became even more maniacal in their attacks on the Jews. Some of them, including papers of high standing, like the *Novaya Vremya* and the *Grazhdanin*, openly encouraged the pogrom-makers. It was known that these papers were in the confidence of the highest government circles, and it is not difficult to imagine the agony of fear in which those cities lived which had not yet been visited by a pogrom.

A single scene epitomizes for me the experience of that time. The High Holy Days of the year 1881 drew near. The *yishuvniks*, the Jewish dwellers in the surrounding villages, were in a state of perplexity. They were afraid to leave their village homes and come up to Svislovitz for prayers, as was their wont at this season. Some of them came to the *Rav* for counsel, and he advised them to put their faith in God and follow their custom. Rosh Hashanah passed in peace. The villagers returned to their homes and found everything as they had left it. On the eve of the Day of Atonement they came up to town once more; they reported that peace still reigned, as hitherto, but that there was something odd in the behavior of the peasants; nothing definite, only looks, intimations, gestures, hints of hidden thoughts and intentions. And it so happened that there came to Svislovitz on that same evening an unusual number of gentile carts, which drew up in the center of the marketplace. Nothing more was needed to give birth to the rumor that the peasants of the surrounding villages were assembling for a pogrom on the Jews of Svislovitz. No one dared to speak out openly; there were only whispers; the reports passed closely from mouth to ear; the secret was carried from house to house by adults and children. Everyone went about as on tiptoe; it was as if the Angel of Death, with his thousand eyes and his drawn sword, had been glimpsed.

The sun went down, on that hot day, a ball of fire in a heaven of blood. Without arrangement or consultation the homes were emptied during the hours of prayer. Grandfathers walking side by side with their sons led their tiny grandsons by the hand to the synagogue; they came silently from all the streets, grandmothers and mothers carrying sucklings in their arms. Not an infant was left in the cradle. They did not hasten, for who can run from his destiny? That evening the entire Jewish population of Svislovitz was assembled in the synagogue; the last comers could scarcely squeeze their way in. The tall white candles guttered in their sockets; the men stood silent in their white kirtles, and the children clung to them for protection. The *Rav* went up the steps of the ark, drew forth the scroll with its silver crown, turned to face the congregation, and said, in a low, trembling voice: "Jews, we are in the hands of God. Pray to Him." And with these words there broke out a lamentation the like of which I have never heard again in my life. The old wept, the young, the children; and the lament was taken up by the tiny ones in the arms of their parents and grandparents. In this bitter plaint there was felt a protest that was directed not against the makers of the pogroms, but against our own God.

"Art Thou not He who is called the Guardian of Israel? And is it not written, Behold, the Guardian of Israel neither slumbers nor sleeps? We have left our possessions, all that is ours, in our homes: with empty hands we have assembled here, in Thy House. Do with us according to Thy will."

The Day of Atonement, too, passed in peace. That something odd in the eyes of the gentiles had been the reflection of the terror of the Jews.

CHAPTER SIXTEEN

Messianic Days

IT WAS only later on, when the pogroms had passed into their third stage that the Jews realized the truth, namely that the government was instigating the pogroms and using them as a safety valve. And it was still later, when the first Duma met in 1906, that Prince Urusov revealed that truth to the whole world. The Police Department, which was under the control of the Ministry of the Interior, was the organizing center of the pogroms; from that office exact instructions were issued on the objectives and the method of attack; here the limits were set and the extent of the pogrom fixed.

The only ones who pretended to understand nothing, who toadied more than ever to the government and tried to induce the Jewish population to adopt the same tactics, were the wealthiest Jews, those who claimed to speak in the name of their people and actually did play the leading role as our representatives—the *shtadlanim,* the self-elected notables who negotiated for us behind the scenes. They trembled lest any word or action of theirs should reflect on the quality of their patriotism, and when the most sensitive interests of the Jewish people were in the balance, it was the patriotism of the *shtadlanim* that turned the scale.

When the Jews petitioned for permission to resettle in the large eastern territories of the empire, the government returned the cynical answer: "The western frontiers of Russia are open." But many Jews had not waited for the reply. They pressed, in thousands, through the open frontier. This was not enough for the Jewish notables. They held secret meetings—secret, that is, to the Jews: the government knew all about them—in which they resolved against the organization of emigration. Emigration was to be neither encouraged nor regulated, for that would contradict the principles of patriotism. It was our good luck that the Jewish notables could only play at history: they could not make it. Their philanthropies, conducted without consulting either the recipients or the historic need of the moment, were impotent, and the iron course of history has passed over them. They refused to reckon with the soul of the people and the future does not reckon with them. Even their names are forgotten.

During the autumn of 1881 a strange phenomenon arose. Almost every day, between afternoon and evening prayers, a wandering preacher, one of the *maggidim*—those troubadours of the Jewish exile—appeared in the synagogue. We were of course familiar with these figures; during that season, however, they followed one another almost without a break. It was their hour. The spirit of the Jews was almost broken, they were ready to listen as they had never listened before, and now was the time to find a way into their souls. The majority of the *maggidim*, following their ancient tradition, continued to preach in the purely moral vein; but there were some among them who undertook to fulfill a new function. They became teachers, and tried to explain to the simple masses the significance of the events that had come upon them with such shattering effect. They poured out the unexpressed rage of the Jews upon their implacable enemies, and brought a ray of hope into the lives of their hearers. They became the "comforters of the people," and their task was to prevent the spirit of the Jews from sinking into depths from which it might never rise again.

They spoke, as was their wont, obliquely, and gave new meanings to old phrases; they implied, they hinted, they used parables. To speak openly was more than they dared, even in Svislovitz and even in the synagogue. So during this period, the parable acquired an importance unknown before. And the *maggidim* could rely on their audience to understand them. Jews like a parable in and for itself; they like it better even than its application. And after all, what sense was there in mentioning, in terror and trembling, the name of Alexander III, Emperor of Russia, when it was just as easy to speak fearlessly of Pharaoh, Emperor of Egypt? What would be the point of referring to "emigration" and daring such lions as the Günzburgs and the Poliakovs of St. Petersburg and the other notables who had forbidden all mention of that word? Was it not simpler to tell the story of the Exodus from Egypt? Was it not safer and more effective to pour scorn and contempt on Dathan and Abiram, rich Jews, notables, who, while in Egypt opposed tooth and nail the plans of Moses and later, in the desert, made a league against him with the rebel Korah? What else should those notables of old have done? They were close to the court, intimate with the ministers of Pharaoh—what reason had *they* to encourage the Exodus? And in the same way the *maggidim* spoke of others whose names might be uttered only in a whisper. What need to say "Ignatiev" or "Pobedonostsev," the two bitterest persecutors of the time, when the Bible had so thoughtfully given us Haman as a symbol and so provided us with countless legends about him?

So the *maggidim* travelled from village to village and taught the Bible. They dragged from their graves the ancient enemies of Israel. They reminded the Jews of the fate of Pharaoh; they recalled how Haman had ended up on the gallows and how Nebuchadnezzar had eaten the grass of the field for seven years. And the Jews understood. Patience, patience. There are still seas enough for all the Pharaohs, trees enough for all the Hamans, and more than enough grass for all the Nebuchadnezzars.

During that summer I was so swallowed up by the great events that I remember little about myself. For that period the village, with its lakes, fields and forests, has vanished from the theater of my consciousness. Had someone come, years later, and told me that I had passed the summer of 1881 in some other place than Svislovitz, I should not have been astonished. All I recall is that the summer was hot and dry and that everybody around me was, like myself, steeped in fear. My memories resume only with the fearful scene in the synagogue on the eve of Yom Kippur.

Little or no change had come over our house. My father had been absent for some time in Ekaterinoslav and Kremenchug, the pogrom districts, and did not return till the High Holy Days; but he said little about conditions there. Our employees carried on as heretofore; they went through the villages and hired peasants as if nothing had happened since the last season; and again during the long winter evenings the peasants would gather in our house. The samovar stood on the table and the assembly drank tea and told and listened to stories.

Only one change had taken place—in my mother. She became even more pious than before. She stayed longer in the synagogue, and she added to her prayers. But it was not in prayer alone that she expressed her intensified piety. She also added greatly to the number of her fast days. Fasts had, in fact, become a widespread custom or fashion in those days. To almost every new pogrom the Jews retorted with a general decree for a fast. In these fasts children twelve years old and over also participated. It was a peculiar sort of hunger-strike, directed in part against the cruelties of the Russian people and government, but more against God, who had closed the gates of heaven and abandoned His people to destruction. On one occasion a fast was decreed for three days, but such decrees were of course not local affairs. They came from headquarters, in Vilna and Kovno, and the authority with the greatest influence was the *Rav* of Kovno, Rabbi Isaac Elkhanan Spektor.

In the matter of saintliness Rabbi Israel Salanter perhaps took precedence over Rabbi Spektor, but the latter was regarded not only as a mighty scholar and saint but also as a Jewish statesman, whom the Russian government had more than once invited to serve on commissions for the study of Jewish affairs. The authority of Isaac Elkhanan Spektor was universal and unchallenged, and a decree issued by him was obeyed without a murmur—particularly when it related to fasts, in which the Jews have been the greatest adepts from earliest times.

And so a war was conducted between the two headquarters. The pogrom headquarters were probably in St. Petersburg, those of the fast were in Kovno. No sooner did pogrom headquarters launch an attack than fast headquarters counterattacked. True, the weapons were unequal, but the Jews had one advantage: their ammunition was cheaper and they were never afraid of a shortage. A curious economist might go into this question and discover that during the pogrom years the Jews of Russia saved a vast amount of money through their fasts—a new instrument of competition with the gentile population.

But for my mother these communal fasts were insufficient. They did not satisfy her "hunger"; and so she added private and supernumerary fasts of her own—sometimes one and sometimes two a week. There were arguments between her and my father. "Elke, is it your business to provide the whole world with piety?" And my mother used to reply: "Let me fast, Samuel Chaim; let me get some sort of pleasure out of life."

In those days my mother talked a great deal about Palestine and the Messiah. She averred that the messianic days had begun—hence these tribulations. She knew that before the Messiah could appear in person the Jews would have to pass through a purification: first the Messiah ben Joseph would come, and he would be slain; then the true Messiah, the Messiah ben David, would lead the Jews back to Palestine. Were there not other signs, too, that the messianic days were upon us? Were there not reports from every corner of the exile that even now young Jews were organizing to migrate to Palestine? Was it not reported in the papers that a great Englishman, Sir Laurence Oliphant, was negotiating with the Sultan for the purchase of Palestine? True, Sir Laurence Oliphant was not a Jew, but was it not written in our books, black on white, that in the days of the Messiah the peoples of the world would come bearing the Jews on their cloaks, an offering to the Almighty? Were other signs needed that the fulfillment of the ancient prophecies was at hand?

Nor was it my mother alone who was caught up in this mood of the messianic days. The mood was everywhere. Scholars began once more to study the apocalyptic prophecies of Daniel, and mystics resorted to the deep, ingenious speculations of the Cabalah on the end of all things. Even in our little Svislovitz the old men would sit for hours in the study house of the synagogue, speaking of the approaching End. They pondered the Book of Daniel, in which it is written: "There shall stand up in his place one that removeth the oppressor, the glory of the Kingdom: but within a few days he shall be destroyed, neither in anger nor in battle; and in his place shall stand up a vile person." What could be clearer? The glory of the Kingdom, he that removed the oppressor, could be none other than Alexander II, for he had removed the serf-owner and had liberated the slave; and now he had been destroyed, neither in anger nor in battle. It could not have been in anger, for he was a just king, and we knew that he had not fallen in battle. And now it followed of itself that the vile person in the prophecy could be none other than the monarch who had succeeded him. . . .

Even my old teacher, Judah Artzer, was drawn into these feverish speculations, and he too paid special attention to the last chapters of Daniel, that favorite hunting ground of mystics and eschatologists. When, in later years, I became acquainted with the history of the false messiahs, and particularly with that of Sabbatai Zevi, I could understand without difficulty how such things could come to pass.

There were two among our old men who were especially strong in the conviction that we were living in the days of the Messiah. They were Meyer the Old One, and Zelig the prayer-reader. Meyer was in his eighties, while Zelig was over ninety, but the title of the Old One had been bestowed upon Meyer because Zelig had been known too long as Zelig the prayer-reader. Zelig had an only son, also a prayer-reader, some eighteen years younger than himself, so that, about the time I am writing of, the son too was no fledgling. But his father still persisted in treating him like a boy, and refused to let him speak in the presence of the sages. Zelig read the late morning prayers on the High Holy Days, Hirschel, his son, the early morning prayers. Joseph Bear Schatz the cantor, was more ritual chicken-slaughterer than cantor, and he got only fragments of the service on the night of Yom Kippur and the day of the Black Fast.

Hirschel was famous for his observance of the Sixth Commandment: "Honor thy father. . . ." He was universally admired, and considered a model son. When Zelig entered into the nineties and his strength began to fail, he changed roles with his son; Hirschel took the late morning prayers and Zelig the early morning prayers. Hirschel wept like a little child, for he saw in this change a sign that his father was growing old. He now became tenderer and more attentive to his father than ever before. And on Friday afternoons the following extraordinary scene was to be witnessed in the streets of Svislovitz: one graybeard carrying another pickaback. It was Hirschel, carrying his father Zelig to the bath in honor of the Sabbath. The baths stood behind the hill, close to the Svislo. One winter's day, when Hirschel was carrying his father downhill to the baths, he slipped, and nearly threw his load to the ground. Zelig flew into a rage with his son, and exclaimed: "You'll grow up a disgrace to the family!"

Zelig loved, above all, to gather a group about himself and tell stories of his own incredibly remote childhood, of Alexander I, of the war with the French, and of Nicholas I, "may his name and his memory be blotted out." Old Meyer would help him from time to time. Sometimes they told a story in partnership, a sentence each in alternation, and neither would interrupt the other. They told how in Svislovitz the Jews had been entirely on the side of the Russians, and how they had prayed every Sabbath for the victory of Alexander and the defeat of Napoleon; and they had prayed so long, and so fervently, that Napoleon had finally been defeated. And so, story by story, they would creep up toward modern times, and Zelig the prayer-reader would wind up with: "Children, have no fear. We have lived through greater tribulations. We survived a Haman like Nicholas I: we will also survive the Vile Person. . . ." It was unnecessary to mention the name. "And I tell you that before the Vile Person shall close his eyes, the Messiah will be among us, and it may even be granted to me to look upon him."

I loved to listen to the stories of our ancients. These were stories not to be found in the books; they were the living thread, incorporated in living persons, binding us to the past. Once, when Zelig told us what Svislovitz had looked like nearly a century before, how there had been no bridge across the Svislo, and no post, I dared to ask him a question: "If there was neither bridge nor post," I asked, "how did one send a letter?" And this was the answer I received: "You are a child and do not understand anything. If the letter was really an urgent and important one, they sent it by special messenger. And if the letter was not so important, they just waited a couple of weeks, and then there was no need to send it at all."

The days crept slowly, coldly, like the waters of our two rivers when they are covered with ice. The shopkeepers opened their stores punctually every day; the peasants felled the trees in the forests; the Jewish peddlers loaded their heavy packs and, bowed under the burden, left for the neighboring villages; the *rebbis* went on teaching the sacred Torah to their young charges, and the boys of the study house sat swaying over the huge volumes of the Talmud and filled the room with their mournful, monotonous chanting. But to every man and woman it was clear that the catastrophe had not run its full course; they knew that the Russian bear was only lying in his winter sleep, sucking his paws, like his brother in the dense forest. Soon the spring would come, the waters would melt, and the bear would wake out of his sleep.

We were the more certain of this because the official, like the semi-official press did not for an instant suspend its fierce assaults on the Jews: the Jew was responsible for the poverty of the drunken peasants—he encouraged them to drink; the Jew had ruined the magnates—he lent them money and encouraged them to lead dissolute lives; the Jew was undermining the Russian army—as official purveyor he delivered rotten goods; the Jew through his secret international organizations, robbed Russia of the fruits of her military victories—as in the Russo-Turkish War. And, finally, the Jews were the revolutionary power. True, they did not venture into the front line themselves, but they were the organizers and inspirers. And the proof was: Hessie Helfman. It was in her house that the assassination of Alexander II had been planned. In a word: were it not for the Jews, Russia would be the happiest and gayest country under God's blue sky.

It was impossible for the Jews to believe the official declarations of the Russian government that no more pogroms would be permitted; but they did put their trust in the cold weather; even the devil would not make a pogrom in the depth of the Russian winter. And so they felt a temporary relief, like a debtor whose note is renewed.

The event quickly undeceived them. In December, 1881, a pogrom broke out where everyone believed pogroms to be impossible, namely Warsaw, the capital of Poland. While with its own subjects the Russian government might do as it pleased, it did have some regard for foreign public opinion. It was therefore necessary to prove to the world that not the Russian peasant alone, but non-Russian peoples too were prepared to carry out pogroms. The experiment was first tried out in Warsaw, the westernmost province of Russia, and almost foreign territory. The population was non-Russian. What better proof that the Jews were hated everywhere?

The effect was excellently calculated. The Russian government killed two birds with one stone: Poland, an oppressed country, stood badly in need of the good opinion of the world, but the rabble of Warsaw had not the moral strength to resist the blandishments of the Russian *pogromshchiks* who were imported for the occasion. On the Jews the effect was doubly shattering, especially in our district of Lithuania. As long as the pogroms were being perpetrated only by the *katzap*, the Russian hooligan, we had hoped they would not penetrate to our region. Our peasants were, after all, of a different type. But the distance between Warsaw and Vilna is small, and Vilna is Lithuania. If pogroms were possible in Poland, we too were no longer certain of our lives.

On the day when the news of the Warsaw pogrom arrived, my father received a visit from the commissar of the local estate. For two hours they were closeted together, and we knew that this was no business visit. Later my father explained that the commissar had come to offer apologies and excuses for the Warsaw pogrom. It had been imported, he explained, by the Russian government; he did his best to calm my father's fears, assuring him that the relationship between him and the nobleman who owned the estate would remain unchanged.

By degrees we lost our faith in the government, in individuals—and even in the winter. Man was our enemy and nature would not protect us; the earth was not ours, we had no portion in it. So we lifted our eyes to the heavens; perhaps they would vouchsafe a reply. But I know that for my own part the result of the pogroms was not a religious reaction. I fasted with the others, said midnight prayers with them. But with every new pogrom I felt the heavens closing, and the conviction grew in me that if there was any salvation it would have to come from ourselves.

All winter I continued my studies, but without special joy. I wrote, imitating the Hebrew articles of Smolenskin, Lilienblum and Yehalel. In poetry I was completely under the influence of Judah Leib Gordon, but I was deeply wounded by the fact that he, our greatest poet of the time, stretched out his hands not to the East, but to the West, to America, whereas even our Yiddish-Russian poet, Simon Frug, had sung of the Jordan, of Carmel and of Lebanon. Tormented by a thousand questions, unable to disentangle myself, I would go out late in the night and visit the Talmud students in the study house of the synagogue. Not all of them had reacted in my fashion to the events of the times. There were some who barricaded themselves behind the huge tomes of the Talmud and of the later rabbinic literature and gave themselves up with vehement and exclusive faithfulness to their studies, just as if nothing had happened. I used to stare at their lean, hungry bodies, their white, withered faces and burning eyes, and I was bewildered. What secret was locked away in them? Were *they*, perhaps, the real heroes, the true descendants of the stiff-necked people, who ignored all catastrophes and obdurately kept on weaving the thread of our continuity?

My relationship to my Russian studies was a purely formal one. I was by now able to read, with the assistance of my teacher and a dictionary, a Russian book or a Russian newspaper, but I had not even crossed the threshold of the gigantic and inspiring temple of Russian literature. I felt no inner urge toward the language; if anything, there was a repulsion. I did not dream at that time that my later entry into the great world of modern culture would be via the literature of Russia.

Spring returned, and with every awakening throb of nature a throb of terror passed through the Jews. The Easter days have always been, in unquiet times, the most critical. All year round, it was averred, the Jew sucked the blood of his neighbors; at Easter time, when the Passover came, he drank it. I cannot remember clearly the ceremonies of that particular Passover; but I do remember than when the moment came for us to fling open the door and welcome in Elijah the Prophet, none of us would stir. We were only too glad that no one opened it from the outside.

There were two great problems before me. The Jewish people had to be saved once for all from their exile, and I had to be saved from Svislovitz in order that I might prepare myself for the great day. I must confess that the first problem seemed to me to be the easier one. The gates of Russia were open; the exit troubles that had faced us under Pharaoh would not recur this time. Nor was there a wilderness to traverse; we had only to go on board our ships and disembark in Palestine. As to the Sultan, we would undoubtedly come to an arrangement with him; it was a matter of a million more or a million less. It was thus that I envisaged the liberation of the Jewish people: a simple, primitive and smooth process.

The big task, it seemed to me, was my own liberation. Svislovitz had become impossible. Had I been a few years older I would have run away to Odessa and boarded a ship bound for Palestine. Then one evening I opened my heart to my parents, I told them I wanted to go out into the world and begin my studies. I wanted to become an engineer. In my imagination I was already at work among the mountains of Carmel and Lebanon, between Shenir and Hermon. (I was bitterly disillusioned when I learned later that neither Hermon nor Lebanon had ever belonged to us.) I saw myself throwing bridges across the Jordan, which I imagined to be broader and more majestic than the Dnieper.

My parents reacted so coldly that I dropped all talk of engineering and put forward the most modest of proposals. I would go to some place where I might continue my Jewish studies—Talmud and ritual—and where I could get better instruction in Russian, and perhaps German. I also hinted that I wanted to see something of the larger world. This my parents found reasonable, and my father promised me that soon after Passover he would take me over to Beresin; there he would install me for a term or two, as an experiment.

There were reasons enough behind my parents reluctance to let me acquire a worldly education. We were a good, middle-class family, with a high tradition of Jewish education, but no relative of ours had ever ventured into the Western schools. It was not easy to overcome the inertia of generations. It was, further, a well-established fact that children who left Jewish homes and threw themselves into secular studies at the high schools and universities almost invariably became alienated. A deep gulf opened between them and their parents—a gulf that was never bridged. A professional man, a doctor, lawyer, or engineer, who still retained a relationship with Jewish religious tradition was, in the Russia of the sixties and seventies, a very rare phenomenon. Almost as rarely did he take an interest in our purely social and secular problems. The division was sharp and clear: on one side a facade without a structure, an intelligentsia without a folk behind it; on the other side a folk without an intelligentsia. Little wonder that parents of decent families were unwilling to send their children out in the world of Western culture and learning.

In the eighties of that century, however, there came a radical change. Under the pressure of the persecutions, which did not distinguish between classes, or between degrees of westernization, the intelligentsia started to turn back to the people. But at the beginning of the persecutions the process of assimilation was in full swing; and there were well-authenticated cases of children of assimilated Jewish parents who had suffered in the pogroms asking in bewilderment: "Haven't they made a mistake? Are *we* Jews, too?"

There was in Svislovitz a family, the Getzovs, which had originally lived in Minsk. The youngest boy, Bendet, had been my rival for the leadership of the small fry when we were both *cheder* boys. In his Jewish studies he was a long way behind me, but his mother, Hannah Neche, had resolved "to make a man of him," as she put it, and she sent him to an older son in Gomel, to enter the *gymnaziya*. That Passover, Bendet returned to Svislovitz, to visit his parents. He came in his royal robes, that is, in the smart uniform of the Russian student: a blue jacket with silver buttons, a high collar with silver stripes, and a silver badge on his regulation cap. I cannot describe the profound impression the brilliant uniform of my old friend and rival made on me. He was the first Jewish *gymnaziya* student who had ever appeared on the streets of Svislovitz. One day we met in the synagogue. I greeted him: "*Sholom aleichem*, Bendet." He answered me in Russian: "*Zdrastvui!*" I thought I detected a certain haughtiness in his bearing, and on a sudden I was filled with fury. "Ah! The change has set in so soon. *Sholom aleichem* is not good enough for him. *Zdrastvui!*" But I believe that my fury had little to do with the *sholom aleichem* and the *zdrastvui*. The truth was that I was consumed to the marrow with envy. The whole of that Passover was spoiled for me. The silver buttons and the silver badge haunted me.

In the old days our friendship had not been too intimate, but now I sought him out as often as I could and gave him all my free time. I devoured him with my eyes—or rather I devoured his buttons and badge. I told him that I, too, would be leaving Svislovitz; I was going to Beresin after Passover. Of my further hopes and plans I said nothing, fearing they would reach my parent's ears. But I hoped he would understand that Beresin was only the beginning; thus I tried to assuage the agony of my envy. But Bendet's brother Leivik had overheard me. Leivik was an ignorant man, a drayman; his job was to carry the mails to and from Svislovitz and Osipovitz. He was prouder of Bendet's uniform than if he had been wearing it himself. "Beresin!" he exclaimed contemptuously. "And what kind of place is Beresin? Have they a *gymnaziya* there?" I bit my lips and said nothing more. But I took an oath silently: "Wait! My turn will come."

On the eve of the last day of Passover we assembled in the synagogue and sang the Song of Moses, which glorifies the God of Israel. "The horse and the rider has He cast into the sea . . . the peoples have heard, they tremble." And on that same evening there took place in Balta the most horrible of the pogroms of that time, a forewarning of the type of pogrom which began again with Kishinev twenty-two years later, a pogrom in which the lowest and most bestial of human instincts were suddenly let loose and abominations without a name were committed against fellow human beings.

And I must confess that in the midst of the tumult and horror the silver buttons of Bendet still swam before me. I was ashamed of myself: how could a son of the Jewish people think, at such a time, of the uniform of the gentiles? But I found consolation: "My eyes are fixed on the idols and vanities of the gentiles, but I seek in them only the weapons for the defense of my people. My dream lies beyond the uniform and the silver buttons: my purposes are high and pure."

A week later I got into the wagon and, with my father at my side, set out for Beresin.

CHAPTER SEVENTEEN

Beresin and Flight

MY ENTRY that day into Beresin was like a prologue to my entry into the great world. On either side of the street was a long row of lofty, thickly-leaved trees, and through the trees peeped magnificent houses—some of them with two stories—built of the finest wood, with grand windows that were actually set in cut-out frames and richly ornamented with brasswork. I saw for the first time a harmonious complex of trees and houses and felt for the first time a genuine aesthetic thrill. My father told me that the whole street was occupied by the younger generation of the Seldoviches, those wealthy timber merchants who ruled the roost in Jewish Beresin and who employed my grandfather Mendel as one of their agents. The older Seldoviches also had a street of their own, called the Golden Street, but their houses were not so fine. The older generation was the richer, but was more modest and did not delight in "making people stare." That phrase was very popular during the pogrom days. The Jewish press was filled with denunciations of Jews who displayed their wealth ostentatiously and was forever warning against the danger of "making gentiles stare."

I was left by my father under the protection of my uncle Chaim Eli, a son of grandfather Mendel Astrakan, and was immediately at home with the family, which consisted of two sons, Bereh and Nissan, and the "baby," Zireh, a girl who was a year or two younger than myself. A third son, Isaac, was already married and had set up house for himself. The Chaim Eli family belonged to the more educated circle; the three younger children had received a more modern training than was customary with the Jewish middle classes. I was at once provided with a teacher of Russian and German and a teacher of Talmud. My education in Hebrew was regarded as completed. The young Astrakans, who became my new friends, were also good Hebraists and kept me supplied with the Hebrew literature of the Haskalah period, as well as with the latest publications.

The ramifications of my mother's family in Beresin were no less broad and no less complicated than my father's in Svislovitz. A great number of houses were thus thrown open to me—uncles, aunts, cousins, relatives by marriage and relatives of indeterminate degree. I was embarrassed by the multiplicity of invitations. The homes were all those of the decent middle class, and though I was welcome everywhere I did not find them particularly interesting. The one house where I felt perfectly at home was the one I lived in—Uncle Chaim Eli's.

The influence exerted on me by Beresin was immediate and powerful. Compared with Svislovitz this was a city; the streets were livelier, the people quicker. For the first time I was in a place where I did not know everybody. In Svislovitz my position had been unique. I had permitted myself to behave as I liked, speak as I liked, uttering whatever came to the tip of my tongue. In Beresin I had to create a position for myself. I became more thoughtful, I paused before I spoke and I ordered my thoughts in advance. The break in the tempo of my being was hard on me, but I was endowed with a deep feeling of responsibility. I grew up very quickly.

The largest element in this change was my friendship with the youngest generation of the Seldoviches. They were boys of my age, or a year older at the most. But from their earliest childhood they had been admonished never to forget—not for a moment—who they were: Seldoviches. They were taught to bear themselves with a certain pride, to walk slowly, with measured steps, to speak slowly, with measured words. I mentioned "friendship," but it was hardly that. The refusal came from their side; they could not accept me, there was too great a difference in the social status of our respective families; and it was quite a concession on their part that they let me approach them and bathe in the glory of their presence. I owed this concession to my Talmud teacher, who had spread the rumor that I was an extraordinarily gifted village youth, with a rich education in all branches of Jewish knowledge, Hebrew in particular.

I grew older, therefore, in another respect. In Beresin I knew for the first time the bitter taste of class distinction, and learned the role that money played in Jewish life. I suffered. I observed that the friendliness of those young people toward me was purely external, courtesy rather than friendship, manners rather than feeling. I had no special respect for them; the great majority were mediocrities, some, in their Jewish studies, downright ignoramuses. True, they knew Russian much better than I, and some of them even had a smattering of German; but this could not compensate for ignorance in Jewish studies. The distinction was therefore one of money: their parents were richer than mine. But what did that have to do with us? Was I asking favors of them? Did money questions ever rise between us? No, it was just the presence of money, the mere association with it, which created the ineradicable distinction. It was an attitude of genuine idolatry. I now felt that there were two exiles for poor Jews. All Jews were in exile among the nations, and the poor Jews were in exile among their own people—an exile within an exile.

What I had heard about before regarding the Seldoviches and the Jews of Beresin I now saw for myself. I perceived how complete was the domination exercised by the many-branched Seldovich family, how complete was the self-abasement of the community. The middle classes lay as prostrate as the poorest Jews, and in the presence of a Seldovich no one else was of any account. There awoke in me a deep contempt for the oppressed and a hatred of the oppressor. But when, unable to restrain myself, I spoke out to my friends Bereh and Nissan, they smiled. They did not laugh, they only smiled, as if to say: "A village boy like you comes to live among us for a few months and breaks out in bitter criticism. We were born here and have always lived here and we are silent. Neither you nor we will change the order of things, which scores of generations have set firmly."

It must be borne in mind that I came upon this "order of things" at a time which should have created a new feeling of solidarity among Jews; for all Jews, without distinction of class or rank, were living, even when at a distance from the scenes of the pogroms, under a common threat. But the rich, snobbish Jews could not bring themselves to admit that in any respect whatsoever they could be classed with their poor co-religionists. In that hour of terror they insisted on trembling apart.

Observing the life of this tiny provincial town I got an insight into the attitude of the Günzburgs and Poliakovs and the other wealthy Jewish notables of the capital who pretended to direct the affairs of the Jewish people. I began to understand why the best Jewish writers of the time were unanimous in their derision of the politics and actions of the wealthy Jews, and in that miniature world I learned how deep the gulf was between the wealthy Jews and the masses.

I will cite a single illuminating fact. The *Chibath Zion* movement began to take form at the time of the pogroms. At first individuals and then groups joined the ranks. The movement made a stir in Beresin, but *not a single member of the wealthy classes was among the recruits.* Later I was to learn that this phenomenon was common to all cities. The wealthy Jew, even when he remained true to what is called traditional Judaism, stood off from the masses and away from the interests of his people.

My Talmud teacher in Beresin was called Mottel the ascetic. He had lost his first wife and had taken in second marriage my cousin. Besides being deeply versed in talmudic and rabbinic literature he was a man of keen intelligence and wit. He kept no *cheder* but confined himself to instruction in the richest homes. He never had more than two or three pupils in a group, and to be a pupil of Mottel the ascetic was a distinction. This man had, by his brilliant gifts and his learning, obtained in his adolescence his rabbinic diploma and could have aspired to one of the very highest posts in his profession. But he turned from the rabbinate and remained a *melamed.* All day long he went from one rich house to another, yet he lived in dire poverty, occupying a tiny apartment in one of the buildings of Grandfather Mendel's home.

I wondered why he had chosen the miserable profession of a *melamed,* and when I had become more intimate with him I put the question to him point blank. He could not blush, for he was so dark-skinned that he might have passed for a mulatto, but clearly the question embarrassed him, and his answer was evasive. I had not asked out of idle curiosity. My early decision not to follow the path that led to the rabbinate had been based chiefly on one consideration: I did not feel myself to be pious enough for a *rav,* and my heart told me that Mottel the ascetic was in the same case as I. I noticed that on those passages in the

Talmud that deal with the logic and justice, Mottel expended all his energies and ingenuities. He went closely into all the arguments, quoted all the commentaries and was not satisfied with anything less than an exhaustive examination of the problem. But when he came to the passages dealing with purely theological matters, the laws of the Sabbath, of the Holy Days, of the prayers, he ran through them rapidly and indifferently. In short, he was interested in the laws that regulate the relationship "of man to his fellow-man," not in those which deal with the relationship between "man and his God." But a *rav*, or rabbi, must be interested in both sets of laws.

In my later contacts with the rabbinate I observed that the greater the jurist, the smaller the theologian, and vice versa. The explanation is simple: with the emancipation of the Jews, the juridical side of the rabbinic training had lost its living importance. The *din Torah*, the settlement of disputes according to Jewish law, fell into disuse; there remained therefore only the theological side, and the freer spirits among the rabbis did what they could to fit Jewish theology, in its turn, to modern conditions. Thence was born the Reform movement. The conservative element, in compensatory reaction, barricaded itself more strongly than ever behind the theological content of Judaism. The most violent fanatics in regard to external piety were the German rabbis who had their spiritual center in Frankfurt am Main. But in Russia the time was not yet ripe for reform, and therefore not for a reaction toward the extreme orthodoxy of the Frankfurt school. Russia therefore produced freethinking scholars and Germany pious ignoramuses.

Like my two former teachers, Mottel the ascetic belonged to the type of freethinking scholar, and he, together with them, fixed permanently my attitude toward Jewish learning; to be more exact, they helped along that development which had been set in motion by the best of all my teachers, Judah Artzer. In this respect I was exceptionally fortunate: there was not, in my development, a spiritual break such as occurred with others as they passed from teacher to teacher.

My Russian and German teacher in Beresin, Joseph Mazeh, was a well-educated and intelligent man, more inclined toward the German than the Russian culture. He used to translate German into Russian for me, and Russian into German, and I limped badly in both languages, or rather, I limped in Russian and crawled in German. But of course, like every Yiddish-speaking Jew who knows no German I thought I knew a great deal. I was strongly confirmed in this conviction by the following circumstance. Among the workers in the forests round Svislovitz there were large numbers of Germans. Once a week they would come from the woods where they lived with their families, to lay in provisions. Most of all they frequented the store of my sister Hannah Braineh, and she spoke with them in German—at least, so she thought. I was often present and I understood nearly everything the Germans said to my sister and she to them. Years later, when I was a student in a German university and came home for a visit, I went to see my forest Germans. I was astounded to learn the truth. Neither my sister nor the other storekeepers of Svislovitz had learned to speak German: the Germans had learned to speak Yiddish.

I had hardly mastered the German alphabet when I came to my teacher with a request for German books; not beginners' books, made up scraps and shreds, but real books, the body of German literature. I argued that since I knew the language and had now learned the alphabet, I was ready for the best. Whether in jest or in earnest, my teacher read out to me the first few lines of Goethe's *Die Leiden des jungen Werthers*, and asked me if I had understood. Of course I had not understood a single word; ashamed, I answered that our Germans back home had a quite different pronunciation. And now for the second time I had to sit down before a book that began: "The cat is in the garden. The pen is on the desk. The pupil sits and learns."

It became evident to my teacher, at about the same time, that my Russian was not much in advance of my German. My vocabulary was small, my pronunciation grotesque. My teacher had to stop me at every word. At last I could stand it no longer and burst out, impudently: "In Svislovitz we have a different pronunciation." My teacher shouted with laughter, so that my friends Bereh and Nissan and Zireh Astrakan came running in from the next room. They laughed till the tears ran down their cheeks. How were they to know that years later I would have to toil long hours to eradicate the traces of my Beresin pronunciation of Russian?

My teacher began to read to me Gogol's *Taras Bulba*, that marvelous picture—the most marvelous in Russian literature—of the old Cossack life. It did not grip me; it was too alien, too characteristically Russian. From Gogol my teacher passed to Pushkin, and this time he was more successful. We read *Eugene Onegin*, and though I did not always get the details, there was some appeal in the general human effect. After *Eugene Onegin* we read Shakespeare in Russian, and suddenly I awoke to a new pleasure. This was remarkable enough: the life pictured in *Hamlet* was even more remote from me than that pictured in *Taras Bulba:* the heroes were even more alien. Yet from the beginning I felt that I had before me something of elemental greatness. I seemed to hear in *Hamlet* an echo of the Bible. I do not know how many years later I read in Heine that he had found but two human creations that might stand the slightest comparison, in power of expression, with the sacred books: Shakespeare and Homer. For the first time a book in the Russian language filled me with joy—and it was a translation of Shakespeare. Later I read, in the Hebrew translation of J. A. Salkindson, the apostate and Christian missionary, two more plays of Shakespeare: *Romeo and Juliet* and *Othello*. I was filled with boundless enthusiasm. I was captured by the marvelous harmony between word and thought, and I understood now why Smolenskin had written in *Ha-Shachar*, when these translations appeared: "Today we revenge ourselves on the English. They took our Bible and wove it into the structure of their literature. We have taken their Shakespeare and given him a place in the front rank of ours. A genius for a genius."

The fragmentary and accidental character of my education may be gathered from the fact that it never occurred to my teacher to broach any subject other than Russian and German, such as arithmetic, geography or history. In this too could be traced the influence of the Seldoviches. These magnates did not plan to send their children to universities; they did not need it. They had wealth enough and honors enough; studies were therefore superfluous. But languages were needed for the regular annual trips abroad.

When I left my native Svislovitz, the talk was all of pogroms, of those that had been and those that were yet to come. In Beresin they talked little about pogroms. First, the times had become quieter; second, and more important, was the psychology of the town. Such was the belief of the Jews of Beresin in the might of the Seldoviches that they considered a pogrom in their city inconceivable. The Seldoviches would put their foot down, and that would be the end of it.

Two weeks before the Jewish New Year my father came to take me home. My cousins were sorry to see me go; they told my father they liked me because of my happy temperament. And Zireh Braineh turned a fiery red when it came her turn to bid me goodbye.

We travelled the whole night in a rustic cart and early the next morning arrived in Svislovitz. I did not go to sleep. As soon as I had breakfasted I went out into the street. Nothing had changed. There was our house, opposite the Orthodox church; there in the center of the square was the old communal well; there to one side was the broad street, and to the other Castle Hill, with its four proud old birch trees. But at the well stood a little girl of the same age as I, she who never called me Shmerel, but Shmerelle. She too turned red, and told me she had been waiting there for me. Very naïvely I asked: "How long have you been waiting?" She answered: "All the time."

I was welcomed back joyously to Svislovitz and for the first few weeks I avoided the question of the future. But the old, impatient longing to continue my education did not die down, and I was afraid that my father would press me to follow my brother's example—and his own—and become a timber merchant. My mother, on the other hand, began pleading with me to go to the famous yeshivah of Volozhin. *My* inmost wish was to be sent to Minsk, to the *Realschule*. There was also a *gymnaziya* in Minsk, but I knew by now that languages came to me with difficulty. The *gymnaziya* was a more classic institution, whereas the *Realschule* specialized in mathematics and demanded only German in addition to Russian. Instead of the storm of opposition which I expected, I met with what sounded like a reasonable proposal from my father. He was going to Bobruisk for two weeks. I was to wait for his return. I could not believe my ears: "You mean, then," I exclaimed, "that as soon as you get back from Bobruisk I shall go to Minsk?" "I did not say that," my father answered. "I only meant that when I get back from Bobruisk we'll take up the matter again." In that instant was born my plan to run away from home.

I laid my plans carefully. I would not go to Minsk—it was too close to Svislovitz. I would go instead to Dvinsk, to my uncle Meyer Vendrov, he who had befriended me in childhood and rescued me from the wretched *cheder* system of Svislovitz. My uncle Meyer had remarried after the death of his first wife, my father's sister Lyube Henye, and had transferred his family to Dvinsk. His oldest son, Gershon, who had been my schoolmate in the little *cheder* of Judah Artzer, was now preparing for the *Realschule*. It was a wonderful opportunity.

The day my father left for Bobruisk I went over to my sister

Hannah Braineh and told her that Father had sent me for twenty-five rubles which he needed for the immediate payment of a debt. My good-natured sister suspected nothing and gave me the money without a word. From my sister I went to Reuben the drayman and told him to have a cart ready early next morning—not too early, but about the time when my mother would be at morning services, and my younger brothers sleeping. My older brother, Meyer, was away in the woods. My plan was perfect, and worked like a dream. As for the money I had fooled out of my sister, I refused to regard it a theft. But neither was it aboveboard. In any case, there was no turning back now.

This was not the only thing on my conscience. I was running away from home. In this wise, probably, Jacob planned his flight from Esau and his flight from Laban the Syrian: he stole away from them. But I was stealing away neither from an Esau nor a Laban, but from my own parents, who loved me heart and soul. Again I comforted myself: I was not *stealing* away, only departing somewhat precipitately. After all, they knew that my heart was set on the kind of education I could not get in Svislovitz; and *I* knew that the event would justify me, that some day my parents would be proud of me and even rejoice that I had gone away without their consent.

In the darkness I put some things together and packed them in a travel-basket. I sat through the night open-eyed till I heard my mother get up and go to the synagogue. A few minutes later, as if he had been a conscious conspirator, Reuben the drayman drew up to the house. I went down into the yard, mounted the cart, and told Reuben to drive me to Osipovitz, the nearest railroad station on the line which led to Minsk, Vilna and Dvinsk.

CHAPTER EIGHTEEN

Wanderings

DVINSK was the first really big city I had ever seen. With its population of 100,000, its seemingly endless streets of stone houses, massive and unshakable, it made me breathless with wonder. Even Beresin, which had made such a prodigious impression on me, was a village by comparison. I walked the streets for hours, drinking in the atmosphere of power and permanence. This was a revolution indeed. The old world had been softer, weaker, more yielding; against this new world axes, hammers and saws would be of no effect: nothing short of bombs and heavy guns could do anything here. The stone walls of the great fortress were a human symbol too; in such a city the people were harder and firmer.

My uncle received me kindly, somewhat surprised at my explanation that my father had been too busy to write. He certainly suspected something, but held his peace. I was at once adopted into the family and given a room to myself. In this large house order reigned; there was nothing like the old haphazard life of my Svislovitz home. We rose at a given hour, the rooms were cleaned at once, the meals were served at fixed times, and there was no deviation from the program. Uncle Meyer was methodical by instinct, and his young wife, Esther, the daughter of my other uncle Meyer, was as exact as he, with an added touch of severity. I suffered at first. This external exactitude and discipline was not to my liking. I longed for the old "freedom." But within a few weeks I was not only well broken in; I conceived an affection for the economies of the regime; I fell in line happily with the other four children of the house.

Two weeks later my father arrived in Dvinsk, and put up at a hotel. It was a principle with him never to stay with relatives —not even with his children. He had other strict principles of that kind, which he tried to inculcate in us. One was: "Never bargain with a workingman. If you go into a store you may bargain as much as you like with the merchant. He is a merchant and did not make the goods; he only deals in them. But a workingman has put his own body into the thing. Therefore go, when you need, to an honest workingman, and do not argue the price with him." Nor do I remember a single occasion on which my father, who bargained frequently enough on the sale and purchase of timber, ever argued with a workingman. He told us further: "Never buy secondhand things, even if they look whole. All old things must sooner or later get holes in them; it may be that the thing you are buying is just ripe for the first hole, but doesn't show it yet. Don't look for bargains and you will never be fooled."

There was no scene between my father and me. He did not even reproach me; indeed, he treated me with great kindness, and this, I do not doubt, I owed to Uncle Meyer, who had written him immediately after my arrival and had persuaded him to let me study for the *Realschule*. Nor do I doubt that the turn of events had not displeased my father. He had never been too certain that he wanted me to be a merchant. He had four other sons who would follow in his footsteps; was it perhaps not better that I, more gifted than they, should tread a new path? I was amazed and delighted by the smoothness with which everything went off. My father only told me that my mother was unhappy, and I promised to write her often.

My cousin Gershon was far in advance of me in his studies; he had been receiving systematic instruction in Russian and other subjects. His teacher, a young student in the upper classes of the *Realschule*, was assigned to me; his name was Friedland, and he was remotely related to the great Friedlands who played much the same role in Dvinsk as the Seldoviches in Beresin. On first examination he declared me raw material, and it was his opinion I would need two years before I could enter the third class in the *Realschule*—and by then I would be too old for the third class.

Fortunately my teacher miscalculated. I was raw material, it was true, in secular studies. But I already had the mind of a man, ripened by a complete Jewish education and sharpened in the best of schools. Nor did my teacher know that this sharpened mind was seconded by an iron will. One incident will illustrate to what extent he had miscalculated. In the fourth month of my studies I took up geography. I argued that geography could not be more difficult than the Talmud, and I sat down to the subject as I had once sat down to the Talmud. I studied solidly through three nights. On the fourth day I came to my teacher and told him I had completed the year's work in geography. He looked at me incredulously and picked up the book. He examined me page by page and discovered that I had simply learned the book by heart. He was dumbfounded. He had never been a Talmud student, and had never been a witness of these feats.

But this was simply a *tour de force*. I had crammed the stuff into myself. Cramming is good for geese immediately before the slaughter and for students immediately before examinations. And in fact when examination time came around I had to learn my geography all over again. But in other subjects I made substantial progress. In three months I had caught up with my cousin, in another month had passed him. Arithmetic and algebra I learned not by memorizing rules, but by analyzing the laws and principles. My teacher informed my uncle that he needed only one year to prepare me in mathematics for the fifth year in the *Realschule*. With some pressure he could bring my German and history up to the same standard. There remained the miserable question of Russian.

Here neither logic nor hard work helped. A language is an organism. To digest it one must, paradoxically, be swallowed up by it, and one cannot be swallowed up by one language when one lives continuously in the atmosphere of another. I could not enter into the spirit of the language. In the house we spoke Yiddish, the subjects of our conversation had no relation to the material which through centuries had built up the Russian language. My teacher worked hard with me, we read the best books, and it was all of no avail. There was but one solution to the problem, a radical solution: to place me in a home where Russian was the natural language. But this solution was unthinkable; never would I be put into a world where I might become alienated from a full Jewish life.

And thus I, as an individual, went through the long torment that millions of Jews have endured, through the generations, when hunger and destiny drove them from one land to another and compelled them to adapt themselves, in various parts of the world, to new languages and new cultures. Every Jewish history is filled with stories of persecution, oppression and massacre. Little has been written of the inner sufferings, the spiritual torments, that accompanied the passage of a people from one language to another. If the mental energies the Jews have expended in forgetting old languages and learning new ones could have been harnessed to some more useful end, they might have sufficed to build whole worlds.

I had no inner compulsion toward the Russian language. I had never felt that Hebrew, the language with which every fiber of my being was organically bound up, was too narrow for my spiritual needs. I could have imagined myself the child of a normal people, living in a land of its own, speaking in a normal way its own language. I might then have wanted to learn Russian, or German, or French—but as foreign languages. I would not have felt that a perfect knowledge of them was a matter of life and death, that I had to transfer myself to them completely, bend my soul to their will, empty myself of my old way of thinking and fill myself with *their* inherited turns of mind.

I yielded. I abandoned, for the year I stayed in Dvinsk, my Hebrew studies. I kept a teacher for Talmud, but he came for an hour a day, and even that hour was little more than a sop to my conscience. I knew that I was committing a crime against my authentic "I." I was turning my back on it, and I asked its forgiveness, promising that the separation, dictated by dire necessity, would be a brief one; I would return to it with the original love, and more. "For I have betrothed thee unto me for ever: I have betrothed thee unto me in lovingkindness and in mercy."

I gave up my Hebrew, and even my interest in the Jewish problem and the fate of my people. I made no friends and spent little time with those I already had. And yet my progress was slow and painful. My teacher decided that I was gifted only in mathematics; for languages I had no talent whatsoever. But he consoled me; he had had other pupils as slow as I, and they had managed by sheer effort to break through in the end.

I lived the life of a hermit, fastened to my books. The Sabbath was my one day of rest. Early every morning Uncle Meyer would leave for the fortress, where he was busy with the erection of new buildings, but on the Sabbath he would accompany us to the synagogue, which stood in the courtyard of the

Friedlands, the great contractors who employed my uncle. The Friedlands were a widely ramified family; the heads had settled in St. Petersburg, but some of the children lived in Dvinsk. I have compared the Friedlands of Dvinsk with the Seldoviches of Beresin, but the comparison is limited. Dvinsk was a large city, with Chassidim and Misnagdim and several rabbis. It was impossible for a single family to dominate the community completely. Besides, there were other rich Jews, who had their say in communal affairs. Still, the Friedlands did tower above them in wealth and influence, setting the tone of Jewish life.

In the Friedland synagogue I became acquainted with part of the modernist Hebrew youth, as well as with the older *Maskilim*, the carriers of the Enlightenment. The boys were about my age; like me they had studied much Hebrew and Talmud, and had not yet decided what they were going to do with themselves. Though Dvinsk was a big city with a distinct European atmosphere, its Jews had not yet caught up with the practice of giving a modern education to the young generation; and so the average boy, unless he was sent away to a yeshivah or harnessed to business, was condemned to idleness in the most productive years of his life. These young idlers went under the general name of "children of good family," which meant that they did nothing but wait till they were ripe for marriage; then after marriage they would have to find some sort of occupation. They were a strange lot, completely devoid of the happiness of youth. Almost every one of them complained that he did not know what to do with his free time—a dolorous affliction which rose out of the depths of the wretched life of exile.

I labored in vain. The month of August drew near, the time for the entrance examination, and my teacher declared himself against taking any risks. He feared that neither Gershon nor I would pass and he advised strongly that we wait another year and try to make a higher class. Gershon was short on mathematics, I on Russian.

It was a heavy blow. I had not the endurance for another year of preparation. Besides, my stay in my uncle's home had become unpleasant. His wife, my cousin Esther, was gradually developing into a *grande dame*, with a taste for rule and, what was worse, pretentions to Russian culture. As soon as the bad news broke, I decided to look for an easier approach to my goal. I had no plan; I was only confident in an obscure way of being able to crawl out of the uncertain situation.

I acted now with the independence of an adult, consulting neither my uncle Meyer, nor my teacher, nor my parents. I decided first to try my luck in Vilna, at the Jewish Teachers' Institute which had been founded by the Russian government. It was not a wholehearted decision. The institute had only one purpose: the steady production of rabbis who would lead the Jewish masses in the right direction, namely, in accordance with the wishes of the government. The Jewish masses disliked the Institute and the rabbis it manufactured; they knew that the government was following consistently one deep and unalterable plan: the destruction of everything that was Jewish; and these newfangled rabbis were another blow at the integrity of the Jewish people. Against my inclinations I decided to try and enroll at the Vilna Institute because I revolted from the idea of returning to Svislovitz without anything to show for my year in Dvinsk.

I had no relatives in Vilna. I stayed in a hotel and for two lonely days I tramped the streets, admiring the great houses and the great shops and approaching no one. I learned for the first time the curious feeling of loneliness which belongs to the big cities. It seemed incredible to me that among these thousands and thousands of people there should be not one who cared about my fate.

By the third day I had prepared my application to the principal of the Teachers' Institute. I had learned the formula before leaving Dvinsk, but I was greatly exercised by the question whether I ought to address the principal as "Your Excellency" or as "Your High-Born." After much reflection I chose the higher title, feeling it was safer to err on the side of generosity. I wrote and rewrote the letter a dozen times, perfected each phrase and improved the writing until I was completely satisfied. Then I went off to the Institute.

Like the provincial I was, I came an hour early, and so I walked about the garden and the neat quandrangle of the Institute. The buildings were not particularly imposing, but I was impressed by the people who came and went: they looked dignified and important. The teachers were all distinguished by their special governmental uniforms, but what puzzled me was that while all of them wore the same uniform some of them had no badges on their caps. I stopped one of the students and asked him what this meant. He told me that the teachers without badges were Jews. The badge was the symbol of full civil service status. The most unimportant Christian official wore the badge, the most important Jewish official, the examiner, was without it.

At twelve o'clock I stood before the principal in the reception room. He was a middle-aged, distinguished-looking man. My letter of application lay before him, and while he read it he kept lifting his eyes to me, as if to compare the contents of the letter with the man who had prepared it. When he had finished he treated me to a lecture on the importance of knowing the Russian language thoroughly and he began to point out all the errors, many of them gross ones, in my letter. Then he said that he could have passed over the errors if not for one which made it evident that I was not only ignorant of the language but alien to its spirit. I had wanted to say, "I place my application before you," meaning "I submit my application" but I had used for the word "place" a variant which had a different connotation—that of placing a dish on a table or a ladder against the wall. And that was my undoing. Mistakes of orthography or grammar, said the principal, were not fatal, but this lack of *feeling* for the language ruled me out. I left the room defeated, carrying with me the application that had betrayed me.

Again the Russian language had blocked my entry into the world of learning. It stood before me like the seraph with the flaming sword turning in all directions before the gates of Eden. And my misery was the more profound because it seemed to me that I had been defeated by a single word: by less than a word, by a participle. Had I written "*pred*" instead of "*pri*" my whole future would have been different. What? Could a man's fate be decided by a single participle even in the modern world? Why, then, did they criticize our Jewish laws for their fine distinctions and fateful niceties? Why had our great poet, the satirist Judah Leib Gordon, written with such gusto the story of two lives that had been wrecked because the obstinate orthodox authorities had refused to pass over the miswriting of the tiny letter *yod* in a bill of divorce? Was the modern world he admired any better?

I returned to Svislovitz, a failure, broken in spirit. All my plans, all my dreams, had come to nothing; my proud demands ended in the familiar, wearisome monotonous life of an obscure village.

The life of Svislovitz flowed round me as of old, but now it was thinner and duller than ever. It was a tiny trickling streamlet, and I had looked on the mighty rivers which roll down to the ocean. I had nothing to show for Dvinsk, and I was ashamed to tell about Vilna.

My mother said she did not recognize me, and again she began urging me to give up my dreams of a secular education and return to the Talmud. Perhaps, she argued, this obstinate resistance of the Russian language was not mere accident: God was standing guard over me, He wanted me to achieve greatness only among my own people, His children. But my father, who for all his severe and formal exterior, understood his children well, refused to throw the weight of his authority in the balance. Thus, at a critical moment in my life, I had to fall back on myself. Unable to enter on a rabbinical career, unwilling to follow that of a merchant, I finally pulled myself together and decided to make another assault on the Russian language.

Perhaps Shneur, the *Rav*'s son, had something to do with it. He had been a brilliant Jewish student, able, gifted and industrious to a degree. Yet he was wholly untrained for the world. He was good at everything—and good at nothing. He might become a merchant, he might become a teacher—and he would be an all-round failure. But apart from being a warning example, Shneur undertook to become an active influence. He was a first-class Hebraist, with a profound love of the Prophets, whom, however, he scrutinized in the spirit of a historian. He had undoubtedly developed his views from books which he would not let me see—probably German books of the Higher Criticism. Very cautiously he breathed into me this spirit, of which I was then wholly innocent. I stood firm on the old traditional grounds: when one and the same prophet spoke as a contemporary of Sennacherib, King of Assyria, and of Cyrus, King of the Medes and Persians, I refused to ask questions, though I knew quite well that the two monarchs were separated by a gap of centuries. When King David, who was the undoubted author of the Psalms, sang of the captives by the waters of Babylon, I only marvelled at the divine gift of the royal singer who could foresee events that were to take place hundreds of years later. I was firmly convinced that King Solomon had composed both the Song of Songs and Ecclesiastes. The differences in language did not trouble me. Had not the sages of old declared that when Solomon was young he had sung of life, and when he was old he had pondered on its vanities?

This naïve faith, Shneur, the *Rav*'s son, undermined in me. He approached his task gently, carefully, like a skilled proselytizer. He began by bringing to my attention passages in the Talmud and in subsequent rabbinic literature from which it was clear that even our sages had entertained somewhat freer views regarding the individual authors of the Bible. Step by step Shneur became more open and insistent, his criticisms became sharper and more far-reaching. I would not budge at first, and answered him with orthodox arguments on every point; but as he had logic on his side, and I only repetition, he overcame me. I began to look more closely and more curiously at the criticisms. I felt something in me undergoing painful dissolution; a deep loss was about to occur. Yet the transitional stage did not last long, and in fact I soon convinced myself that I was losing nothing. On the contrary, I was gaining something.

I remained in Svislovitz some three months, and it was in my backward and forlorn village, of all places, that I got my first touch of modern scepticism. I lost my childish and naïve faith; but there was created in me a new and firmer citadel. There unrolled before me something I had never perceived before: the long *perspective* of the Bible. It expanded before me. I stood in the presence of a gigantic structure to which one generation after another had contributed its row of stones. The heavens came down a little lower for me, but the earth was lifted in proportion. Fewer miracles descended from heaven, but greater glories went up from the earth. My new outlook on the Bible taught me a new relationship between heaven and earth. I understood more deeply the significance of the passage in the greatest of poets: "Give ear, O heavens, and I will speak, and let the earth hear the words of my mouth." Heaven alone was not enough; earth too had to bear witness. Let the earth become heavenly and heavens earthly; let the two mingle and be lost in each other, so that "truth may blossom from the earth and justice shine down from the heavens."

But now a deep and unexpected change took place, utterly

amazing to me. When, more than a year earlier, I had torn myself away from that which was my own, my Hebrew, I had felt like a criminal; now I thought I could abandon my Russian without the slightest regret. I was wrong! During these three months of absorption in Bible and Talmud I felt something missing—the Russian book. This was the first sign that a relationship had been established between us, and when I recognized it for what it was I returned decisively to my original plans. I told my parents finally that I would neither enter a yeshivah nor join my father's business. I had made up my mind to renew the attempt in Minsk—but this was really going to be the last gamble. I set everything on this effort and played *va banque*.

This time there was no need to obtain money by a trick. My father, who was very sparing when it came to his own needs, was openhanded when it came to his children. He sent me out with enough money to cover the first few months. My mother, having resigned herself, prepared me for the journey by baking and roasting food for several days, as though I were going into a wilderness. And I left Svislovitz, the second time, accompanied by the blessing of my parents and the good wishes of all my friends.

CHAPTER NINETEEN

Minsk

MINSK is today the capital of the White Russian Republic. In my time it was a Russian town, with all the peculiarities and attributes of a provincial cultural center. There was a classic *gymnaziya*, a *gymnaziya* for girls, a *Realschule*, and a Greek Orthodox theological seminary. But when I say that Minsk was a Russian town I speak only of the dominant Russian forces. In population Minsk was more Jewish than Russian, a city filled with scholars and *Maskilim*, great *yeshivoth* and famous rabbis. Yet here the tendencies among the upper classes were distinctly Russian. The young generation was set on a Russian education, Russian literature occupied the first rank, the Russian language had worked its way deeply into the Jewish upper classes.

I began in Minsk to swim with the stream that led to cultural assimilation, and that stream was wide and powerful. And it would be well to correct here an impression that is as universal as it is false. Almost every Jew believes that the cultural assimilation of his people was strong only in western Europe, while we, the Jews of eastern Europe remained unaffected.

This is altogether inaccurate. We came to this stage later than the Jews of western Europe, but when we reached it our participation was no less decisive. The youth among the upper classes threw itself upon Russian literature with all the fury of its famished desire for education, and the same passion awoke in great numbers of the lower classes.

There were young people whose lives were a profound tragedy. They were wretchedly poor, and lived in dire and unrelenting need. Many of them went along for months on a diet of dry bread, cheap cheese and tea; a piece of herring was a red-letter occasion. Even after the spiritual revolution had swept them from their old moorings they were constitutionally the same yeshivah boys, the same ascetics, holding body and soul together with a minimum of nourishment. From one point of view I pitied them; from another I regarded them as heroes, and envied them their hardness against themselves. I saw in them a higher type than myself, created for higher purposes. I was simple flesh and blood: they were steel.

When I became more intimate with them—and I was drawn toward them more than toward any others—I discovered that at least in one respect we were alike; we shared the same misfortune. For them, as for me, the great obstacle was the Russian language. Most of them had sat twice for their entrance examinations and had twice failed. Looking on them, I made a resolution that for the six months which preceded the examination I would not speak a word of Yiddish, I would not look into a Hebrew book. It was a heroic decision. But I could not carry it out.

Because of my numerous relatives, as well as because of my father's reputation among the timber merchants, I was soon thoroughly at home in Minsk. And it was here that I developed a talent that I had never before had a chance to test: I made my first public speeches.

The *Chibath Zion* movement was at that time—the early eighties of the last century—in its swaddling clothes. It had taken hold of small, picked circles, mostly of *Maskilim.* The normally orthodox elements were at first passive to the movement, the more extreme orthodox hostile. The latter felt vaguely, but strongly, that the movement was motivated by a rebellion, a protest against the destiny of the Jewish people, and against the divine power which had imposed that destiny. Such a protest was next door to atheism.

The hostility of the rich Jews rose from an instinctive fear of all radical and revolutionary tendencies. They were concerned with their own status quo, and the prospect of a change terrified them. As for the Jewish masses, they had as yet been little affected either by general political ideas or by those of the *Chibath Zion* movement. There were left, as the only ready proselytes, the Hebraist modernizers, the *Maskilim.*

Despite my youth I soon acquired a reputation as a young *Maskil*, and the doors of the small circle of the elect were opened to me. I was admitted as a full-fledged member, and all the secret hopes and dreams of the *Maskilim*, those that they dared not parade openly, were uncovered to me. There was no formal and regular organization. There was no central office, no central program. There were just groups, each with its own methods and program. Interestingly enough, the *Chibath Zion* movement in Minsk began first with pure "territorialism"—a home for the Jews in any territory that could be acquired. It was only under the influence of Perez Smolenskin that it swung round and fixed upon Palestine as its unalterable goal. The same evolution characterized, later, the Zionist development of Leo Pinsker and Theodore Herzl. But the change had taken place by the time I joined the group and I never once heard serious mention of any territory for the Jews other than Palestine.

We used to meet several evenings a week, mostly in the house of Joshua Benenson, who was widely known for his hospitality, and who used to sing duets with his daughter Leah, the fiancée of one of the young men of the *Bilu*, the first group of pioneers to leave modern Europe and colonize Palestine. We used to do a lot of singing, but we used to speak more, and argue most. The main themes of our discussion were nationalism and assimilation, and we were agreed that nationalism was the only possibility, while assimilation was to be crushed mercilessly. We differed, however, as to the weapons. Some held that the most sensible plan would be to argue it out with the assimilationists, show them clearly that their ideal was an impossible one, that an entire people could not assimilate; whence it would follow that they were impractical Utopians. Others were for a general assault on the moral front, exposing the baseness of the philosophy of assimilation. A third party believed in ignoring the assimilationists altogether, letting their movement run its course to the inevitable, disastrous end.

As a singer I was not a success, and if I ever asserted myself during the musical part of the evening's program I was gently advised to listen attentively. But when the discussions began I opened up. I was not content with the usual phrases, I had to deliver an entire speech, full of passion and invective. I would forget that I was in the midst of my comrades and that my fury was wasted. I could not speak calmly on the subject of assimilation, for it was as if the word evoked the enemy and he stood before me. There they were, the assimilationists, the cowards, the renegades; before I could proceed with the address proper I had to let them have theirs. So much for the exordium; after it I came to the point: *how* to combat assimilation. But it was my exordium that was most effective, and it took up two-thirds of my address. No one ever protested against my procedure; on the contrary, I remarked that I made a distinct impression even on my older friends. Before long I was, in that circle, an acknowledged speaker, and recognition soon took the form of an important assignment; I was to address a propaganda meeting in one of the larger synagogues.

I remember that I accepted the assignment without a tremor. I had only one worry: I wanted my *thoughts* to follow logically on one another; I wanted them to be strung like beads on a thread. If only my thoughts followed one another, I knew I would find the words.

My first public appearance was a great event in my life, and it occupies an important place in my memories. Two speakers preceded me. The first, I thought, used too many literary and oratorical clichés; his phrases were artificial and had something of the boudoir about them. The second was more solid and more logical; his difficulty was that the words came too slowly; they had neither fire nor force, and seemed to be frozen on his tongue. When my turn came I did not introduce myself or the subject, but plunged straight into the argument, and at once I was aware of two things. It seemed to me that the audience had an active relationship to me; it was on the alert, anxious to catch my words and even to help me get them out. Second, I had the feeling that not I spoke, but another. *He* spoke, *I* controlled him, I guided him, so that he might not let fall the thread of his thoughts. The audience signified its approval by applause, but my gratitude was not for the applause; it was for the spirit of cooperation; and I was grateful to that other self who had spoken from within me, and who had proved so tractable to my control.

This first experience of mine in the Minsk synagogue set its stamp on my destiny as a public speaker. I was not intoxicated by my success with the audience, nor exhilarated by the compliments of my friends; I simply felt that on the platform I had found my element. I did not have to exert myself; my thoughts were born of themselves and emerged completely robed in words. And I easily worked out for myself the first rule: before I mounted the platform I was not to think about words, only about thoughts; the words would come of themselves. I saw that the "what" was more important than the "how," for as far as the "what" was concerned, I was my own master, but the "how" was in God's hands, and I had no power over it. Later, as I became a more practiced speaker, I worked out other rules. Until this day I have not read a single book on the art of public speaking, and the rules I have worked out have nothing to do with the manner of speaking; they are concerned with the construction of the speech, with the architecture, not the phraseology. What I desired most was to remain myself; what I feared most was to slip into the stereotyped manner and become someone else.

I have two subsidiary rules on the structure of a speech; if you have lost one of your thoughts during the course of the speech, do not return to look for it. Second, make a definite mark where you want to stop. Ecclesiastes says: "Better is the end of a thing than the beginning thereof." Woe to the speaker who cannot cut his speech short where he intended. He approaches the close, hesitates, loses control, and turns into a verbal ruminant, chewing the same words over and over again helplessly. The spectacle is not pleasing to the audience and it is less pleasing to the speaker.

The *Realschule* of Minsk, for which I was preparing, had at that time no lower classes. It began with the fifth year. The majority of my friends were preparing for this school instead of for the *gymnaziya;* like me, they were afraid of the classic languages. We had found the battle with Russian difficult enough; to tackle, on top of that, the Slavonic mother language, with its harsh sounds and its marvelously complicated grammar, was unthinkable.

There were forty Jewish students preparing that year for the *Realschule*. The number of Christian students was smaller, and of these the majority were children of the Polish magnates. They never became friendly with us; they considered themselves our superiors because they knew that the first vacancies belonged to them, and we would divide among ourselves those that were left. This was not yet the formal law of the land, for the liberal decrees of Alexander II were still on the statute books. But the oral law, as is usually the case, had already taken precedence over the written law: the principals of all the high schools and the rectors of all the universities had been circularized "unofficially" pending the formulations of the new laws.

At that time we used to pray that as many Christians as possible might flunk even the easy examinations prepared for them —then more places would be left for us. Later, when the *numerus clausus* was introduced—so many Jewish students for every hundred Christian students—we used to pray that as many Christian students as possible might be admitted. Then, more than once, a wealthy Jew would collect ten Christian students and prepare them for the examinations, and pay their fees, so as to create one place for his own son in the government school.

My chances were considered weak because of my Russian. Neither my own resolutions nor the urging of my comrades could make me take the logical step: give up Yiddish and speak nothing but Russian. I was already finding too much fulfillment and satisfaction in my *Chibath Zion* work. I studied obstinately yet with a sense of futility; but my evenings were happy and consoled me for the days. We used to meet almost every evening and live for a few hours in a purely Palestinian atmosphere. The *Bilus* were already at work in the homeland; letters came regularly from Gederah, the first colony, and they were filled with such joy and enthusiasm, with such colorful descriptions, that we read them over and over again. They described Palestine as an earthly paradise. About the Arabs they told stories that came straight from the *Arabian Nights*. First, they spoke a language which was almost Hebrew; second they admitted freely the right of the Jews to Palestine. In fact, an old sheikh had told a colonist that he knew personally of the imminence of the Messiah. What more could we ask for? I was happy beyond words that I too could play a part—that of the propagandist awakening the Jewish masses—in the great drama. And when I returned from some meeting late in the night, and mounted to my room, the books on my table were reminders of something trivial and meaningless.

The examinations began on a lovely summer day. Two hours before the hall was opened the Jewish students, nervous, noisy, were assembled before the doors. The Christian students came much later and their bearing was calmer—they were more confident of the outcome. The first item of the examination was the writing of a theme, in Russian of course. What the theme was I do not remember, but I know that I began my essay with: "Our sages have said . . ." and followed it with an ingenious quotation from the Talmud. I had forgotten for whom I was writing, I was only anxious to find interesting thoughts, and they came to me from my own world, the Jewish. I remember, too, that I was continuously translating, and with great difficulty, Hebrew thoughts into the Russian language. We had four hours for the writing of the essay. I saw with horror that some of the examinees were through in an hour; they rose radiant, and handed in their papers. And throughout the period students kept leaving, after two hours, after three hours. . . . I remained there till the end of the fourth hour, translating, crossing out, and translating again.

Russian was followed by German, German by mathematics. It happened that the geometry teacher had set a problem which was beyond the limits of the course. Translated into algebraic symbols it emerged as a complicated equation of the second power, and we were not supposed to have prepared solutions of the second power. In this subject we again had four hours, and again most of the students left earlier. I remained till I was alone in the room with the mathematics examiner, and with his assistant Kurilko, who was teacher of mechanics in the *Realschule*. The latter came to my desk and watched over my shoulder. I had covered twenty pages with calculations, but I was happy. I had found a solution which was logically consistent throughout. The mechanics teacher picked up the paper, said "*Otlichno*"—"Excellent"—and made some remarks in a low voice to the principal examiner.

Of the forty Jewish students seven were admitted. I had flunked in no less than three subjects—Russian, geography and history—and yet I was one of the seven. I was a stranger in the town and had no pull. But I learned afterwards that Kurilko had exerted himself strongly in my behalf. Not one of the students had solved the geometry problem. Some had managed to reduce it to a quadratic equation, and had immediately given it up as lying outside the curriculum. I, however, could not hide behind that excuse. There was the problem, and it had to be solved. So I perspired, covered sheet after sheet of paper with experiments and arrived at the solution by the sheer force of logic. Kurilko declared at the council of teachers that he would take me in on his own responsibility.

Who was it came to my rescue in the examination room that day, drove me without mercy to analyze the problem into its simple elements, and build them up again, level by level, in mathematical form? It was not the student of Dvinsk and Minsk, but the *cheder* boy of Svislovitz, whose mind had been trained and sharpened in childhood on Jewish studies. My gratitude went out to my earlier self—and to Kurilko.

During the days that followed the announcement of the results I went about like a man who has drawn the winning number in a big lottery. How was it possible not to believe in pure luck? If the mathematics teacher had not committed a serious error and included a question outside the curriculum, I might never have entered the *Realschule*, and all my development would have followed a different course. Together with my elation there was an element of confusion: pure chance had broken the chain of logical cause and effect—and precisely where logic alone reigns, in mathematics! What could have been more paradoxical than this juxtaposition?

I came to know Kurilko more intimately during my student years. My first private visit took place when I learned that he had been the man to intercede for me. When I tried to thank him he stopped me abruptly. "What I did was purely in the line of duty." I felt that this was not mere courtesy. He was, in fact, the most severe of teachers and the most just—and for that reason the best-beloved. He was a mathematician in every fiber of his being; nature seemed to have designed him mathematically, too, for he was all straight lines and angles. He demanded two things of his students: industry and exactitude. "In mathematics," he would repeat, "a dot plays a more important role than anywhere else in life."

A totally different type was Alexandrov, who taught Russian language and literature. He was a native of Moscow, and in the Minsk *Realschule*, where eighty percent of the students were Poles and Jews, he felt himself in an alien atmosphere. He did not like the homely, provincial Russian that even the remaining twenty percent spoke. He suffered much from his Russian students, more from his Jewish students, but most from his Polish students who seemed to take a national delight in revenging themselves on the grammar of their conquerors.

To me his attitude was friendly, and he listened to the story of my growth sympathetically. But he begged me, above all else, to give up my habit of beginning every essay with: "Our sages say . . ." followed by a quotation from the Talmud. "After all, Levin," he said, "I am a Russian teacher. What do I care what *your* sages say? Haven't we sages of our own?" Poor man! He did not realize that I had the same complaint to make. What did *I* care about *his* sages?

We came across little anti-Semitism in the conduct of the school. Nor would it have been easy for the teachers to be consistently anti-Semitic and retain their self-respect as teachers. The best students were Jews; in my class there was a sort of conspiracy that no gentile student should ever be permitted to enter the *minyan* (group of ten) at the top. Even in the Russian language the Jewish students led. Their form was weaker than that of the Russian students, but the contents of their essays were infinitely more substantial. I ought to say, however, that the competition was weak. The Russian students were mediocre, and the children of the Polish farmers had not the slightest chance when pitted against former yeshivah students.

One more teacher should be remembered in this story: Ossip Hurwitz, the religious instructor. In the Russian schools there were always men appointed by the government to look after the welfare of young souls and instill in them the fear of God which would make them better citizens. I do not know how successful the government was with its Greek Orthodox and Catholic priests, but with its Jewish religious teachers it achieved the opposite of its purpose. The religious books given us were as dull as multiplication tables, and the teacher, a graduate of the former governmental rabbinical seminary, which had been replaced by the Vilna Teacher's Institute, was steeped in the spirit of assimilation. After the majority of us had spent years in the study of Bible and Talmud it was ludicrous to expose us to the wisdom of a shallow teacher and to texts that consisted of silly questions and sillier answers, most of them detached and badly translated verses that we knew thoroughly in the original. But the Russian government believed it was displaying a commendable generosity in allowing the Jewish students a religious instructor of their own. The action even smacked of equality. The teacher was, of course, supported by the Jews; his salary came out of the kosher meat tax. And of course it would have been going too far to put the Jewish religious instructor on the same level as the Catholic and Orthodox priests. *He* was not a government official; he was merely an employee, a servant of the government paid for by the Jews.

Ossip Hurwitz, or, as we called him, Father Hurwitz, was a well-educated man, even in the Jewish field, particularly from German sources. But he was of the old type of government official. He served the government first, and then the Jewish people, and he was touchingly anxious to stand in well with his superiors. It goes without saying that no intimacy or friendliness ever sprang up between him and us.

The Russian government stood, at that time, before an insoluble problem. It wanted to educate and to suppress the youth at one and the same time. Remarkably enough, the government seemed to know that the educated youth was bound to develop in the wrong direction, and what was true of the student youth generally was doubly true of the Jewish sector, which was Semitic, and alien to the Russian spirit, and had the impudence to regard itself as part of an oppressed nation.

In the villages, where the vast majority of the Russian people lived in a half-primitive stage of civilization, bound to the soil and to unremitting labor, the task of the government was easier. It simply turned the schools over to the Church, and the village priest, almost always a man of little education, was about the best instrument the government could have found. But in the cities the priests were not good enough, and the secular teachers could not be trusted. They were busy men; with the best intentions, they could only answer for their students during school hours. But what of the evenings? What of the free days?

To take care of these periods the government instituted, in all its secondary schools, a special police. The official name was: "Assistant Class Educators." These men had no relationship to education in any sense of the term. They were ignorant and incapable, the sweepings of the educational system. They had a double duty. During school hours they were an open police; after school hours, in the streets, or in the homes of the students, which they often honored with unexpected visits, they were nothing more nor less than spies. Ostensibly they came to help the student with his homework; actually they were on the lookout for forbidden books, and in their conversations they would throw out innocent feelers on the life of the students outside of school, their habits, the company they kept, and so on.

In the eighties of the last century the Socialist movement in Russia was in the embryonic stage, particularly among the Jews. There was as yet no clear line of demarcation between Marxists and Social Revolutionaries, and the war between the two philosophies had not yet broken out. A Socialist, in those days, was roughly one who was dissatisfied with things as they were. The government, tyrannical toward all its subjects, was murderously inclined toward the Jews. Its vices and deficiencies cried out to heaven, and by its actions it provoked and strengthened the spirit before which it trembled. To the Jewish youth, educated in the Prophets and in the later classic writings, the Socialist movement had a special appeal. Those who had learned the Bible, and knew almost by heart the famous passage in the First Book of Samuel: "This will be the manner of a king," were hardly likely to be shocked even by the sharpest criticism directed against a crowned head; and they were equally familiar with the scorn which the Prophets had poured out on the rich. Apart from this, the Jewish youth had reasons enough of its own to long for the overthrow of a government committed to the shameless persecution of its people.

Among the Jewish students a struggle went on between the Socialists and the Zionists—this term is an anticipation, for the word was not yet coined—with myself as spokesman of the latter. My chief opponents were the students Seideman and Dugovsky. Both had become assimilated down to the marrow —that is, they had not the remotest interest in the affairs and problems of the Jewish people, and they were not at all aware of the vehemence of their new Russian nationalism. Both were under the closest surveillance of the "Assistant Class Educators," Seideman having been compelled to live with one of them—a severe penalty. More than twenty years later, in 1905, I met Dugovsky again, when he was released from the Schlusselberg fortress, where he had passed five years in solitary confinement. I do not know how it was, but we were friendlier than in 1884. I know that I had not become more Russian; it is possible that he had become more Jewish.

Some of my schoolmates could not make up their minds whether to stand with Seideman and Dugovsky or with me. They belonged to the type which fears decisions—in the Yiddish folk-phrase they are "guests at all weddings." Driven by the zeal of the missionary I exerted myself to win these neutrals over, and to that end even founded a "Neutrals' Club," consisting of some fifteen students. We used to meet once a week, making the rounds of our homes. We would read papers on the burning questions of the day and follow up with discussions. The meetings had to be secret, and in particular we were afraid of the school police. I must admit that from my point of view the Neutrals' Club was not a great success, but I obtained valuable practice in two important activities. I had to prepare most of the papers, and to that end read a great deal in the literature of our antagonists; and whenever I prepared a paper I did not read it, but learned it by heart.

I was not content with my work among students. Seideman and Dugovsky had organized groups of yeshivah students and of young artisans—the Jewish type of factory worker was practically unknown at that time—and carried on an educational campaign. They taught these groups Russian, history and geography, and discussed social problems with them. The *Choveve Zion* organized similar groups for their purposes, and three of them were entrusted to me. The Socialists always conducted their lectures in Russian, though it would have been infinitely easier for them to convince their hearers in Yiddish; but they had a double objective: they were teaching Socialism and they were combatting Jewish culture. Thus they made it appear that a lofty ideal like Socialism cannot be explained in Yiddish. We, in response, were compelled to conduct our courses in Russian, too. I remember how fantastic the whole business looked: I, among my old friends, the yeshivah students, and among plain, everyday Jews, tormenting myself and them with a language that was not natural to any of us.

I need hardly say that if the police had broken in on one of our meetings they would have arrested everyone present. At the trial it would not have been easy to explain to the local authorities what we had been talking about. They were not up to such wild and complicated questions, and could never have decided whether this fantastic "love of Zion" was legal or illegal. In any case all meetings, even of a private character, had to have a permit. It was much easier to get into a Russian prison than out of it; first would come the arrest and the presumption of guilt; then, while you remained in jail, the higher officials would slowly and laboriously disentangle the philosophy of Zionism and what punishment should attend the spread of it. There was current in the Russia of that time an anecdote illustrating the general police policy. In a certain town the chief of police issued an order that all hares should have their left ears cut off. Why hares, and why the left ear, we did not know—such was the fable. The Jews were terrified by the decree and declared a communal fast: any police officer might catch you on the street and cut off your left ear—after which you might proceed to prove to him and to his superiors that you were not a hare.

CHAPTER
TWENTY

Ruler and Inquisitor

THE NOMINAL ruler of Russia in those years was Alexander III, but the power was concentrated in the hands of its evil genius, the learned and reactionary Inquisitor—so he was called by the educated classes—Constantine Pobedonostsev, former professor of civic law at the University of Moscow, and for many decades Chief Procurator of the Holy Synod. Pobedonostsev directed, without control or criticism, the spiritual and mental evolution of the greatest people in Europe, numbering at that time over a hundred million. By his consistent policies he undermined the creative energies of the Russian people, broke its morale and brought it to the verge of collapse. The historian who undertakes to review the latest developments in Russian history will have to devote more space to Pobedonostsev than to any of his contemporaries; it will become evident that he was the embodiment of the destructive forces of Russia, the first among the band of scoundrels and fanatics who were responsible for the ruin of that country. The Rasputins and Iliodors who followed him found a ready and responsive field for their activities: the preparations had been made by their great model. A foul odor of corruption and oppression went up from every corner of the land.

Pobedonostsev hated all the foreign elements in Russia, but his hatred of the Jews was frantic. He hated them on national grounds and on religious grounds. He had worked out a plan, which he later made public, for the solution of Russia's Jewish problem. Conditions had to be created, he said, in which one-third of the Jewish people would perish, one-third would have to migrate, and one-third would be swallowed up in the Russian people. In its naked brutality this plan is reminiscent of one of the darkest passages in the Prophets: "And thou, son of man, take thee a sharp knife, take thee a barber's razor, and cause it to pass upon thine head and upon thy beard: then take thee balances to weigh, and divide the hair. Thou shalt burn with fire a third part . . . and thou shalt take a third part and smite about it with a knife; and a third part thou shalt scatter in the wind."

For the Jews of Russia there set in again a true medieval era —a new edition, improved by modern ingenuities. Every day brought new decrees and new discriminations. And yet the government was at a loss as to its strategy. All nationalist movements were put down by an iron hand, but with regard to the Jews what the government wanted was to stimulate emigration, and emigration automatically augmented the nationalism of the Jews who remained. On the other hand, the government was occasionally tempted to make a partial exception in favor of Jewish nationalism in the hope that the Jewish youth, absorbed in the problems of its own people, would cease to take any interest in the affairs of Russia. This last point was often thrown up to us by our Socialist opponents, and I must admit that we were embarrassed. To have anything in common with the intentions of the government was a shameful thing. But what were we to do? We could not renounce our ideals solely because the Russian government was able to make indirect capital out of them. Indeed, it needed a special variety of moral courage to work for a movement that entailed less danger. But it must also be admitted that many of the Jewish youth did choose the nationalist movement because it was the less dangerous.

Apart from the students, we concentrated our efforts on the shopkeepers, and I was assigned to a street—actually a narrow alley without a name—lined by the poorest shops. The sun never came that way, except perhaps toward evening, when a dying beam entered briefly as if in conscious pity. In this pent and dark prison the Jewish shopkeepers passed their lives. It was a semi-subterranean world in whose perpetual twilight families were raised, marriages celebrated, and social distinctions established.

In Minsk, as in every other large Jewish city, there were countless such burrows, and the moles that inhabited them lived literally from day to day: the earnings of each day decided the character of the family "dinner." Very often the "shop" consisted of half a barrel of herrings, a few thin loaves of bread, a dozen cheeses, a box of nails and a hunk of soap from which the shopkeeper sliced pieces for a kopek (half a cent) or half a kopek. I have seen with my own eyes a customer enter such a shop, in Minsk and in Svislovitz, and buy a herring for a kopek, and half a kopek's worth of herring-juice, called *lyak*. The herring he wrapped in a piece of paper and for the herring-juice he brought a cup. The *lyak* would be the staple of the family dinner that evening. The mother would add a lot of water and throw in pieces of bread. Among the poorest Jews of Lithuania this was the favorite dish.

I visited almost every shopkeeper in that alley, and from one of them I once received an answer that I have not forgotten till this day. He happened to belong to the "upper" class in his area, which is to say that his entire inventory could have been bought up for three hundred rubles, that is, one hundred and fifty dollars. From the proceeds of this shop he raised a family of five children and according to the standards of the place and time he was a decent and successful citizen with nothing to complain about. His life was perhaps pinched, but it was not beggarly. The man was a halfway *Maskil*, too, and between one sale and another would dip into a Hebrew book.

I was quite certain, before I went to him, that I would meet with little difficulty. I made a frontal attack: no need for tactics here, I thought. First I drew, in the blackest colors, the picture of our exile, dwelling on every detail of the horror and misery of our life. Then, abruptly, I passed to the picture of our future life in Palestine, and evoked a world filled with color, happiness, and the joy of creation. I spoke as if I had just returned from the land flowing with milk and honey; and I wound up with a glorious peroration on the virtues and joys of freedom. But I remarked that my lofty style and fiery phrases were making no impression. This prisoner of the store, this mole of the underworld, who passed all his life among barrels of herrings and boxes of nails, returned a calm, unmoved gaze. His answer was short: "Young man, you are wasting your time. We shall never exchange Europe for Asia."

One meeting well worth a description was held soon after the Kattovitz conference of 1884, when for the first time Eastern and Western Jews, representatives of thirty-five independent *Chibath Zion* groups, met to plan common action. They organized, under the extraordinary name of "The Moses Montefiore Memorial Foundation in the Holy Land," an ostensibly philanthropic instrument which was in fact the beginning of our political activity. The leadership was taken by Dr. Leon Pinsker, whose famous pamphlet, *Auto-Emancipation*, appearing in 1882 in the German language, had made a deep impression on educated Jews. We, the students of Minsk, decided to celebrate the event on a grand scale. We arranged the affair in a brewery belonging to a Jew, and over a thousand people jammed the hall. I no longer remember whether the incident I am about to describe took place before my speech, or in the midst of it, or after it; but I do remember that the meeting had reached its highest point, the faces of the audience were shining with enthusiasm, and the atmosphere was tense. Suddenly, and without any warning, the lamps began to go out. The police had arrived. I and my fellow students were in the greatest danger, for we wore our easily distinguishable uniforms, and the punishment for participation in the meeting would have been expulsion from the school. In the darkness I and a fellow student who was the other speaker were seized by strong hands and thrust toward a doorway which led into the hop cellar of the brewery. No steps led downward from the door, which was swiftly closed behind us; there was only a ladder which stopped abruptly halfway. We hung on to the last rung for an hour or so, and our strength began to give out. Finally, having got rid of the police one way or another, our friends remembered us. They opened the door and brought lights. We then perceived that we had been hanging with our feet a couple of inches from the floor.

In 1886 I was graduated from the Minsk *Realschule*. I did poorly in Russian and German, but for all that I stood near the top of the list. A proud and happy son, I returned to my parents' home in Svislovitz, and there I passed the remaining months of the summer. My time was my own; no examination stood over me with whistling whip. I could read freely, write freely; I could walk again in the fields and forests of my childhood; I could spend hours in the company of my old teacher, Judah Artzer, and of the *Rav*. During these few months I recaptured, for the last time, the spirit of my lost childhood. I felt again, as I have never felt since, the early consciousness of faith. I relived vividly the days when I had believed earnestly, naïvely, that God had created the world for His people

Israel, that the other nations were just generous additions to creation; that were were passing through a period of darkness and tribulation only that we might be purified and attain to the highest level of goodness and piety.

One cloud cast its shadow over that summer—the unsettled problem of my future. My father began once more to speak to me seriously about going into his timber business. He did not compel me, but did everything short of it in his arguments. My mother, now convinced that there was no hope of my becoming a rabbi, joined with him and pleaded with me to remain at home. Even Judah Artzer urged the same advice on me. I spoke of engineering, but Judah believed that as a merchant I would be more certain to turn to my pen than as an engineer whose professional duties absorb all his mental powers.

My father could not be persuaded to send me abroad, and I could not be persuaded to become a businessman. In the end we settled on a temporary compromise. I returned to Minsk and took a post-graduate course in physics. It was a pleasant interval for me. The work was interesting, my teacher was my favorite, Kurilko, and my friends of the *Chibath Zion* were happy to have me back. There was much to do. The movement was at that time on the defensive on several fronts. The periodical *Voskhod*, round which were grouped the foremost spirits of the assimilatory intelligentsia, was now conducting a systematic and sustained campaign against us. *Ha-Zephirah*, which as a Hebrew periodical could not very well advocate assimilation, was negative in its attitude toward us. But the bitterest and most active of our enemies were the heads of the *Chalukah*, that ancient charitable institution which, with its collectors travelling through the communities, had turned Palestine into an old folk's home. For them Palestine was a land reserved exclusively for aging pietists devoted to the study of our sacred lore. The means employed by the agents of the *Chalukah* were unscrupulous: calumny directed against the colonists who were working the land, and against the land itself. It was a war in which poison gas and stink-bombs were used without hesitation or shame.

Meanwhile the work of the arch-anti-Semite Pobedonostsev was bearing fruit. Mine was the last generation of the Jewish student youth to enjoy the benevolence of the old regime. In July, 1887, the government issued a decree for the regulation of the numbers of Jewish students to be admitted to the elementary and secondary schools and the universities. Within the Pale of Settlement, to which most Jews were confined, the percentage of Jewish students was fixed at ten; outside the Pale, at five; in Moscow and St. Petersburg at three. There were far-sighted statesmen like Count Palen who warned the government that it was digging its own grave—that the Jewish student youth, locked out of the Russian schools, would flock to the West and return to Russia as the most dangerous of the opponents of the regime. The warning was ignored, and the prophecy was fulfilled.

The girls' schools were for the time being excluded from the decree—a marvelous repetition of history. "And the king of Egypt spoke to the midwives . . . and he said: When ye do the office of a midwife to the Hebrew women, and set them upon the stools, if it be a son, ye shall kill him; but if it be a daughter, then she shall live."

It must be borne in mind that the Jewish population was almost exclusively urban. The Jews were not admitted to the villages, and even those that had been living there were largely driven out by the decrees of 1882. In certain towns within the Pale of Settlement the Jewish population made up eighty percent of the population. The brutality of the new decree is revealed by these figures: only a tiny fraction of the ablest Jewish competitors could look forward to an education.

The flight of the Jewish student youth to the West had its obstacles. Most of the foreign universities and technical schools would not admit students without the graduation certificate of a secondary school. There arose in Russia a new type of student: the "externe." For the time being the government still permitted students who did not attend the secondary schools to take the examinations. Every year the externe came to the examination, until he had worked himself up to the graduation certificate. Actually, few of these externes ever reached their goal. One who had failed three times in the final examination could not try a fourth time. I have known externes of the age of thirty, still struggling for the certificate which would admit them to a Western university. They were called "the eternal externes," and the anti-Semitic press found them dangerous, as well as comical.

I fell into a mood of deep depression. I foresaw that only a second miracle would open the doors of a Russian university to me, and I had no faith in a second miracle. I felt I was being choked, and I wanted to protest. So I did—through a most illogical act. Without any grounds—that is, official grounds—I came one day to school and asked for my papers. I was one of the best students in the school, and in another four months I would have completed the course. But I could not continue in that oppressive atmosphere. I had no hope of entering one of the higher institutes of education in Russia. For a foreign university the graduation certificate I already held sufficed. I would not wait to be turned down by Russia: I preferred to withdraw of my own free will. This is the revenge of the condemned criminal who will not give the executioner the satisfaction of inflicting the death penalty, but anticipates him by committing suicide.

CHAPTER TWENTY-ONE

Confusions and Folly

BETWEEN the time of my resignation from the Minsk *gymnaziya* and my flight to the West lay a period of confusion and indecision, marked by two incidents: I became a Russian soldier, and I fell in love. My career in the first was brief and unimportant; the effects of the second were lasting; and the two incidents have an accidental geographic connection.

I did not have to join the army. My eyesight was poor, and when I first presented myself at the barracks in Bobruisk, the military headquarters for Svislovitz, the doctor rejected me out of hand. To his amazement I asked him to reconsider. I told him that I wanted to be a soldier at all costs—and I hinted that I would make it worth his while, or that others would do it. I did not explain my motives, for he might never have understood them. In the matter of military service the Russian government did not treat the Jews with niggardliness; on the contrary, it conscripted them lavishly, though always without prospect of promotion. The proportion of Jews serving in the army was considerably higher than was warranted by their ratio to the general population. It did not matter that most

Jews—and for that matter most non-Jews—did their best to evade military service. A certain total had to be made up, and the number was based on the statistics compiled before the time of Jewish emigration. I knew that if I did not serve, someone in Svislovitz would have to take my place, perhaps an only son, the sole wage-earner in the family. I could not tolerate the thought, and by persistence I got the doctor to pass me. It took about three weeks and cost me almost as much as it cost others to keep out.

My military career lasted some four months in all, for my defective eyesight was discovered as soon as we went out on the range. But during my preliminary stay in Bobruisk and my brief period of service I made the acquaintance of the young *Choveve Zion* of Bobruisk, among them Leon Lozinsky and his sister Anna. At my first meeting with Anna I knew that we were meant for each other, and my life, which had been running such an irregular course, seemed suddenly to have acquired its permanent direction and purpose. Before I entered the service I saw her frequently and though neither of us spoke of love, I felt we had reached an understanding. During the months of service I saw her only on leave, but I used to see her younger sister Manya almost daily. The Lozinskys had a provision store in the Bobruisk fortress, and Manya was the manager. I would go in there as often as I could, and though she knew that I did not come for her sake, she received me with all friendliness. I felt vaguely that if I looked lovingly enough at Manya, something of my glances would carry over to Anna in the evening. In these matters I was even younger than my years. It seems that what Anna and I needed was an old-fashioned marriage broker, a *shadchan*.

With my discharge from the army I could see Anna freely again; and now, walking in green fields and under trees in blossom, along paths that led far, far from the city, we spoke of our love. She spoke of it simply and directly, but for me this time of fulfillment evoked all that was dearest and most deeply rooted in me. All the biblical pictures and stories that had been engraved on the tablets of my mind in childhood rose before me, and when I wanted to speak, the verses of the Bible danced on my lips. It seemed to me that whatever I had learned, whatever I had drawn into me, no longer was mine, but belonged to Anna, whom I had sought throughout my life without knowing that I sought her. Often it seemed to me, in the moments when my soul was flooded with happiness, that till then my life had been a dream. It seemed to me that I was surely the first man, Adam, and Anna the first woman, Eve. We were, then, in Paradise, and I was waiting for Eve to pluck the apple from the tree and share it with me. But I wanted no snake to come between us.

Our love would have run a smooth and happy course if, into that early Eden there had not come, not indeed the snake, but the calculations and commonplace interference of an older and more corrupt world. Leon, now my most intimate friend, was content with the bond between me and his sister; so was Manya. But Anna's mother was opposed from the first. A widow, she wanted for her daughter a man who was fully prepared for marriage, a man with an income. I was still a boy; true, a promising boy, with every likelihood of making good if I found the right path. But Anna's mother was practical, and had no use for ifs. Slowly, by pressure and persuasion, she began to win Leon over to her point of view—and he, in turn began to introduce new subjects into our conversation: my personal plans, my prospects—practical matters in no way related to the Song of Songs. Yes, even he, the *Chovev Zion*, who believed that an entire disinherited people could create a new life for itself if it only had the will, turned exceedingly cautious when it came to the question of the individual, that is to say, of me, his closest friend.

I was suddenly confronted with a new world of petty

worries of whose existence I had had no suspicion. I had been, till then, my father's son, lacking nothing that I desired. If I had given thought to the future, it had always been in loftier terms. I had believed that life was to be lived, and everyday questions answered themselves. I still clung to my plan to study abroad, and I took it that there would have to be a waiting time of five years before Anna and I had to consider "practical" things.

And it was here that I committed, for Anna's sake, the betrayal of all my life's purposes as I saw them. I went to my father and asked him to take me into his business. Nothing was said about my reason for this *volte-face*, though my parents knew it and, with a delicacy that awakened my deepest gratitude, refrained from mentioning it. Thus passed the summer and autumn months of 1887, and the winter of 1887-88. The merchants with whom I came in contact did not interest me. Their educational level was very low and I felt myself a stranger amongst them. But business took me to Bobruisk two or three times a week, and there I could see Anna. We no longer met in her home, but in the house of a cousin of hers.

The sacrifice I brought to my love was a false one, and I did not know how dearly I would pay for it. Anna loved me, but she had not the courage to strengthen me against myself and bid me not to yield. I lost my spiritual balance, and with it my self-respect. The dream that I was destined to come to the aid of my unhappy people was now covered as with a mist. It was a miserable winter for me. I had frequent occasion to be in Minsk on business, and there, instead of pursuing my Zionist work, I wasted evenings and nights at the card table. My business affairs drew me into the circle of the gilded youth, into whom card-playing had eaten like a disease. I fell a victim to it, and though after every session I would take an oath to myself, invoking the image of my pious and God-fearing mother, and of my Anna, who loved me with the pure love of a child, I would break my oath at the next invitation. I did not understand until years later how grave the danger had been and till this day I do not know how I saved myself. There is an old legend that when Joseph was tempted by Potiphar's wife, he suddenly saw the picture of his father. Evil pulled him in one direction, the image of his father in the opposite direction, and it was Jacob's image that triumphed. Perhaps I too was saved by my sacred images.

I understood suddenly that my original resolution to study abroad had also been a compromise. I said to myself: "If you are really a *Chovev Zion*, go out and become a pioneer. Take this bitter life upon you; sow, plant, reap; do not hide behind excuses; do not pretend that you wish to be more useful to your people. No one is more useful than the pioneer."

At first I entrusted my new plan only to Anna and her brother Leon. Their responses were strange. Anna was clearly frightened, and though Leon gave me his support, it was not in the capacity of a future brother-in-law. I had become dearer to him as a comrade, but at the expense of my status as the future husband of his sister.

I laid my new resolve before my parents, and again they reacted with moving delicacy. They only asked me to think again and again before I put my resolve into execution. Inwardly my mother even sympathized with me. Had she not dedicated her most secret dreams and prayers to the messianic ideal? How could she have stood in the way? She saw me as one of a countless host of young Jews suddenly seized with the fever of the ideal and streaming toward the sacred city of Jerusalem, in which the Divine Glory receives the prayers of the Jews when they turn their faces to the east. Before long the rumor spread that I was going to Palestine, and I was lifted to a new level among my friends and comrades.

In Minsk, which I continued to visit frequently, I became acquainted with Nachman Syrkin, a young man of about the same age as myself. We were related by marriage; my older brother, Meyer, had married a cousin of his, also a Syrkin, of Minsk. Nachman himself already had an interesting past. First, he had been expelled from the *gymnaziya* of Mohilev, not for lack of ability, but for insolence toward the principal. It was not a personal clash. The principal had made a remark directed at Syrkin's Jewishness, and Syrkin's retort was haughty and defiant. Second, Syrkin had already passed some time in London with a troupe of Jewish actors, and had even manufactured some dramas for the Yiddish stage. He already spoke both as a fiery Socialist and an ardent Jewish nationalist, propagating the synthesis of the two ideals which subsequently became the philosophy of the Labor-Zionist party. Later Syrkin and I were students together in Berlin and shared a room for some time.

In Minsk I also became acquainted with another rising star in the Jewish nationalist movement, Menachem Mendel Ussishkin, who today, after nearly half a century of service, is still one of its leading protagonists. In contrast to Syrkin, Ussishkin never racked his brains for syntheses, for he was never aware of antitheses. He never knew the inner torment of a competition between Jewish nationalism and any other ideal, and his conviction of the rightness of his views was never troubled by a single doubt. As a student in the Moscow *Realschule*, from which he had been graduated in the late seventies, he chose his friends only among Russians, for the Jewish students were all from assimilated homes. Ignorant of the meaning of compromise, he preferred a complete non-Jew to a half-Jew. Later this monolithic unity of his expressed itself in his fight against Yiddish. He formulated his view in a slogan: "Either Russian or Hebrew." When I met Ussishkin I knew at once that this was no ordinary man. His appearance was impressive. He was strongly built, with handsome features and a bearing which expressed the will to command, something Napoleonic, purposeful, and obdurate. Such was the young man with whom I worked, later, for decades, often in a parallel sense, and more often at a sharp angle with him.

My preparations for Palestine absorbed two months. It took several weeks to obtain my passport, and there were the endless farewells with my family in Minsk and Bobruisk, on top of which came the affairs in my honor arranged by the *Chibath Zion* groups. These last were filled with fiery orations in which I was extolled as the hero of the day and an inspiring example to Jewish youth. I wriggled under this torrent of exaggerated praise, for I knew that if it had not been for my unfortunate love affair I would have obtained a visa not for Jaffa, but for Berlin. My leave-taking from Bobruisk, if less uncomfortable, was darker and more oppressive, for my heart told me that I was running a great risk with Anna, but after those festive farewells there was no turning back. My leave-taking from my family went off normally, and my mother begged me to write often and to fill my letters with details of the life in Palestine.

I left Bobruisk by railroad for Gomel, and from Gomel went by boat to Kiev, first on the Saj and then on Grandfather Dnieper—a glorious experience. I understood now why Gogol had dedicated his loveliest prose to the Dnieper, and why it is called the Jordan of Russia. He who travels on this river begins to feel why so many races have loved it to the point of idolatry. Kiev, too, cast a spell on me. It is a city not only physically beautiful but filled with a spirit of graciousness and aristocracy. I stayed there for two weeks, dodging the police, for I had no permit; but it was not for the beauty of Kiev that I risked arrest. I had begun to sober up and to examine my plans more realistically, and the question of what I was to do when I got to Palestine emerged with brutal sharpness. I knew of the harsh trials that our first pioneers had to endure there, despite their first glowing letters, and I hit on the idea of obtaining from the Brodskys, the great flour and sugar magnates of Kiev, an agency in Palestine. It would have been a good idea if the firm had not already had an agent there; but seeing the mighty Brodsky in person (I was given an introduction by Professor Max Mandelstamm, the famous eye-specialist and one of the earliest Zionists) was in itself an experience. The moment I explained what I had come about, Brodsky opened his eyes wide and stared at me as if a freak were sitting before him; and I, forgetting that I had come to ask for a favor, remembering instead that the Brodskys did not agree with the *Chibath Zion* movement, launched into a terrific propaganda speech, in which I furiously denounced the Poliakovs and Günzburgs and all the other wealthy Jewish superpatriots—including by implication the Brodskys—for their toadying attitude toward the government. If I got no agency, I got a great deal of satisfaction from the fulfillment of an old desire—to tell one of these magnates what I thought of them.

I had a disappointment of another kind in Kiev. I sought out the famous Hebrew poet Yehalel—Judah Leib Levin—accounted second only to the great Judah Leib Gordon, and instead of the distinguished figure I had expected, I saw before me a typical Jewish employee, with nothing about him to inform the world that he belonged to a higher type of being. Nor was he very friendly, though I considered myself a fellow poet, and was a passionate admirer of his writings.

From Kiev I went to Ekaterinoslav, where I spent some time with my brother Meyer, and there I received a letter from my father, who was then in Kherson. His business was in a critical condition. He had bought up a large forest, larger than he should have tried to handle by himself and for the first time in his life had fallen into the hands of moneylenders. He had no recourse at the moment but to try and renew his notes, wholly or in part. There was no talk of bankruptcy, his assets were more than enough to cover his liabilities, but he needed time. My father suffered; he hated to have another man's kopek in his purse. He was undecided as to the course he ought to follow. If, as he wrote to me, he extended only part of his notes, he might find himself short of capital for the transaction. It would cost him an effort to renew all of the notes, though he was sure that within two years he could pay off all his debts, with interest. Believing that I had a clear head in these matters he sought my advice, and when I had thought the matter over I sent it to him in a single line consisting of a popular quotation from a talmudic commentary. The subject of the comment is Sarah, the wife of Abraham, of whom the commentator says that when she was a hundred years old she was as beautiful as a girl of twenty, and when she was twenty years old she was as pure as a child of three. The Hebrew phrasing runs: "At a hundred as twenty for beauty, at twenty as three for innocence." The hint for my father was: If you are to renew the notes, twenty thousand and three thousand are the same as regards the innocence of your intent; and a hundred thousand is just as nice to have as twenty thousand. My father renewed all the notes, and later, when he was out of debt, he used to show my line around as being the shortest business letter he had ever received and the one packed with most meaning.

I wrote to Anna almost every day, but in Ekaterinoslav I began to mark that her answers were growing more and more reserved. I felt that something not to my benefit was taking place in Bobruisk, and I would have gone there if I had not been ashamed to show myself there after those eternal farewells. I went instead to Kachova, near Ekaterinoslav, where Anna's brother Leon was in the employ of a firm of grain dealers, and it was from him that I received the bitter news. Anna had become engaged. I uttered not a word of complaint, but concentrated all my inner forces on concealing my feelings in that critical moment. When I found my speech I took to talking feverishly of my Palestine plan: now I would be able to dedicate myself completely to my ideal, untroubled by personal motives. My friend seemed to be delighted by my attitude; but what I felt was a poisonous feeling of vengefulness.

From Kachova I went to Odessa on the Black Sea, the proud and beautiful city which stands on the southernmost point of Russian soil. Its sunny mood casts a spell on the visitor, and from its towers he catches a glimpse of the Near East. But the radiance of the city was lost on me. I was driven by sick motives to actions that were unnatural to me. I wanted to dull a pain that I could not uproot, and I did not understand that what was happening to me would cut across the rest of my life.

I knew not a soul in Odessa, even though it was the center of the *Chibath Zion* movement. The famous Moses Leib Lilienblum lived there. His writings, in Hebrew and Russian, had exerted a powerful influence on the national-minded Jewish youth. Equally if not more famous was Leon Pinsker, the president of the movement. Perhaps more famous than either was the lion of Odessa Jewry, Mendelle Mocher S'forim, whom Sholom Aleichem was to call the Grandfather of Yiddish literature—and it is by that title, *der Zeideh*, that he has been referred to ever since. Not so famous as these, but soon to surpass them, was Asher Ginsberg, known now throughout the Jewish world by his pen name of Ahad Ha-am. These were men that I had long dreamed of meeting, and had I been my normal self I would have thrown myself at once into a round of introductions. But I was wretched beyond words; I could neither find the strength to move on to Palestine, nor the interest to plunge into the Jewish life of the city. Some time passed before I could resolve to face the men whose ideal I was supposed to incorporate in my decision—now moribund—to become a pioneer in Palestine.

Lilienblum was the one I sought out first. I had read everything he had published, down to the most insignificant articles.

Judging the man from his writings, I expected to meet a combination of hot-headed enthusiasm and high, logical discourse, for he was perhaps the most important intellectual force in the propagation of the new national idea. I was thunderstruck to see before me a man of middle age with features which reminded me irresistibly of some village rabbi, some helpless *batlan* or *shlimihl*. Neither his bearing nor his speech had any sort of relation to the picture I had carried around with me for so many years. He was cold, phlegmatic, without a spark of enthusiasm or a tremor of excitement. When I told him hesitantly of my intention to become a pioneer, he asked simply: "How much money have you?" The depressing effect of this reception was not mitigated when some Jews interrupted our conversation and in my presence began to bargain with Lilienblum about the price of a funeral and of cerements . . . . Lilienblum was at that time the secretary to both Leon Pinsker and the Odessa *Chevrah Kadishah*, or communal burial society. I felt as if I had been personally insulted. On the one hand the revival of a people, on the other hand the burial of Jews and a squabbling over the price of graves and cerements.

Altogether different from him was Leon Pinsker, with his pleasant and aristocratic bearing. Though a Russian Jew, and the descendant of a line of famous Jewish scholars, his outlook was that of a west European. He had made a name for himself in medicine, had won the respect of the non-Jewish world, and came to his Judaism from the outside, as it were, free in his nationalism from any trace of a theological background. In the ranks of the *Choveve Zion* there were elements that were dissatisfied with his leadership, in particular the orthodox rabbinical world, to which he was a stranger, but his standing was such that an open fight against him was impossible. In his relationship to the movement Pinsker was a precursor of the second leader who came—in his case literally—out of the Western world to be accepted by the Eastern masses, namely, Theodore Herzl.

My friendliest reception was from Mendelle Mocher S'forim (Mendelle the Bookseller: his real name was Sholom Jacob Abramovitch). He was among the first Yiddish writers my old teacher Artzer had introduced me to, but I was even more intimately acquainted with his Hebrew works. He invited me to attend "his" services of the New Year and the Day of Atonement—that is, the services of the Odessa Talmud Torah, of which he was the secretary. His company was a delight. He was torrential in conversation; an irresistible stream of stories, quips, anecdotes and puns issued from him, and on his features a satiric, Mephistophelian expression was always at play.

Incontestably the greatest of the men I came to know in Odessa was the young manufacturer with the commonplace name of Asher Ginsberg. He was already spoken of, among the elite, as a rising star in the Jewish heavens, and there were those who uttered his name with the reverence which in Chassidic circles is reserved for the *rebbi.* I was brought to his home one Friday evening, after dinner, and a considerable company was gathered there. The instant I set eyes on this frail little man I realized that I was in the presence of greatness. There lay upon his features, simple and festive, a strange spiritual radiance. They were open and expressive features, across which the passage of his ideas marked a clear, unmistakable path. In contrast to Mendelle, he spoke little, leaving the burden of the conversation to his guests, who conducted themselves in his presence like disciples in the presence of a master.

It was shortly after I met him that Asher Ginsberg published a sharp, almost annihilating criticism of the *methods* of the *Chibath Zion* movement, in an article which is now a classic of Hebrew literature and of Zionist history: *Lo zu ha-Derech* (*Not This is the Way*). The pen name he chose for himself was Ahad Ha-am, One of the People. It is quite certain that he chose the pseudonym out of instinctive modesty, but while an author may choose a name, the significance and interpretation of it is later supplied by the public. *Ahad Ha-am* came to mean "The One Who Represents the People." Asher Ginsberg, quiet, modest, retiring, became the spiritual leader of Zionism. He did not seek the leadership: it sought him out. There was not in him the shadow of a desire for greatness, but he was a great man. For me, personally, he was to become and remain *the* leader and guide. It was one of the luckiest circumstances of my life that during the greater part of it I was thrown together with him in a work that was dear to both of us; and it is a source of pride to me that I never forgot, even for an instant, that I was the contemporary of the great thinker and the still greater Jew, Ahad Ha-am.

Years were to pass before I touched the soil of Palestine. I lingered on in Odessa, suspended between its attractions and the reproaches of my conscience. At one point I so far pulled myself together as to book passage for Constantinople, the halfway point to Jaffa. Then my father turned up in Odessa, harassed and distraught, and begged me to remain with him for a time. I made a great but affectionate show of resistance. My obligations! How could I default on them? Then my father turned my advice to him against me. Had I not persuaded him to renew his notes? Was he not asking me to do the same now? It sounded plausible, even though there was one decisive psychological difference. *His* obligations had been toward others, mine were toward myself. If we human beings only treated our moral obligations toward ourselves with the same respect, the same fear of consequences, as we treat our legal obligations, if the voice of conscience were as imperious as the voice of public opinion, our lives would be far more decent than they are.

I gave way, and I left without saying farewell to a single person in Odessa. I had by this time fallen to the lowest point that can be reached by a young person. On the way home I stopped in Bobruisk and saw Anna, and there awoke in me again a longing for vindication and revenge. I cannot, even at this distance, say other than this: I had lost all pride and self-respect. I became engaged. It was a dull affair, banal, without taste. I was demonstrating that my love for Anna had not been more substantial than hers for me. I wanted no one to pity me. But the greatest element of meanness lay in this: I was exacting revenge not with my *own* resources, but by involving a third party. To punish Eve the First I had to humiliate Eve the Second.

If there is any truth in the aphorism that man was given language in order to disguise his thoughts, I demonstrated it at that time with artistic distinction. I took myself as a model, forged my own handwriting, plagiarized my own style, and imitated the letters I had originally written to Anna Lozinsky. For a time I took some interest in my father's business, but I gradually withdrew from that, to find refuge in study. There I began to find spiritual peace. My letters to my fiancée became more infrequent, then stopped altogether. I worked consistently and closely, reading intensively during the day, writing poetry through most of the night. A dear and lovely interlude finally set in for me. In my native village of Svislovitz I was again sheltered by the visions of antiquity. A marvelous silence took hold of the townlet in the nights, a silence of retreat and isolation, steeped in such peace, in such longing for work, that I hated the coming of the day and resented the first rays of the sun.

When I had accumulated a whole sheaf of songs, I sent them to Judah Leib Gordon, and back came a prompt reply: the foremost Hebrew poet of our time praised my songs! He stated distinctly that I had talent. All I needed was practice and greater neatness of expression. It was widely known, alas, that Gordon's habit was to praise all beginners, but I took him seriously and resolved forthwith to publish a volume of poetry. And need I confess that beside my natural desire to appear in print there was the need to show Anna Lozinsky whom it was she had thrown over?

For so crucial an event as the publication of my poems I had, of course, to go to Warsaw myself, and there, in the first world-city of my experience, I spent two months. Twice the size of either Kiev or Odessa, Warsaw had its own character. Kiev is outspokenly Russian Byzantine, steeped in the sacred atmosphere of heroic legends and ancient history; its beauty is inward, distilled by many generations. The beauty of Odessa is outward; it has an Italian gaiety mixed with the impudence of the parvenu; it does not look back at Russia, but outward, toward the Mediterranean and the Near East. Warsaw is wholly and thoroughly occidental. It has taken as its standard—and not as its final goal, either—three cities: Paris, Berlin and Vienna. There is very little of the Slavic in Warsaw, less, in fact, than in Prague.

In Warsaw I felt for the first time that I was abroad. Two circumstances contributed to this feeling: I knew no Polish, and even the Yiddish that is spoken there sounds very different from the Yiddish of Russia proper. The Russian administration, the Russian military, and even the Russian cathedral lifting its five triumphant cupolas on the beautiful Saxon Square—did nothing to weaken the Western impression. They did not mingle with the rest of the city; Warsaw remained Polish, and the Russifying elements stood out like brutal patches on the body of Poland. The Russian language was to be heard everywhere on the streets, but it was universally regarded as the language of the administration and the soldiery. A peculiar situation had been created for those Jews who had been driven by persecutions and restrictions out of interior Russia into the commercial centers of Poland, principally Warsaw and Lodz. Their language was Russian; and without any desire to help the Russian administration in its violent campaign of Russification, they became an instrument in the hands of the anti-Polish authorities.

They were better Russifiers than the regular officers and officials in two respects: they got no pay, and they did not succumb to the influence of the Polish population. Of the higher Russian officials it was said that they made better pupils than teachers: they learned to speak Polish—the young ladies they were supposed to teach were altogether too charming. Moreover, the indigenous Polish Jews did not feel particularly friendly toward the newly arrived Russian Jews who, through no fault of their own, did a good deal to worsen the already hostile relations between the native Jews and the Poles.

Warsaw was also a prime center of Hebrew literature. Because of my volume of poems, which appeared under the simple title of *Ten Songs*, I soon found entry into the city's Jewish literary circles and was introduced to some of the foremost figures.

The dean of that little world was Chaim Zelig Slonimsky, the editor of *Ha-Zephirah*, a patriarch of eighty, who had retained an extraordinary degree of youthful freshness. Slonimsky was a living legend in the Jewish world. His mathematical gifts had won him the prize of the Prussian Academy of Science, and he had invented a method for sending four messages simultaneously over one telegraph wire. But he had achieved his greatest popularity, especially in orthodox religious circles, by his thirty years' war on behalf of the Jewish calendar. The struggle was not as bloody as the Thirty Years' War of Germany, but it evoked and sustained the interest of the entire Jewish world. Slonimsky had proved mathematically that in their establishing of the festival dates the Jews of the East had to base themselves not on the meridian of Greenwich, but on that of Jerusalem, and he defended this view—to the great satisfaction of the orthodox—with the strength and ferocity of a lion.

There was something leonine in his appearance, too. He had an enormous, square-shaped, snow-white beard, ornamenting a face that was almost devoid of wrinkles and out of which shone the clear, intellectual eyes of a Jewish scholar. I could never look my fill at him, and I could never decide which to admire most, the giant spirit or the body that contained it.

Ha-Zephirah was at that time in the fifth year of its publication. While Slonimsky was the nominal editor, the real editor was the young, amazingly gifted and even more amazingly industrious Nahum Sokolov, already famous for his encyclopedic range of knowledge and his incredible productivity. Work after work issued from his pen, like one edition after another of the man himself, every edition an improvement on the last. But these works still remained—encyclopedias, covering an enormous area of information and touching on a thousand and one subjects. Every problem that Sokolov treated—and what subject did he not treat?—emerged from his pen polished and balanced; but the interior remained unorganized. Sokolov was a swift swimmer in a calm sea, but he was no diver and he never brought up the pearls that are under the surface of the waters. He envisaged all life, but did not penetrate it; he was witty and intelligent, but not passionate.

For a long time he was the leading spirit both in *Ha-Zephirah* and the Jewish Polish *Israelita*. His was the political part of the work. He treated the questions of the day, but however burning these might be his articles were cool, quiet, deliberate, and fair to both sides. He, who later became a foremost Zionist figure, was at that time openly and consistently opposed to the *Chibath Zion*. Steeped in Jewishness as much as any of his contemporaries, filled with Jewish history and Jewish knowledge, he could not identify himself with the men who led the movement in Poland. He looked upon them as idlers, chatterers, whose ideas had not the remotest relation to world politics. It was only with the coming of Herzl, who transformed the *Chibath Zion* into a modern movement, and gave it a sweep and power it had never before possessed, that Sokolov was drawn in, and then he exerted himself to the utmost to wipe out the debt he had contracted in the years of his hostility.

Sokolov, too, received me with great friendliness. He was, indeed, friendly to everyone, even his opponents—at all times the personification of the gentleman. But Slonimsky was not overfriendly toward him: there was a struggle between the declining and the rising power. The story was told that one day Slonimsky lost his temper completely, then, recovering his balance, shrugged and said: "Well, he can't live for ever, can he?" The old Jewish astronomer and mathematician had become too accustomed to being alive; the old calculator of the calendar had lost his own sense of time.

Before long there appeared in *Ha-Zephirah* a long review of my book, in two installments. The reviewer was not a professional writer, and he had never before attempted to review a book. He made this one attempt as a favor to me. I did not even consider him a good critic, but nothing could mar my satisfaction with the review. I sent copies of it to all of my friends; to Leon Lozinsky, two . . . one for him and one for his sister.

Now that I had got to know the leading Jewish spirits in Odessa and Warsaw, and now that, as I thought, I had myself become part of their world by the publication of my book, I definitely relinquished all thought of a business career. Had the literary career constituted a profession in those days I would have given myself to it immediately and abandoned the search for another. But only a tiny handful among the many Hebrew writers made their living by the pen, and they had editorial positions on one of the two Hebrew papers. All the others had to find their livelihood elsewhere; and had anyone dared to prophesy that within twenty years there would arise a whole army of Hebrew writers living solely by their craft, he would have been regarded as a lunatic. But if I was not going to live by my pen, I was certainly not going to become a merchant. The future was still vague; all I knew was that I had only one path to follow—westward, for an education that would provide me with an intellectual profession. My parents no longer objected. When I came back to Svislovitz before setting out for Berlin they treated me like a beloved and important visitor. I was, after all, the author of a book.

My stay was brief. My mother, as usual, baked and cooked as if to provide for a transcontinental caravan, and I left my home weighted down with her provender and the high hopes of everyone. I made two stops on the way to Berlin: in Pinsk, to get my passport, and in Kovno to get the blessing—at my mother's urgent solicitation—of Rabbi Isaac Elkhanan Spektor. I stayed in Kovno only one day, for the venerable scholar and thinker received me at once. I told him why I had come, and what my plans were in regard to my Jewish studies. I told him further that I did not know to what use I would put these studies; I might remain a writer, I might become a rabbi; but whatever I became I wanted to have his blessing. I expected that this idol of the masses who had also won the respect of the intellectuals would make some effort to impress me with his importance. Above all I expected a quiet exhibition of piety. Nothing of the sort took place. His blessing was given in the simplest form, gently and affectionately, as though he had known me and liked me for years.

Thus closed the second of the three periods that constituted my *Wanderjahre*: from Beresin to Dvinsk, from Dvinsk to Minsk, from Minsk to Bobruisk, and then my stay in the two Jewish centers, Odessa and Warsaw. From the beginning I was the incarnation of the wandering Jew. Wherever I set foot I came in contact with the various levels of Jewish life, and everywhere I became part of the worries, the hopes and the dreams of the Jewish soul. The last and third period of my wander-years I passed in Germany: a different world, different people, different Jews.

CHAPTER TWENTY-TWO

Student Days in Berlin

FOREIGN LANDS! No modern on either side of the Atlantic, no man who has passed many years in a halfway civilized country, can ever taste the magic and mystery which lay (and alas still lies) for the Russian intellectual, and particularly for the Russian Jewish intellectual, in the word "abroad." It was not and is not the primitive emotion of curiosity or the ordinary desire for change. In the Russian intellectual it was and still is the profound desire for freedom. In the heart of every Russian there was a longing like a prayer to break free, if only for a moment, from the prison which was called Russia; to fill his lungs deep, if only for once, with the breath of freedom; to see with his own eyes how human beings walk about unintimidated; to hear men talking as they wish concerning God and man, devil and government, unterrified by their own thoughts.

When we recall that "abroad" did not necessarily imply France or England or the United States, that for the modest Russian it was Prussian Germany or Austria that represented an earthly paradise, we shall appreciate in what sort of hell he lived, and how relative were his concepts of freedom. However much he reads about that incredible land, the non-Russian still cannot picture the extraordinary reality. The sense of freedom was possible in Russia only to one who himself belonged to the oppressors, or else to the idiot.

The instant I passed the frontier and arrived at the village of Eidkuhstadt, I already felt like a liberated slave. Had I been of a pious turn of mind, I would have recited the prayer of the freed prisoner, and if I had not been ashamed I would have embraced and kissed the Prussian gendarme who now boarded the train. That the Prussian gendarme, too, could prove to be a nasty customer; that he, too, was not exactly a fount of pure justice, and that even in his presence it was just as well to observe a certain degree of caution, was something we learned later, when our concept of freedom became a little more advanced and Prussia ceased to be our idea of paradise.

Joyous thoughts danced in my brain, keeping time to the jolting of the wheels on the sleepers. I wanted to dance with my thoughts and with the rhythm of the wheels; and since this too was not possible, I pulled out the huge supply of things my mother had cooked and baked and fried, and invited all the travellers in my car to join the feast. I knew German, or at least I thought I did; in any case the Germans understood me perfectly, and after every mouthful said: "*Prachtvoll!*" By the time I reached Berlin the basket was almost empty. I told my fellow travellers that these good things my mother had prepared with her own hands, and the Germans praised my mother to the skies and I myself was in seventh heaven.

In the darkness of an early autumn morning I arrived in the city of Berlin. I was received there by my friend Nachman Syrkin, who was already a student at the University of Berlin. The huge electric lamps in the Friedrichstrasse station made on me the impression of suspended terrestrial suns which turned night into day. I moved, weirdly, in a sea of light—and accepted it as an omen. Syrkin refused to let me take a droshky or a carriage; it cost too much, and it was not fitting for a student. He had, in fact, ordered his landlady to come down to the station with a small cart drawn by a dog. In the cart there was just room enough for my baggage; Syrkin and I went on foot to his lodgings, like pilgrims approaching a shrine.

The dog pulled away at the cart, the landlady drove the dog, and Syrkin and I strolled two or three miles through the streets of Berlin to his lodgings in the northern quarter of the city. I cannot truthfully say that my entry into the imperial city was majestic or imposing, but according to Syrkin this was the proper thing for students. His room was on the fifth floor of a typical workers' tenement, a vast structure housing a huge swarm of lodgers. The room was large, well-lighted, and decently furnished. Until my arrival Syrkin had been paying fifteen marks (three dollars and seventy-five cents) a month for room and breakfast. The two of us would now pay twelve and a half marks each for the same service.

Breakfast, as I soon learned, consisted of a cup of coffee and two slices of black bread thinly smeared with butter. By way of variety the student could order two white rolls *without* butter. During the week Syrkin contented himself with the black bread; on the Sabbath he sacrificed substance for elegance —a memorial of the Sabbath white bread of his far-away home. The landladies were, in almost every case, workingwomen or the wives of workingmen. The average earnings of a workingman in Berlin, in those days, was between seventy-five and ninety marks a month, and the income derived from a student lodger counted heavily in the family budget. Students were always treated with consideration and respect.

Immediately after my first Berlin breakfast, Syrkin conducted me to the Russian Reading Rooms, two moderately sized rooms poorly furnished, but supplied with all the Russian papers of a liberal tendency. The reactionary papers were excluded. The Jewish press was represented by the Russian *Voskhod.* It was only some time later, after a bitter struggle at open meetings, a struggle that lasted for months, that the club agreed to subscribe to the Hebrew papers too. The readers were ninety percent Jewish, ten percent real Russian or Polish. It was Jewish students, therefore, who thought it their duty to express their abhorrence of nationalist chauvinism by refusing admission to the Hebrew press. *Ha-Melitz* and *Ha-Zephirah*, they argued, were reactionary by virtue of their language alone. Practically expelled from Russia for being Jews, they no sooner arrived in exile than they proclaimed themselves Russians, and repudiated violently anything that bound them to their own race and people.

In the nineties of the last century Germany was drunk with her great victory over France and with dreams of world-power. In primary school and university, in village and metropolis, in the local club and in the Reichstag, the burden of all music was *Deutschland über Alles*; and if this song did not sufficiently express the rising temper of the country there were the famous words of the Iron Chancellor, Bismarck: "We Germans fear no one but God." The meaning was: "We Germans ignore the opinions of mankind; we are the sole judges of our acts. We do not deny the existence of God, but our account with him is private and confidential. And since we are the greatest power on earth, as He is in heaven, we shall no doubt easily reach an accommodation with Him."

This general spirit in the Germany of the nineties was not without its effect on German Jewry, which felt itself compelled to take over the moral rulership of the Jews of the rest of the world. Objectively, German Jewry was in fact entitled to first place, being the largest group among the emancipated Jewries of the West. But it had another, more important ground for the claim. It was, after all the creator of the *Jüdische Wissenschaft*. Its record was rich with names like Mendelssohn, Zunz, Geiger, Steinschneider, Jost, Fürst, Graetz.

But German Jews were totally ignorant of the achievements and activities of Russian Jewry; they were ignorant of the great renaissance and of the new Hebraic literature which had begun to blossom, as well as of the organized political struggle taking place within Russian Jewry. As for Yiddish literature, that was beneath their notice. They called Yiddish *Maushel*—Sheeny language.

I had two possibilities open before me. One was the Theological Seminary of Dr. Asriel Hildesheimer, the representative of extreme orthodoxy, the second the *Hochschule für die Wissenschaft des Judenthums*, which prepared rabbis for the liberal wing and also admitted students who did not intend to enter the rabbinate. I knew that the Seminary of Dr. Hildesheimer was as good as closed to me; I therefore enrolled in the *Hochschule*. Its address was on the Unter den Linden—on paper, at least. Actually it was lodged on the third floor of a building in an interior courtyard, and its three dingy rooms would have been a disgrace to an elementary school. In its teaching staff the *Hochschule* was almost as poor as in its housing, its one bright spirit being Dr. Herman Steinthal, famous for his philological studies. I must confess that in the field of Jewish knowledge I learned more from the Christian professors in the University than from the Jewish scholars in the *Hochschule*.

There was nothing surprising in all this. After the era of Zunz and Geiger, German Jewry fell away from Jewish scholarship with extraordinary rapidity. The Zunz-Geiger group, which achieved great things in Jewish research, had made it their object to display to the world the spiritual and cultural treasures of the Jew of the past. Zunz himself had stated clearly that the road to emancipation lay through *Jewish* scholarship. But the old scholars died and no new ones rose to take their place. Things had reached such a pass that of the dozen or so rabbis of the United Community of Berlin, three-quarters had been imported from Hungary.

Again, most of the student body, which consisted of thirty

members, came from Galicia and Hungary. There were four of us from Russia. The German Jewish students were astoundingly ignorant, their level of education being about that of a *cheder* boy at home in his second or third term. Yet they were looked upon as the leaders in the seminary and were treated with special tenderness by the professors. The fact that they spoke German—and without an accent—covered a multitude of deficiencies. I knew certain young German rabbis whose equipment fitted them better for a Protestant church than for a Jewish temple. But the Jews of Germany felt more comfortable when German chauvinism was preached to them by a native Jew rather than by an imported Hungarian Jew.

The Russian student colony in Berlin lived a life apart from the German student body. Nor could the Russian student—meaning, for all practical purposes, the Russian Jewish student—have any share in the political life of the country. Germany, it must be remembered, was never a center of immigration. The stranger arriving in America regards himself as part of the country from the moment he enters it; he can begin to build at once, without hesitation or afterthought. No wonder many east European Jews, setting out for America, provided themselves in advance with American flags. France and England were not countries of immigration to the same degree as was America, though even there the immigrant found it possible to take a lively interest in the politics of the country from the day of his arrival. In Germany the alien Jew, especially if he came from the East, had to rely on time. His *children*, perhaps, might become citizens of the country. Yet the Russian youth streaming into Germany were passionately interested in politics. There was only one door open to them—the Social Democratic Party.

But this had its dangers. The Jewish Socialist students in Berlin had their own organization, but they were subject to restrictions and dangers from which their German comrades were free. It was, for instance, dangerous to become a subscriber to the German Socialist daily, the *Vorwärts*. It might lead to a refusal on the part of the police to renew the residential permit of the foreigner. It was curious to note how the German police regarded the political activity of the foreign student not as an internal German matter, but purely from the Russian point of view. In a completely inverted sense the Prussian government extended to Russian students in Germany the extraterritorial "rights" generally reserved for ambassadors and their entourage. Russian students in Germany were subject to Russian law!

The Jewish nationalistically inclined students were much better off. Since the Russian government was not interested in Jewish nationalism, Prussian liberty, unadulterated by Russian interference, sufficed for us. We could found an organization and hold open meetings after observing certain simple formalities. So in time there was founded the *Russisch-Jüdisch Wissenschaftliches Verein*, which drew into its ranks the ablest of the nationalistic forces of the Jewish student youth and became a center of attraction for the student body as a whole. It became also the arena for the struggles of the two main forces in the Jewish student life of Berlin. Leo Motzkin, famous in the Jewish world as the president of the Jewish delegation which fought for Jewish rights at the Paris Peace Conference of 1919, was one of its founders.

The *Verein* held its meetings on Saturday nights, but the mass of our work was done daily, continuously. It was genuine missionary work—the catching of souls. Not content with "working" the enrolled students, we organized to catch them as they arrived. Every morning the train would bring into Berlin, from the eastern frontier, new and unsuspecting students; and Socialists and Nationalists lay in ambush for them. These newcomers were green; for the most part they did not know where their sympathies lay, and their future would be decided by the first contacts. The competition was fierce. The agents of the two parties would be standing in the station before sunrise, under the flickering arc light. The Jewish student coming from Russia was easily recognizable, if not by his appearance, then by his marvelous collection of bundles and baskets and packages. The scene is still engraved in my mind. The station is either the Friedrichstrasse or the Alexanderplatz. From a fourth-class carriage a student creeps out, dragging his packages after him. Two young men detach themselves from the crowd and make for him: each claims the honor of leading the newcomer to his lodgings. There they stand, the three of them, gummy-eyed from lack of sleep. The newcomer is in a stupor; in the land he comes from Jews are accustomed to receiving blows; here he sees people coming to blows over a Jew.

It was the rule for every student organization to have its regular locale, generally a side-room in a restaurant. The German restaurants were for the most part beer halls, for beer-drinking was a German cult—the modern expression of the early German spirit which turned heaven itself into a magnificent brewery, with attendant angels in the form of *Valkürie.* Every student had his daily ration to consume, and he performed his duty with Teutonic piety and thoroughness. When a German student complained: "I haven't had my beer today," he did not mean that he had not drunk any beer; had this been the case he would have been sent to a doctor. All he meant was that he had not reached his quota; if he was one short of his fifteen glasses he went about feeling a strange lack or emptiness. But with the German Jewish students the question of beer-drinking was a bitter one. They were anxious to keep pace with the real Germans, but there was a trifling difference between them: the German had to exert all his willpower in order to keep away from beer; the Jew had to exert all of his in order to drink an appreciable quantity. The atavisms of the

Jew refer back to a land flowing with "milk and honey," not beer. To the honor of the German Jewish students let it be said here that they made fantastic efforts, but a distance always remained between them and the real Germans.

The question of beer-drinking played an almost fatal role in the history of the *Russisch-Jüdisch Wissenschaftliches Verein.* It goes without saying that the moderate success achieved by the German Jewish students after generations of training and selection was altogether beyond our reach. We Jews had lived in Russia since time immemorial and had never caught the trick of a manly drink of vodka: how could we be expected to acquire overnight the art of beer-drinking? Our drinks used to be mostly chicory masquerading as coffee; when we felt riotous we took a glass of raisin wine—drinks you could order in a German beer-hall only at the peril of your life. Our great trouble rose from the custom of the restaurants in regard to the student societies. A locale was set aside for them free of charge in every restaurant; the proprietor made his rent on the drinks. Twenty German students could shift, in one evening, between three and four hundred glasses of beer. Now, our meetings, even at the beginning, would draw a crowd of over a hundred. When we so informed the proprietor of a restaurant he eagerly offered us a room; but the first meeting was enough to disillusion him. The more than one hundred of us were not worth half a dozen decent Germans. We were therefore driven from restaurant to restaurant, from beer hall to beer hall. Our society took on the wandering exilic character of the Jewish people. At every meeting Motzkin used to beg the students, almost with tears in his eyes: "Friends, for God's sake, drink more beer. Have some consideration for the Society." It was useless. Not only were we averse to beer, but the majority of us were poor. In the end we made up our minds to *pay* for a room, and thus be free from the eternal torment of what and how much to eat and drink.

But if our Society was the most primitive in Berlin in regard to the consumption of food and drink, we made up for it by the wealth of the problems we brought with us and the passion of the discussion which after every lecture would last far, far into the night—not infrequently until the quiet morning star was shining on the roofs of Berlin. This too was a source of misunderstanding between the Germans and the Jews. The Germans saw fellow students, the "wild" Russians, who drank neither beer nor wine, but who shouted and argued as if they were half-drunk, while their faces shone and their eyes glittered with a fierce enthusiasm. Sons of a sated people, they could not understand that for us words were enough to bring on a more lasting intoxication.

Our Society was founded by and for the Jewish Nationalists: it turned into a rallying center for the Socialists and anti-Nationalists, who came there to sharpen *their* arguments on us. They attended every debate, and whatever it began with it always ended up with Socialism versus Nationalism. The Socialists had one advantage over us. Whenever they were short of forces they would bring to their assistance well-known figures from the Socialist world to crush us with authority if they could not do it with argument. Our debates became famous, and the number of students frequently ran into several hundred. Then it was less a debate than a genuine battle between two philosophies in the presence of eager and passionate spectators.

One of the deadliest debaters on the Socialist side was Parvus, who had even in those days achieved a considerable reputation as a Marxist theoretician. In debate he was swift and merciless, and his vocabulary was more fitted for a barroom than for a scientific Society. He always spoke with a terrible immediacy, as though the barricades were rising in the streets of Berlin and the mortal struggle between the classes had already opened. I remember one of his addresses—the picture comes back to me after more than forty years. Parvus was thundering, as only he could, against the meaninglessness of Nationalism. He cited Marx, history and philosophy, and then, feeling that these arguments were too vague and academic, he grabbed hold of his own coat and roared: "The wool in this coat was taken from sheep which were pastured in Angora; it was spun in England and woven in Lodz; the buttons come from Germany and the thread from Austria: is it not clear to you that this world of ours is *inter*national and even a miserable thing like a coat is made up of the labor of ten different races?"

The argument and, still more, the illustration, were extremely effective. You could almost *feel* the stream of intellectual sympathy turning in Parvus' direction. Hands were lifted to applaud—then something unexpected happened. Parvus' coat was too small for him. In the fury of gesticulation, while pulling his coat about to point his illustrations, he had ripped the right elbow, which now showed a stretch of white shirt. Right opposite Parvus sat Nachman Syrkin, his eyes burning with rage and contempt. Just at the moment when Parvus had completed his argument, Syrkin, unable to contain himself, rose to his feet and shouted: "And the rip in your sleeve comes from the pogrom in Kiev!" The effect of that interjection was marvelous. Parvus had worked for an hour to reach his climax of the international coat. Syrkin had undone him with a sentence. The hands that were lifted to applaud Parvus seemed to swing over. We *knew* they were applauding Syrkin now. A fearful tumult rose in the hall. Parvus roared idiotically that he had never been in Kiev, and that at the time of the famous pogrom he had been in the Baltic countries. Nobody cared where he had been. For that evening at least, he was undone.

There were other figures at our meetings who were destined to rise to prominence. Tugan Baranovsky, the Russian economist, was one of us; Berdyayev the mystic, and Peter Struve, already a scholar, were also there. I did not know, of course, that in later years I would be together with Struve in one of the parties in the Russian Duma. I had not changed by then, but he had. Originally one of the most brilliant Marxist theoreticians, he later became a liberal and wound up as one of the right-wing leaders of the Cadets.

The year 1891 was marked by an incident which created—or revealed—a profound crisis in the history of Russian Jewry and shook world Jewry to its foundations: the great "expulsion from Moscow." This infamous act of the Russian government made clear to all humanity that the five million Jews of Russia were outcasts and outlaws. The mob pogroms had left the Russian government with a pretext: they were outbursts of elemental hatred, a folk-movement which had grown up through the centuries. In this case the folk obviously had nothing to do with it. It was direct government action; the plans were laid in St. Petersburg by a general staff under the direction of von Plehve and Pobedonostsev. Thousands of Jewish families that had been living in Moscow for decades were suddenly arrested, dragged out of their homes, and transported under police guard to remote corners of Russia.

The order was carried out on a bitter cold night, and the refugees travelled from filthy prison to filthy prison, until they were set free at their destinations—to starve. Even Russian Jewry, which had resigned itself to pogroms as regular periodic events, was thrown into a frightful panic. The faint glimmer of hope that the Russian government would put an end to the pogroms now died, and the wave of emigration broke out with elemental fury. Of the quarter of a million Jews who crossed the ocean from the Old World to the New in the year 1891-92, the vast majority came from Russia.

They set forth, these hundreds of thousands, almost at a day's notice; they sold the last of their possessions under the pressure of the moment; with the meager returns they bought fourth-class tickets and, unorganized, unprotected, they took to the open road once more. World Jewry had not even that degree of organization which it has today, and was not prepared to meet a *national* catastrophe.

The path of the emigrants lay across Germany, and from the German border there streamed toward Berlin a furious tide of migrants, as many as two or three thousand a day. The Prussian government was anxious that they should all arrive safely in America, and that not a single one of them should be dropped on German territory. It was then that German Jewry came to itself. Philosophies, rationalizations, theologies were thrown overboard; no one asked whether the Jews are a nation or a religious sect. It is proper to record here that no one who witnessed the swift reaction of German Jewry to this overwhelming situation can describe it as anything short of wonderful.

And now the opportunity presented itself to our Society. Motzkin became the organizer of the work; more than one hundred of us placed ourselves at the service of the committees which formed spontaneously in Berlin, and were supported in every part of Germany. Money flowed in toward the center, and in Berlin, groups of distinguished and refined women took over the actual labor at the railroad stations. The emigrants were tongueless as well as helpless. They did not know German, and they were terrorized. In every person who approached them they suspected one of those criminal "agents"—they were without number—who sprang up at that time to prey on these wretched wanderers. We students were the intermediaries between the emigrants and the committees, and it was our first opportunity to become more closely acquainted with the German Jews. Many of my prejudices vanished forever. I saw that deeper than all theories and pretenses lay the immovable instinct of race; blood was stronger than ideology.

As against this, our own position changed in the eyes of the German Jews, who realized that we were not simply babblers, and that we were concerned with a fundamental problem which even they could not escape. Had Palestine in those days been a possible center of immigration, we could easily have persuaded the German Jewish Committee to divert part of the stream of wanderers in that direction. But at that time the little, new settlement in Palestine was passing through a crisis. The *Chibath Zion* was too small in scope; Palestine had not yet developed as an immigration center and it could not yet respond to the magnitude of the historic task.

At this point there rose on the horizon a star of hope. Baron de Hirsch, the great philanthropist, had begun negotiations with the Russian government as far back as 1888. He had set aside the sum of fifty million francs to carry out plans for the improvement of the condition of Russian Jewry. His plans envisaged the founding of a far-flung net of trade schools and agricultural colonies. But the Russian government was not particularly overjoyed by Baron de Hirsch's offer; its object was not to better the condition of the Jews, but to get rid of them. It therefore made a counter-proposal to the Baron. It was prepared to sacrifice itself to the extent of accepting his fifty million francs, but on condition that it alone should have the direction of the fund. Baron de Hirsch refused the condition and the plan fell through.

The Baron's next step was to found the I. C. A., the famous Jewish Colonization Association, with the Argentine as the chief center of immigration. The plan won the support of nearly all the rich Jews of Russia, and of part of the intellectual group; that is, of the assimilationist elements. Since the Argentine meant nothing to the Jewish people *as an idea*, it was safe—and it counteracted the *Chibath Zion* movement.

Thus it was that an "Argentinian" movement was born. Baron de Hirsch was hailed as the new Jewish Messiah, the counter-Messiah to Baron Rothschild, who was the main support of Palestinian colonization, and the Jewish world was divided into two camps. The antagonism between "Argentine" and "Palestine" grew from day to day and filled the Jewish world, penetrating to our Society. It penetrated even to our little Svislovitz, whither I returned in the summer of 1891, my first visit since leaving for Berlin. And there, as in Berlin, I devoted most of my days to *Chibath Zion* propaganda and the struggle against the "Argentine" movement.

I went out also to the neighboring towns, including Bobruisk, and with my comrades labored in the preparation of a petition to Baron de Hirsch, imploring him to ignore his assimilationist advisers. The idea that Jews could become colonists, and remain colonists, in the Argentine, we pointed out, was a false one. We urged that whatever our personal relationship to the idea of Palestine, we had to recognize that *as a sentiment* it alone was capable of endowing Jews with the strength and endurance needed for a task so exacting and so difficult as changing the uprooted city dweller into a tiller of the soil.

When we reassembled in Berlin that autumn we discovered that this handful of students had collected over forty thousand signatures to the petition. We sent it off—and that was the last we heard of it. It is remarkable that in spite of the tremendous philanthropic gift of the Baron, the Jews who reported for Argentinian immigration were few in number. The great mass streamed toward the United States. Baron de Hirsch's promise to the Russian government that within twenty-five years he would relieve the country of three million Jews was shown to be an exaggeration within the first year of operation.

In 1891 the periodical *Ha-Maggid*, the Hebrew organ of the *Chibath Zion* movement, edited by the devoted and energetic David Gordon, moved its headquarters to Berlin. The new editor was Jacob Fuchs, a young man, born in Bialystok and now half-Germanified. Fuchs was simultaneously editor, chief (and assistant) article- and newswriter, publisher and errand boy. His great ambition had always been to be a publisher, but this ambition was backed by neither material nor intellectual resources. The only faculty which he did possess—and this to a marvelous degree—was that of being hungry. It was by starving, in fact, that he kept *Ha-Maggid* going. Unfortunately Fuchs's needs were small, so that if he did save on food and clothing, it amounted to little. He was forever borrowing, and his loans were small: ten marks, fifteen, twenty . . . all of them levied on lovers of Hebrew and devotees of the movement. He also borrowed from students. The loans were known technically as "maximum-minimum" loans: the minimum he could do with, the maximum we could offer. We also called them "internal" loans.

Fuchs extended to me an invitation to become a contributor to *Ha-Maggid*, promised me payment for my articles, and on the strength of the honorarium for the first article made a loan from me. But if Fuchs had only known how eager I was to be printed, he need not have promised any honorarium, and could have obtained a much larger loan into the bargain. One day Fuchs brought me an English Jewish periodical in which one of my articles—something on the Exodus from Egypt with obvious allusions to the flight from Russia—had appeared in translation. I was enormously impressed. I became more important in my own eyes; so did the English language. In gratitude to England I determined to learn the English language and began on the spot. Meanwhile, until I had mastered it, I spelled out my article word by word until I had learned the English translation by heart. However, my decision to learn the English language was not carried out until some decades later.

I produced an article for *Ha-Maggid* every week. This was in 1891, when I was occupied with many other things. It was during this period that I made my first attempt to prepare myself for a scholar's career. I had, fortunately, a rare capacity for work. I could go months on an allowance of three hours sleep nightly.

The thesis I chose for my first treatise was the *Metamorphosis of Concepts*—an investigation in the field of folk-psychology—a subject which has always had an extreme fascination for me.

I completed the thesis in a few months and brought it to Professor Steinthal. His comment was brief and to the point. He called me in, told me I obviously had a capacity for research, then took down a book from the shelf and showed me that my work had been wasted. This aspect of the subject had already been covered by a scholar of the name of Karl Abel!

My disillusionment was bitter in the extreme. I should of course have known about this work, and the fact that I did not showed the incompleteness of my devotion to my studies. This incident was perhaps the chief single influence in my choice of a career. It became clear to me that two such exacting roles as the scholar and the warrior could not be played by any one man.

I did not realize this at once, of course. I continued my studies. I attended the lectures of Zeller, Dilthey, Paulsen and Lazarus. In particular, however, I was fascinated by the lectures of George Simmel, who dealt with various philosophic problems. Simmel was a Jew, and it was widely held that he would long since have become a full-fledged professor if he had been anything but a Jew. What attracted me in Simmel was not so much the substance as the manner of his lectures. I heard in him the echo of generations of talmudic scholars, their way of illuminating points, their method of clinching an argument. It was only in his latter years that he rose to a professorship, not in Berlin, but in the University of Bonn.

In the fall of 1892 I transferred to the University of Königsberg. Life in Berlin was too tumultuous, too exciting, for a man of my temperament. I needed a quieter center for the prosecution of my studies, and I believed I would find it in Königsberg. I was not mistaken; yet it was in Königsberg that two decisive and symbolic events closed, as with a double lock, the first two periods of my life and left me facing my full manhood. It was there that I "ended" my education and took my degree, and it was there that I married.

Heine says somewhere that he who loves for the first time is a god, he who loves for the second time is a fool. The bitter wit of the remark conceals the taste of the deeper truth it carries. It is a rare thing for a man to be content with loving once, hence the proportion of gods to fools is miniscule. But we should note that our first love is not a matter of chronology. Life does not proceed chronologically; events belonging to different psychological epochs are embedded in the same time-stratum. When one of Chekhov's characters says that his first love affair came second, he is talking chronological but not psychological nonsense.

There is an old Jewish legend that forty days before a boy or girl is born, a Voice is heard in heaven crying: "This man belongs to that woman, this woman to that man." The souls are paired off, every Adam to every Eve. But the question on earth is, by what sign shall Eve recognize her Adam, Adam his Eve? Neither the antique nor the modern artist has the reply. Probably to the end of all time every man and woman will have to make answer according to an obscure personal impulse, and few will ever know whether the impulse led them to the truth.

The young woman I married, Helena Conheim, was an orphan. Her three brothers were in America, the oldest, Herman, already in business for himself. Helena was five years younger than I, and this difference in years, small as it was, sufficed to create in me a feeling of protectiveness and responsibility toward her. The marriage took place quietly in Krantz, a summer resort near Königsberg. The guests were few. My parents came from Svislovitz and Herman Conheim from America. The two families were strange to each other, the relationships were formal, courteous; and after the wedding the group scattered again, almost to the ends of the earth.

The years of my apprenticeship to life were over; from now on I was to be the independent artificer of it.

BOOK III

THE ARENA

CHAPTER TWENTY-THREE

The Battlefield

IT WAS the custom, particularly abroad, to speak of Russian Jewry as of a close-knit unit, held together by a community of interests, mores, education and political fate. This was one of the misconceptions fostered by the position of Russian Jewry as an object of compassion and charity. Western Jewry did not think it necessary to make a genuine study of the spiritual, cultural life of six million Jews on the other side of the frontier. It was as if the river Sambattyon of ancient fable lay between.

I doubt whether there was anywhere another Jewish group as heterogeneous and as motley as was Russian Jewry before it was practically destroyed by the great revolution. Ignoring the shadings that were to be found even in small localities, we may take three huge divisions: Polish Jewry, northwestern or so-called Lithuanian Jewry, and southern Jewry, which included New Russia, the Ukraine, Bessarabia, and the Crimea. Each of them had between one and a half and two million souls. Each of them also had its own character, the product of the human environment in which it lived and of its historic development.

There was a great difference between the Lithuanian Jew

and the southern Jew. The northwest was a poor district; the earth is lean and the peasant can barely wrest a living from it. Its one natural resource is timber. The vast forests were cut down pitilessly, and it came about that while the Polish nobility were the destroyers, the well-to-do Jews were nearly always the purveyors. The Ukraine, on the other hand, is blessed with a marvelously fertile soil. Its fields provide not only for Russia, but for many a country besides. The Lithuanian peasant, then, was a depressed, worried creature; when he sang it was of want and hunger. His brother of the Ukraine was well-fed and carefree, and he sang of joy. The difference between these great peasant groups was reflected in the Jews. The Lithuanian Jew was a pessimist, his brother of the Ukraine an optimist. The former sought refuge in speculations on a world to come; the latter found joy in this world. Lithuanian Jewry produced the Gaon of Vilna, the pure intellectualist; Ukrainian Jewry produced the Baal Shem Tov, the founder of Chassidism and the mystic lover of this life.

And yet the difference between these two groups was minor as compared with that which divided both of them from Polish Jewry. Poland was a conquered country, yet it had always remained foreign. The Russian citizen needed no passport to go to Poland, but when he got there he found himself in a strange country. The same foreignness was felt by the Russian Jew among Polish Jews. Even their pronunciation of Yiddish was so different that often they had difficulty in understanding each other. Lithuanian and Ukrainian Jews could mix and be lost in each other; but in Warsaw, as in other parts of Poland, two groups of Jews lived their distinct and separate lives. The line of division did not lie between Chassidim and Misnagdim, but between Russians and Poles. The division became particularly sharp in the nineties, when Warsaw was flooded with the refugees from Moscow and other interior districts. The majority of the ejected Jews were of Lithuanian origin.

All southern Jewry stood under the influence of Odessa, while Polish Jewry turned toward Warsaw. Lithuania had no center of its own at the time of which I am writing, for the days of Vilna's greatness had long departed and did not return until the coming of the Socialist Bund. Lithuania therefore looked to the Jewish community of St. Petersburg, which fulfilled a double function, for Russian Jewry as a whole and for Lithuanian Jewry in particular.

This brief analysis of the fragmentation of Russian Jewry will indicate what a fearful task this group had before it in its struggle for cultural and political emancipation. I doubt whether any other people has ever been faced by such a discouraging combination of circumstances. The Jewish thinker who wanted to address himself to his people had to bear in mind its three languages, two of them its own, one alien. It is impossible to calculate how much physical, nervous and mental energy this fact alone accounted for. One great Jewish leader has characterized the Jewish problem as a struggle with geography. He might as well have added that it was also a struggle with philology.

All these difficulties loomed large before me when I stood at the crossroads, compelled to make my choice of a career. My studies in Germany had uprooted me from my own locality; for the third time I had begun my life anew, and I could not deny that this third life had taken a powerful hold on me. Five years had sufficed to develop in me a deep affection for the German milieu. I admired the orderliness of German life in general, and I was touched by the deep German striving for knowledge. But I loved even more the German language and literature, which had become dearer to me even than the Russian. Another circumstance strengthened the bond: Germany was Protestant. I had studied the Bible under Christian professors, and I had been deeply moved by the passion and earnestness which they brought to their researches in our ancient literature. I had more than once visited their churches and had been amazed to mark the awe and reverence with which they spoke of our heroes and Prophets.

True, I still felt myself a stranger in their midst, without a portion in their mighty heritage. But was I not a stranger in Russia, too? Was I any nearer to the authentic Russian than to the authentic German? As it happens, I found myself accepted and more humanely treated in the land to which I came than in the land where I was born. I was in the midst of a people that made no pogroms!

I had friends and connections enough in Germany. The dean of the faculty of philosophy in the University of Königsberg urged me to stay on and promised me his moral support. But something pulled me back to Russia: not the country, but my people. Again, I might have made my peace with the genuine German world, but the world of German Jewry, with its imitative Teutonism, I found intolerable. I longed for the millions who lived in oppression and need, but who had not sold their souls.

Among the three Jewish centers of Russia, my choice fell on Warsaw. I had no "right of residence" in St. Petersburg, though I might have taken a "job" with some well-known magnate, ostensibly as doorman or butler. That was what the famous poet Frug had done. Or I might have got an artisan's certificate and paid monthly graft to the police. But I was repelled by the shifts and dodges of the fugitive's life. Odessa was too distant and too strange to me, while in Warsaw there had formed a considerable group of "my" Jews, Lithuanians, among them many *Choveve Zion*, and not ordinary ones, but members, like myself, of the secret order *B'nai Moshe*, Sons of Moses, founded by Ahad Ha-am. My choice, then, was along the line of least resistance; I settled in Warsaw.

The Jewish world of thought stood, in those days, under the sign of Ahad Ha-am. I have told of my meeting with him in

Odessa, five years earlier. Within that interval his name had risen to the first place in the Jewish intellectual world. Around Ahad Ha-am had gathered a small circle of kindred spirits, who looked to him with reverence and affection as the personification of all that was best and finest in Jewish thought. In this restricted circle the idea was born of an organization of the elect, of men who sought the path of spiritual purification, who desired to build a new future for their people not because they wanted to be "like all the other nations" but because *inner* necessity drove them. The *B'nai Moshe* was founded on the seventh day of the month of Adar in the year 1889. We chose that date because according to an ancient tradition the great leader was born on that day, and on that day he died.

The *Chibath Zion*, which had begun with mighty dreams of a general Jewish exodus, had retreated step by step into petty worries and by the end of the eighties it had shrunk into a philanthropic institution. The Odessa center, directed by Pinsker and Lilienblum, had become the collector of pitifully small donations, which were boomed in the press as if they represented a great folk movement. Pinsker, in his *Auto-Emancipation*, had spoken of an enlightened Jewish manhood which should take upon itself the task which tradition used to assign to a half-divine leader, and as a collectivity should play the Messiah to a people living in slavery and shame. Lilienblum had been even more specific. He had written:

"We must try to colonize Palestine so rapidly that in the course of one generation the Jews as a whole shall be able to leave hospitable Europe; we must be able to settle as a mass in the land of our fathers, the land to which we never lost our historic right simply because we lost our freedom."

There had indeed been times when the movement had a messianic element in it. But those moments of brilliant illumination soon failed, and a mood of sobriety succeeded. As long as an idea is abstract, time and space disappear, and the path leads smoothly forward. When reality sets in, the stones and thorns on the road multiply. A noble idea, a lofty concept, enlists a thousand enthusiasts; when the labor begins, a tiny handful of the choice remain.

The *B'nai Moshe* was in a sense a counterweight to the *Chibath Zion*, and the two movements reflected the opposed but complementary personalities of their directors. Superficially it appeared that Lilienblum was the optimist, Ahad Ha-am, the pessimist. But the opposite was the case. For Lilienblum assumed that what the Jewish people then was, it would remain forever; it could not be trained to accept the discipline of a great effort. Ahad Ha-am, who saw the condition of the people as it actually was, believed profoundly in its latent forces. It was this belief in the possibility of awakening to creative action the almost atrophied capacities of the Jewish people that stamped the philosophy and life-activity of Ahad Ha-am. In his first public utterance he demonstrated, with the merciless logic that was peculiarly his, that the methods chosen by the *Chibath Zion* would not lead to success, that the way to the reconstructed land led first through the reconstruction of the will of the people.

A second principle ran parallel with the first: whether it was the preparatory work in the exile or the experimental work in Palestine, quality had to precede quantity. Had there been a possibility of transferring the Jewish people to Palestine in an instant (a generation is of course an instant, historically speaking), it might have been permissible to yield a point here and there. But since the delay was in its very nature for the purpose of education, every action had to be of a quality that would train the intelligence, the dignity and the discipline of the people.

Within the Order itself Ahad Ha-am applied equally rigidly principles of quality. He had worked out a system of exacting rules of conduct, and every member had to take a solemn oath to apply them to every circumstance of his personal and public life. In the days of its greatest extension the Order of *B'nai Moshe* did not comprise more than a hundred members, and for Ahad Ha-am even that number sometimes seemed too high.

One element was lacking in the make-up of Ahad Ha-am. He was a great teacher but not a political leader, a guide but not an organizer. A moral personality alone does not suffice in political action. The political leader must have, in the first place, a passion for leadership. He must desire to master and command. He cannot consider too closely the wishes of those he leads. He must be able to decree, to impose his will. Ahad Ha-am was not cast in this mold. The leadership of the Order was thrust upon him. His one wish was to remain free, to devote himself wholly to the task of his life, the cleansing of the national ideal from the superfluities and the undesirable features which had accumulated in it. A people purified, he argued, can think clearly, and a people that thinks clearly acts clearly. The first report of his visit to Palestine in 1891 (the stormy days of the *Chibath Zion*) ends with the following characteristic passage:

"Filled with melancholy thoughts after what I had seen and heard in Jaffa and the colonies, I arrived on the eve of Passover in Jerusalem, there to pour forth my sorrow and my rage before the stocks and stones, the remnants of our former glory. I went first, of course, to the Wailing Wall. There I found many of our Jerusalem brethren standing and praying in loud voices. Their haggard faces, their wild, alien gestures, their fantastic clothes—all harmonized with the ghastly picture of the Wall itself. I looked alternately at them and at the Wall, and one thought filled my heart: these stones are the witness to the desolation of our people; and which of these two desolations is the greater? For which of them shall we shed more tears? When a land is destroyed, there may yet arise a Zerubabel, an Ezra, a Nehemiah, and, bringing a people with him, restore the land. But when a people is destroyed, who can come to its rescue?"

During its eight years of existence the *B'nai Moshe* was under constant attack. Militant Jewish orthodoxy was not in those days an organized power in the modern sense; but it had its groups in every large city, and it stood on guard against every manifestation of energy that might endanger the ancient traditional outlook and way of life. The center of orthodoxy was Kovno, and its adherents called themselves the Pillars of the Law. Their leader was Jacob Lifschitz, the secretary of Rabbi Isaac Elkhanan Spektor.

The reader will have gathered from my brief description of him that the Rabbi himself was not a fighter. His extreme piety had given him almost the status of a saint, yet he was known to be amongst the most tolerant of the rabbis, and he took no part in the struggle between the old ideas and the new. But Lifschitz used his name freely, and it was the general impression that whatever Lifschitz did had the approval of Rabbi Isaac Elkhanan. In the camp of the opponents of orthodoxy this center was called the Black Cabinet, and this Black Cabinet declared war to the death on the *Chibath Zion* movement. Its methods were not of the choicest; they included libel and slander and that most repulsive of tactics: the denunciation that Jewish nationalism was not only against the powers of heaven, but against those of earth too.

This was the battle waged by ancient, orthodox Judaism, a Judaism petrified to the core, compact of servility, against the revolutionary spirit which sought a way into the open, and called the Jewish people to action and daring. But apart from purely ideological motives, arising from a genuine conservatism and even reaction, there were factors of an economic order.

To these I have already referred briefly when speaking of the *Chalukah*—the charitable institution which sent its agents out from Palestine to make collections for the pious old Jews who had gone to spend their last days in the Holy Land. Reactionary Judaism saw them as *its* pioneers—heroes of prayers and fasts, the only kind fit to bring the Day of Redemption. Immobile, passive, slavish, the supporters of the *Chalukah* could never conceive of earthly self-help. It saw in *our* pioneers a formidable competitor—both in the raising of funds and in the Redemption itself. The Mount of Olives—the Jewish cemetery in Jerusalem—and the Wailing Wall shifted into the background, and the foreground was occupied by talk of colonies, of fields sown with grain, of trees heavy with fruit. From Palestine the leaders of the *Chalukah* issued an open civic denunciation of the entire *Chibath Zion*, and did not rest until they had brought about the imprisonment by the Turkish authorities of the man who symbolized in Palestine the new spirit of Jewry—Eliezer ben Yehudah, the great reviver of spoken Hebrew. The excuse was an innocent article which ben Yehudah had printed in his Hebrew newspaper in honor of the Feast of Tabernacles. Here he made allusion, in the ornate circumlocution of the time, to the glorious deeds of the Maccabees—and that was enough for the *Chalukah* leaders. To the task of hastening the appearance of the Messiah, the heroes of fast and prayer added a second—that of defending the throne of Abdul Hamid against Jewish "revolutionaries."

The *B'nai Moshe* was in the thick of a complicated struggle. The Pillars of the Law were our deadly enemies, but the *Chibath Zion*, itself the enemy of the Pillars of the Law, had no great liking for us, either. We had the same ultimate objective as the *Chibath Zion*, but to most of its old members our high standards and criticisms seemed merely destructive. We were critical of Baron Edmund de Rothschild, the only supporter of the new settlement in Palestine; and Aham Ha-am denounced in unmeasured terms a regime which destroyed the initiative and energy of the colonist and turned him into a lackey of the Baron's local administrator. But we were not merely critical. Through the efforts of the *B'nai Moshe* was founded the first *self-supporting* Jewish colony, Rehovoth, today one of the finest and largest in Palestine. We were also creators in the cultural field at home. We were responsible for the founding of two Hebrew publishing houses and for the first modern Hebrew schools, which contributed greatly to the Hebrew renaissance.

Meanwhile we were conducting a ceaseless battle on another front, against the *shtadlanim*. In these days of popular Jewish movements it is almost impossible for a newer generation, especially if it has grown up in the democratic West, to understand the role played by these men. The *shtadlan* was born of the utter helplessness of the Jewish masses. They were abandoned to the random, irresponsible private whim of anyone who had money and influence and cared to use them for what *he* thought was their good. I doubt whether there is the equivalent of the word *shtadlan* in any other language, for I doubt whether any other people has ever thus been at the mercy, not of rulers—that would be commonplace enough—but of backstair negotiators without a genuine status.

I do not wish it to appear that I consider the *shtadlanim* to have been corrupt or evil men. There were undoubtedly among them individuals of larger caliber and cleaner mind, who desired solely to serve their people and would have been happy if they could have appeared in the role of the properly elected representatives of Jewry. But they saw no such possibility before them; to serve at all they had to serve as *shtadlanim*. History, however, cannot pause over the occasional individual. Whatever a *shtadlan* might be here or there, the system was one which could not but be corruptive of good intentions. It need not surprise us that the *shtadlanim* of Russian Jewry should have fought tooth and nail against the emergence of a democratic will, especially when the attitude of the government toward the masses is taken into consideration.

The government liked the *shtadlanim*. From time to time it even let them know that it was prepared, out of sheer benevolence, to administer some sort of relief to the Jews—always, of course, in homeopathic doses, so as not to arouse the resentment of the Russian masses. The situation was one on which no traditional Jesuit could have improved. Through her thousands of secret agents the Russian government carried on a continuous campaign of slander and incitement against the Jews. At the same time the government cited this "folk anti-Semitism" as an excuse for its attitude toward the Jews. The *shtadlanim* were of course unable to break this vicious circle at any point; they did their best, therefore, to instill in the Jewish masses the treacherous philosophy preached by the government. Unwittingly they became the agents of the government, and the Jewish masses, without directives or leaders, were compelled to follow the only light they saw—the *shtadlanim.*

This was the condition until the time of the pogroms in the eighties. Shaken to its foundations, Russian Jewry lost every vestige of respect for the *shtadlanim* and began to organize its own awakening forces. This revolt found expression in the double phenomenon of the Jewish labor movement and the Jewish national movement. Both of them were symbols of the break with the past, of the sudden thawing of our frozen strength, the setting in of a new epoch, perhaps the greatest epoch of activity in all the history of the Diaspora.

The national movement, first appearing in the *Chibath Zion*, and later as political Zionism, had no direct connection with the struggle in Russia itself. It simply sought an exodus. As to the situation within Russia, the labor movement ignored the struggle for Jewish emancipation, denying from the outset that there were such things as separate Jewish interests. It was only when the leaders came in intimate contact with the Jewish masses that they discovered their error. But the two movements, labor and nationalist, changed profoundly and forever the foundations of the general movement for emancipation. For the first time in the history of their struggle for human rights, the Jews spoke as a national entity.

It would, however, be quite wrong to credit the new epoch in Russian Jewish life solely to these two movements, labor and nationalist. To get a complete picture of the changes in Russian Jewish life we must consider a third factor, perhaps the most important, namely, the general spirit of the time.

The written theory of the eighteenth, and of part of the nineteenth century was the theory of cosmopolitanism, according to which the nation is a purely fortuitous phenomenon, destined to pass away in the course of history. The greatest thinkers, artists, and statesmen of that epoch dreamed not of an international order, a harmony and cooperation of various nations, but of the disappearance of the differences which constituted the nations themselves. They dreamed of a world inhabited by man the common denominator, the abstract man, the citizen of the world, a stranger to any of the bonds of race or origin. It was, perhaps, a beautiful dream, but it was nothing more; for the illusion on which it was based ignored the organic nature of the human being and of the course of history. They went on dreaming and life went on weaving its own pattern. The process of nationalizing, which began about the time of the Renaissance, reached its highest intensity precisely in the nineteenth century. And now new thinkers and artists, and particularly scholars in the field of culture, exalted the nation as the crown of human achievement. The nationalist factor came into its own.

The formulation of the new theory was bound to take place in those countries where it was needed most. England, France and Germany were almost homogeneous units in the matter of population. The picture in Austria and Russia was vastly different. These were states specifically built up of diverse nationalities. Thus it came about that in England, for instance, the concept of nationality did not differ from the concept of state. The bearer of a British passport was known to be, and thought himself to be, British by nationality too. In Russia, on the other hand, no Jew, and for that matter no Tartar, would ever have conceived that he was of Russian nationality—not even if he had assimilated. In Austria the situation was such that it led the assimilating Jew into strange self-contradiction. Wishing to escape into something, he would sometimes designate himself as of Austrian nationality. But there was no such thing. The state consisted of seventeen nationalities. Thus, the Pole, the Czech and the Magyar always knew to what nationality they belonged.

It was therefore natural that the scientific theory of nationalism should have emerged in Russia and Austria. A long list of theoreticians and of practical statesmen attests to this truth, and every name represents both a man and a school. I cite a few. There were Potebnia, Gradovsky and Vladimir Solovyov in Russia, Masaryk and Springer-Renner in Austria. Each of these men was a pathfinder and a teacher. Among the Russian Jews too there were those who helped clear the road for national freedom. They came along convergent paths from scattered points, but they came together in their task of teaching Russian Jewry a new method and a new understanding.

One of these men was Dr. Chaim Zhitlovsky. His nearest parallel is the Austrian Springer-Renner. He issued first from the Socialist point of view but came to understand that it is impossible to realize Socialism while ignoring the nationalist factor. Another was Simon Dubnow. It took this man a long time to rid himself of the cosmopolitan hypnosis, but the deeper his researches took him into the significance of history, the more clearly he saw the significance of the nationalist factor. There is a strong similarity between Dubnow and Masaryk in the development of their ideas. The third, and most powerful of the Jewish figures is Ahad Ha-am, and there is, again, a parallel between Ahad Ha-am and Solovyov. For both of them nationalism was above all an ethical problem, a question of supreme justice.

For me the Order of *B'nai Moshe* was a sort of temple, served by an incomparable high priest. Time did not weaken this feeling; the more intimately I came to know Ahad Ha-am, the more I admired his clear insight, his simple, healthy logic, and his sharp power of analysis. But most of all I was drawn to him by the purity of his mind and of his intentions.

It was long after the *Chibath Zion* had yielded the stage to the Zionist Organization that the *B'nai Moshe* disappeared silently—like the leader of olden times whose name it bore. No man knoweth the place of his burial. Political Zionism, tumultuous, vigorous, held the attention of world Jewry. The founders of the Zionist Organization denied that Zionism was simply a development of the *Chibath Zion* idea. They always asserted that Zionism was a brand-new movement, beginning with its own Book I, Genesis. I have passed through both movements, almost since the birth of the first, and I must confess that I cannot distinguish the principle that divides the two. The dream of a Jewish state is characteristic of both of them. In the *Chibath Zion* the cultural element played a larger role than in the Zionist movement. The explanation is simple. The *Chibath Zion* was dominated by the Jews of eastern Europe, who were the strongest Jewry in the cultural sense. In the sense of leadership, it was the Western Jews who dominated the Zionist movement. The idea of a Jewish state simply became more clear, but the result was a compromise in the cultural field.

Not all the members of the *B'nai Moshe* accepted the new features of the national movement. Ahad Ha-am himself was less satisfied than anyone. His apostle and adjutant, Joshua Eisenstadt, remained unsatisfied too. Twenty years after he had inducted me into the Order, I visited Eisenstadt in Jerusalem, where he lived in a modest little room on an obscure side street. He had withdrawn from public and political life. The apostle was silent. He spoke no more of the far-off future; he reverted instead to the days that were gone. He told me that he had sworn me into the Order on his own responsibility, and that the directors of the Order had looked askance upon my membership, because of my youth. But he had believed in the strength I would yet develop. I gave him my thanks—belated by almost a generation.

CHAPTER TWENTY-FOUR

Finding Myself

I TOOK quarters among my more intimate friends, on a side-street off the Nalevkis, the main artery of the tumultuous life of Warsaw. Here life raged not less furiously than on the Friedrichstrasse of Berlin, but reminded one less of Western commerce than of an Oriental bazaar. The Jewish merchant had not the habit of sitting patiently in his store, waiting for the buyer. He had a hatred of loneliness, and the interior of the store was lonely. He was drawn to noise, the rush, the chaos of the street. He wanted the mass, the crowds, where he was not condemned to silence between one customer and another, and where he could talk himself out. It may be that this was a genuine reversion to the Orient; in part it may have been the long life of the ghetto, where Jews had always lived close together and where the feeling of security was associated with the multitude.

With the help of some friends, Helena and I were soon settled in a roomy apartment, large enough, in fact, for small gatherings—an important matter in view of the restrictions on meetings of all kinds. Every householder, without exception, was watched by the police. The houses in Poland were built round courtyards. To enter the house it is always necessary to pass the porter's lodge at the main gate on the street. Now this porter, or *strusz*, as he is called in Polish, was in nearly every instance instructed by the police to keep a sharp eye on the tenants: to mark the number of guests and their character, to learn something about the occupations and associations of the tenants; wherever possible it was his proper business to eavesdrop on conversations and get a line on the ideas of the people living round him. If he thought he heard anything suspicious, he was to report to the police at once. He was supposed to be at the service of the tenants, and he was in fact treated as a low-class servant. In reality he played the sneak and stool-pigeon for the police. In the hierarchy of the Russian espionage system he was the lowest among the low; and yet he was the foundation of the whole structure, for he stood in constant and, so to speak, intimate contact with the population, and he was a man not easily avoided.

It goes without saying that the majority of these porters were gross and ignorant creatures to whom a political conversation was simply jabber; but the grosser and more ignorant they were, the more dangerous they were to the population which factually lived under their supervision. A word torn out of context, a harmless phrase misunderstood by an illiterate, might be carried to the police and result in much discomfort. It was therefore the first law of life in Warsaw that relations with the porter must be friendly, and the friendliness must, if necessary, be purchased.

The monetary cost was trifling; the feeling of humiliation was hard to bear. My friends instructed me how to go about making friends with the porter. It was a mistake to give him too large a tip and to seem too anxious for his goodwill. He was to be treated with a diplomatic mixture of condescension and consideration, as though no one suspected him of being anything but a servant, but a servant of somewhat higher quality. In brief, he was to be made a friend, but a not-too-friendly one.

My house, tastefully furnished by Helena, became at once a gathering place not only for the *B'nai Moshe,* but also for my friends among the Hebrew writers. Helena was the soul of hospitality; she was a skillful and friendly hostess, though at first she treated my intimate friends as though they too were "guests." It was my desire to keep the kind of house my father had kept—no ceremony; my friends were to come and go freely, without the feeling that they were guests—and it was difficult to make Helena fall in line, for she liked doing things for people. My friends saved the situation by perceiving that Helena's friendliness was not artificial, and they got used to the idea of being treated every time with the care and thoughtfulness bestowed on a new guest.

But this related only to the outer side of our social life. Inwardly Helena was unable to find, among those who frequented our house, the satisfactions to which she was entitled as a young and intelligent woman. She was the daughter of an orthodox Jewish home, but she had grown up in another world. She had been educated in a Russian high school for girls. She had been nourished on the literature of modern Russia, had followed the stream of thought of the better type of Russian society, and dreamed of a small circle of comrades devoted to the Russian movement of liberation. Her relationship to the Jewish people and its destiny depended insecurely on her relationship to her father's house and his Jewish friends. Jewish knowledge, the language, history, and literature of the Jews, remained alien to her, and it was only because of her earlier contact with some friends who had belonged to the Jewish national movement, and because of her relationship to me that her attitude toward the movement was not without sympathy. Yet it is probable that in a purely Socialist world she would have suffered from the absence of Jewish interests. But her participation in such a world would have been more intensive, if only for technical reasons. She wrote and spoke an excellent Russian, she knew Russian literature thoroughly, and she had a profound and earnest relationship to the Russian liberation movement.

At the meetings which were held in our home the old chief topics of discussion were Jewish problems, Hebrew literature, the new life in Palestine; and I could observe how Helena exerted herself to create an inner relation between herself and these subjects. But I saw too, that it was a sacrifice on her part; it seemed to me at times that in the midst of all the excited talk she was dreaming of her girlhood years, when, among companions who shared her education and her views, she had not only listened but had also shared freely in the debates.

Helena was good to me. She was by nature independent, yet she admitted tacitly that the foremost place in the house was to be given to *my* world, and this is the greatest concession that any woman can make. When alone, she and I spoke Russian, yet the atmosphere of the house was nationalistically Hebrew. The content did not agree with the form: both of us lived in perpetual translation. For me the translation consisted in the language, for Helena in the content.

The old saying, "We don't see the wood for the trees," is just as good in reverse. We do not see the trees distinctly for the wood. In Warsaw, for the first time, I came up against the harshness and brutality of life. Till then I had lived in the forest and had had little to do with the trees. I lived in a movement and had eyes only for that. I saw the army of those that made up the movement, and it did not occur to me that the individual units, those marching figures which kept step rhythmically, were in a sense detached, that each one had a path of its own to follow, an individual struggle to face. I never descended to the man. Even with my most intimate friends, I had never discussed the question of my personal future. Nor did I think about their private lives, their means, their plans. I was criminally carefree in this respect, pathologically optimistic; the idea of "settling down," the question of "feathering a nest"—the primordial occupation of the modern world—did not exist for me. I was the typical Talmud student, repeating: "Do not make the Torah a spade to dig with." The Tree of Knowledge bore fruit, but not fruit to be eaten; learning was its own reward.

A little commonsense would have told me that I had no right to found a "house in Israel." I was not equipped with means or a profession. The extraordinary thing was that neither my parents and relatives nor Helena's asked me what I intended to do about it. Helena's brother, the "American," probably did not even entertain the question. If I was founding a house I was probably entitled to do so.

My parents, Russian Jews, saw it all otherwise: a Jew must found a house in Israel—then God will help him.

I had some means at first, and used them till the shoe began to pinch, and for the first time in my life I began to worry about livelihood. I began to examine my friends as individuals, and observed, somewhat to my astonishment, that every one of them had a regular profession or occupation which provided him with bread and butter. The profession or occupation left him with a certain amount of freedom which he was able to devote without afterthought to the public good. My Warsaw friends, all of them industrious, practical people, were also the first to discuss with me this question of "the future." They may have thought me better off than I really was, but they argued with me earnestly to look for a source of income. But finding a source of income is, I need hardly say, more easily said than done when there is no regular profession to do it with.

Under normal circumstances a person like myself would apply for and probably obtain a government job. In the big machinery of a state there is always room for a man of good education and industrious habits. Such doors were of course closed to Jews. On top of this, I was extremely fastidious. I would under no circumstances accept work, however dignified in itself, which would not be connected, however indirectly, with the ideas that made up my intellectual and emotional life. Business? I could have chosen such a career before, without having spent so much of my life in study abroad. Warsaw and Lodz, in those days rapidly expanding centers of commerce and industry, absorbed masses of our young people of academic training, and turned them into efficient businessmen. But from this path I turned resolutely.

I hit at last upon something that seemed to me to contain an element of originality. I was going to open a *cheder* of the modern type and become a *melamed*—a simple *melamed* and comrade to little children. When I proposed the idea to my friends they looked at me openmouthed. At first they took it for a kind of jest; finally I convinced them that I was in earnest and that I wanted them to help me realize my plan.

The idea satisfied me in all respects. As a faithful disciple of Ahad Ha-am I shared his views on "the preparation of the generation." With him I believed that before we built Palestine we had to build the people. A generation was to be brought up which did not strain toward Palestine simply because of persecution and discrimination, but because of a desire to loose the soul of the Jew from the chains that held it down—and not less in the lands of so-called emancipation than elsewhere. Among the most masterly passages in the writings of Ahad Ha-am are those which deal with the slavery of the Jewish soul in the lands of outward freedom. And there was not a better point to begin at than with the very young, the clean and still uncorrupted.

It was not the idea that was new, for the modern *cheder* was already in existence. The newness lay in the fact that a man of Western education was willing to take upon himself the name of *melamed*. Etymologically the word means simply "teacher," but as the reader has had occasion to learn, it had by association become a comical and odious title. I wanted, among other things, to restore to the word "*melamed*" its original dignity, and to lift back the word "*cheder*" to its old estate.

My friends did not believe that I could find a secure livelihood in the *melamed's* profession; they foretold distress and disappointment, they spoke of obstacles on the part of parents and of the government—particularly the latter. The government was opposed on principle to raising the standard of the *cheder*, which it was prepared to tolerate as a primitive religious school but not as an institution which might impart even the rudiments of a decent education.

In Russia proper the *cheder* was forbidden to teach Russian and arithmetic, history and geography. To the ordinary folk or public schools, the Jewish child was rarely admitted, and the *cheder*, which the Jews supported out of their own pockets, was hampered by cruel restrictions. But the province of Poland had other laws. Here the teaching of Russian in the *cheder* was *obligatory*! Every *melamed* had to pass an elementary examination in the language before he was permitted to open a *cheder*. The explanation of the paradox is quite simple: denying the Jew his rights in Russia proper, the government so far relaxed them in Poland as to make him an odious instrument of forcible Russification.

In spite of this wretched situation, and in spite of the discouragement of my friends, I persisted in my resolution. The *cheder* became an *idée fixe* with me. I was convinced that this was my life career. Later on, when I did become a teacher, I understood that it was a healthy instinct that had driven me to think with such persistence of becoming a *melamed*. I had a genuine affection and gift for this work—perhaps the result of my intense admiration for my teacher Judah Artzer.

I found a decent room in one of the most thickly settled Jewish sections of Warsaw, furnished it with the necessary benches and desks, and approached the task of obtaining pupils. My friend Zev Gluskin, a fellow member of the *B'nai Moshe*, was my guide. He introduced me to the prospects and gave me a good character, assuring the parents that I had no ulterior motives or sinister designs, and that I really wanted to teach the children by modern methods. He strongly advised me to wear a silk hat when calling on my prospects, as there was nothing more impressive, not even my doctorate of philosophy from a German University. He further advised me to speak to the parents in pure or "*goyish*" German, so that they should not understand me wholly. The best thing would be to bewilder them slightly—and for this purpose a silk hat and high German were excellent adjuncts. My friend said all this with great seriousness, but I felt that he was mocking me; he saw the absurdity of my project, but did not care to be open about it.

My plans came to nothing, but the deciding factor appeared unexpectedly from another quarter. My father came on a visit to us. We tried hard to persuade him to stay with us during the visit, but he remained true to his old maxim: "Don't stay with relatives, not even with your own children. Take your meals there if you like, but nothing more." Our apartment was on the fifth floor, and while I was accompanying him upstairs for the first time I observed with a dreadful pang that my father was growing old. He found the steps difficult and had to pause for breath at every floor. I tried to cover up the sad pauses by accelerated conversation, but my eyes must have given me away, for when my father turned to me on the top floor he said, curtly: "We don't stay young forever."

It may be that in my terror there was that inevitable touch of self from which there seems to be no escape. Till now I had been utterly dependent on my parents, and I saw the prop beginning to yield. It was a lightning-flash revelation of responsibility: the time had come for me to think seriously of the future, in a purely material sense.

My father stayed in Warsaw several weeks and spent most of the afternoons with us. He asked me a great many questions about my plans and hopes. When I told him I was going to become a *melamed* he smiled, as one smiles at a foolishness uttered by a child. He began to explain that I had to look at life like an adult; he would continue to help me, as he had always done, but I was a grown man, I had a wife to look after, I would have to change. There was, he granted, something very fine about the idea about working for the benefit of one's people, but no man could serve his people unless he looked after himself first. He begged me, then, to drop this idea of a *cheder* and to find a serious occupation.

For the first time I can remember I yielded at once to my father. Never had I felt so strongly his worldly superiority, or the genuine and loving concern in his voice. And the short scene on the steps had left an indelible impression on me. My father was no longer the young, all-powerful figure of my boyhood. He was bowed under a burden of years and responsibilities, and among the latter were many of my creation. And because my father was bending under the years I bent before his will. He told me, too, that he and my mother were feeling their age and that the coming summer, God willing, they were going to take a rest abroad, at some cure.

I felt as though someone had thrust cold steel into me. It is a good thing if children can live in the vicinity of their parents, so as not to see them growing old. For the last few years I had not seen my parents. I had left him, as I had left my mother, a youthful, vigorous and energetic person; and I trembled at the change.

I gave up the *cheder* nonsense and concentrated on another idea, one that had long floated about vaguely in my mind: to become a rabbi in some important congregation where I would have the opportunity to go on with my nationalist work. In the meantime I would intensify my activities in the field of propaganda and literature.

I became a member of that group of young writers which had founded the modern publishing house, *Achiasaf*. It had one employee on a regular salary, ben Avigdor, and the pay which writers received was meager indeed. Ben Avigdor was literary editor for the house, and also its bookkeeper. He was a man of tremendous energy, and his will to produce books for the Jewish world was boundless, but though he was a member of the *B'nai Moshe* he thought more of quantity than quality. He was irked by the restraints we placed on him and finally broke away to found another publishing house, *Toshiah*; he did more to increase than to enrich Hebrew literature.

How it came to pass I do not know, but once in the *Achiasaf* group, I began to write poetry again. I had prudently divorced the muse in early years; now I fulfilled the Jewish law which exalts the remarriage of a divorced wife as a special act of piety. I also wrote polemical articles in a light satirical vein, and here I was faced with a difficulty. I was afraid to put my name to them, it was so easy to acquire a reputation as an irresponsible humorist, and I wanted my work as a publicist to be taken seriously. But I also wanted to make my mark, and a *nom de guerre* would leave me still unknown. I consulted the gifted poet, David Frischman, one of our contributors, and he advised me: "Choose a fantastic name vaguely reminiscent of your real name. Jews are fond of riddles; they won't rest till they've found you out. If you want to remain wholly hidden, choose a simple name that won't arouse suspicion."

He went on to tell me the story of a name. A young man had brought a short story to the editor of a periodical. After many months he got a reply—a rejection. The editor liked the story but refused to print something by a writer with the utterly absurd name of Kugelmacher. Not that he objected to Jewish names generally, but why Kugelmacher? The young man ran breathlessly to the editor and implored mercy and advice, which were granted freely. Why not choose a somewhat more aesthetic-sounding name, at least for writing purposes? The young man confessed: "As a matter of fact my real name is Tschalendtopf, an awful one, I know. But I wanted something that wouldn't wholly hide me, so I chose Kugelmacher, and you don't know how long it took me to think it up."

There is something in our nature that prevents us from running too far away from ourselves. Even the criminal has an impulse to remain somehow identified with his crimes. The comparison is not too far-fetched. No person revisits a book more frequently than its writer, and he alone can never quite get over his admiration for it. I have read somewhere of a great counterfeiter whose banknotes were masterpieces of imitation. For a long time he passed them off successfully, but in the end the forgery was detected by an expert. In a tiny corner of text a letter *i* had remained undotted. The counterfeiter was tracked down and at the trial the question was put to him: "How could you possibly make so gross a blunder after showing such amazing skill?" The counterfeiter, deeply wounded, answered as an artist: "It wasn't a blunder. I did it on purpose. If not for the undotted *i* even I could never have distinguished between real notes and my counterfeits."

In the end I adopted the simple pseudonym of Joachim Hurwitz. Behind this name my identity was safe; but it was a wrench.

The sages of all peoples have sung the praises of the man who settles down to one craft and becomes a master in it. If God has given you one shred of talent, work with it; be happy and do not look for successes elsewhere. I do not mean to say that everything else must be neglected, but over-concentration is better than scattering. The dilettante suffers from an over-developed appetite, and a little success in one direction makes him eager to extend in all directions. I am speaking not of the genius, but of the ordinary man of talent, who among Jews has a specific leaning toward becoming a Jack-of-all-trades. He is a type of scatterbrain who never wins through to a higher craftsmanship.

I myself was such a scatterbrain, and I still mourn the fact. I was driven by the exilic restlessness to try everything at least once, and to neglect the one field where I could have developed to my maximum capacity. In Warsaw I began two pieces of literary work that should have absorbed all my energies and all my powers of concentration. Had I followed them up in the right spirit I would have consolidated my talents in the literary field. As it was, I carried on with the pieces till they were fairly well developed, and then dropped them to follow other ambitions. I promised myself earnestly that I was only interrupting myself, but knew all the time that I would never take them up again.

The first was an anthology of Hebrew songs from the earliest times to our own day. The second was a new Hebrew dictionary, complete in all branches, with all the old treasuries and all the new creations. Ahad Ha-am worked out the program, I was to prepare the material in concentrated form. I gave two years to this enterprise and got as far as the seventh letter, *zayin*. Both works were, as I have said, abandoned in the middle. It is true that there were technical difficulties; the finances of the *Achiasaf* publishing house were shaky; yet the fault was still mine. Had I not been pursued by the imp of dilettantism, I would have managed to overcome even the technical difficulties. I do not pretend that the completion of these works would have meant the intellectual salvation of the Jewish people; but I myself would have been whole and I would not have been haunted for years by the sense of abandoned creations which still implored me to complete them.

My preparations for a scholarly career were respectable. I had a good knowledge of modern and ancient literature, the latter through translations. I had mastered three languages, Russian, German and Hebrew, though of course not in equal measure. The first two never became for me—not even after years of study and exclusive use in daily life—what Hebrew was. With regard to speech, Russian and German were as native to me as Hebrew; this was natural, since Hebrew was not a language of daily use. I had the illusion that I also thought in all languages alike, but the test—when I sat down to write—contradicted the illusion. No sooner did I begin to muster my ideas for an article in either German and Russian than the Hebrew language at once presented itself to me, unbidden, as if to say: "At most I will allow you to translate me."

Much observation has strengthened me in the belief that an *organic* relationship can exist between a person and only one language. The belief is common, too, among authorities on the subject. Languages may be acquired to perfection, but they are acquired on a foundation that cannot be shaken, namely, a man's original language. In that one language the man feels at home; other languages are like inns in which the host may suddenly appear to advise him sternly that he has unwittingly broken one or another of the house regulations.

I have omitted Yiddish from the list not because I consider this language unimportant. On the contrary, it has played a role second only to Hebrew in the life of east European Jewry, and is in every sense fully a folk language. But at that time I did not use Yiddish as a written medium of expression.

It is important to remember that in the nineties Yiddish literature played a very small role in Jewish life. It had not yet been admitted to the drawing room and was ignored in intellectual circles. At best it was regarded as an unliterary phenomenon: a translation of what was good in Hebrew for the benefit of those who had not received an adequate Hebrew education. At first even the Yiddish writers assumed an apologetic tone, and explained frequently the causes that drove them to use this language. In those days no one suspected that Yiddish was about to develop a genuine rivalry with Hebrew and make a bid, not for equality, but for priority—and even for monopoly. The best writers of Yiddish, the creators of a Yiddish style, Mendelle Mocher S'forim, Sholom Aleichem, Peretz, Ravnitsky, and in poetry Frischman and Frug were, with the exception of the last, masters of Hebrew, and nothing was further from their minds than the raising up of a rival to their own first medium.

Among the founders of modern Yiddish literature, one must be noted especially, not merely because of his supreme talent, but because of the singular role he played. Sholom Aleichem was a master of Hebrew, and some of his stories originally written in that language can serve even today as models of a rich and charming style. He had a profound respect for the Hebrew language and its literature. It had been the first medium for the development of his talents. It had nourished him in childhood, formed his taste and encouraged his growth. Yet among all these figures Sholom Aleichem was the first to transfer the center of attention from Hebrew to Yiddish not for a negative but for an affirmative reason. It is true that Mendelle, too, had a genuine affection for the Yiddish tongue, but Sholom Aleichem's love was bound up with jealousy. He wanted the first place for the object of his love, and his Yiddish Folk Library may be regarded as the first signal of the new age, the gauge of an impending battle.

Sholom Aleichem was not, like Peretz, a natural fighter. In life, as in his writing, he loved the gentle, the charming, the witty. Yet he must be regarded as the foremost fighter for the supremacy, as opposed to the simple vindication, of Yiddish. His jests, his playful descriptions of men and things, and his infinitely amusing juggling with Hebrew texts did more to raise the prestige of Yiddish than all the arguments and apologetics of his contemporaries. Nor must we forget, or underrate, the fact that Sholom Aleichem was the first to seek out as his collaborators the most gifted of the Hebrew writers, and to reward their work liberally. Frischman revealed, for instance—and with half-concealed pride—that for his song "*Ophir*," which he contributed to the Yiddish Folk Library, he had received payment at the rate of only a little under a ruble a line: an utterly undreamed-of rate of remuneration in those days. And since the poem was quite a long one, the public counted the lines, envied the poet, and gaped at the publisher.

Sholom Aleichem was by nature a spendthrift. He hated niggardliness as much in money matters as in his devotion to art. As long as he was well-to-do—there did happen to be such a period in his life, a very short period, naturally—he squandered all he had, right and left, on Yiddish literature. He loved a good jest, and it was a good jest to him to be able to say, in deeds if in not so many words: "The mother may be older and more snobbish, but the daughter is both younger and richer." The jest lasted no longer than his money. The prodigal supply of funds ran out, but not the prodigal talent.

I used to meet Peretz frequently in the circle of Hebrew writers. He had once been a passionate supporter of the *Chibath Zion* and one of its best propagandists. In my time he had withdrawn from active service, more because he could not agree with the leaders than because of a basic change of view. Even as early as my Warsaw period, before he had become the acknowledged leader of a new generation of writers, it was Peretz' wont to talk in mystic hints, in half-phrases, allusions, fragmentary quotations, almost like a real neo-Cabalist. There was in his eyes a bright, hard laughter, an intellectual joy, a radiant perception of something beyond the physical. His presence was a mixture of the gracious and the masterly.

We used to gather in the house of Nahum Sokolov, whose wife had refined hospitality into an art. In that house we talked of everything, beginning with Hebrew and ending up with world politics. In the conversation the central figure was always Sokolov himself. Even in those days we used to say of him:

"He has memorized all knowledge." He was thoroughly grounded, even then, in ten languages, and he never had to work to acquire one. It is no exaggeration to say that he was capable of learning any language in three months. One day I found on his table an Arabic grammar. I asked him whether he also understood Arabic. He answered: "I keep Arabic only for odd moments when I have a little superfluous energy."

At one of those gatherings there was talk of a young poet who had just appeared on the Jewish horizon—a one-time yeshivah student by the name of Chaim Nachman Bialik. The poem which had attracted much attention was called "The Bird." When analyzed coldly, it betrayed neither an extraordinary style nor an extraordinary richness of content; and yet its effect was electrical. To this day I have never been able to explain how this song touched us all, and at once, with a premonition of greatness about to be revealed in our midst. It may have been the elemental integrity that breathed in it. The premonition was not falsified. Bialik has fulfilled all the hopes that were reposed in him and has furnished Hebrew literature with one of its great and eternal figures.

CHAPTER TWENTY-FIVE

Exile and the Rabbinate

In modern social literature much has been written about the immigrant type, the individual torn out of the soil in which he grew to maturity and transplanted to the soil of another people. But it is in his social aspect alone that he has been treated, from without, as an element to be adjusted, not from within, as a soul to be understood. He was a factor to be reckoned with in the economic machinery of peoples, but the human tragedy he represented has been mostly ignored and repressed. That tragedy is, simply put, that a grown individual must turn back to the processes of his own birth and must be simultaneously newborn child and midwife.

I will not enter into the details of this transplantation; it is enough to say that the immigrant must uproot many things that have become a living part of himself, and every uprooting sends a shudder of pain through him; nor does he ever make a thorough job of it. At best the rebirth takes place through a series of substitutions; piece after piece is replaced until the total is more or less a new person.

Infinitely more complicated is the phenomenon when we pass

from the small group to the totality of a people, the highest group form. The difference is not merely one of quantity, but of quality. A small group detached from a people and placed in a strange environment does not carry within itself a sense of responsibility for the survival of the soul of a people. Whatever the homesickness of a group detached from its source, the pain does not compare with that of an entire people facing extinction.

A generation does not suffice for the complete transplantation even of the small group. There is not room enough in the body of a person for two souls, and as long as memories and fragments of the first linger in its texture, the second expands in the midst of torment. Perhaps the second generation may witness the total obliteration of the past, but as a rule an entire series of generations is involved in the completion of the process. Much more laborious, much more complex, is the case of an entire people. It is my firm belief that no people that has once acquired a complete group personality can ever assimilate as a people. The group personality persists, carries on an obstinate battle with circumstances and, until the last chance of physical survival is removed, forms a perpetual guard round its cultural and spiritual inheritance; then from the struggle emerges a dualism that is one of the most interesting of cultural historical phenomena.

In the history of the Jews this dualism runs like a thread across all the ages, from the Babylonian epoch down to our own, expressing itself in law and in mores, in institutions and in language.

Let us take one illuminating instance—our sacred festivals. A festival is one of the luxuries of a people's life; it is always associated with additional expense. Simple logic would therefore dictate that whatever a people permits itself, on its own soil, once it goes into exile it will cut down on its expenses. But what has happened in the case of the Jews? As far back as the Babylonian exile we see a doubling of the three chief festivals, Passover, Shevuoth and Succoth, each of which received two days in the place of one. There is a formal explanation, namely, that the calendar was not fixed and there was danger of an error in the observing of the Holy Days. The real explanation lies deeper, in the psychology of exile. It was the outward expression of the dualism into which the inner life of the people was split. Life now consisted of two halves: the surrounding world of actuality, and memory—a thing distinct from and not connected with the surrounding world; and each half created its own system. The first day of the festival was a tribute to the organic past, the second day a tribute to the present which had no connection with it. And indeed, that second day was known from of old as the Festival of the Exile.

The explanation goes even deeper. There has come into play the elemental instinct of self-preservation which drives the poor man to have more children than the rich man. The rich man is not afraid—he can guard his children from danger; the poor man has no such feeling of security—he must take refuge in numbers.

The same phenomenon appears in the realm of language. Of the two languages, the second is the support in exile. It was out of deep anxiety for the survival of Hebrew that the Jewish people provided it with the prop of Yiddish. The first language was locked away in the security of books; the second was for daily use. The second language was made Jewish, of the people, by the transference to it of all the thoughts that were contained in the first. The foremost living authority on the Hebrew language, Chaim Nachman Bialik, has said that the Yiddish language played a role of the first importance in the preservation of Hebrew.

The festivals split, the language split, and a third institution split similarly. To this I must devote more attention because out of the resulting situation emerged one of the problems of my own life. I am speaking of the rabbinate.

It was Russian Jewry, with its extreme folk-consciousness and its concern for the preservation of national values, that created the second type of rabbi, namely, the *Kazyonne* or State Rabbi. The very name was ugly and humiliating. It meant the rabbi who belongs to the government, the scapegoat rabbi. The government had demanded that the rabbis should satisfy it in regard to their general education, so that through them it might control the community. The Jewish people refused to acknowledge such a situation, so instead of combining in one man the requisite Jewish scholarship and the demanded general education, it bestowed them separately on two individuals. There was one rabbi for the Jews, and one for the government. The distinction in the folk mind was almost as sharp as between kosher and unkosher meats. The State Rabbi became a ludicrous figure, a buffoon, almost, put up to distract the attention of the non-Jews.

I doubt whether the government got much value out of *its* rabbis, for their influence on the life of Jewry was insignificant. But the Jews had much to lose and little to gain from the split. No one was strong enough to hold back the forces that were at play in Jewish life. New problems were created by new situations, and the most difficult problem of all was the education of the young. Here questions arose that the old school of rabbis was not able to answer and the new school obviously even less. In the spiritual life of Jewry there was chaos: the *cheders* were decayed, the communal Hebrew elementary schools were in ruins. There were no trained leaders, and the youth, devoid of guidance, was forced to grope blindly for ways of its own.

In the larger Jewish centers, and particularly in those communities which were situated in government towns, the Jews were compelled to elect a rabbi for show purposes. It was demanded of him that he be able to deliver the right kind of address on public occasions and that he be able to formulate the requests of the community more or less intelligently. The candidates for this office were the graduates of the old Russian rabbinical seminaries. Often enough, there were candidates from the German seminaries. But wherever they came from, they were looked upon as unavoidable evils, the rabbis forced upon the people by the government.

In the south-Russian Jewish communities, life was not yet as rigidly channelled as in the rest of the country. They were comparatively new, their history not going back further than the reign of Catherine II. Here a third type of rabbi emerged. He had actually nothing at all to do with the original concept of rabbinics; he was created simply as the director of the social, non-religious cultural and philanthropic activities of the community, and can best be compared with the social workers of the Old and New Worlds. But police supervision compelled the community to exalt this function—which was not recognized by law—by conferring on it the title of Rabbi.

Now this new, third type of rabbi was more likable than the State Rabbi of other areas. There was less of the disingenuous about him and he did, as a matter of fact, fulfill a need in the community. Also, he was less intended to fool anybody. Whereas in Lithuania a State Rabbi was expected to have a smattering at least of higher Jewish learning, it was the usual thing to discover, in southern Russia, "rabbis" who knew less about Judaism than one might find in a hedge priest. They might, however, be excellently educated otherwise, as doctors, engineers or lawyers. Some were exceptionally able men, first-class directors of communal affairs, tolerant leaders of the youth, going, in this respect, beyond the call of their obligation to the community. Some of them even became famous in the Jewish national movement. Yet to the observer it seemed queer enough: a rabbi who could not read two words of Hebrew! But the whole picture was queer: three types of rabbis, the first authentic, the second imitative, the third not even an imitation.

The rabbinate wrote into my personal history a chapter I would gladly wipe out of my memory. I can still feel in my mouth the aftertaste of that episode. I have occasion to hear remarks—as others in my case do—about the "sacrifices" I have made for the sake of the national movement. Such tributes always grate on me, not because of my modesty, but because of the simple fact that I have never known what it is to make "sacrifices." It is for me an obvious truth that no matter how great a man's "sacrifices" for an idealistic movement, he cannot contribute to it more than a fraction of what he receives from it.

I can think of only one exception in my own life, and this exception, too, was never understood: I am referring to the time I spent in the rabbinate, during which I felt not so much that I was sacrificing something, as that something was offering me up as a sacrifice. And my slavery was not the less real because the communities which I served, in Grodno and Ekaterinoslav, treated me with courtesy and consideration. For them I have only gratitude. My slavery was inward. I had taken a false step and I continued on the false path because I lacked the courage to turn back.

There was, first of all, the title itself: *Rabbiner*, a parody almost on the fine old title of Rabbi. In accepting it, I seemed to acquiesce in the tragicomedy of the Jewish evasion. Also there were certain duties bound up with this type of rabbinate which could poison the life of any honest man. From the first day of my appointment I carried on a steady war against them, and in part with success. But I regretted that I had ever been brought in contact with them; for this, not even my warfare could console me.

My first position, in Grodno, came to me through the initiative of my friend, Bezalel Jaffe. The vacancy was created by a death, so that my appointment was at no one's expense. When my friends heard of Jaffe's first steps they insisted unanimously that I submit my name. That the Grodno community should be contemplating the replacement of the former rabbi by a young man of modern education created a mild sensation. The whole question of the rabbinate came up anew for discussion, and the Hebrew press was strongly in favor of the change. The loudest demands came from the Zionists, and it is remarkable enough that all the young rabbis who entered on their careers at about the same time as I were Zionists. I say this was remarkable because the explanation is by no means simple. Officially the communities were anti-Zionist rather than Zionist. The leaders —meaning the rich—were usually hostile. The Zionist groups were small, composed of young people who had no say in communal affairs. It was an illustration of the old truth that a minority knitted together and inspired by an idea counts for more than a majority. Nor does the intrinsic merit of the idea matter, for it is not by the convincing power of the idea that the minority triumphs. Indeed, after all the Zionist victories, the communities remained practically as anti-Zionist as before.

The preparations for the election in Grodno lasted nearly a year. During that time I paid several visits to the community. I felt like a prospective bridegroom on a visit to the in-laws chosen for him through a marriage-broker. However, a young rabbi can also do his own choosing—again, like a young man in search of a wife—by prudence. I have tried both ways, and they are very different. Often I have wondered that life should always offer us these two ways, the way of love and the way of the marriage-broker. Can it be a deliberate check on our conceit that a good choice can be made either way?

The Grodno appointment was not a love-match; that came later with the Vilna community. There, indeed, though I had not the old title, I felt myself to be a rabbi, and was therefore happy.

The possibility that I would finally enter the rabbinate had occurred to me even before I went to study in Germany. It was this possibility that induced me to enter the *Hochschule für die Wissenschaft des Judenthums* and to occupy myself with rabbinic literature. I cannot pretend that this possibility represented to me the maximum ideal, but it did seem to offer a many-sided, active, creative life. I did not dwell on the negative aspects; but on my visits to Grodno during the year of my candidacy, I heard from the leading worthies of the community such opinions concerning the duties of a rabbi and his role in the education of the youth that today I cannot understand why I did not abruptly withdraw my name.

From one of the richest and most prominent of the communal leaders of Grodno I heard the following anecdote—true or apocryphal. In a certain city the Jewish leaders elected a stammerer as rabbi. Obeying protocol, they conducted him to the governor of the province in order to introduce him. The governor, who happened to be neither a vulgarian nor an anti-Semite, made a little speech to the newly-elected rabbi, calling on him to become the spiritual guide of the Jewish youth, and to teach it its duties with eloquence and passion. The rabbi trembled and turned pale, but there was no getting out of it: a reply had to be made. But the going was slow, his average speed being about three words a minute. The governor at once understood the caliber of the eloquence that was to be expected from this State Rabbi, and he too turned pale—with resentment. Very sternly he asked for an explanation. A member of the deputation, more courageous than his colleagues, answered, simply: "Excellency, the law forbids us to elect a mute to the office. We've done the next best thing and chosen a stammerer." The hint from the Grodno worthy was clear enough.

The duties expected of me in connection with the communal Hebrew schools were unfolded to me by another important notable of Jewish Grodno. He told me, briefly, that the methods of the neo-Hebraists were no good at all. They were artificial and they smacked of revolution. There was no sense in trying to educate a young generation without frequent application of the strap. I saw before me a reincarnation of my first teacher, Mottye the bean, and I wondered how the soul of that miserable village *rebbi* had come to occupy the body of a wealthy manufacturer. To both communal leaders I offered some mild objections, but for the most part remained reserved. This was my first lesson in remaining silent. My comrades in the movement insisted that this was now my role, and from their point of view they were right. Arguments alone are not the instruments of conquests. But I was not cut out for politics, and I suffered.

I spoke with Helena about my impressions of Grodno, and we decided to visit my parents and get their advice. In Svislovitz I was received with the honors due a man who has achieved the highest distinction possible to a mortal: so young, and already—or nearly already—a rabbi in a great city like Grodno! My father was frankly interested in the material side. What prospects did it offer? My mother was a little dazed; she did not know whether to rejoice or mourn. I considered it my duty to make clear to her the difference between a real rabbi and a *rabbiner*. She said: "My child, perhaps you had better wait, and you may have a chance to become a real rabbi." She understood that the position of *rabbiner* had little to do with hopes of Paradise, and though she agreed that I ought to accept the position, she felt like a housewife who has known better days, and who prepares for the Sabbath a piece of herring in place of the big pike she can no longer afford. My mother, too, was learning the difference between the ideal and its realization.

My rabbinic experience in Grodno was one of the bitterest disappointments of my life. It is true that I entered on it with little relish, yet I had hoped that somehow, in the movement of things, I would find enough to absorb my energies. What I found, however, was that my position was an actual barrier, almost designed to prevent me from doing any work. If I managed to acquire some influence in a few corners, it was in no wise connected with my official position.

There were a few homes in Grodno where my history was known; my wife was better known there than I, for her family came from Grodno. There was also Bezalel Jaffe, my comrade in the movement, who had initiated the idea of my coming to the city. In addition, there was an important group of the *Chibath Zion.* But in a rabbinic post the esteem of friends is not a substitute for the right relationship with the public, and this was lacking. I knew that the general attitude of suspicion and reserve were directed, not at me, but at my office. Nevertheless I felt myself personally insulted. If I had not believed that I could be of service to the community, I would never have accepted the rabbinic post. I sought neither honors nor monetary rewards, and though in respect of the latter I could not be wholly indifferent, all I wanted, and this for the first time in my life, was to earn what I needed for myself, my wife, and the daughter that was born to us shortly before we came to Grodno. It was generally assumed that I was adequately paid, but when I told my friends what I actually received they were incredulous. I lived decently, without extravagance of any kind, but my income sufficed for about a third of my needs. It was my father who helped us out during the two years I spent in Grodno. The other rabbis in Grodno were even more wretchedly paid than I.

What contributed greatly to my unhappiness was the fact that all my dreams of bringing new views to the younger generation, of instituting a new system of education, vanished almost completely. I had to look elsewhere for my contact with the youth. We tried to organize a study group among the pupils of the middle-grade government schools, but we met with little success: at the time of which I am writing the competition of the Socialists was much too strong.

Addresses on Jewish topics at large were not favored in Grodno. The only place where a meeting could be held was the synagogue, and here the difficulty of language arose. Russian in a synagogue would have sounded outrageous to the older generation, beside which the police would have learned that the synagogue was being used for other than religious purposes. Yiddish would have given my address too much of the tone of a sermon. There remained only one way, the way I had pursued in Warsaw: to address secret, illegal meetings in the homes of friends. What, then, I asked myself, was the use of my rabbinic position? Without it I could take greater risks and do more. I could also approach the youth more easily. But there was a second question that was even more painful: of what earthly use was I to the Jewish community of Grodno. Why, indeed, had it not found a stammerer with nothing more than a knowledge of the Hebrew alphabet?

CHAPTER TWENTY-SIX

Grodno

ALMOST at the moment when Theodore Herzl had perfected his plans for the creation of an organization of world Jewry devoted to the construction of a Jewish homeland, there was held in Vilna the first constituent meeting of the General Jewish Workers' Bund (Brotherhood) of Lithuania, Poland and Russia, which became known in Jewish history simply as the Bund. These two great organizations were born twins; and though among other peoples the respective tendencies which they represented have harmonized, they followed in the Jewish people the general rule of twins and quarreled from the day of their birth. The pity of it was that in these futile quarrels much positive energy which could have served either movement well was lost forever. It is not my purpose to assign the blame; the loss came largely through mutual misunderstanding and obstinacy rather than through a genuine clash of ideals.

Superficially seen, and from the technical point of view, the two foundation meetings, held in Basle and Vilna respectively in 1897, were diametrical opposites of each other. The Basle gathering of the first Zionist Congress was held in the city casino, which was decorated for the purpose; it aimed to attract the maximum of attention. The delegates numbered several hundred, and they came from every corner of the world. A host of newspaper correspondents from the chief European countries followed the proceedings and telegraphed them home. The Bund gathering was held in a cellar in an obscure street of Vilna, and the "delegates" made certain that not a word of what happened there would leak out. They were few in number, since few were to be trusted. Every man was a tried servant of the movement, known for his devotion—and for his skill in dealing with the agents of the government.

A superficial glance also revealed a contrast of philosophies. The Congress at Basle declared to the world that the Jewish problem was national in character and could therefore be solved only through the application of a national remedy—a country for the Jewish people. The Bund, representing the principles of Social Democracy as then understood, simply ignored the nationalist factor as an element in the development of history. And if it did recognize the nationalist principle as a phenomenon, it denied its applicability to the Jews. Of course this attitude provoked the logical question: "Then why are you forming a separate Jewish Socialist organization?" The only answer the Bund could find at first was: "For convenience of language—Yiddish." Only later did the Bund add the more cogent reason—the particularity of the Jewish social structure and the peculiar problem of the Jewish worker. And from that it was a step to an admission—fully made in the course of time—that the nationalist principle applied to the Jewish worker, too.

The evolution of the Bund teaches us again that it is dangerous to rely on the interpretation of events as made by those who participate in them. An author is often the last man to understand the significance of his own work, and men engaged in political enterprises are the last judges of the historical significance of their activity. It is shallow to consider the program of the organizers as the index of a movement. Not what *they* intended, but what the mass did, is the criterion. But it happens that the organizers of a movement are also, very often, its historians, and the first histories of a movement almost invariably overstress the intentions of the founders and underestimate the element of the masses. We see it in the case of Herzl. Herzl was a powerful personality and a great leader. His intention was to found a purely political movement, without any cultural problems. In this he failed, and with every passing Congress the founder of political Zionism had to make concessions.

The same emergence of the latent will of the masses, triumphing over the rigid program of the founders, was to be observed as a parallel process in the Bund. In spite of appearances, the Bund was something more than an organization for the improvement of the condition of the Jewish working classes. It was impelled by a desire to raise the status of the Jewish population as a whole, both in the matter of civic rights and in the matter of cultural interests, to whatever extent the latter go hand in hand with Socialist interests. It took seven or eight years for these facts to be understood and to be added to the platform of the Bund, but though they were acknowledged late, they had existed from the beginning.

The question of the Yiddish language cannot explain the tremendous risk and labor that were bound up with the creation of a separate and additional secret Socialist organization with an autonomous constitution. And even if we were to accept at face value the protestations of the founders, it would be shallow to regard language as a mere technicality. The leaders of the Bund were, as a matter of fact, at home in the Russian language, but the Jewish masses they led resisted the intrusion of Russian. They did this not because Russian was less convenient for them, but because they felt that their identity was bound up with Yiddish. Resistance of this kind is nationalist in character. In the case of the Bund the leaders were compelled, year by year, to yield to the insistent will of the masses and to accept the transformation of their organization into a national instrument. There was of course a desperate struggle, but the theoreticians had to give way before living forces.

It should be noted that the Bund was founded before the Social Democratic movement in Russia had crystallized into a firm organization, but friction arose between the Russian Social Democrats and the Bund. Lenin and Plekhanov were both opposed to the Bund. They declared at once that it was a Jewish national organization with which true Social Democrats could not sympathize. Plekhanov expressed his view in a jest: Bundists were Zionists who were afraid of a sea-journey. It was a poor joke; lack of courage was not among the failings of the Jewish Socialists of Russia. They paid the largest toll of sacrifice to the Russian government, which detested Bundists even more than ordinary non-Jewish Socialists, and in its sentencing of those it caught expressed its hatred of both Socialism and the Jewish people. The government did not take the pogroms into its account, and it was indifferent to the Bundist attitude toward Jewish nationalism. Its motto was: Once a Jew, always a Jew. But men like Lenin and Plekhanov also held that view, and were therefore suspicious of a separate Jewish organization. They asserted that within the Socialist movement there was no such thing as nationalism. Ostensibly they defended an internationalist point of view. Actually they preached cosmopolitanism, which within a few years was seen to be inapplicable to Socialism. The Bund was not the only body to evolve into conscious nationalism. In the world Socialist movement every territory developed, under the pressure of events, along the same line. Everywhere life was stronger than the theorists.

The necessity of defending itself externally against the charge of nationalism set in motion a compensating mechanism within the Bund. It expressed its irritation by its attacks on Zionism. Indeed, the bitterest enemies of Zionism, Jews or non-Jews, were the Jewish Bundists. In this Jewish civil war it was the Bundists who were the aggressors. I myself suffered greatly watching the struggle. I was never able to see any contradiction between the nationalist principles of Zionism and the Socialist principles in the program of the Bund.

Grodno is a few hours by train from Vilna, and Vilna was the center of the Bund. Yet I had no means of knowing whether there was a branch of the Bund in Grodno. The Bundists were master conspirators. They led the lives of political Marranos; they worshipped almost literally in catacombs—their substitute being the cellar. But I knew many of the Bundists as individuals, and I cannot remember that I felt bitterness or antagonism against any one of them. I did detest the assimilationist, independently of his political views, whether he was a temple-goer or a Socialist. My only bitterness was against those who laid the dead weight of their inertia in the scale of Jewish decline.

Life in Grodno was sickeningly monotonous. The petty worries of the congregation did not interest me. When I was invited out of politeness to its meetings, I felt myself to be among strangers. However, I was quite aware that there were smaller, more intimate congregational meetings to which I was not invited; the feeling of indifference was apparently mutual. The city notables and I spoke a different language. The "better" classes spent their evenings playing cards, in which they were joined by the professional classes, to whatever extent their time allowed. I had given up cards since that wretched time in Minsk. The card-playing intelligentsia wrote this down among my shortcomings; a modern rabbi was in fact expected to be able to take a hand when called on. There only remained for me the circle of the Zionists, and this was not enough.

The chief cultural personality of Grodno was Tatiana Ilinisha

Greenberg. Her education had been rather ordinary, her looks were rather below ordinary. But she occupied the first place in Grodno society, and not among the Jews alone. She had achieved her social position through her extraordinary gift of friendliness and her readiness to help without asking questions. She excelled at listening to the woes of others and at working out plans to help them if help was at all possible. She was busy all day long, either in her home, or in her husband's large dry-goods store or in the town. The Greenbergs had lost their only child, and they lived like people who found more in common in their business than in their family life. Tatiana Ilinisha once told me how an unhappy Jewish woman had gone to Governor Batiushkov for help. He told her that he himself could not help her, but that there was a woman, an angel, who helped everybody, and he sent the woman with his card to Tatiana Ilinisha. The poor woman thought she was going to see, almost literally, an angel: the Governor-General himself had said it. When she saw the "angel," a rather plain-looking and unpretentious creature, she was so disappointed that, involuntarily, she spat and exclaimed: "What? This is Tatiana Ilinisha?" She disappeared without telling her story.

Tatiana Ilinisha conducted a salon. In one room sat her husband and friends, playing cards; in another were the assembled intellectual spirits of Grodno. I learned there, once again, how remote the Jewish intelligentsia was from our classic sources, how little it was to blame if it drifted daily further and further from them. It was there, too, that I became acquainted with individual Bundists, among them a remarkable girl by the name of Fisher. It was from her arguments with me that I learned of her affiliation with the Bund, and I envied a movement which could attract such a woman. Tatiana Ilinisha mothered all of us. If the argument went too strongly in one direction, she intervened; she would have no victors and vanquished in her house. She loved ideas as such, and her greatest happiness was to be among people who were attached to ideas. What the ideas were did not matter.

Grodno was one of the oldest and proudest Jewish communities in Lithuania. It had already played a role in those far-off days when a large measure of autonomy had been granted the Jews under the *Vaad Arba Aratzot*, the famous Council of the Four Countries. This Council had had a theocratic touch, first, because it resembled the Slavic governments of that time in its stress on religion, second, because more particularly it was a reflection of the Jewish religion, in which the distinction between the secular and the religious is less easily established than elsewhere. Yet it would be wrong to look back upon this Council as a regulator only of the religious life of the Jews. It played a larger and more general role, affecting the economic life of the Jews too. When we study the scope of the Council, we are amazed by the *decline* of Jewish rights, even in the countries of emancipation. The civic rights of the individual have swallowed up the political rights of the community.

After the fall of Jewish communal autonomy, the Jewish plutocracy rose to power. The rule passed out of the hands of the spiritual leaders into the hands of the rich. The transference did not take place without a struggle, and for a long time the conflict between tradition and wealth, between reputation and gold, filled all Jewish life. In the end the new power triumphed. The fight was not, of course, characteristically Jewish. It had its parallel in the struggle between the baron and the merchant, between the feudal lord and the capitalist.

In the Jewish field, an excellent illustration is afforded in the marriages which were arranged between families of standing, and by the role which pride of descent played on the one hand and pride of gold on the other, with the ultimate disappearance of the marketable value of pride of descent. It is a great pity that the movies came just a little too late to catch this war.

As a boy I was in the thick of the atmosphere of calculated matchmaking; if there had been preserved an authentic picture of the scenes and persons, it would have given the world an excellent résumé, under a specific form, of the struggle between an hereditary nobility and an emergent wealthy class. There was, with the passing of the years, a regular, almost systematic regression of the value of a distinguished genealogy. At first, a long family pedigree of scholars easily held its own in the scales against a heavy bag of gold. Later on, the gold could be replaced by silver. Still later a handful of copper coins was considered the equivalent of a long and honorable descent. Finally the worth of aristocracy fell to nothing, and the article disappeared from the market.

In Grodno I witnessed the last agonies of the struggle. Today, after years of observation in the New World, I understand its deeper significance. Retrospectively, I see that it was a struggle between Europeanism and Americanism. But it is a mistake to think that Americanism was born in America, that the displacement of the hereditary nobility by the self-made man—considering them as two types of rulers—is a specific American product. America, itself the product of a powerful protest against the petrified worship of the hereditary principle, was naturally the aptest soil for the development of the new outlook, for in America the activities of the individual found no barrier, and almost no limit to their scope. It was a whole continent that was offered to them. But it was not necessary to export the type to Europe. It arose there independently. It could not develop with the momentum it acquired in America, but it was distinct and undeniable. I first got to know the new type in Grodno. Later I met it in more developed form in southern Russia, in Ekaterinoslav, where a genuine Americanism—in the sense used above—developed on a rich virgin soil.

There were three ruling families in Grodno, and every family had its supporters and its rabbis. The community was, one might say, a triangle, with a rabbi in each corner to give religious authority to the views of the group. The three families were the Bregmans, the Frumkins and the Shereshevskys. The richest among them was Eliezer Bregman. Aristocracy he had none at all. He came from a simple, small-town family near Grodno, and was in all respects a self-made man. His character was generous. Like Frumkin, he was a government contractor, but on a larger scale: Shereshevsky had made his money as a cigarette manufacturer. Bregman was a man of iron will and large ambitions, but he had sense enough to know that in social standing he could not measure up to the Frumkins nor, like Shereshevsky, provide a living for thousands. He therefore competed for status by means of his donations and thus acquired the first place in the community.

Of the three men Bregman was the most progressive. He still observed all the old Jewish forms, but there was something in him that we now call "American." The new did not terrify him. He was in the swim and he knew which way the currents of the time were moving. The two others were extremely conservative, and looked with envy on the parvenu whose generosities put them in the shade.

It was Bregman who had insisted on bringing me to Grodno. He had really intended to introduce, through me, something new into the life of the community. If nothing came of his intentions, he was not to blame. He remained my champion until his death, which occurred a few months before I left Grodno. I myself did not show the necessary resolution to break through the walls of prejudice in Grodno, the less so as I realized that this was not the town for me.

During the first period they used to call me "Bregman's Rabbi"—a title not much to my liking. I was not permitted to work for the community as a whole, and the idea of working for a clique in the community was repugnant to me. I adopted an attitude of equal friendliness to all three groups. The Frumkins readily admitted me to their circle, partly because of their friendship with my wife's family in Königsberg. Shereshevsky was friendly for a reason of his own. The influence of the Bund was being felt among his workers, and the first attempts were being made at the formation of a union. Shereshevsky thought it wise to have some sort of connection with the intelligentsia—it might be useful some day. I think I may safely say that my sympathies were continuously and consistently on the side of the workers in their efforts to better their position. I lay no claim to particular virtue in this matter: a profound respect for the meaning of work and for the worker had been inculcated in me in my childhood by my pious and old-fashioned father. To this day the touchstone of genuine Jewish piety is, for me, the attitude toward the worker.

In Grodno I made my first acquaintance with the Jewish factory worker, a type distinct from the independent Jewish artisan. The latter, as I had long known him, had always been a machine, but a self-contained and complete machine. The factory worker is only part of a machine. The psychological difference expresses itself in the loss of individuality on the part of the factory worker. When I would see the half-grown girls who used to pour out from the Shereshevsky factory each evening, their lungs filled with tobacco dust, I could hardly regard them as so many individuals. I saw only the mass, the machine. I learned a great deal about life in the factory from a young doctor, and from my friend Miss Fisher. It was a life of continuous and elemental struggle. And yet there were countless candidates for jobs in the factory. Even in those days the servant problem was beginning to be felt in Grodno, and girls had to be imported from the surrounding townlets. Economically the servant girl was on a surer footing than the factory worker; yet every girl in Grodno who had to work for her living preferred the factory. The social stigma of the servant was beginning to be felt more and more strongly.

My most intimate friends in Grodno were the Jaffes. Their family was not among the richest but it was certainly among the most distinguished. Ber Jaffe, the head of the household, was the son of the famous Rabbi Mordecai Gimpel Jaffe, who had passed the last years of his life in Palestine, and had played an important role in the pre-colonization community there. Ber Jaffe himself represented the finest type of aristocratic Jewish family, but the moving spirit in the house was his wife, Chaya Leah. For years she was a victim of rheumatism, and kept to her bed. But even from her bed she directed the household and the family business—a distillery for Passover whisky. When I made the acquaintance of the family she was already a confirmed invalid, and I used to spend hours by her bedside in the company of her children. She had a tongue that an orator might have envied, and as she was unable to make the rounds of Grodno in person, she used to do it verbally—and by the time she had completed a "tour" there was very little left of the town. She did not simply talk about people, she used to give something like a theatrical performance—thus Frumkin spoke, thus Bregman, and thus Shereshevsky. She was more than a mere mimic—she was a wit. She could catch the manner of thought no less than the manner of speech. Her husband, to redress the balance, was almost wordless. Whether he was so by nature or whether he donated his part of the conversation to his wife, I do not know.

During my first year in Grodno I did a great deal of literary work, chiefly on the Hebrew dictionary. My assistant, young Joseph Klausner, also lived in Grodno. He left before long to pursue his studies in Heidelberg, where he obtained his doctorate. He showed early the promise, later fulfilled, that he would become a scholar of note. In his youth he had received no systematic education, but for all that he mastered several languages, together with their literatures, leaping over the elementary stages and plunging at once into higher studies. Two faculties saved him: a remarkable memory and a no less remarkable industriousness. I had the impression that young Klausner never permitted himself a single hour of relaxation or amusement. He was obsessed by the ambition to become a scholar, and this attitude did not desert him either at Zionist meetings or in the company of girls. His primary public interest was the revival of Hebrew as a living tongue; he wanted to bring it out of books into daily circulation. In this respect he modelled himself on the famous Eliezer ben Yehudah, and it must be admitted that his contribution to the cause was considerable.

And yet I cannot help saying that there was something slightly unpleasant about these young apostles of the Hebraic revival. Often enough they used to speak as if they were the creators rather than the revivers of the language. I remember once reading a feuilleton in the *Neue Freie Presse* of Vienna concerning the art of breakfasting. The feuilletonist grew rhapsodical over an acquaintance of his who had become a great master in this recondite art. He lived in one of the most distinguished hotels in Vienna, and breakfast was usually taken in the palm gardens. The atmosphere was one of grace, charm and comfort. The faces of guests and visitors alike shone with the freshness of morning. The rolls had just arrived from the baker; they too radiated warmth and light and newness. The steaming coffee sent out an odor suggestive of the most delicious spices. The breakfast artist sits at the table, and on his face are written contentment and joy. He strokes the rolls gently—not like a housewife investigating their quality, but like an artist feeling their texture. He breathes in the scent of the coffee, like a worshipper sniffing at the fumes of the swinging censer carried by an acolyte. The waiter brings him two eggs. He does not eat them. He looks at them, curiously, smiling; he turns them over in his hands; he admires their shape, their whiteness, their luster. He is proud of them—he is so far carried away by his artistic spirit that he forgets who laid them. I remember how, at a public meeting, a Jew once spoke of the "discoverers" of the Hebrew language—ben Yehudah, Klausner, and the others. Like the breakfast artist, the speaker had forgotten the hen.

From one circumstance I suffered particularly in Grodno: I seldom had the opportunity to develop my gifts as a speaker. The little Zionist meetings we held were secret, and therefore only Zionists could attend. As a result I felt myself inhibited; there was lacking the goad of the opponent. During all this time I delivered only two addresses that satisfied me, and these were delivered not in Grodno, but in Vilna and in Bialystok, whither I was invited by the Zionists to lecture to the public.

I have special reasons for remembering these two occasions. In Vilna I met Isaac Goldberg, one of a group of three members of the *B'nai Moshe*. Goldberg exerted a remarkable influence over his comrades. He was a poor speaker, but he imposed himself on his surroundings by his singular devotion to the movement and to Palestine. He was one of the few who understood in those early days that the first necessity for the individual Zionist was to make a personal connection with Palestine and gradually, through this connection, to transfer the center of gravity of his life to the Jewish homeland in the making. But more important than this personal experience for me was the effect which Vilna had on me. It was during this visit that I fell in love with the city, and began to dream of making it my center—a dream that was ultimately to come true.

Bialystok I remember particularly for my first contact with Dr. Chazanovich, one of the most astonishing personalities I have ever come across. I have always regretted that no one has been found to write his life as it deserved to be written. As a lover of mankind he was in the front rank of the saintly; as Jew he had forgotten all self-interest in the pursuit of the welfare of his people. He was the initiator and founder of the Jewish National Library of Jerusalem, which today measures up to the finest in the world. He launched the idea on his own responsibility, and whatever he earned—he was one of the foremost physicians in the city—he spent on old volumes. He maintained contacts with antiquarians all over the world, interested strangers as well as friends, added book to book, keeping them in excellent order, cataloguing them as best he could, packing them in crates and sending them off to Jerusalem. He did all this with a quietness and modesty which made one think of a sacred service. No one ever heard him boast about his work. At the Zionist Congresses he would be found withdrawn into a corner. He gladly relinquished leadership to others, and his attitude toward Herzl was one of wordless reverence. One thing he did permit himself: he once asked Herzl to try and see to it that there should be less speaking.

I visited Chazanovich several times and had the opportunity of looking over some of his collections. As the external symbol of his eternal bond with Palestine, he used to wear, when at home, a fez. But no one wondered at the things Chazanovich did. One day I met him in the house of Rabbi Samuel Mohilever, and he invited me to lunch, but explained that he never ate before two o'clock. Mohilever took me aside and advised me quietly to have a bite before I went to have lunch with Chazanovich. I ignored the advice, and regretted it, for I got nothing to eat until three o'clock—and what I got was two rolls and a glass of milk. "You see," said Chazanovich, "I eat simply. I'm a vegetarian. I find it healthier for me—and healthier for my library."

It was told of him that once, while examining a patient, he paused, became abstracted, then sighed and said: "Too bad, too bad." The patient was badly frightened until Chazanovich explained. The patient was all right—only a slight cold. But it had just occurred to Chazanovich that without Palestine the Jews would come to nothing.

Two of the best years of my life were given to Grodno, years of desire to work, years of creative impulse—and nothing came of them. Materially I had not advanced at all; I was still dependent on my father on the one hand, and on my brother-in-law Herman Conheim on the other. My parents were perhaps overgenerous, for they never uttered a single complaint and seemed to accept the situation as something obvious, but Herman Conheim had been brought up in an American atmosphere, and the thing was by no means obvious to him. He could not understand, to begin with, how a man could venture into marriage without being assured of a livelihood; and secondly, the whole situation seemed fantastic to him: a State Rabbi in a Jewish community of twenty-five thousand souls, and not even a modest living. If anything was needed to convince him finally that Russia was a wild country, and its inhabitants half-crazy, this was it. He did not offer any protest; he only seemed bewildered.

My financial helplessness had a depressing effect on me, the more so as I derived no satisfaction from my work. Even in spiritual matters I seemed not to be earning my living. Often I longed to get a refusal from my parents, and to be compelled brutally to shift for myself. Once again I placed the responsibility on others: it was I who should have made the break, and mine should have been the refusal. I was like the Jewish woman who offered this prayer on the Day of Atonement: "O Lord, provide me this coming year with a decent living; and if you do not I may as well tell you that I shall go and live with my rich sister."

During my two years in Grodno I did not once visit my parents. I looked for all sorts of reasons to make the journey impossible. I was ashamed to go home—and I surely had little enough to boast about. However, Helena and my little Esther, or Enya as she insisted on calling herself, did go to Svislovitz. My mother at once fell in love with her granddaughter, but between Helena and my mother there was the gulf which separated two worlds. Mother-in-law and daughter-in-law could not bridge it.

CHAPTER TWENTY-SEVEN

Ussishkin and Ekaterinoslav

MY LIBERATION came sooner than I expected. One friend, Bezalel Jaffe, had brought me to Grodno; another, Menachem Mendel Ussishkin, liberated me from it.

Ussishkin and I were friends, though I had met him only once, and that ten years before, in Minsk. Our common activity had held us together. In those ten years—the period during which the old *Chibath Zion* was swallowed up in the new World Zionist Organization—Ussishkin had grown into one of the most important figures in the movement. His influence was felt everywhere, and at the Zionist Congresses his opinions carried weight. The closer friends of Herzl regarded him as an opponent of their leader, because he symbolized the old days when Zionism was centered more on Palestine than on the political setting, the days when—as they used to say—a goat in Palestine counted for more than the promise of a minister. But Vienna, the center of the new movement, was compelled to treat the representative of the old order with respect and sometimes to meet him halfway, for behind Ussishkin there stood, with few exceptions, all the ranks of the Russian Zionists.

Ussishkin was an authentic leader by nature; he was a gifted organizer and he understood the art of commanding men. This is more than a technique; it is a gift that is difficult to understand. Often enough we meet men who seem to have all the elements that go into the making of a leader, and who yet remain within the ranks. And often enough we meet men who are not more gifted than those they lead but who possess that indefinable something which turns them into leaders. Sometimes it is called moral force, yet it is not very clearly related to what we call the moral element in life.

Ussishkin was famous for his obstinacy. Oddly enough, his house was situated at the corner of two streets, one called Obstinate Street, the other Iron Street. The house belonged to Ussishkin's father-in-law, an engineer. I believe that when Ussishkin married, the symbolic properties of this house were included in the marriage portion. Ussishkin's obstinacy went so far that he refused to bend even before the laws of grammar. Having passed through a Russian secondary school and a higher technical institute, he spoke with a perfect Russian accent, but he never submitted to the dictates of Russian grammar. Later, when he turned to Hebrew, he treated Hebrew grammar with the same ruthlessness. But he was forgiven these little sins for the sake of his genuine oratorical gifts. Yet Ussishkin cannot properly be called an orator. We can only say of him that his speeches were often more effective than those of the most gifted orators. He spoke with an elemental force that overpowered and convinced.

Ussishkin's great rival was Dr. Yechiel Tschlenov, a cofounder of the *B'nai Moshe*, of Moscow. Tschlenov was a complete contrast to Ussishkin. First as to appearance: he was slight of build, the typical "fine young man" of the Jewish tradition, with mild eyes and gentle facial lines. His bearing was of a piece with his appearance. Ussishkin commanded, threatened, issued ukases in the style of a Russian tyrant; Tschlenov explained gently, requested, even implored, like a doctor pleading with his patient to be reasonable and take his medicine. Yet Tschlenov in his own circle was not less effective than Ussishkin in his. Both men were respected and loved. Behind Ussishkin's hardness was felt the soul that suffered, and behind Tschlenov's gentleness the firm will of the natural warrior. In Herzl's immediate circle Tschlenov was far more welcome than Ussishkin. It was true that Tschlenov, too, clung to the principles of the old, practical Zionism, but his harmonious nature impelled him to seek a synthesis between "practical" and "political" Zionism, and wherever a compromise was possible, Tschlenov found it. At the Congresses, as well as in Russia, Ussishkin and Tschlenov were regarded as equal leaders. When it came to specific problems, however, the Russians leaned more to Ussishkin and the Western Zionists more to Tschlenov.

It was a curious division. The center of the movement was in Vienna, but the masses of the movement were in Russia. Russia was divided into districts, and at the head of each district was a sort of parallel to the governor. There was thus created a special Zionist Russian geography, and when one Zionist asked another under whom he served, the allusion was not to the Russian governor, but to the Zionist head. However, it was not the Zionists alone who had created a new geography. In Poland, Volhynia and Podolia there was also the Chassidic geography, and in this system the governor was replaced by the Chassidic saint or wonder-working rabbi. Under Tschlenov's "regime" were to be found those sections of Russia in which Jews had no right of residence. His "territory" therefore stretched from Moscow to Vladivostok in the Far East. When Russia swallowed up Manchuria, Tschlenov at once informed his new "subjects" that thanks to the success of the Russian arms, Manchuria had also been brought under Zionist rule.

Vilna was "governed" by the calm and moderate Goldberg.

Elizabetgrad belonged to Vladimir Tiomkin, and the whole of Bessarabia was assigned to Dr. Jacob Cohen-Bernstein, a revolutionary who had turned Zionist. One of his brothers, too, had at one time been amongst the most active of the Social Revolutionaries; he had been sentenced to imprisonment with hard labor and together with his fellow prisoners in far off Irkutsk had risen in a rebellion that shook the whole of Russia. He met death heroically on the scaffold together with his comrades. Dr. Cohen-Bernstein never talked about his brother, but his fate had instilled into him the steadfast rage of a revolutionary. In addition to the administration of his district, he had also the dangerous task of directing the so-called Post-Bureau. This was the center from which there went out regularly the theoretical letters to all the districts. The author of these letters was Cohen-Bernstein himself, and through them he acquired a great influence over the younger generation.

Ussishkin was the head of the Ekaterinoslav district, and of all districts this was the best organized. He had introduced an almost military discipline among the Zionists, and he was less the leader than the imperator.

At one of the meetings of the All-Russian Zionist Organization, Ussishkin proposed to me that I submit my name for the post of rabbi in his city. I told him how dissatisfied I was with this type of work, but he assured me that there was no comparison between the rabbinate in southern Russia and in Lithuania. In the former the rabbinate could be made the instrument of a wide-spread nationalist activity, and the spoken word could be made the medium of a powerful influence over the masses and the youth. The proposal was made to me not out of friendship, but for the advancement of the movement.

This was the period when Herzl had proclaimed the new slogan—the Zionist "conquest of the communities." It was, in fact, Herzl's concession, though in disguised form, to Ahad-Ha-amism. At the beginning Herzl had had only the vaguest notions about Jewish life; he had really believed that no preparation of the masses was necessary in order to carry through the Zionist idea. He was of course prepared for opposition from the Western assimilated Jews, but he believed that he had only to approach the masses of the Eastern Jews in order to be accepted. He was badly informed on the movements and tendencies within Eastern Jewry. When he came down to realities and made a serious study of the situation, he realized his error and proclaimed the principle of the conquest of the communities as a step in the forward march toward his goal. This was the first break in the pure political front of his original form of Zionism, and through this break there began to enter the application of the principle of "the work of the present"—*Gegenwartsarbeit*. It was the beginning of a new epoch in Zionism, an epoch in which there would not be the same sharp division between the general Jewish needs of the present and the continuing Zionist program.

To this day I am grateful to my friend Ussishkin. In Ekaterinoslav I grew not only in will and in energy, but in my struggle with the Jewish and the non-Jewish society of the locality, spiritually and intellectually. It was here that I made my first contacts with non-Jewish Russian society, which, until then, I had known only in books. I met for the first time the Russian intelligentsia, a great world, fascinating and provoking. In Lithuania the Jews really lived in a sort of ghetto. The reason was that the upper classes among the non-Jews were mostly Polish. The Polish intelligentsia was absorbed in its own problems, and was concentrating its energies on the task of removing the Russian yoke. There was hardly any common ground on which it could meet with the Jewish intelligentsia. The Russian upper stratum consisted almost exclusively of officials, who treated the whole of Lithuania like conquered territory, and they felt that it was part of their program to keep themselves at a distance both from Poles and from Jews. In Ekaterinoslav I had easy access to the Russian intelligentsia, in part because of my official position and in part because of the extra-rabbinical tasks I assumed. I began, therefore, to understand the realities of Russian life: I came in contact with the covert forces of the Russian people, forces which were at that time beginning to break into new, tumultuous expression.

Along the lower half of the majestic Dnieper, there are countless little scenic paradises, and in one of them there had sprung up, as under a magician's wand, the marvelous city of Ekaterinoslav. It is a city as broad, as open, as kingly, as the Dnieper itself; a city that draws its character from the mighty river and from the broad, powerful earth of the Ukraine. Ekaterinoslav, with its youth, its freshness and its gaiety, took my fancy by storm. The buildings, the trees, the people—all seemed radiant. I had been accustomed for a long time to Lithuania, an ancient land, with ancient cities and villages; the dust of generations lay upon it, and the worry of old age was like a visible shadow: it was a land that looked to the past. Even my little Svislovitz made the impression, by contrast with the newly developed south, of an ancient, undersized gaffer, bowed under a burden of countless generations. Who could remember the birth of Svislovitz, or the name of the man who laid its corner-stone? That northern country was one in which beginnings were no longer made; men could only continue what the anonymous and forgotten past had begun. But here, in the virgin city of Ekaterinoslav, the generations had not preempted everything, a man could still write his name into something. Many years later I experienced the same thrill of renewal, when I came in contact not with a new city, but with a new world—America.

When the worthies of Grodno invited me to their city, they advised me that silence was the first prerequisite of a good rabbi. In Ekaterinoslav they told me to speak—and to speak much. This was all the encouragement I needed. Ussishkin had me come a few weeks before the election to the rabbinate. The old incumbent, who had stood in the way of the Zionist movement, was fighting for his position and the city was divided in a lively contest. But not the Jews alone were interested; the Russians too caught the infection. There were at that time two big dailies in Ekaterinoslav; one, the more conservative, was for the old rabbi; the other, the more liberal, was for me. But the latter did have one objection to me—I was known as an outspoken Zionist. The liberal press of Russia was either neutral toward Zionism or hostile. But the liberal newspaper of Ekaterinoslav felt itself compelled to support me in spite of my Zionism, probably, in the first place, because the other newspaper had chosen to support the old rabbi. I was astonished when I read for the first time, in Russian newspapers, long editorials on the duties and functions of a Jewish minister, and on the standards which ought to be set by a Jewish community. It occurred to me that we ought to have the same right to say something about the choice of Christian priests.

The old rabbi, Shochor by name, a graduate of the Vilna Rabbinical Institute, had many friends and supporters. He was a decent and kindly soul, but like many of his colleagues of the Vilna Seminary he was deficient in one trifling matter: he had absolutely no inner relationship to his calling, or to the problems of the Jewish people. With his gentle nature, he only wanted things to go on drifting. At the mention of movements, whether Jewish or general, he became panicky. He considered movements as such superfluities; human beings could do very well without them. The Jewish notables and the Russian administration regarded him as an ideal type of rabbi. Socially he was extremely popular, and was considered one of the most gifted card-players in town, his specialty being the game of *préférence*.

In addition to these two elements, a third was strongly on his side: the baptized Jews. Ekaterinoslav was a city of Jewish apostates, and the majority of them were to be found in the upper classes. At that time, as I remember, there were around a dozen baptized Jewish lawyers in Ekaterinoslav. In a certain sense these men could be called Marranos, or secret Jews; not that, like the Marranos of old, they were the bearers of a genuine tragedy, conforming outwardly to Christianity and longing inwardly for their old Jewish life. Their lives remained the same as before: they were neither worse Jews nor better Christians. They had only succeeded in evading all the obstacles that the Russian law placed in the path of the intellectual Jew. It is not easy to say whom their sudden change insulted more, the Jews or the Christians. However, there was one obstacle that their change could not overcome—the social one. Russian society remained cold to them even after their baptism. This is perhaps easily explained. The genuine anti-Semite is surely not prepared to change his attitude when the Jew adopts the simple device of calling himself a Christian. On the contrary, it must look to him like the shabbiest sort of trick. And later I became acquainted with Russian intellectuals quite free from anti-Semitism, who regarded these baptized Jews with profound contempt as weaklings and renegades.

The baptized Jews of Ekaterinoslav provided me with an excellent study of certain aspects of Jewish assimilation. Here I need only note that, being excluded from higher Russian society, they were compelled willy-nilly to turn to the Jews, and willy-nilly they had to take an interest in Jewish affairs. The entire group of baptized lawyers stood staunchly with the old rabbi. The reason was clear enough: as long as Judaism was interpreted only in the religious sense, as long as it was regarded as a matter of dogma and ritual, they could make peace with their consciences. These dogmas and rituals had meant nothing to them even when they had been Jews technically. In passing themselves off as Christians they had repudiated nothing. True, there was a slight inaccuracy in this new nomenclature, but that was for the Christians to worry about; it surely had nothing to do with the Jews.

The situation became quite different as soon as Judaism was

interpreted as a national reality. Then the question bit deeper and a man's identity was at play. It might have been put thus: "You did not share the religion of your people, and therefore you repudiated it. Did you also manage to repudiate your people, cut yourself away clean?" Put thus, the question worries even men of less tender conscience.

There was one man who put this question sharply and, having given the right answer, demanded loudly and openly that the renegades be excluded completely from contact with Jewish affairs. This man was Menachem Mendel Ussishkin. He argued: "We have no defense against their treachery, but by admitting them into our affairs after they have repudiated us, we are condoning their act." It was not an easy battle to wage, for it drew in some of the most distinguished "Jewish" families in the city. But I have already indicated that Ussishkin was not a man of compromises. With Ussishkin as my champion in Ekaterinoslav, and myself as a fighter in the movement which he symbolized, it was inevitable that the opposition to my election should be desperate.

I delivered, on the average, something like one address a day, making the rounds of the synagogues. I was in fact more interested in making these addresses, in living myself out at last, than in the result of the election. Had there been the slightest possibility that the old rabbi would remain at his post, while I came in as preacher and lecturer, I would gladly have embraced it. Unfortunately there was no such division of functions. It was only many years later that my dream of such a division was realized.

The elections were democratic, though not direct. There were six hundred electors, and I was elected by a large majority. It was not my victory, but that of Ussishkin, and not so much his as that of the movement.

But the democratic election was not enough; there was still needed the ratification of the administration, and the administration had been openly on the side of my opponent. I do not know whether my election would ever have been ratified but for an utterly unforeseeable accident.

Years before, during my student days in Berlin, I had had a friend by the name of Boris Brandt. He came to Berlin a graduate of a Russian law school, with a two year scholarship to study international financial law. He had come to the favorable attention of no less a personage than the Finance Minister himself, Count Witte; and Witte, as is well known, was clever enough to gather round himself gifted Jews—taking talent wherever he found it. When Brandt had completed his studies in Berlin, he was given a post in the Ministry of Finance, and when I came to Ekaterinoslav, he already occupied a high position. He had been a convinced Zionist when he came to Berlin, and remained one, not passionately so, but firm and objective in his views.

This was the first half of the accident. Now comes the second. The Governor of Ekaterinoslav was at that time Prince Sviatopolk-Mirsky, one of the noblest and most distinguished personalities I have ever met. Ussishkin, who was friendly with Brandt because of their common Zionist interests, persuaded the latter to speak on my behalf to the Prince, and a short time after the interview my appointment was ratified.

The two years I had spent in Grodno were entered upon the calendar, but they passed over my life without leaving a trace. They were shorn away from me with as little effect as the shearing away of one's hair. They had, however, one virtue. They made my parting from Grodno a light one. The worthies of Grodno said they were sorry to lose me. They also said they could not blame me. A poor town like Grodno could never match rich Ekaterinoslav. Their sweetness did not please me at all. I told one of them that I suffered less from the fact that Grodno could give me so little than from the fact that the Jewish leaders had not permitted me to give *them* anything at all.

My wife and daughter remained for a time in Grodno, and I transferred myself, full of hope and courage, to my new place. My friends, and particularly the family of Bezalel Jaffe, were genuinely happy for me. On the way to Ekaterinoslav I visited my parents. They too were happy, first because of the honor that had been shown me, second because they believed that Ekaterinoslav would do better by me than Grodno had done. My father had business relations with Ekaterinoslav, and he had been told that the rabbinate in that city was exceptionally well paid, and such was to be expected of a Jewish community of sixty thousand souls in the center of a rapidly developing region. However, both my parents and I were to be disappointed in this respect.

If I had been asked, before my Ekaterinoslav days, what were the relations between me and Russian society, I could hardly have found an answer. Social relationships imply a common area of contact. In Grodno, as in other towns, such an area did not exist for Russians and Jews. If we except occasional card parties and occasional contacts in the city clubs—confined on the Jewish side to a few privileged individuals of the professional and rich merchant class—there was no social relationship. My official position in Grodno enabled me to develop a stiff and formal acquaintanceship with a few Russians, mostly among the higher official class, and that was all. Not one instance could I observe, among my Russian acquaintances, of a human interest or a desire for friendlier intimacy. Per contra, I was often enough able to observe a consciousness of condescension. The natural result was that I remained equally reserved. Moreover, I found nothing to interest me in these official circles; I did want very much to become more closely acquainted with Russian social life, but it was quite clear that I could not satisfy my desire there.

I had a Jewish as well as a purely human interest in the

Russian world. Russia at that time contained some seven million Jews. I felt that the fate of these seven million would for many generations be bound up with that of the country. No one, not even among the Zionists, believed that these millions could be lifted out and transformed somewhere into an independent national entity. It is true that we saw in Zionism the *only* possible solution to the Jewish question, but the effects of Zionism were to be qualitative rather than quantitative. We saw the Jewish problem not only under the economic and civic aspects, but also under the political and psychological aspects. What we attacked was the *homelessness* of the Jewish people, wherein we saw the chief cause of the disastrous Jewish situation throughout the world. The creation of a Jewish homeland, even if only for a fraction of the Jewish people, would remove the reproach, with all its psychological consequences. The individual Jew living outside the Jewish homeland would then feel like the member of any other people who finds it necessary to leave his homeland. It might be that even under these circumstances there would continue a certain hostility toward the Jews, the result of a profound difference in life-outlook that has expressed itself in differences of religion, customs, and manners. But it was the attitude of contempt toward the people that was the greatest evil.

It was obvious to me, and all in my circle, that in Russia the condition of the Jew would change for the better only with a change in the regime. But we did not think of that change in the form of a social revolution; we thought it sufficient if we could achieve a constitution like that, for instance, of England or France. And I must confess—though the confession does not reflect favorably on our outlook—that we might even have been content at first with conditions as they were in Germany. For all these reasons I was anxious to make contacts with the circles of the Russian constitutionalists. From contemporaneous Russian periodical literature, which stood on a high intellectual level, I got the impression that something earnest was afoot, but the literature alone was not enough for me. I wanted to meet the men who wrote and read it, the men who were preparing a brighter future for the seven million Jews of Russia.

During my Grodno period I hardly had the feeling that I was living in Russia. The Russians I met were not, for me, representative of the Russian mind that was disclosed in Russian literature. It was in Ekaterinoslav that I formed my first living concept of Russian society. Curiously enough, I was helped to this concept by the very highest Russian official of the locality, the Governor-General, Prince Sviatopolk-Mirsky. When I came, according to the custom, to present myself, he received me, in the presence of a considerable number of important guests, more like an old acquaintance than a new official. I imagine that Boris Brandt had gone to great lengths on my behalf. The man I had come to meet had an open, intellectual face, on which were clearly written the qualities of gentleness and honesty. At first blush I could hardly believe that such a man could be a Russian governor. He wore, at that interview, the uniform of a lieutenant general and aide-de-camp to the Czar. His breast was covered with the insignia of academic titles and military orders. Neither the uniform nor the decorations accorded with that tired, spiritualized face, which seemed constantly to be saying: "These things I have had to put on, or rather, I have submitted to having them put on me. I would much rather wear the plain clothes of an ordinary citizen."

His warm reception of me, which was interpreted as a demonstration of friendliness toward the Jewish community, made its impression on political circles, and I observed that officials actually took pains to be friendly toward me; but while the friendliness of Sviatopolk-Mirsky was natural, theirs was forced.

I soon became acquainted with the Russian religious hierarchy, including the Archbishop and the upper clergy, with the judges of the Ukrainian Supreme Court, and with the representatives of the nobility and *Zemstvos*, or local councils. In brief, I got to know personally all the circles that made up the government of Ekaterinoslav. I was interested in the mechanics of their organization, and in the motions of their component parts. The nobility played the leading role and set the standard; whatever failed to agree with it was removed. The two principal parts of the machine were the priesthood and the army. The same material was used to cast the church bells and the heavy artillery; whatever the first failed to achieve by persuasion, the second achieved by force. The schools, more particularly the public schools, were placed somewhere between the two; on one side the priest, on the other the soldier. The directors and inspectors of the schools, whom I soon got to know, were the darkest of all the forces, in some respects worse than the gendarmerie. They were men, I soon realized, who had not the slightest interest in education and pedagogy as such. They had one objective in view: to make more difficult the already difficult task of the teacher, to keep him constantly aware of the fact that he was watched, that his every word was weighed.

My reception among the Jews of Ekaterinoslav was a mixed one. The minority defeated in the election maintained an unfriendly attitude. Their dislike of me was, for the most part, not personal; they were simply smarting under defeat. But there were some who understood in advance the program I had set myself and who were determined to keep up the fight against me. Perhaps I myself would not have noticed the opposition particularly, if my friends had not frequently and insistently told me about it. Every day these "friends" came to me with detailed reports as to what this one had said, what the other thought, and what the general attitude toward me was in the opposing camp.

But there was a small handful of people who did give me the kind of reception I wanted, with genuine moral support in my work. Without talk, without bluster, there grew up between us a silent bond. Before I entered on my principal task, which had to do with the reform of the Hebrew schools of all grades and the education of the Jewish youth in general, I held long and serious counsel with them. It was their share of the work to prepare the ground in the community and to make my assault easier.

I cannot apply the simple word friendship to my relations with Menachem Mendel Ussishkin. It was a relationship of absolute trust and confidence, built on an unshakable foundation of understanding. I saw in Ussishkin a reincarnation of those old Jewish heroes who had concentrated in themselves the will of an entire people. I was not blind to his faults and weaknesses, and they occasioned me much suffering; but they never disturbed our relationship. I admired his consistency and his oneness. The only son of a well-to-do father, in a turbulent, parvenu city where men were amassing fortunes in grain, iron and coal, Ussishkin withstood all temptation and devoted the strongest years of his youth and manhood to the Zionist ideal. He could have become a rich man; I believe, moreover, that he wanted very badly to be rich. But he fought an inner as well as an outer battle, and came through the victor in both.

Another reason compels me to take Ussishkin out of the general ranks of my friends. As Zionist head of the province of Ekaterinoslav, he was in a sense my superior. He was accustomed to asserting his authority with a strong hand, and more than once I had occasion to feel his severity; but I always admired him and submitted to discipline.

The immediate circle of my friends was a small one, but it consisted of authentic, strong individualities. The oldest and the youngest in the circle was Michael Maidansky, well known throughout Russia as one of the cleverest and most active figures in Jewish public life. He was nearly eighty years of age, a man with a snow-white head and a broad, snow-white beard. His eyes, which would have suited a young, temperamental hero, shone out of their setting like unnatural suns. It was hard to tell whether the eyes were mocking the snow-white hair or vice versa. Vigorous, lively, Maidansky concentrated in himself intellectually the best in the old type of neo-Hebraist. He was crammed with knowledge of our old and modern literature; he had a remarkable memory for his own experiences, too, and seldom faced a situation for which there was not a helpful parallel in his past. He was a wit of the first order, and where opposition could not be broken by assault, he melted it. He was loved and respected by Christians and Jews alike. No important function that had to do with Jewish life was complete without him; even the government often found it necessary to consult him.

Strangely enough, this man had been in his youth a fanatical Chassid; he had even been the "repeater" of a famous chassidic rabbi: as such it had been his function to repeat the sayings of his rabbi to larger audiences, sometimes in popularized form. He also acted as publicity agent for his rabbi. What incident, or series of incidents, was it that caused him to exchange the mystic, ecstatic world of Chassidism for the sensible and modern world of public service? This was his secret, and he never revealed it. He had no enmity for the world he had left; indeed, he had no enmities at all—there was no room for them in his joyous, optimistic nature.

During my five-year stay in Ekaterinoslav I met this happy old man nearly every day, since he belonged to the directorate of the main synagogue in the city. There were three in this body: the president, the scholar and the treasurer. The rabbi belonged *ex officio*. According to Russian law, the rabbi was at the head: in actuality he was, as a rule, content to be admitted at the bottom of the list, a long way below the others. Michael

Maidansky was the "scholar" of the directorate. He played a considerable role in the *Chibath Zion*, and when Herzl transformed the movement into its political form, the old man kept pace with the younger generation. Our acquaintanceship passed early into intimate friendship. He called me by the familiar "thou" and wanted me to address him similarly. I could not bring myself to do it: I always spoke to him in the third person: "What does the Grandfather say?"

One day my eighty-year-old friend turned up at my house at seven in the morning. He knew that I was an early riser. Seeing me startled, he reassured me with: "Don't be afraid. It's an important matter, but nothing tragic." Then he went on: "There's a Jewish girl in town whom the Christians have persuaded to accept baptism. For the time being she's in a convent." The old man had been to see the archbishop, with whom he was quite intimate, and had asked him to have the girl, who was little more than a child, released and returned to her parents. He had been successful in his mission. Why had he come to me then, at this early hour? There was a second matter.

"You see," explained the Grandfather, "I don't need your help now. But I had an intimate discussion with the archbishop on the relative merits of Judaism and Christianity, and while I was talking I remembered an anecdote in this very connection. It was a beautiful anecdote. It tickled me all over, but I didn't dare to tell it. But I had to tell it to someone. You know, I'm an elderly man, and my memory isn't what it used to be. I was afraid I would forget it altogether, and then it might get lost. But I feel sure that in your hands the anecdote will be perfectly safe."

I need hardly say that the anecdote was salty—much too salty for an archbishop, too salty, in fact, for a plain, ordinary bishop. If I hadn't been ashamed, I would have kissed my eighty-year-old friend. Sometimes one reads of such high spirits in an old man; to meet an instance is an unforgettable experience.

Old Michael loved little children. He could play with them by the hour and hold them hypnotized with his stories; and the children responded by idolizing him. At the meeting of the two extremes of life a marvelous harmony was created. For my little daughter Enya he had a special love, and once when she was ill he made it his business to visit her every day. On one occasion he brought with him a canary in a cage and, sitting down by her bed, began to spin stories about birds.

The most important and most influential Jew in town was Moisse Judovich Karpas. He resembled in many respects Eliezer Bregman of Grodno. As a type he was American, full of energy and initiative, always ready to take a chance with something new. He was creative and far-seeing in his social activities, but not drunk with success, knowing his own abilities and measuring them soberly. In this he was unusual. I have had occasion to meet many rich Jews, some of them wonderfully good and gentle persons, always ready to help people in a big way. Their good intentions seldom came to anything because God, who blessed them on the one hand with the means, punished them on the other with the ambition to possess a philosophy of their own, and their lean philosophy used to eat up their fat donations, as the lean cows in Pharaoh's dream ate up the fat cows, and of the latter we are told that "it was as if they had not been."

If Moisse Judovich Karpas did have an ambition, it was to see Ekaterinoslav become a model Jewish community. He was prepared to back his ambition with money, but as to his ideas and suggestions, he never failed to consult his co-workers, or obtain the most expert assistance; and when it came to questions of education he kept modestly in the background. Himself with next to no education, he made up for it by natural intelligence and mental honesty.

A very different type was the father-in-law of Ussishkin, Sergei Pavlovich Palei. "Sergei" had originally been Shmarya and "Pavlovich" Feitel; and Feitel Palei came from one of the old-fashioned Chassidic families. Shmarya himself had received a purely Jewish education, and it was only after his marriage, when he was the father of two children, that he suddenly abandoned the world into which he had been born and turned to the books of the moderns. He recast his whole education, went through a high school course first, then passed successfully through the aristocratic Institute for Transport Engineers in St. Petersburg, of course under his new Russian name. With that name, Sergei Pavlovich, he returned from St. Petersburg. He educated his children solely in the Russian culture—not a word of Yiddish or a sign of Hebrew. The grandfather understood the grandchildren with difficulty, the grandchildren the grandfather not at all. I mention this as an instance of kaleidoscopic changes of the Jewish generations during my own time.

Sergei Pavlovich was the manager of his father's business—a large steam mill for grain and a large sawmill equipped with the most modern machinery. As Sergei Pavlovich was an only son, the public regarded him as the head of the firm. In the business world he was known as a man of absolute integrity, but very hard. He was by nature skeptical and pessimistic—not the kind of stuff out of which public-spirited men are made. But under the imperious influence of Ussishkin, Sergei Pavlovich did enter Jewish public affairs, and even to some extent Zionist affairs. He lacked both the magnanimity of Karpas and the optimism of Maidansky. But his brilliant mind was of great use to us, particularly as a controlling element.

The Jewish community of Ekaterinoslav was much more democratically organized than that of Grodno, where only a couple of rich men directed communal affairs without any representation of the masses. There was here a genuine public opinion. In part this was due to the Russian newspapers, which devoted considerable space to Jewish matters. To this they were really compelled by the preponderance of Jewish readers.

The Jewish population was only a third of the total, but its readership was far higher than the Russian. Among the latter there was a large class of workers, chiefly in the iron works and the railroad shops of the well-developed Ekaterinoslav lines. There was also a large element of the lower-middle class. Neither the workers nor the lower-middle class had reached the cultural stage where a newspaper is a daily necessity.

In Ekaterinoslav I was for the first time drawn into ordinary charitable work. The community had assumed the responsibility for the poor, and begging from door to door was forbidden. It was not a self-evident responsibility. On the one hand there was much opposition on the part of important Jews, who rather liked handing out their gifts to the poor in person. On the other hand there was much opposition from the poor themselves. It was no use explaining to them that the new system was better, more decent, more reliable, that someone would take an intelligent interest in their troubles. They did not want these impersonal donations; they would rather depend on the moods God inspired in the hearts of the donors. I took part in the reorganization of the charities. The new system involved much research into individual cases, and with my colleagues I paid frequent visits to the poorest Jewish quarters. I did not meet in Ekaterinoslav such poverty as I had observed in Lithuania. Indeed, there were many receivers of our help who might have been envied by some of the smaller householders of Grodno. They did not eat the heavy black bread of the Lithuanians, but tasty white bread; instead of the eternal herring and onion you could smell in their houses beet soup and meat. The houses were roomier, the clothes more decent. I did not meet those pale, despairing faces to which I had become accustomed in the north, the expressions of hunger and want endured since earliest childhood. I learned from this contrast the meaning of Schleiermacher's famous phrase: *Der Mensch ist was er isst*—man is what he eats.

The fact that Jews usually have a larger number of philanthropic institutions than others has been accepted as evidence of a superior kindliness among them. The true explanation is rather more one-sided. It lies less in the character of the Jew than in the historical development of the people. The Jews have seldom or never been the recipients of whatever degree of care governments bestowed on the poor. They therefore learned early to exercise voluntarily those social functions which the government performed for non-Jews; and it is a curious fact that if we examine Jewish philanthropic institutions we shall see that nine-tenths of them are devoted to pathological cases, and the rest to constructive work. Hospitals, orphan asylums, homes for the aged, old-clothes societies and the like are repeated over and over again. Only of late has Jewish philanthropy turned to the care and education of the young, but the disproportion is still striking. Whatever the explanation may be, this is certainly a sign of weakness, and even of sickness, in the people.

During the first year my position and my work were both insecure. I had, it is true, won a following through my numerous public addresses, but the general public remained either cold or reserved. I knew the unpleasant feeling; I had already experienced it in Grodno. But here the situation was more difficult. In Grodno I had been a stranger personally, but as a type I was flesh of their flesh, bone of their bone—an authentic Litvak. The reverse was the case in Ekaterinoslav: the silent hostility was directed against the type, the Litvak, and not against the man. Between the Litvak, or Lithuanian, of the north and the warmer Jew of the south there was traditional enmity dating back to the religious break of the eighteenth century. The generous and emotional Chassidic sect had been born in the south and taken root there, and its opponents were the cool, dry intellectual types of my homeland, Lithuania.

That revolution had expressed the rebellion of the simple, ignorant masses against the trained scholars—not a new phenomenon in Jewish history. Lithuania was looked upon as the nest of the sceptical, over-intellectualized scholar; the south was the home of the ecstatic religionists. The division thus created extended through all Jewry, and it took several generations for the mutual hostility to relax. The migrations of the Lithuanian Jews to the south produced a mixed population in the larger centers. There was another equalizing circumstance —the common wave of Russification which passed over all Jews, Chassidim and Misnagdim alike. But historic wounds are not so easily cured. Even in my time the scars were still open; the original cause of the dispute had in reality disappeared, but phrases and emotions outlived the reality. In brief, I felt that it was as a Litvak that I was being rebuffed, and it was as such that I would have to conquer this place.

In my public addresses I always avoided the question of Jewish divisions; I treated Jewry always as a whole, and my theme was always the liberation of the national entity. It was the creative entirety of the Jews, made manifest in their achievements of the past, which was the earnest hope of their happier future. I spoke little of nationalism and Zionism in direct terms—the name did not matter as long as the substance was there. In this I was guided by the principles which had been laid down by my master, Ahad Ha-am. I used as my material the accumulated treasures of Jewish history, and in particular the midrashic literature, with its simple stories profoundly conceived and skillfully pointed. I aimed at the creation of spiritual values, and often the public read more into these stories than I myself had put into them.

I managed at last to break the ice. A friendlier atmosphere surrounded me. I did not take the public by storm; it was a hard struggle, and every step was marked by great labor.

But if I found pleasure in my public speaking, I found even

more in my work as a teacher. My Warsaw dream achieved realization in Ekaterinoslav. To my functions as rabbi was added that of teacher in one of the higher government schools for girls. It was not, God forbid, a regular government job with pay—to this privilege no Jew in Russia could aspire. It was the unpaid position of religious instructor, and even this was regarded as a great concession. The local government actually permitted me to teach Jewish girls the Jewish religion!

The school had eight classes, and I taught the upper four, in which the ages of the girls ranged from fifteen years to twenty, that is, from late childhood to early womanhood. As regards their Jewish knowledge, however, they were all of the same age. They had not the remotest idea that there were such things as Jewish history and a Jewish literature. Very few of them knew the Hebrew alphabet. These, it must be borne in mind, were children that came from the richer homes—their ignorance could not be written down to economic deprivation. It was the result of a criminal attitude on the part of their parents toward the Jewish education of their daughters. The Jewish girl, the future Jewish mother, grew up like an exotic plant in her parents' house, and often enough her Jewishness consisted solely of a fear of pogroms. It was only with the growth of the national movement that some attention began to be paid to the Jewish girl. But one generation could not catch up with the lapses of many. If the Jews had only known what contempt was aroused in Russian intellectuals by *their* contempt for Jewish culture, they might have changed their attitude.

In my curriculum I decided at the outset to leave the beaten path, to ignore the dry catechism, the dates, rules, and so on, and to concentrate on the cultural history of the Jewish people. As textbooks I chose the histories of Simon Dubnow, but expanded the material considerably. I did not want my pupils to learn anything by heart. I seldom examined them. The course would have to be intrinsically attractive and interesting. Parallel with the history of the people ran the narrative of the literature and of the spiritual tendencies which it reflected. It was hard work, made the harder by the fact that my pupils did not understand a word of Hebrew, and I had to prepare all my quotations in Russian. There was not even one good Russian translation of the Bible.

It was a happy period of my life. The attitude of my pupils toward me was one of gratitude. Poor Jewish girls! They became aware of the fact that they belonged to a people which had a fascinating past and a great literature. There were some among them who even came to my house to express their gratitude, and many of the parents became my supporters.

My success aroused the envy of my Russian "colleagues," the two priests who gave religious instructions to the Christian girls. One of them was a man with an academic training, and with him I got along well; we often had long discussions on theological subjects. The other had only been to a seminary and had a weakness for the bottle. I ought to observe that it was by no means a rare thing for a teacher to turn up in class somewhat the merrier for a couple of drinks. This second priest had no luck with his classes. As often as they could his pupils cut classes, and often he addressed almost empty benches. He took an aversion to me from the beginning, and made no bones about it. One day, during a session of the staff, when the subject of the theological courses was being discussed, he made a provocative remark: "I would like to know, Samuel Chaimovich, what kind of magic you've invented to hold your pupils as you do." The tone in which he said it made his meaning clear: he was an old man, I was young. I answered him first with the biblical verse: "There is no magic in Israel." Then I went on to explain that *his* courses were obligatory, that is, he had the help of the police; mine were not obligatory, I had no police to help me, so I had to rely on myself. I added that the great characteristic of Judaism was its freedom from compulsion.

CHAPTER TWENTY-EIGHT

Herzl and the Congresses

HERZL, the creator of political Zionism, had pinned his greatest hopes on England. He neglected no opportunity to lay the claims of his people before all rulers, but in his eyes England was the future bulwark of the movement. In this he showed the mixture of the artist and the *Realpolitiker*. England was the leading world power, but England was also the country which had known how to reproduce with strange fidelity the spirit of the Old Testament. In no other European language are the influences of the Bible and of biblical phraseology as pronounced and as organic as in England, and no other literature has produced a book like *Daniel Deronda*. Herzl understood that the element of the marvelous, almost of the fabulous, would find its strongest echo among these northerners. It was not an accident that among Herzl's first great helps was the pious Englishman, the Reverend William H. Hechler, one-time liberal tutor of the children of the Grand Duke of Baden. This man, who looked like a biblical Patriarch, saw in the Zionists the savior of mankind. He was forever praying that to his England might belong the merit of bringing about the fulfillment. At Zionist Congresses, and at all important Zionist gatherings, Hechler was to be seen, with his snow-white hair and long, white beard, with his huge cape, the wings of which spread out like the wings of cherubim—a symbol of the fact that Zionism was something more than a merely Jewish affair.

All the financial instruments of the Zionist movement were created under English law and had their headquarters in London. Had it not been for the technical difficulties of language and distance, most of the Zionist Congresses would have been held in London. In point of fact only the fourth, in 1900, was held in the British capital.

This was the first Congress I attended, and I went openly as a delegate, refusing to ask for a vacation in general. I told Prince Sviatopolk-Mirsky that I preferred not to use some pretext and attend the Congress incidentally. I must record the fact that this extraordinary man, the governor of a province with a large Jewish population, had no idea, when he came to Ekaterinoslav, of the disabilities under which the Jews labored. He did not know that there were so many special laws designed to make Jewish life intolerable. At every new revelation he would open his eyes as if to say: "Is that really so?"

The Congress was a thing of marvelous contrasts. A nation that was politically the weakest in the world, which was geographically scattered over five continents, was coming to the capital of the greatest empire known to history. Hundreds of Jews from remote townlets and villages in forlorn provinces were staging their embryonic parliament in the city of the Mother of Parliaments. And, finally, persons who during three Congresses had gone through considerable torture to adapt themselves to the official language—German—were now cast into a milieu in which their broken German was useless.

It would be difficult to describe the sufferings of the delegates in the matter of lodgment. Had the headquarters been in Whitechapel the difficulties would have been of another kind—

the absence of decent rooms decently furnished. At least we would not have had to wander around the streets like deaf-mutes, inventing for the occasion a new sign language which the English, alas, found as incomprehensible as we found their speech. But it was Herzl's intention to impress the English world; besides which he hoped that a dignified and imposing Congress would break the stiff-necked opposition of the rich Jews of London. The Congress was therefore held in one of the finest sections of the city, namely Regent Street. The headquarters were in the famous Queen's Hall. It was task enough to find a land for the Jewish people; we did not want to be looking every day for the Congress hall in the gigantic labyrinth of streets. We were afraid to try the big hotels; they were said to be hideously expensive. So we went looking for furnished rooms as near as might be to Queen's Hall, and at last we were duly quartered. A few of the delegates had been clever enough to make a preliminary study of the English language, but it did them little good, for their pronunciation concealed the words from everyone but themselves. My wife came with me to this Congress, and was certain that in a day or two she would be quite at home. She had studied English in the high school of Königsberg, and could quote "To be or not to be" from beginning to end. But after we had wandered around for a whole day, and were faced with the final decision whether to be or not to be lodged for the night, my wife found Shakespeare to be quite useless for our purpose, and we had to fall back on our sign language.

But for all that, the Congress must have made a profound impression on any observer. He would have been compelled to admire, first of all, the extraordinary talents of the leader. To bring together, in the capital of England, the representatives of a scattered people, and to impose upon them a parliamentary discipline which would have done credit to any nation—this was indeed an achievement. It called for great skill in organization and a very high degree of moral force. With the very creation of the Congress, Herzl dealt a deathblow to the famous legend—current particularly among Jews—of the undisciplined character of east European Jewry. The rapidity with which the east European Jew adapted himself to the rules, regulations and wrinkles of parliamentary procedure, even becoming an expert in their manipulation, was remarkable.

On me the impression of the Congress was ineffaceable. The praesidium on the tribune, with the majestic figure of Herzl at its head, called up in my mind the descriptions of the ancient Sanhedrin. I forgot for the moment our condition, helpless and unprotected. I only saw before me the representatives of an ancient cultural people, and I believed that with the power behind them they would move mountains and build up worlds. It seemed to me that the meeting was being held not in London, but in some forlorn and desolate place: outside the building the millions of Jewry waited; within, the resolutions would be adopted, the word would be passed to those that waited, and in an instant millions of hands would be transforming the desolation into one of the world's centers.

I cannot forget, either, the occasion when Nordau delivered his address on the subject of the Jews of Rumania and the new persecutions instituted by the Rumanian government. Queen's Hall was packed. Below, in the parquet, sat the delegates, above, in the galleries, the thousands of guests and visitors. Nordau did not deliver an address; it was, rather, a moral ultimatum, the protest of generations. It was not the voice of a living man, but that of thousands of the dead. Nordau spoke in German. I do not believe that the majority of the guests could follow him completely. But it hardly seemed necessary. The words cut through the air and through the barrier of imperfect understanding. The anger of the prophet sounded in the voice. Nordau pictured the situation of the Jews of Rumania, but what the audience heard was the story of the fate of a people.

On the tribune, not far from Herzl, sat a living illustration of Nordau's protest—Dr. Moses Gaster, Chief Rabbi of the Spanish-Portuguese community. As scholar and philologist he had added more than any other Rumanian of the past or present to the language of his country. As a mark of gratitude the Rumanian government had exiled him. True, she later recalled him, but it was too late.

The second great occasion was the mass meeting in the Whitechapel district. The dignity and beauty of Queen's Hall had not served any purpose. The Jews for whom Herzl had made his arrangements remained at a distance, and the so-called Jewish aristocracy was unmoved. Indeed, some of the members of the latter even found it necessary to make unprovoked public declarations of their disagreement with the entire movement. The one exception was Sir Francis Montefiore, the nephew of the great Sir Moses Montefiore, that legendary figure among the Jews of eastern Europe. Sir Francis was good decoration, but apart from his name he represented no element in British Jewry. The other nephew of Sir Moses, Claude Montefiore, a rising scholar, would have been something more than a decoration, but he elected to remain among our opponents. Zionism had little luck among the rich and satisfied Jews—satisfied, that is, not only in material things but with their situation. They were quite alien to the meaning of the words "the national hunger."

The picture underwent a radical change when the Congress turned round and faced the Jewish masses. Among the rich Jews we exerted ourselves in vain to touch them with Zionism; among the poor we had to exert ourselves to instill into them something more than an instinctive response. The entire leadership attended—Herzl, Nordau, Zangwill, Gaster, Professor Mandelstamm of Kiev, Ussishkin, Tschlenov, Cohen-Bernstein, Vladimir Tiomkin—all of them imposing figures. At first there were short addresses in English or German, but the audience caught fire only when it was addressed in its own language. With the first Yiddish phrase of the speaker: "Greetings to you from your brothers on the other side of the water," a thrill went through the audience, and when the speaker went on: "We have become weary of being a nation of wanderers," the audience was in the hollow of his hand. When the meeting was over the audience would not go home; groups accompanied the delegates to their lodgings through the dark midnights streets.

The debates at the fourth Congress were vehement. There were already strong oppositionist factions within the movement: on the one hand a number of rabbis who wanted to place a religious stamp on it; on the other the respresentatives of radical-democratic youth. These demanded that within the Zionist program be included a wide range of social and cultural activities for the Jewish masses. The leaders of the young democrats were two of my friends, Leo Motzkin and Chaim Weizmann. The latter was younger than I by several years, but he belonged wholly within our group. He had already made a name for himself as a deadly debater. It was apparent to all that in this young man there was latent a leader of unusual power, but it occurred to no one that he was destined, in later years, to take the place of Herzl.

I shall say little about the impression Herzl produced on me. I was not astonished by the strength of it, for I came prejudiced in his favor. And yet it was even stronger than I had anticipated, and this was true in spite of the fact that I actually got little more than a glimpse of him. I was present at a session, held prior to the opening of the Congress, of the *Permanenz Ausschuss*—the Standing Committee, the chief committee of the Congress—and was deeply absorbed in a debate then in progress. Suddenly the door opened, and a tall, slender figure stood there. I heard the announcement that as the Congress would open in the afternoon instead of in the morning, the delegates would have to come in morning clothes instead of in evening dress. This was the rule in England. The figure then disappeared. Everyone had risen to his feet, with the exception of myself. Motzkin, who had been sitting by me, nudged me and said: "That was Herzl." I felt a sudden wave of emotion pass through me. I sprang to my feet, but it was too late.

The Congress closed with a banquet in the main hall, a formal, frosty affair after the English fashion. At the table on the dais sat a number of ladies in extreme décolleté: among the guests moved waiters with the traditional English sideburns. The atmosphere was icy. One of the strong champions of the orthodox wing in the Congress, Akiba Rabinowich, a rabbi of Pultova, was outraged by the ladies in décolleté and left the hall in protest. We did not believe either in the sincerity of his words or the genuineness of the protest. A little later we discovered him in one of the loges upstairs, staring at the ladies through his balled hands. I went over to him and said: "Rabbi, don't strain your eyesight. You can come closer." He afterwards developed into one of the ugliest opponents of Zionism.

At last the Congress was over. The hours of exaltation had ended. It was time to return home. Not all of the delegates had their fare. No one will ever know with what difficulty a great many of them had scraped together their expense money.

A few days before the opening of the Congress, there was also opened in London the new "tube," the deeper of the two underground systems. Shortly thereafter, when the Congress was in session, one of the trains got stuck in a tunnel for several hours. The company, anxious to avoid difficulties, handed a gold sovereign to every passenger as he emerged from the train. Such, at least, was the story that reached the Congress delegates. Then a second story was told, having to do only with the delegates, namely that several of them took to riding the tube diligently in the hope that the accident would be repeated. The old saying that there is just one step from the sublime to the ridiculous is not quite accurate. The two always run parallel.

This is the way of history: when it has accepted a plan and defined a goal for itself, it does not set out in a hurry. Slowly it assembles the necessary forces, and gives, or rather hints, a warning of its purpose. Its purpose is not its own; it is bound by laws which it must fulfill; but it is not wholly ruthless, for the wise may take the warning and prepare themselves. Later, when the forces are all assembled and the fulfillment is at hand, the purpose becomes more and more insistent. Finally the day of reckoning comes, when those who would not read the signs and have refused to prepare themselves are broken and cast aside.

The time I am now about to describe embraces only a few years, but they were years of crisis and of judgment, and in them are gathered the processes of the ages. It was the beginning of the end of a long, long epoch of slavery, and the approach of a period of freedom which had already given its first signs in the seventies of the last century. How much time must pass before that freedom is realized, no one can tell. But when I concentrate on the few most critical years, there rises before me a remarkable picture. As a rule, if we turn to look at the past, we see the steady stream of the years, smooth or stormy. But the four years embracing 1903 through 1906 are a double picture of two streams: for the Russian people the tempestuous waters flowed upward, for the Russian government they flowed downward.

As always, seen from the outside, the government presented itself as a huge, impregnable fortress. But this was a facade; within the building were chaos and decay and despair. In its blindness the government hastened its own doom, and did more damage from within than the waiting masses did from the outside. In their panic, the rulers of Russia lost every vestige of decency and shame. More like a gang of desperate adventurers than a class responsible for the well-being of a country, they embarked on mad enterprises of which disaster could be the only reward.

The final collapse of the Russian imperial government began with the Kishinev pogrom. The reader will suspect in this statement the one-sidedness or the chauvinism of a Jew who looks at history under the Jewish aspect. But I feel quite free from this tendency. I do not exaggerate the role which the Jews played in Russian life—and no one accuses them of having played a small one. But I regard the Kishinev pogrom of 1903 as the beginning of the collapse because it revealed with breathtaking suddenness the ghastly rottenness which had eaten into the system of the government. It is quite true that in the earlier pogroms too the government had played its part, but the pogrom of Kishinev was all its own. It was born in the black brain of von Plehve. Every detail was worked out in the dark rooms of his ministry. Even the instructors were sent down from St. Petersburg. The hooligans were a home product, and as good a crop could be found in Bessarabia as in any other part of Russia. There is an ancient Jewish legend which tells that Pharaoh the persecutor became a leper, and his advisers told him to bathe daily in the blood of Jewish children. For the leprosy of the Russian government von Plehve prescribed and arranged a blood bath of Jews of all ages. But perhaps the reader will ask: "How was it possible for a government to exist at all if at the head of it stood men with the education of corporals and the psychology of lynchers?" That very question, in those very words, was asked in the first Russian Duma by Prince Urusov. I do not know the answer, but the Kishinev pogrom may well stand as a warning to sundry governments today.

The civilized world, accustomed as it was to pogroms against the Jews, was horrified by the Kishinev pogrom, which went beyond all others in its bestiality. A cry of protest went up from the whole world, and loudest among the voices were those of non-Jews, who demanded the intervention of their respective governments. The governments could not intervene. The slaughter of Jews, Armenians, and others is "an internal affair," and according to the international etiquette book it is not proper for an alien government to step in. Within Russia itself the protests were few, but among them was that of the man who had been excommunicated by the Russian Church, Count Leo Tolstoy. I do not know what effect it had on the Russian masses; the Jews did find a little comfort in it.

The Jewish world, particularly that part of it which lay beyond the seas, was shaken to its foundations. In addition to the immediate thrill of sympathy, there was the reflection: "If not for an accident, it might have been us. *They* might have fled from Russia; *we* might have remained there to meet their fate." The helplessness of the Jewish people was once more revealed in all its revolting nakedness. In a poem of rage and misery which the Kishinev pogrom inspired, Bialik poured forth the anger of the Jewish people against the pogrom hooligans, against itself, and against its own God. Like a flash that poem travelled from end to end of Jewish Russia, and everywhere the Jews learned it by heart.

The Kishinev pogrom preceded very closely the sixth Zionist Congress, the one in which the Uganda question almost shattered the movement, not only from the organizational but also from the ideological point of view. The leader himself, Herzl, had been badly shaken by the pogrom. He who had kept his eyes fixed only on the big future, who for the sake of it had rejected small colonization plans, and had thereby made himself a host of enemies, suddenly realized that the claims of the present could not be ignored. He began therefore to look for a side path, an indirect approach to his problem. He was ready to compromise. He would accept, as a halfway station, the territory of Uganda offered by England's Colonial Minister, Joseph Chamberlain. He declared, indeed, that it *was* nothing but a halfway station; but this was the first time he had spoken in half-terms. In a critical moment he lost his balance. It is thus that I see the connection between Kishinev and the Uganda proposal. It was thus that I saw it then, when I was in the midst of the conflict.

Shortly before the Uganda Congress, as it came to be called, Herzl undertook a journey through Russia and had a long interview with the Minister of the Interior, von Plehve. If Herzl had been properly advised, he would never have undertaken this journey, though not because of the storm of protest which it aroused among Jewish radicals, who regarded von Plehve as a man not fit to be dealt with. Herzl was, after all, acting in the capacity of the foreign minister of the Jewish people, and it happens often enough that in such a capacity a man of the finest character must deal with a man of the meanest. The journey was inadvisable simply because the most solemn promise of von Plehve was utterly without value.

On his return journey Herzl made a stop in Vilna. The Jewish community gave him a royal reception, the kind it had given many years before to Sir Moses Montefiore when the latter visited St. Petersburg to discuss the Jewish situation with the Russian government. As then, the Jewish community came to greet the guest with a Scroll of the Law—the highest honor that can be bestowed on anyone. It was in Vilna that Herzl made his first contact with the simple Jewish masses. This was the one positive gain of his visit to Russia.

Once again the Zionist delegates came together in the beautiful and hospitable city of Basle. Once again the wandering parliament of the wandering people held its sessions in the casino. It was an impatient horde of delegates, conscious of the fearful emergency, that waited for the Congress to open. But something more than impatience was written on their faces: worry, uncertainty, and the sadness of hope deferred.

Six years had now passed since the leader had called them to the first Congress and had startled and inspired them by his first appearance and his first speeches. Six whole years—and of all the hopes he had then inspired not a single one seemed a jot nearer fulfillment. The Jewish magnates were still deaf and dumb; an earlier offer of the British government, of the El Arish desert area above Egypt, had come to nothing. And meanwhile? Meanwhile there was Kishinev.

It was widely known that the leader had something of great moment to reveal to the Congress, but the nature of that something was a closely guarded secret of the inner circle. It was the Uganda offer. I must repeat over and over again, as Herzl did, that he considered Uganda only a stepping-stone. It was not Palestine; but for the sake of their present sufferings the Jews ought to accept this offer with gratitude. I was sitting, when Herzl revealed the whole matter to the delegates, on the platform of the Congress, being one of its secretaries. I was therefore able to watch closely the effect produced by the announcement on the faces of the listeners. It was one of almost agonized attention. On the faces were written astonishment and admiration—but not a sign of protest. I do not believe that any of the delegates realized at the moment the significance of what had happened. The magnanimity of the British offer sufficed, during the first instants, to obscure all other considerations. And yet the astonishment and admiration were not such as might have been expected. It was only when the general session broke up, and the various groups assembled in caucus, that it was realized that a crisis had appeared in the Zionist movement.

The Russian delegation was the largest in the Congress. Its leader was Yechiel Tschlenov, for Ussishkin was not at the Uganda Congress—he happened to be, at that time, on a visit to Palestine. Tschlenov, as I have indicated, was not a man to look for battle. Also, he was a passionate admirer of Herzl. He opened the deliberations of the Russian delegation, but did not venture an opinion; all he did was to analyze the significance of the offer. After him spoke Weizmann, who even then exerted considerable influence over the younger and more radical elements of the Congress. He was known for the swiftness of his ideas and the devastating wit with which he defended them. But he too, on this occasion, did not find himself so easily. Even the delegates noticed his uncertainty.

I was the third to speak. It would be untrue and ungenerous to insinuate that either Tschlenov or Weizmann lacked the Zionist courage to give the decision for which the delegates were waiting, and that they had therefore left it to me. It happened to be my good fortune that I spoke third, when all of us had had a little time to gather our thoughts. With the rest, I had already sobered up from my first bewildering impressions, and the general mood of clarification helped me, too, to think clearly. I caught, and out of conviction reflected, the mood. After me others spoke, like myself, in a spirit of the strongest opposition to the Uganda offer. But there were some just as strongly for it. The session became tense. Interruptions like "Suicide!" "Criminal!" "Treachery!" began to fly from all sides. Without being formally chosen I became the leader of the Russian opposition to Uganda.

In the general sessions of the Congress we passed through hours of storm. Max Nordau, in principle opposed to Uganda—though we learned this only later—submerged his own views out of loyalty to Herzl, and defended Uganda in a speech that was more remarkable for its wit than its power to convince. Leopold Greenberg, for several decades the editor of *The Jewish Chronicle* of London, was one of the staunch defenders of Uganda. It was he who had brought Herzl into close contact with the British government. European Jewry was divided into two almost clean-cut parts: west European Jewry was for the project, east European Jewry against it. Of course there were exceptions, for it must be remembered that the division into west European and east European was psychological as well as geographical. It is a remarkable fact that the majority of the orthodox rabbis were in favor of the project. There was even one delegate who made a bet in advance that this would be the case—and he won. For the orthodox rabbis, Uganda was a real find. The building of Palestine by profane means had contained an element of competition with their favorite concept of the Messiah, while Uganda could be built without interference in Messianic affairs.

The vote was taken by roll call, and every delegate had to answer either "Yes" or "No." The No-sayers shouted more loudly, but the number of Yes-sayers was greater. Out of some five hundred delegates, only one hundred and eighty-five voted No. It was therefore decided that an expedition be sent to the territory of Uganda to report on its possibilities. Without any further announcement the minority rose as one man and left the Congress. On the faces of many there were tears; they felt they had lived through a third Destruction.

On several occasions during the Congress Herzl invited me, with other leaders of the opposition, to meet with him in the council room. He tried to soothe me. I observed his face, and I did not envy him his victory. He understood well enough: one more victory of that kind, and the Zionist Organziation would be done for. But those who stood near to him did not see it thus; they did not understand that they were undermining the sources of the Zionist impulse. They were playing politics not for but with Zionism. They had weakened the moral power of that immemorial Jewish demand upon which Zionism was based.

When, in the Congress hall, the map of Palestine was covered by a map of Uganda, the delegates felt as though they were watching a total eclipse of the sun. The last night of the Congress no one slept; in particular, the oppositionists held an all-night session. Late in the night the leader appeared in our midst and asked to be heard. A resolution had to be passed before he was given permission; while the resolution was being passed, he waited in the corridor. The proud leader humbled himself before his followers. Entering, he assured us once again that Uganda was not a substitute for Palestine, but only a halfway station. He produced no effect, there was no applause. We had faith in Herzl—but we had no faith in Uganda.

Herzl delivered the closing address of the Congress. His last words were those of our forefathers when they swore eternal faith to Jerusalem by the waters of Babylon. He uttered the words as if they had been written for him for the occasion. That speech was his swan song. The oppositionists organized themselves under the leadership of Ussishkin, and the war against Herzl was conducted with too much bitterness. With a little softness we might have achieved the same results.

After that Congress, Herzl's heart became weaker from day to day. In the midst of its growth, the loftiest Jewish tree of many centuries toppled and fell. I was present at Herzl's funeral in Vienna, the greatest procession I have yet seen. In my imagination I followed the unresting chain of events that had led to that moment: von Plehve-Kishinev, Kishinev-Uganda, Uganda–Herzl. It seems as if when Herzl went to see von Plehve he went to face his doom. He rose into the Jewish heavens like a comet and like a comet he disappeared from them.

It is here, perhaps, that I may most fittingly tell of another loss, more personal and perhaps more significant as a marker in my life—the almost simultaneous death of my parents. I had seen little of them during their latter years. The journey from Ekaterinoslav to Svislovitz used to take, in those days, nearly forty-eight hours. For me it was difficult to spare the time; for my parents, difficult to stand the strain. I felt that we were drifting apart, and I suffered. A new factor had entered into our relations. I was no longer dependent on my parents, as in the days before Ekaterinoslav. True, things had not turned out as I had expected, but with my many activities I did manage to make a living. I was writing a great deal: at first for *Der Yud*, a good literary weekly edited by my friend Joseph Luria, and then for *Der Freind*, edited by another friend, Saul Ginsburg. I also wrote in Hebrew for *Ha-Zeman*, edited by ben Zion Katz, and for Ahad Ha-am's monthly, *Ha-Shiloach*. Yet I was ashamed to admit to myself that my material independence had anything to do with the increasing alienation between me and my parents. I thought it was merely the years, which wear down everything, including love. But whatever the cause, it was clear to me that my parents no longer occupied that place in my thoughts which had once been theirs. They still occupied, formally, the place of honor, but somehow the place of honor was not as impressive as it used to be.

For some years before his death my father suffered greatly from a disease which affected his feet and made it almost impossible for him to get about. He was taken to various places abroad but to no effect. I found my father, when I visited him, in pain, and raging against the doctors. But beside his physical anguish, my father also suffered mentally in his last years. Of this latter side of his distress my brothers and I suspected nothing—we only knew that something was on the mind of our pious father. His closest confidant was my brother-in-law, Asher Shafrai, the great scholar and still greater *shlimihl*. Suddenly my father began to spend many hours together with him, in intimate talk. None of us asked Asher what the subject of these secret conversations was. My brother-in-law only used to say that we had never understood what a saint our father was, and to what extent he remembered every act of his life and weighed it in the balance of his conscience.

My mother bore all this in silence and humility. She too was ill, with diabetes, but she forgot her own illness in her worry for my father, and if she had only been able she would have added his pains to her own. But she was helpless, and she had to sit by and watch the life ebbing slowly from her Samuel Chaim.

During all the years of his illness my father had a special servant assigned to him, but my mother did not relax her attention for a moment; she would even miss synagogue services for his sake, and that was her greatest sacrifice. In the hall of our house there used to hang a large, hand-drawn portrait of my father. A couple of times I saw my mother standing before it and praying, not out of the prayer book, or audibly, but silently, as Hannah, the mother of Samuel, prayed in the tabernacle. That was strange to me: a pious, God-fearing Jewish wife standing in prayer before a picture, even though it was not to the picture, but for the subject of it, that she prayed.

For herself, she had made her peace with God, but she prayed for one favor—that her husband might live another two years and fill out the seventy years promised by the psalmist. It was not out of love of life that she prayed, for their sufferings were too heavy, but out of piety. Her prayer was not accepted. My father died between his sixty-eighth and sixty-ninth years. There was no consolation in this world for my mother. Her life had been bound to my father's since she had been a child of fourteen, and she survived him by only fourteen days. A little while before her death she was taken to Minsk, in the hope that her life might be prolonged a little, and there she died. Among Jews it is not the custom to transport the dead. "Where the tree falls, there let it lie." My mother lies buried in the cemetery of Minsk.

We were assembled in Svislovitz, four sons and a daughter, and nearly a score of grandchildren. In the old house of my father, and in the village of my birth, lying peacefully between its two rivers and among its fields and forests, nothing had changed. We felt like the branches of a tree when the trunk has fallen. In that moment we felt closer to one another, tried to be gentler and more thoughtful than was our wont. But it was just this added touch of gentleness which made us feel that we had lost the strongest thing in our life. The power which had sustained us all these years, the power of Father and Mother, was suddenly gone, and gone forever.

The "baby" of our family had always been my youngest brother, Eliezer. In the latter years of my father's life, it was he who had conducted the business, which was not as big as it had once been. My older brother, Meyer, who had a large family, had had to shift for himself. A younger brother, Joshua, a dentist, was going his own way. It was Eliezer who inherited the business and the traditions of my father's house; that is to say, he saw to it that none of the employees should be dismissed, and that the families that had made their living by the business, and particularly the family of my sister, should continue to derive a living from it as before. So when we sat together after my father's death, our eyes turned to the youngest among us, to him on whom the burden of responsibility had fallen heaviest. We trusted him to continue decently the tradition built up by my father, together with the house, in so many years of labor.

This was my last visit to Svislovitz. I never saw the village of my birth again. I said farewell to the people, to the rivers and fields and forests, and in my heart thanked them for the marvelous memories of childhood with which they had filled all of my life.

Soon after this doleful episode, another change came into my life. I received the offer of a position in Vilna. This Jewish community, a center of Jewish scholarship for the last four hundred years, was a continuation of Nahardea and Pumbedhita, the great centers of Jewish learning in ancient Babylonia. But the name by which it was glorified was not of a Babylonian city: they called it the Jerusalem of Lithuania. Vilna was first a talmudic center, and afterwards a center of the Hebrew renaissance in the nineteenth century. I believe that for this happy development much credit must be given to the giant figure, Elijah, the Gaon of Vilna, the spiritual leader of the community in the eighteenth century, whose spirit still broods over the city. This extraordinary man had, without any influence from the outside, and aided only by his incomparable knowledge of Jewish lore, prepared the way for the modern enlightenment. It was he who had had the courage to declare that without a knowledge of Hebrew and of Hebrew grammar—the latter a thing taboo to his contemporaries—it was impossible to attain to a true knowledge of Judaism. Even more daringly, he declared that those who wished to understand Judiasm also needed to study worldly things like geography, mathematics, astronomy and medicine. He went further. He demanded that a decent measure of education be provided for the Jewish girl, not less than for the Jewish boy. The neo-Hebraists who came after Elijah of Vilna found their task made easier by his authority.

My official position in Vilna was to be that of preacher to the Congregation *Taharat Kodesh*, which had distinguished itself by its attention to the education of the youth, and it was in this latter field that my principle duties would lie. I was to be preacher and educator, without being a rabbi—a unique position in Russia at that time. I accepted the offer readily and gratefully; and as chance would have it, at about the same time Prince Sviatopolk-Mirsky resigned his position as governor of Ekaterinoslav to be appointed governor of Vilna.

CHAPTER TWENTY-NINE

Jerusalem of Lithuania

IF I were to give my two years in Vilna the place they occupy in my memory, I should have to devote at least a full volume to them; and if I were to reproduce the tone of my memories, I should have to leave the prose form. In the life of most people there are, besides the regular festivals observed by all, private festivals and High Holy Days. The great Pentecost of my life was Vilna.

Before I came to Vilna I had had frequent occasion to change my place of residence, and every change had been bound up with a time of adaptation—lost time, lost energies. My two years in Vilna began, as it were, on the eve of my arrival. It is perhaps because of this fact that the Vilna period of my life seems so long and full.

Vilna fitted me like a glove. I loved the landscape around the city, reminiscent, as many have remarked, of Switzerland. I loved the castles of the old city, which breathed the spirit of a proud past. I even loved the little alleys with their gray, huddled buildings, which brought with them memories of the Middle Ages. Most of all I loved the Synagogue Yard of Vilna, dotted and surrounded with tiny study houses, the memorials of the great spirits that have given Vilna her name. They still lingered above the vast tomes that lined the shelves, above the benches and lecterns, built massively, as for eternity, above the brass candlesticks and seven-branched candelabra, and above the mighty stoves, in which, it almost seemed, the Divinity itself had lingered on long winter nights to hear the voices of Jews in study. I could wander for hours in that ancient courtyard, pausing at the door of some house of study to listen to the traditional chant of the Talmud student, itself the carrier of a host of stories out of the past. The same feeling, I suppose, comes over the sensitive Englishman when he wanders among the colleges and cloisters of Oxford. The Vilna Synagogue Yard was the Oxford of a people in exile, and the study rooms were its colleges.

I was happy, too, in the small circle of friends which formed round me to help me in my work. The first place among them was taken by Isaac Leib Goldberg, who had been instrumental in bringing me to Vilna. He belonged in reality to the business world, and was much occupied by his affairs. Yet he had made for himself a home which conformed to the instructions laid down in the *Ethics of the Fathers:* it was a meeting place for the sages, that is, for the intellectuals of the city. Whoever came there found enough to eat and drink, and guests enough to make good conversation. Goldberg possessed the valuable knack of being able to put everyone of his odd moments to practical use; moreover, he could divide his time and occupations so as to do five days' work in one. His fullest efforts were given to Zionism, and he found time to read all the latest books and periodicals. He remained modest, quiet, and retiring. Another of my helpers was Arkadi Naishul, who also belonged to the business world. It was a generation of businessmen which has now died out in the Jewish world—individuals who regarded business only as a means that would enable them to serve the community.

In our intellectual world, which was not Zionist throughout, the outstanding figure was Simon Dubnow. He held the view that it was necessary to create in Palestine a cultural center to serve as a beacon to world Jewry, but he also believed this to be only one of the tasks of the Jewish people. For him the center of gravity of the Jewish problem lay in autonomous rights in the Diaspora. This view he defended with the double equipment of a historian and a publicist. He believed in the possibility of independent Jewish cultural evolution in the Diaspora, and he carried the principle of Jewish minority rights to its logical extreme.

Simon Dubnow lived the classical life of a scholar. In his house there was peace. It was like a temple dedicated to search and meditation. The priestess of that temple was his wife Ida Efimovna, a modest, gentle soul, devoted to her husband's work. With Dubnow I became friends as soon as I arrived in Vilna, and the two families became closely united.

Among the many rich types who formed part of the intellectual circle, and who were frequent visitors in my house, I have space here but for three: Joshua Steinberg, Dr. Judah Leib Cantor and Feivel Getz.

Joshua Steinberg was the last of the Mohicans, the representative of the vanished generation of the Enlightenment in Vilna. He was a man of more than seventy years, but as straight and as stiff as the Hebrew roots which were his lifelong occupation. He had been, for no one knew how many decades, a teacher in the old Rabbinical School, and inspector of the Jewish Teachers' Institute. His reputation was founded on his Hebrew dictionaries. As a type, he was a born official, and having all his life studied only grammatical forms, he became in the end as dry and formal as the subject matter of his studies. He considered life something to be parsed and conjugated neatly—but hardly something to be declined, for when he was over seventy he married for the third or fourth time, taking to wife a woman of twenty-odd years. The incident did not create much of a sensation, for in the Jewish world such marriages were not unknown. Often this old scholar was to be seen strolling through the streets with his young wife, leading by the hand his charming little daughter.

Dr. Judah Leib Cantor was chosen in my time as the Rabbi of Vilna, and it was there that I first met him personally. He made a tragic impression. He had been noted as a scholar even in his youth, and was a stylist in Hebrew, Yiddish and Russian. His education was European, he had written much for periodicals and was considered a first-class publicist. Then, in his latter years, he looked around and discovered that he had frittered his life away in many trifling achievements. This had happened because he had observed many movements with light interest and had been passionately interested in none. The same was true of his friend, the poet Frischman, but Frischman had never wanted to be anything more than an artist and to influence the world through his art. Cantor had wanted to win recognition in the field of public activity, and a publicist without a passion cannot make a place for himself. The public regarded him as a sort of cultural ornament to the community. His style and scholarship were praised, his opinions ignored. Cantor was one of the aesthetic sceptics who did not believe that anything serious would ever come of the Jewish national movement. In Vilna he discovered his mistake, but by then it was too late.

The third man, Feivel Getz, would have been recognized as a type in Frankfurt, but in Vilna he was something unique. I, at least, have not met his like in Russian Jewry. He was conservative both in his Judaism and in his political views, and at the mention of radical opinions he trembled from head to foot. He was profoundly convinced that if the Jews only had skillful, silver-tongued orators enough to convince the world of the beauty of Jewish ethics, then all Jewish troubles would come to an end. He considered himself one of those advocates, of whom there were, alas, too few. He polemized with Leo Tolstoy on the views expressed by the latter on Judaism and Christianity. He carried on a long and voluminous correspondence with the great philo-Semite and philosopher Vladimir Soloviov on the Jewish problem. He published large numbers of Jewish apologias with laudatory introductions by Tchicherin and Vladimir Korolenko and others, and believed with all his heart that in this way he was improving the condition of the Jews. The Bundists and other Jewish Socialists terrified him almost out of his wits, and even the mild demands of the League for Jewish Civic Equality seemed to him excessive. He had a job in the Ministry of Education as "learned Jew," and lived in perpetual fear of losing it; and as the times were stormy and the Jewish world was full of movements, this man trembled day and night and was a pitiful object to behold. He was a frequent visitor at the Dubnows' home and at mine. He was forever trying to influence the Jews to be more modest in their demands. Ridiculous figure though he was, it must be said for him that he genuinely believed what he preached.

Of the Socialists, a few used to visit the houses of our circle, but only for social reasons. There was no such thing as an official contact between their organization and ours. It was only a little later, when the political storm broke out in full fury, that the Jewish organizations drew somewhat closer together.

My lectures in the *Taharat Kodesh* drew from the beginning a large audience. They were formulated especially for the youth, but the older people came in even larger numbers. The synagogue could seat no more than fifteen hundred in both sections—that is, of the men and the women—but on many occasions two thousand people squeezed themselves into the building. The place became a deathtrap in case of fire, and the police had to be called in to control the crowds. My work in

Ekaterinoslav now helped me greatly; I had a skeleton ready for all my lectures, and plenty of time in which to prepare the material. It moved me deeply to note how closely the audience followed my lectures, word for word, and if the audience was grateful, I was even more so. This was my own audience, which lay open to me, and which understood my every hint.

I gave little place to formal Jewish history in my lectures. Most of my time I devoted to the history of the development of Jewish culture. I dedicated six full lectures to the Jewish laws concerning the slave, and showed the evolution of Jewish thought on this subject from the oldest times to those of Maimonides, comparing it with the attitude of the Greeks and the Romans. I did the same with the subject of charity, the agrarian laws, and even the regulations for the conduct of war. I worked hard to bring the Jewish youth of Vilna into the spirit of the Jewish outlook in the various epochs of our history. I did not, of course, omit the messianic idea in Jewish history. In addition to my regular lectures, which were delivered on Saturday nights, I occasionally had to preach. But my "sermons" were really additional lectures. The congregation of *Taharat Kodesh* did not need sermons.

I had to be much more careful in the preparation of my material than I used to be in Ekaterinoslav; there were too many scholars in my Vilna audience. Among the listeners were men like Dubnow, Steinberg and Cantor. One of them would have been enough to inspire respect in a speaker. I always liked to have in my audience men who had to be treated with special intellectual respect.

From various sides propaganda was conducted against attendance at my lectures. I was accused of chauvinism. I believe the accusation was unfounded. In any case, it did my accusers no good, for the synagogue continued to be packed. Apart from this propaganda I had not a single complaint to make regarding my career in Vilna; and even in this respect my complaints were purely ideological, for my opponents were men of intellectual standing; the stamp of the city was on them.

The seventh Zionist Congress, the first after Herzl's death, was to make the final decision on the Uganda question. Actually the decision had been dictated by the members of the expedition which had been despatched by the resolution of the sixth Congress. The report was negative; the offered territory was declared to be unfit for purposes of colonization. But out of Uganda had come an independent phenomenon—Ugandism. The finding of a territory other than Palestine, to serve as an immediate source of relief, had become a question of principle. The fight against Ugandism was now taken up by Menachem Mendel Ussishkin, and in this battle he showed himself, as always, hard, almost ruthless. Close by Basle, in the little German town of Freiburg, Ussishkin called a conference of the faithful, who gave themselves the rather clumsy name of the Zio-Zionists, indicating a higher degree of Zionism. He organized the group with iron discipline. At the Congress itself, in Basle, speeches were now superfluous. The delegates spoke with their hands—that is, they just voted. Almost unanimously the Congress turned back the offer of Uganda, at the same time expressing its profound gratitude to the British government, and expressing the hope that when occasion arose, it would still support the Zionist demand as formulated in the Basle program for a Jewish homeland in Palestine.

A group consisting of the English and a few Russian delegates, under the leadership of Israel Zangwill, broke away from the Congress and the Zionist movement to found the Territorial movement. Zangwill defended territorialism as a matter of principle. He believed that the Jewish people had a right to a territory. Palestine was not excluded from the range of possibilities, but it was only one; however, after the founding of the Territorial organization Zangwill even became an opponent of

Palestine, and spent more energy in combating Palestine than in finding a territory.

This is a common enough phenomenon in party life: it is the men with the most similar ideas who fight each other most savagely. A bitter war was conducted for many years between Territorialists and Zionists. Zangwill never lost an opportunity to attack Zionists and Zionism. I took part in this war, and I had only one prayer on my lips: "O God, punish Zangwill and send him a territory!" For then he would be busy with his territory and have less time to attack us. Also he would learn that there is no such thing as a territory without difficulties; only a theoretical territory could be an earthly paradise. There, rain always falls at the right time, there are neither earthquakes nor diseases nor blights, there are no conflicts with the inhabitants, the administration is faultless, life runs as smoothly as a dream of love. Of course, for such a territory only those people are fit who are as innocent as children, and who therefore still run about like Adam and Eve before the Fall. And so I prayed that Zangwill, who was not exactly an innocent child, might be driven out of his theoretical paradise into an earthly territory and come to grips with Mother Earth. To my regret, my prayer was never answered, and the Territorialist dreams continued to float about like soap bubbles until the winds dispersed them. The only service the Territorial movement did for the Jews was, I believe, that several leaders became good geographers.

The death of Herzl left the Zionist movement orphaned. There was not one man to take his place. One individual had indeed gripped the imagination of the Zionists by his many-sided knowledge and the fire of his speeches—Max Nordau; but he lacked the qualities of a leader. None knew this better than he, himself, and he refused categorically to take up the leadership. The Zionist movement was in a difficult position. Its center of gravity was in eastern Europe, principally Russia.

For political reasons the center of gravity of leadership had to be in western Europe. The Congress finally chose a person who in some measure represented both east and west, David Wolfsohn.

This man, who had been born in a little town near Kovno, in Russia, had been taken as a child to Germany; there he had grown up, living at first in the border town of Memel, and later in Cologne, where he founded a large business house. Wolfsohn was a typical self-made man. For everything that he had achieved in life—wealth, social position, and a decent education—he had none to thank but himself. He had enrolled under Herzl's banner at the first call, and had become his intimate friend. Herzl immortalized him in his *Altneuland* as the man of natural intelligence and practical insight, David Litvak.

With that practical insight, Wolfsohn recognized that the Zionist organization as it then was could never carry out the task it had assumed. He therefore attempted to draw into the practical work for Palestine such other Jewish world organizations as the *Alliance Israelite*, the *B'nai Brith*, the German *Hilfsverein* for Russian Jews, and the Jewish Colonization Association (I.C.A.) of Baron de Hirsch. In this he anticipated by twenty years the action ultimately taken by the Zionist Congress. To achieve his purpose Wolfsohn called a conference in Brussels, and there the question of a union of Jewish forces for the work in Palestine was discussed. But the time was not yet ripe for this union; the other organizations still looked upon Zionism as a movement of east European Jews, that is, they patronized it. Besides, all Jewry was in a nervous mood because of developments in Russia.

It was quite clear to everyone that Russian Jewry, once emancipated, would take over the leadership of world Jewry. There were many who believed that the events in Russia belonged to the last act of the drama. Soon the curtain would be rung down on the old regime, and a new order would appear bringing Russia into the family of the civilized nations. It was therefore believed that for the moment the best policy for outsiders to follow was one of watchful waiting. I was present at the Brussels conference and delivered an address on the subject of the various party groups in Russian Jewry and their respective attitudes on the question of emancipation.

Meanwhile, with dizzying speed, the Russian rulers rushed toward their doom. After the Kishinev pogroms came the war with Japan (1904–5). From the outside the two incidents seem to be remotely related; actually they were two manifestations, almost equally important, of one destructive motif. Kishinev was the beginning of a systematic series of pogroms, the purpose of which was to act as a safety valve for the revolutionary restlessness of the Russian people. But a second, more powerful outlet was needed. What Jewish blood could not wash out, the fire of war would cleanse away. It was understood, of course, that the war would end with a Russian victory.

This was the time when the Emperor, Nicholas II, had ceased to consider even the views of his own ministers. He had surrounded himself with a secret cabinet of his own, in which the leading spirits were the gang of swindlers and intriguants, Bezobrazov and company, and it was they who rushed the country into the mad war with Japan. The private life of the Czar had sunk into a mixture of disgusting superstition and mysticism, in which he was deeply influenced by his sick and perverse wife. The court was haunted by religious quacks, of whom the most famous was Rasputin. It is a historical fact that the war with Japan was declared against the united opposition of Count Witte, the head of the cabinet, Lamsdorf, the Foreign Minister, and even Kuropatkin, the War Minister. The advice of von Plehve outweighed that of Witte, and when the latter reproached his colleague, von Plehve answered cynically: "You don't know conditions in Russia. We must have a successful little war in order to stave off revolution."

Few armies have ever made such a contemptible showing

as the Russian army in Japan, and the fleet made itself even more ridiculous. The public suddenly picked up courage. What had been whispered in cellars was now shouted openly in the streets. The mood of revolution was abroad, and the government leaped from one extreme to the other. Von Plehve did not live to see the organic outcome of his policy: the bomb of a terrorist reached him first. After von Plehve came Prince Sviatopolk-Mirsky, and all over Russia the cry arose: "The spring is here! The spring is here!" Higher than anywhere else spirits rose in Vilna, the city from which Sviatopolk-Mirsky was called to take the place of the assassinated von Plehve. Deputation after deputation came to see him off. He assured them that he would, in all his acts, consult the opinion of the Russian people and seek its confidence.

I had come in frequent contact with Sviatopolk-Mirsky in Vilna, too; I was one of his official "learned Jews." He was still the same open, kindly soul that he had been in the past. I was part of the Jewish deputation which came to say farewell to him in Vilna, and on that occasion, too, he spoke like a great gentleman, using no banal phrases, making no vain promises. He only said that he regarded the Jewish situation as the most anomalous feature in the whole of Russia, and that it would have to undergo a radical change. He too dreamed of the Russian spring, but before long it became clear that he had been called in only to be used in the game of chess that the rulers were playing against the people. When I visited him in St. Petersburg he told me that he felt like a prisoner. He had not even the power to change his officials, and there was not a man he could trust to carry through the most trivial reform.

Czar Nicholas only waited for a decent opportunity to rid himself of his unwelcome messenger of the Russian spring. The opportunity soon came. It was Nicholas himself who issued the order to his own palace guards to fire upon the peaceful thousands of Russians who came, with crosses in their hands and respect in their hearts, to implore their Emperor for mercy on his people. The procession was led by the priest who later achieved a unique infamy, Father Gapon. If there were still in Russia naïve persons who believed that by nature the Czar was inclined to lend an ear to the cry of justice, but that he was perpetually being misled by his ministers, that ninth of January, 1905, finally opened their eyes.

The pogroms against the Jews did not cease. A new type of pogrom-maker appeared—the mobilized Russian soldier. The Jewish self-defense, in which both the Jewish Socialists and the middle classes participated, was now well organized in all the towns and villages. For all that, the number of Jewish victims who fell in the pogroms of those years mounted to several thousand. In the winter of 1905–6 I took part in the Jewish self-defense. It was a wretched feeling, to go marching around through the frosty night. In my heart was an inherited hatred of shedding blood, in my hand was the revolver I might have to use at any moment. Vilna was spared an organized pogrom because of the mixed population—Jews, Poles, Lithuanians. The Russians proper were a small minority.

One passing feature of the political struggle of the Jews of Russia calls for explanation. As long as the Jewish Bund was the predecessor of the Russian Social Democratic movement, and played to some extent the role of pioneer, the Jewish middle-class democratic movement lagged behind the Russian. It was only in 1905 that it began to organize. This curious fact—that in one field the Jews led, while in another they followed—cannot be explained solely on the ground of the passivity of the Jewish middle class. The fact was that the Zionist movement had withdrawn a large number of middle-class Jews from the struggle. The Zionist program had been laid down largely by west European Jews, for whom the separate struggles of the various Jewish groups in their own countries lay outside the Zionist field. This point was strongly disputed at the Congresses. Part of the "present work," which so many of the east European Jews demanded to have included in the Zionist program, was the struggle for local Jewish emancipation, as well as the intensification of Jewish cultural work. The Zionists of Russia broke through the program before it was changed by the Zionist Congress.

With this general awakening to political life, there also came the question of the creation of a Russian national Jewish organization for the defense of Jewish rights, and for the first time in the history of the Jewish emancipation a Jewish group emerged openly as a *national* entity. The name of the organization was the Society for the Full Rights of the Jewish People in Russia. The demand was for civic, political and national rights. By "national rights" was meant autonomy in regard to language, educational system, and communal affairs. The phrase "equal rights," which was usual in such formulations, was replaced by "full rights." The phrase "equal rights" implies two classes of citizens: those who got their rights first, and those who got rights equal to theirs: those who have rights and those who have equal rights. The natural effect is to leave a perpetual aftertaste of inequality.

In this connection the reader must recall what I have already said about Russia: it was a huge state composed of a large number of nationalities, and the concepts of "state" and "nationality" were not, as elsewhere, synonymous. The Society for Full Rights—sarcastically called by its opponents the Society of Fullers—was founded in Vilna in March, 1905. The initiative came from St. Petersburg, and the leaders were Maxim Vinaver, G. B. Sliosberg, and Leonte Bramson. The leading place belongs to Vinaver. He was already known in Russia as a scholarly lawyer of high caliber. He had also played an important role in the general Russian democratic movement as it expressed itself in the party of the Constitutional Democrats, generally known as the Cadets. Sliosberg was known as the great specialist in Jewish disabilities, which, as a practical lawyer, he had fought all his life in individual cases. Politically he was the most conservative of the group. Bramson, also a lawyer by training, had long been active in the cultural and economic fields of Russian Jewish life, on which he had written widely. In politics he was a radical and worked with the Russian intelligentsia, which had not yet gone over to the Socialist camp. The St. Petersburg group represented the non-Zionists—actually the anti-Zionists—in the Society. Opposed to them—within the Society, of course—were the Zionist leaders, who laid sharper emphasis on the national demands. Both elements were necessary to the foundation of the Society. Simon Dubnow was the liaison between the two elements. Three Jews of Vilna, Dubnow, Goldberg and I, were elected to the central committee of the Society. Maxim Vinaver, whom even his opponents recognized as the ablest statesman produced by the Jews of Russia, was elected chairman.

It was during the year 1905—the year preceding the opening of the first Russian Parliament, or Duma, and also the most fearful year in the modern history of Russian Jewry—that the so-called Black Hundreds, the dregs of the population, came to the fore. Their organization was directed against the movement for freedom as a whole, but they expended nine-tenths of their fury on the Jewish people. Neither the police nor the soldiery interfered with their outbursts, and it was an open secret that these makers of pogroms were in turn supported by the throne, and that the Czar himself was in personal contact with their leader, supplying him with large sums of money out of the private imperial treasury.

In this frenzy of lawless repression the Czar had the support of the secret cabinet of charlatans he had gathered about him. The *official* central government, conservative and vengeful though it was, realized, during the disastrous Russo-Japanese

War, that some sort of compromise had to be offered to the Russian people. And thus after every defeat on the field of battle it literally compelled the Czar to issue his appeasing manifestos. First came the promise of what was called Buligin's Duma, really an advisory council, to which no Jew would be admitted; then came the second manifesto—the Jews were to be included. Then, in the midst of tremendous strikes, when work in Russia had been practically suspended, when the trains were no longer running, when the factories were shut down and the lighting systems cut off, when everything was at a standstill, the Czar issued the third manifesto, that of October 17, 1905.

I have said something about the effect which this produced—that feeling of spring dawning upon our world. We sometimes read of blind men who suddenly regain their sight. Something of what such a man feels when the light burst upon his brain was felt in Russia when that manifesto was published. Strangers embraced each other on the streets. Men went about pinching themselves to make sure they were not dreaming. The Bastille had fallen! They were not dreaming. Slavery was dead! Russia was to have a parliament, a real parliament, a legislative body with full powers! Tyranny had abdicated.

It was thus that the third manifesto was interpreted by some. The Jews were not mentioned in it, but it was quite clear that from this moment on the discriminatory laws against the Jews were dead. This, at least, was how the Jews saw it. And if there were some who pointed to certain dark and dubious phrases in the manifesto, they were shouted down. The public wanted to be happy, and was.

The happiness did not last long. There was a third way of interpreting the manifesto—that adopted by the Black Hundreds. The week following the publication of the manifesto more than fifty pogroms took place throughout Russia, and in every one many lives were lost. Once more Vilna escaped the wave of butchery, but if it escaped the pogroms, Vilna paid in another way. A day before the issuance of the third manifesto the soldiers shot into a mass of demonstrating citizens, killing five and wounding thirty. Of the five killed, four were Jews. On the day of the publication of the manifesto a cortege of fifty thousand men and women accompanied the five victims to their burial.

That winter there was a kind of lunacy in the air, a chaos in which men could not gather their wits together. Neither side, neither the rulers nor the ruled, knew what it was about. On the one side was the manifesto, which promised freedom; on the other side the Black Hundreds and the pogroms of the soldiers. On the one side preparations were being made for the election of a legislative parliament while the workers and peasants were in revolt; and as an answer to these there was a declaration of a state of siege, the sending of punitive expeditions to terrorize a peaceful population. And to make confusion more confounded, on the one side were the Bolsheviks, calling for an *active* boycott of the elections, on the other side the Mensheviks, proclaiming a boycott against the Duma but supporting the elections themselves as an opportunity for propaganda. It was in the midst of this bedlam that the elections took place.

At the conference of the Society for the Full Rights, held in St. Petersburg after the publication of the third manifesto, there were also heard voices in favor of a boycott of the elections. But the great majority of the members, if not the Society as such, were actively interested in general Russian affairs, and belonged for the most part to the League of Freedom, that is, the Cadet party. The Society itself proceeded at once to the organization of the elections throughout Russia. Only a couple of months before the elections were the names of the candidates announced. Mine was submitted for the city of Vilna.

As part of the election campaign, a number of my friends founded a daily Russian paper with the name of *Novaya Zarya* (New Dawn). The already existing daily of Vilna also belonged to Jews, but it was opposed to the Society for Full Rights. The Jewish Socialists of Vilna accepted the resolution of the Bolsheviks to conduct an *active* campaign against the elections, that is, they tried to prevent the holding of the elections as such. I clashed with them at many of the open meetings. Again I must state that I have nothing to complain of in regard to these clashes. Each side was permitted to present its side of the case peacefully. One fact is worth remembering. During the winter before the elections, the Socialists "took possession" of the synagogues. They made use of them for their propaganda. But regular lectures in the *Taharat Kodesh* continued without interruption.

The elections, and my candidacy in particular, received support from an unexpected direction. The well-known Socialist Hermann Lopatin had been released from prison after the publication of the third manifesto. This man had been in solitary confinement in the Schlusselberg fortress for twenty-five years. Why he chose to come to Vilna after his release I do not know; perhaps the government chose this city for his residence. He was already an old man, with a snow-white beard. There was no sign of suffering on his face—or if there were such signs they were hidden in the deep wrinkles which ran across his forehead. He called on me several times, and also accompanied me to my meetings. He spoke very little. Twenty-five years of solitary confinement can teach a man the art of silence. I looked with awe at this strange, noble Russian, in whose pure, almost childlike eyes shone neither pride nor the light of revenge. He saw in the Duma the forerunner of the Messiah.

Among those who supported my candidacy actively there were two men worthy of note—two different types. Shmarya Gorelik was a close friend, and an intimate in my house. He was one of the chief workers on the *Novaya Zarya.* I have seldom met a man who served the literary ideal in general, and Russian literature in particular, with such knightly purity. For him literature was not the reflection of life, but its substance. He belonged to no political party. As a follower of Tolstoy he abhorred the use or even the very suggestion of force. He lived a lonely sundered life, like a modern Essene.

The other, the opposite of Shmarya Gorelik, was still very young, but he came to Vilna with a complete reputation as a fighter, an able journalist, and a brilliant speaker. I had seen him for the first time at the Uganda Congress, the sixth. There he had delivered an address in Russian—he did not yet know German—against the Uganda proposal. In the course of his speech he introduced many new words, like *equilibristika*, *journalistika*, *publicistika*, and so on. The witty critic Eliashov, better known as Baal Machshavot, dubbed him "the *stika* delegate." Dr. Eliashov did not suspect that the *stika* delegate would in time become one of the stormiest figures in Jewish political life. He came from Odessa, where as a seventeen-year-old boy he had already achieved fame by his stinging feuilletons in one of the leading dailies.

This man was Vladimir Jabotinsky. Arriving in Vilna, he threw himself into the seething cauldron of politics and became the idol of the very youngest generation. He was admired for his wit, his energy, and above all for his extraordinary mastery of the Russian language, which he used as a musical virtuoso uses his instrument; the ready phrases flowed from his tongue so smoothly, so painlessly, so effortlessly. We received him as one of our own, and he became the pride of the Jewish community. It was my privilege to become his first teacher in Hebrew, and I was amazed by his talent. After the first eight lessons, he was able, with an almost insignificant vocabulary, to perform the most extraordinary tricks, something like a gifted actor who is called upon to deliver an impassioned monologue in a language he does not know. More than anything else he loved politics. His favorite slogan was: "Make the bear come out and fight"—that is, under all circumstances, whether necessary or not, provoke the enemy to battle.

When election day came round, the Poles refused to participate. The Lithuanians united with the Jews in my support, and I was elected almost unanimously as the representative of Vilna to the first Duma.

It was at this time that our second child was born—a son. We named him Samuel Baruch, the first name for my father, the second for Helena's. Both of us were happy in the event, I because I had wanted a son, Helena because every woman renews her motherhood with each child. In the midst of all that turmoil the leaders of the Vilna community and many guests from St. Petersburg came to the celebration. We were congratulated on the event and told that the boy had been born under happy auspices—namely, together with the rights of the Jews of Russia.

CHAPTER THIRTY

The Great Swindler

There were twelve of us in all, the representatives of between six and seven million Jews, and I wonder whether any twelve men have ever carried on their shoulders the responsibility of so many hopes and longings. Russia was—as it seemed—about to rise out of the abyss of oppression; the Jewish people was about to rise out of the abyss below the abyss. And these twelve men were to haul it out. To make the task harder, these twelve men had to bear in mind that they had been elected by the non-Jewish as well as the Jewish voters, and frequently there was no correspondence between the work they had to do for their own people and the party needs dictated by their other constituencies. Even if there was no actual conflict of interests, tactics might sometimes bring about a seeming conflict. When a thousand things had to be attended to by this first parliament, and every group was clamoring for first attention, the very order of affairs became an important matter.

The Society for Full Rights assembled in St. Petersburg after the Duma was opened. The Zionists, who formed half the Jewish group in the Duma, proposed that all the Jewish members organize into a parliamentary faction, with the obligation to vote as a unit. The other six members demurred, arguing with some show of reason that, to be consistent, the Jews would have to step out of their various parties. A compromise was struck. It was decided that on all Jewish questions, the Jewish members should come together and try to act as a unit, though without party discipline. As a matter of fact, as will be seen, the discussion was almost purely theoretical.

There were three groups in the Duma. First came the Constitutional Democrats, or Cadets, in which were found the most advanced elements of the old *Zemstvos*, and the finest forces of the non-Socialist Russian intelligentsia. The chief leaders of the party were the historian Paul Miliukov and Maxim Vinaver. On agrarian questions the leftist members of the Cadets took an extreme view which approximated to that of the Social Revolutionaries. The leader of this section of the Cadets was Solomon Gerzenstein, a former Jew, professor of political economy in the Agricultural Institute of Moscow, and a recognized authority on economics and finance. Him the government feared and hated as much as any man, for he was the most adept in exposing the indecent conduct of finances during the Russo-Japanese War. Soon after the dissolution of the Duma the government squared its accounts with him; he was assassinated by the Black Hundreds.

To the right of the Cadets stood the Union of October Seventeenth. It included the mildly liberal elements and the less conservative representatives of part of the large landowners. I doubt whether these men were genuine constitutionalists. They were only cleverer than the other large landowners and made a virtue of necessity.

The third group, under the name of the *Trudoviki*, consisted of the radical elements, Socialists and half-Socialists, who had been elected in spite of the official ban of the party in the elections. This group had no party program, and the only point on which it was united was agrarian reform, but on this point all of its constituent members were extremists. Of the twelve Jewish deputies, eight joined the Cadets, three the *Trudoviki.* One remained without attachments, or as we said, he ran wild.

Among the Jewish deputies I occupied, in a certain sense, a special position, not for my virtues or abilities, but because of one of those fantastic anomalies which were so frequent in Russian Jewish life. I was the only one among them who had no right to stay in St. Petersburg. The others belonged, one way or another, to the class of "privileged Jews," either by academic association or through their standing in the business guilds. But my degree had been taken at a foreign university and I was not a businessman. I was therefore one of the six million who could not leave the Pale. And so I walked around in St. Petersburg as the living symbol of the absurd system, as if to say: "I have no right to be living in St. Petersburg, and I am only here for the purpose of helping to make the country's laws." I did not neglect to point this out in my addresses, both in the Duma and at a meeting in Moscow.

However, there were absurdities enough in connection with the first Duma. One little circumstance, which had to do only with the Jewish delegation, I remember with amusement. Every delegate to the Duma had to register his name, together with his religion and his nationality. We were twelve Jews in the Duma; it was therefore to be expected that the twelve names would be repeated under the list of the religions and under that of the nationalities. But among us there was the well-known journalist and economist Gregory Yollos, for many years the Berlin correspondent and then the editor of the foremost Russian daily, the *Russkiye Vedomosti* of Moscow. Yollos insisted on enrolling himself as a Jew by religion and a Russian by nationality. But it appeared that the old dispensation could not tolerate the disappearance of one of the tribes, so there appeared on the scene the friend of Yollos, the former Jew Gerzenstein. *He* registered as Russian Orthodox by religion and Jew by nationality. Thus the accounts were squared, though, as often happens in accounts, by means of a little cooking. There *were* twelve Jewish deputies, both on the religious and the nationality lists. Yollos, too, it may be noted, was one of the members of the Duma to be assassinated by the Black Hundreds. These two men lived as half-Jews, one with his nationality, the other with his religion; they died as full Jews.

The first official reception of the Jewish delegates was arranged by the Jewish community of St. Petersburg under the leadership of the man who had, for many years, been the chief *shtadlan* of Russian Jewry, Baron Horace Günzburg. He received us in his palatial home and spent a couple of hours with us. More active in his reception of us was his son, David Günzburg, a famous orientalist and the possessor of one of the finest collections of Hebrew books and manuscripts in the world. The Günzburg family easily occupied the first place in Russian Jewry. In the days when *shtadlanut* was still the only means by which anything could be done for the Jews, the Günzburgs set the example—not too often followed—of quiet, modest and selfless service to their people. The old man invited us to his house as a sign of respect to the *elected* representatives of the Jewish people. But in this house the ancient system of *shtadlanut* had for many years found its headquarters, and our appearance there was symbolic of the revolution that had taken place in Jewish, no less than in Russian life. Baron Günzburg accepted us, too, in a spirit of symbolism. He bowed to the new order.

Quite different in character was the reception given to the entire body of the Duma in the imperial palace, where the ruler by the grace of God was to come face to face with the men who, from now on, would make the laws for his empire. In one of his moments of weakness, when he had felt the sword suspended above him trembling in the wind, the Czar had issued his own invitation to the deputies. And it had needed much persuasion, almost compulsion, before he was convinced of this necessity; he regretted the step as soon as he had taken it. But it was too late. The comedy had to be played out until the moment when the supporters of the throne had gathered enough strength to ring down the curtain. And then another play would begin, the play of revenge on those who had forced this humiliation on the elect of God.

The day of reckoning was, in fact, close at hand. The ranks of the faithful were being increased and closed; in the interim the farce continued. Some six hundred of us, therefore, assembled in the palace and there, *standing*, we listened to him. Some two hundred of the country representatives came in their peasant clothes and brought with them into the perfumed air of the palace the strong smell of the Russian earth or, less figuratively, the still stronger smell of newly polished leather. Officials of every rank crowded into the doors and corners of the hall. The Imperial Guard was drawn up before us in two ranks. The Court Marshal entered and struck three times with his baton, to say: "The Czar is coming." And here he comes, an unimposing little figure, accompanied by a great suite. They advance in measured step and the Czar ascends the dais. Some of the lackeys try to raise a cheer. It dies in the hall without an echo. And standing by his throne Nicholas reads forth his speech. He speaks of mutual trust and confidence between Emperor and people. He mentions the Duma and expresses the hope that the great heritage which he has received from his fathers he will be able to transmit to his young heir. Once again the Marshal taps three times with his baton. The Czar marches out. Once more a weak cheer. The ceremony is over.

I watched the man closely, and listened to his words intently. There was no twitching of his face, no tremor in his voice. He had learned his part well, and he played it well. On me he certainly did not make the impression of a weak nature, such as had often been ascribed to him. On the contrary, I felt that before me stood a good actor, who could control his face and expression excellently. He wore a mask. Years later, when I read the memoirs of Count Witte, I came to the conclusion that I had understood Nicholas. The blank face covered a studied desire for revenge. Witte, who knew him better than any other man, says of him that he was the most bitterly vengeful of all the Romanovs.

In the speech from the throne, as in the October manifesto, the Jews were not mentioned. The government believed in adding contemptuous insult to injury: Jews could not be mentioned in important documents like these. The answer to the speech from the throne was composed largely by Maxim Vinaver, and in it appears the categorical statement that there can be no talk of a regular constitution for the country without civic equality for all its inhabitants. Once more, in its reply, the government ignored the point, and Vinaver, in the Duma, made perhaps the strongest speech of his career, declaring openly: "Let the government know, once for all, that without civic equality there can be no tranquility in this country."

The Cadets and the *Trudoviki* were united on this point, but they were divided on the order of procedure. Was the question of civic equality—which meant, of course, the Jews—to take precedence over the agrarian question, which was the burning question of the day for all Russia? The Russian muzhik, who represented more than three-quarters of the population, was crying out for land. The division of land had created injustices which it was difficult to look upon without feelings of revolt and disgust. While gigantic estates had accumulated in the hands of the aristocracy, the peasants were compelled to work tiny plots which could not provide the barest necessities for themselves and their families. Not only the *Trudoviki*, but many of the leftist Cadets, were inclined to place the agrarian question first. But all of the Jewish deputies, and most all of the Cadets, were afraid of the attitude of the muzhik delegates in the matter of equality of rights. In their opinion it would be the wiser course to proceed with the Jewish question first. I took part in the debates in the sessions of the Cadet caucus. Instead of using arguments, I asked the permission of the assembly to tell a Jewish story and, weary with the monotonous debates, the delegates signified their assent.

It was a rather difficult story to tell, for I had first to explain certain Jewish laws and customs. One of these laws is that on the Sabbath the Jew may not kindle a light, even through the agency of a non-Jew. Having explained this I went on to describe the dreariness of the long Friday nights in the winter. At five o'clock in the afternoon the prayers are over and the Sabbath has begun. At six o'clock the family meal is over, and then follows sleep. At twelve they are through with sleeping, and there remain seven or eight hours of darkness. The poor cannot afford to leave a light burning through the night. This is the privilege of the "rich." One such "rich" Jew rose one Friday at midnight and saw to his horror that the light had gone out. He had a gentile servant in the house, but it is forbidden to direct the servant to light the lamp. The Jew cast about in his mind and suddenly called loudly to the servant: "Ivan, how would you like a drop of whisky?" Ivan did not mind being roused out of the deepest slumber for the sake of a drop. "Thank you," says Ivan, "I'd love it." "But it's dark," his master answers, "I can't find a thing." "That's perfectly all right," says Ivan, "I'll make a light." The Jew is delighted; he has not told Ivan to kindle the lamp. The lamp is lit, the drink is poured out. Ivan swallows the drink gratefully, hands back the glass—and extinguishes the light. "Be careful with Ivan," I warned the Cadets. "He may get what he wants and then put out the light again." I was told that my story had its effect. The problem was taken more seriously.

In court circles Count Witte was regarded as the chief criminal in exploiting the defeat of the Russian armies for the purpose of wringing concessions from the Czar, in particular the manifesto of October 17. Shortly after the calling of the first Duma, Witte was deposed as prime minister and his place was taken by Goremikin, a black reactionary of the old school. This incident alone makes clear what was in Nicholas' mind when he issued the manifesto. One look at Goremikin was enough. His eyes were cold and glassy, he wore the old, ultra-orthodox side whiskers of the typical Russian bureaucrat. He was, in all, the personified antithesis of a constitutional government. Goremikin was not the only sign of the real intentions of the Czar, but he was the most revealing.

And still the Duma believed that Nicholas meant well—or, at least, that with the manifesto he had gone so far that retreat was now impossible. And who knows? If the democratic forces of Russia had been united at that moment, they might have emerged victorious from the struggle. But there was no such unity. The interparty struggle, a bitter and obstinate struggle, was not suspended even for a moment, and the energies of the delegates were exhausted before they approached the question as a whole. The leaders of the fight against the government were the most optimistic party. I was at that time a contributor to the *Rech*, the party newspaper edited by Paul Miliukov and Joseph Geseen. The first of these was the leader of the party; the second, a one-time Jew, was one of the foremost intellectual and political forces in the party. I was well acquainted with the entire group that was in the van of the movement: Miliukov himself; Feodor Rodichev, the La Salle of the party; the brothers Ivan and Ilya Petrunkevich, old fighters in the *Zemstvo;* Vladimir Nabokov, son of the former Minister of Justice, a cool, logical and convincing speaker; and the lovable and pure personality of Feodor Kokoshkin. The last two were also assassinated, Kokoshkin by the Bolsheviks, and Nabokov, after the World War, by a former member of the Black Hundreds, who shot him in Berlin. In all the upper circle of the party, composed of the higher intelligentsia, there was the same feeling of optimism. There were times when they spoke seriously of a "cabinet of the Cadet party."

In the Jewish group Maxim Vinaver was the best informed on Russian political questions. The Jewish deputies took their lead from him, some of us because we recognized his greatness, some because we had no alternative. I was of the former. Among the Zionists, and particularly those of St. Petersburg, I was censured for my attitude.

The Zionists had their own salon in St. Petersburg, just as in Vilna. In Vilna it was conducted by Isaac Goldberg, in St. Petersburg by Israel Rosov. But while in Goldberg's house the atmosphere was Hebrew, in Rosov's it was Yiddish-Russian. In this circle the driving force of Zionism was not the power of the ancient Jewish culture and the impulse to a renaissance, but quite simply the intolerable conditions of Jewish life and the brankruptcy of the assimilationist ideal.

The Duma set to work in dead earnest. Commissions were appointed for the framing of laws, and in the full sessions the questions of the day were debated in general terms. But while this went on in the palace which was the seat of the Duma, catastrophe was drawing closer in the country, and once more it sent its shadow in advance in the form of a pogrom. The question of the Jewish pogroms had been brought sharply into the open by an interpellation of the government so formulated as to indicate clearly the government's guilt. The Minister of the Interior, Stolypin, a graceful speaker with elegant manners, promised to give an answer within a month. But the pogrom leaders were impatient, and provided their own answer before the month was over—a pogrom in Bialystok. This was an orgy of beastliness after the fashion of Kishinev: bellies ripped open, heads with nails driven into them, children with their brains dashed out, and the rest. Eighty Jews were killed and hundreds wounded. A tremor went through the Duma. It was not only the pogrom as such, but the hint that it carried. This, then, was the reply of the government to the interpellation. The Duma resolved at once to send a commission of investigation to the scene. One of the members of the commission was the Jewish deputy Benjamin Jacobson, who belonged to the party of the *Trudoviki*.

I had occasion to speak in the Duma on the subject of the pogroms, but I cannot remember whether it was on the general question or in connection with the Bialystok pogrom. I said, addressing myself to the Russian people: "It is well for you to know that we Jews are bound to you, the Russians, like Siamese twins." My meaning was that the destruction of the Jewish people could be accomplished only at the price of the destruction of Russia. I was attacked from both sides. The *Novaya Vremya* accused me of having offered mortal insult to the Russian people; the Zionists attacked me for having insulted the Jewish people. Neither side understood my simile. I do not know whether it was particularly skillful or not, but the sense in which I used it I hold to be true even today. There has been no case in history where a government has done violence to the Jews without doing equal violence to itself.

Between the Bialystok pogrom and the dissolution of the Duma I had occasion to visit the most Russian of all cities, Moscow. I received an invitation from the general Cadet party to deliver an address on the Jewish question. The Bialystok pogrom had acted like a cold shower on Jews and liberal Russians alike, and many had begun to feel that the Duma would not live much longer. The depression was of course deepest among the Jews. In Moscow I had the first occasion to declare the tragedy of the Jewish situation to a huge, pure Russian audience in the very heart of traditional Russia. My two friends, Yechiel Tschlenov, who was very popular among the Moscow Cadets, and Isaac Naidich, a rising public figure in the Jewish community, participated in the meeting. I cannot forget the extraordinary reception that was given me, a Jewish deputy who had no right to be in Moscow at all. The real celebration took place after the meeting, when the leading spirits assembled once more in the Slavianska Bazaar, a famous restaurant, and occupied the place until four in the morning.

On the second day of my stay I addressed a purely Zionist meeting. I took as my theme the question of what would happen after the Jews had obtained their "full rights." My text was the life of Herzl, and I indicated how the impulse toward the building of a Jewish homeland had come not only from Jews who lived in lands of oppression, but from those who had achieved civic equality. That impulse was not born of oppression and did not die with liberation.

The commission returned from Bialystok. Fiery speeches were delivered in the Duma by Vinaver, Jacobson and Rodichev. By an overwhelming majority the Duma accepted a resolution calling on the Czar to dismiss his cabinet, in order that the rulers of the country might disassociate themselves from the disgrace of the pogrom. The atmosphere was heavily charged. The deputies knew that they now stood at the parting of the ways. Two days later, when they turned up at the chamber, they found the doors locked and guarded. Outside was posted the manifesto of the Czar dissolving the Duma.

I went with a group of deputies to the Nevsky Prospekt, the main artery of St. Petersburg. We wanted to see for ourselves the effect which this action had produced on the general public. There was nothing to be observed. There was no sign of excitement. The crowded street looked as it had always looked—countless people hurrying around, intent on their own business. If two persons stopped to hold a conversation, a third was sure to stroll by as if by accident, sidle up absentmindedly, and overhear what was being said. There were agents enough in the capital to provide a third for every two that stopped to talk. Life was "normal" once more. The citizen had reverted to the subject.

We were called together in the club of the Cadet party. The deputies wandered around like lost souls. It was known that somewhere, in some secret place, the leaders were in conference, and there was nothing to do but wait. The hours passed slowly. The mood in the club was like that in a house of mourning before the corpse has been removed. The dead man can never be disturbed again, yet every visitor walks on tiptoe, as if afraid of waking him. It was toward evening that some of the leaders finally appeared. It had been decided that the whole party should transfer itself to Viborg, the nearest town across the Finnish border.

The *Trudoviki* had taken the same resolve. There, in Viborg, the two parties assembled, separately, and hour by hour there came messengers from St. Petersburg, the emissaries of the revolutionary organizations. Stories were circulated of the excitement that reigned in the ranks of the workers of St. Petersburg. Others would have it that the unrest had spread to the barracks. And we ourselves could not make up our minds. Was *this* then the signal for the liberation? Was the dissolution of the Duma the necessary interlude before the curtain was raised on the last act?

The hall in which we are assembled is small and overheated. The faces of the deputies are drawn and haggard, the voices weak. There are still some who preach moderation: this is not the moment for a revolution—peaceful victory is in sight. But the moderates are a small minority. The majority wants action, something to restore the dignity of the outraged Duma. The best speakers of the party follow one another and the deputies listen intently, nervously. Vinaver takes the floor. The time has come, he declares, to ignore party programs. The government has practiced a deliberate swindle on the first representative assembly of the Russian people. The reply of the Duma will have to be fearless and dignified.

It is after midnight when the meeting is called to order. Sergei Muromtzev, President of the Duma, who has become the symbol of Russian freedom, enters, and everyone rises. We stand as if at prayer. The Viborg manifesto of the dissolved Duma is read out. The Russian people is called upon to boycott the Russian government with all the means at its command, to arrest the entire machinery of administration, and to continue to a successful conclusion the struggle for freedom. Muromtzev is the first to append his signature. After him come the other leaders and then the delegates.

The next morning we returned to St. Petersburg. On the train we received the "confidential and reliable" message that round the station in St. Petersburg hundreds of thousands of workers had assembled to greet us, and that there the first open clash with the government would take place.

And sure enough, at the station there waited for us a guard of honor—two rows of gendarmes between which we walked as down an alley. No one else to greet us. When the droshky driver asked, with the famous St. Petersburg courtesy: "Excellency, what address?" we did not know what to answer.

Swindled again. It was the old game once more. It has been described once for all in the Book of Books. Nine times Pharaoh swindled Moses. He was waiting for the tenth plague. And even after the tenth plague he changed his mind and pursued the liberated people. At the Red Sea he got his final answer.

Many, many ages must pass before history changes into legend. But after a long time—I do not know how long a time—the legend will arise of the great swindler who was the last to sit on the throne of Russia. He swindled, and swindled again, and kept on swindling until the Red Sea swallowed him up.